CONVERGENCES AND DIVERGENCES BETWEEN INTERNATIONAL HUMAN RIGHTS, INTERNATIONAL HUMANITARIAN AND INTERNATIONAL CRIMINAL LAW

Series Supranational Criminal Law: Capita Selecta, Volume 24

Recently published in the series:

8. *Collective Violence and International Criminal Justice: An Interdisciplinary Approach*, Alette Smeulers (ed.)
9. *International Criminal Law from a Swedish Perspective,* Iain Cameron, Malin Thunberg Schunke, Karin Pale Bartes, Christoffer Wong and Petter Asp
10. *The Implementation of the European Arrest Warrant in the European Union: Law, Policy and Practice,* Massimo Fichera
11. *The Principle of Mutual Recognition in Cooperation in Criminal Matters: A Study of the Principle in Four Framework Decisions and in the Implementation Legislation in the Nordic Member States,* Annika Suominen
12. *The European Public Prosecutor's Office: Analysis of a Multilevel Criminal Justice System*, Martijn Willem Zwiers
13. *Victimological Approaches to International Crimes: Africa,* Rianne Letschert Roelof Haveman, Anne-Marie de Brouwer and Antony Pemberton (eds.)
14. *The United States and International Criminal Tribunals: An Introduction,* Harry M. Rhea
15. *EU Sanctions: Law and Policy Issues Concerning Restrictive Measures,* Iai Cameron (ed.)
16. *Whose Responsibility? A Study of Transnational Defence Rights and Mutual Recognition of Judicial Decisions within the EU,* Malin Thunberg Schunke
17. *Genocidal Gender and Sexual Violence: The Legacy of the ICTR, Rwanda's Ordinary Courts and* Gacaca Courts, Usta Kaitesi
18. *Addressing the Intentional Destruction of the Environment during Warfare under the Rome Statute of the International Criminal Court,* Steven Freeland
19. *Individual Criminal Liability for the International Crime of Aggression,* Gerhard Kemp
20. *Selective Enforcement and International Criminal Law: The International Criminal Court and Africa,* James Nyawo
21. *The Governance of Complementary Global Regimes and the Pursuit of Human Security: The Interaction between the United Nations and the International Criminal Court,* Andrea Marrone
22. *The Rationality of Dictators: Towards a More Effective Implementation of the Responsibility to Protect,* Maartje Weerdesteijn
23. *Extended Confiscation in Criminal Law,* Malin Thunberg Schunke

CONVERGENCES AND DIVERGENCES BETWEEN INTERNATIONAL HUMAN RIGHTS, INTERNATIONAL HUMANITARIAN AND INTERNATIONAL CRIMINAL LAW

Edited by
Paul De Hert
Stefaan Smis
Mathias Holvoet

intersentia
Cambridge – Antwerp – Portland

Intersentia Ltd
Sheraton House | Castle Park
Cambridge | CB3 0AX | United Kingdom
Tel.: +44 1223 370 170 | Fax: +44 1223 370 169
Email: mail@intersentia.co.uk
www.intersentia.com | www.intersentia.co.uk

Distribution for the UK and Ireland:
NBN International
Airport Business Centre, 10 Thornbury Road
Plymouth, PL6 7PP
United Kingdom
Tel.: +44 1752 202 301 | Fax: +44 1752 202 331
Email: orders@nbninternational.com

Distribution for Europe and all other countries:
Intersentia Publishing nv
Groenstraat 31
2640 Mortsel
Belgium
Tel.: +32 3 680 15 50 | Fax: +32 3 658 71 21
Email: mail@intersentia.be

Distribution for the USA and Canada:
International Specialized Book Services
920 NE 58th Ave. Suite 300
Portland, OR 97213
USA
Tel.: +1 800 944 6190 (toll free) | Fax: +1 503 280 8832
Email: info@isbs.com

Convergences and Divergences Between International Human Rights,
International Humanitarian and International Criminal Law

Artwork on cover: Francisco DE GOYA (1746–1828), Etching, Plate 11 from 'Los desastres de la guerra'

ISBN 978-1-78068-640-0
D/2018/7849/22
NUR 828

GPRC
Guaranteed
Peer Reviewed
Content

British Library Cataloguing in Publication Data. A catalogue record for this book is available from the British Library.

FOREWORD

'Human rights' is an exceptionally strong brand name. In comparison with this giant, international criminal law and international humanitarian law are little-known dwarves. In everyday discourse, as well as in writings by scholars from outside the law, human rights often seems to absorb international criminal law and/or international humanitarian law. For example, in contemporary critiques of the human rights project, criticism of the International Criminal Court holds a central place, regardless of the fact that it is not, as such, a human rights body. In other situations, the lines between human rights law and its next-door neighbours are blurred or contested. A prominent example is found in discussions of the 'war on terror'.

Hence, when human rights lawyers explore the reality of fragmentation and the desirability of integration within the context of human rights law, it is meaningful to include in the scope of the analysis those parts of the broader human rights project that are, technically speaking, hosted by other legal disciplines. There is such a thing as human rights law 'in the broad sense'.

This is why a research project on 'The Global Challenge of Human Rights Integration', sponsored by the Belgian Federal Science Policy (BELSPO, 2012–17), included a work package that focused on 'the fuzzy borders of human rights law'. At the project's flagship conference in Ghent in December 2015, this resulted in a track on 'Convergence and Divergence between International Human Rights Law and Other Branches of International Law'. A selection of the papers that were presented in that conference track has now been assembled in this volume.

In promoting scholarship that adopts a holistic perspective of the (broad) human rights project, the 'Human Rights Integration' project is not pursuing an agenda of unification. Its aim is much more modest and nuanced. An integrated human rights protection system is a human rights system in which the different actors, operating at different levels of jurisdiction, and with different mandates and specialisations, nevertheless share an awareness of being part of that bigger project, and reflect upon their role in it and their relationship to other nodes in the same network. Human rights integration is, in the first place, a matter of mindset and, in the second place, a dynamic. It is about making room for a global conversation on human rights, across sub-disciplines, fora and jurisdictions.

Despite being a young discipline, human rights law is experiencing fast specialisation at the level of scholarship. Only two decades ago, it would have been self-evident that expertise in international human rights law, international criminal law and international humanitarian law was in the hands of the same scholars. Today, in most law schools, these are likely to be spread over two or three different chairs. What is more, most human rights scholars specialise within human rights law – for example, in a single forum (such as the European Convention on Human Rights) or in a specific set of rights (such as economic and social rights, or minority rights). While this is a sign of the maturing of the discipline, and an indicator of increasing depth and nuance in scholarship, it also carries the risk of the trees obscuring the forest (i.e. the bigger picture of the human rights project disappearing from sight). Against that background, the present volume offers an important contribution to the holistic or integrated analysis of human rights law in the broad sense.

Eva Brems
Human Rights Centre, Ghent University

PREFACE

As already noted by Professor Brems in the foreword, this volume compiles a selection of papers initially presented in a track of the 'The Global Challenge of Human Rights Integration' flagship conference, which took place in Ghent in December 2015. More specifically, the track was entitled 'Convergence and Divergence between International Human Rights Law and Other Branches of International Law'. The call for papers required applicants to address the following questions: how does international human rights law (IHRL) relate to and interact with other bodies of international law? How does IHRL have a guiding, gap-filling, expanding or narrowing effect on such other bodies of law? In return, is IHRL undergoing similar effects from other branches of international law? The selected papers explored convergences and divergences between IHRL and the various sub-branches of international law such as international criminal law (ICL), international humanitarian law (IHL), international refugee law, international responsibility law, international economic law and international environmental law. In order to give the volume a focused theme, the editors chose to select only those papers dealing with convergences and divergences between IHRL, IHL and ICL.

IHRL, IHL and ICL are rooted in a similar ideal: respect for the autonomy and integrity of individuals and protecting individuals from misused State authority.[1] They have been represented as circles or rings, each of which overlaps with the other two. Indeed, human rights treaties, such as the Torture Convention,[2] and humanitarian law conventions, such as the four Geneva Conventions,[3] contain provisions regulating individual criminal responsibility.[4] Conversely, ICL instruments, such as the Rome Statute of the International Criminal Court (ICC),

1 D. Robinson, 'The Two Liberalisms of International Criminal Law' in C. Stahn and L. van den Herik (eds), *Future Perspectives on International Criminal Justice*, TMC Asser Press, The Hague 2010, p. 117.

2 See Article 4 of the Convention against Torture and Other Cruel, Inhuman or Degrading Treatment or Punishment.

3 The criminal provisions under the four Geneva Conventions are commonly known as the 'grave breaches': see, for instance, Art. 50 of the first Geneva Convention; Art. 51 of the second Geneva Convention; Art. 130 of the third Geneva Convention; and Art. 147 of the fourth Geneva Convention.

4 S.R. Ratner, J.S. Abrams and J.L. Bischoff (eds), *Accountability for Human Rights Atrocities in International Law. Beyond the Nuremberg Legacy*, 3rd ed., Oxford University Press, Oxford 2009, p. 13.

contain provisions that draw upon both IHL[5] and IHRL.[6] Notwithstanding these significant overlaps and synergies, there is a far from perfect congruence between IHRL, IHL and ICL. What is more, their relationship and interaction have been marked by friction and have, at times, resulted in collisions and impairments of the respective normativity and rationale underlying the three bodies of law. For instance, as described by Darryl Robinson in his piece 'The Identity Crisis of International Criminal Law', interpretive, substantive, structural and ideological assumptions of IHRL and IHL have seeped into ICL jurisprudence and scholarship. According to Robinson, this has distorted the methods of reasoning of ICL and undermined compliance with the fundamental principles of ICL.[7] In a similar vein, the pieces selected for this volume explore frictions, collisions and impairments that arise because of the fact that IHRL, IHL and ICL interact and overlap, but diverge at the same time. However, in addition, the various chapters identify, conceptualise and formulate multiple ways in which IHRL, IHL and ICL can converge – for instance, by complementing, guiding or gap-filling one another.

This volume consists of three main parts. Under the first main part, the contributions by Patrícia Pinto Soares and Gerhard Kreutzer, Damien Scalia and Marina Aksenova explore the convergences and divergences between IHL and/or IHRL on the one hand, and ICL *stricto sensu* on the other hand. ICL *stricto sensu* is to be understood as 'the totality of international law norms of a penal nature which conjoin typical legal consequences of criminal law with a decisive conduct – namely the international crime – and as such can be applied directly'.[8] The four core international crimes for which international law is said to provide direct individual criminal responsibility are: genocide, crimes against humanity, war crimes and the crime of aggression, as incorporated under Article 6 to Article 8*bis* of the Rome Statute.[9] In their contribution, Pinto Soares and Kreutzer tackle an issue that has been relatively underexplored in scholarship: the impact of ICL on IHRL. More specifically, their contribution scrutinises the (likely and/or evident) short- and long-term effects of ICL on the overall edifice of HRL, by giving, inter alia, an overview of the ICC's law and practice relating to fair trial rights. Conversely, in his piece, Damien Scalia studies the manifold ways in which international criminal courts and tribunals have (mis)used IHRL in their judicial practices. Marina Aksenova's chapter explores the relationship

---

5 See, most notably, Art. 8 of the ICC Statute on war crimes.

6 See, for instance, Art. 67 of the ICC Statute on the rights of the accused.

7 D. Robinson, 'The Identity Crisis of International Criminal Law' (2008) 21 *Leiden Journal of International Law* 961.

8 K. Ambos, *Treatise on International Criminal Law: Volume I: Foundations and General Part*, Oxford University Press, Oxford 2013, p. 54.

9 N. Boister, 'Transnational Criminal Law?' (2003) 14 *European Journal of International Law* 961–62.

between human rights law and ICL with specific reference to the principle of complementarity. She argues that judicial discretion is essential when assessing the degree of human rights protection at the ICC.

ICL in the broader sense – or ICL *lato sensu* – includes so-called transnational criminal law (TCL). Contrary to ICL *stricto sensu*, TCL is considered indirect, because it suppresses crimes such as drug trafficking, trafficking in human beings and corruption through international treaties providing for domestic enforcement of these crimes.[10] Despite its practical importance, in scholarship, TCL in general is too often overlooked[11] and also its interactions with other bodies of international law are rarely studied. The contributions by Amy Weatherburn, Valentina Milano and Mirja Ciesiolka in Part II of this volume are thus timely in starting to fill this gap in international legal scholarship by enquiring into the convergences and divergences between IHRL and transnational crimes. Amy Weatherburn's contribution considers the role of IHRL in strengthening and facilitating actions to end forced labour in order to achieve the newly adopted International Labour Organization Protocol of 2014 to the 1930 Forced Labour Convention's aim of a modern approach to addressing forced labour. In her piece, Valentina Milano analyses the extent to which IHRL is permeating the TCL response to human trafficking, and vice versa. Milano enquires, inter alia, whether IHRL and TCL are fundamentally distinct, in terms of not only norms but also monitoring mechanisms. Furthermore, she analyses to what extent they are mutually reinforcing and what their main gap-filling and guiding effects are. The last chapter in this part, written by Mirja Ciesiolka, examines the relationship between IHRL and the United Nations Convention against Corruption (UNCAC). Ciesiolka highlights that the UNCAC's aim of containing corruption is an essential element of international peace and security. She posits that the tensions between this aim and ensuring the enjoyment of civil and political rights are also a reflection of structural and general problems that come along with the phenomenon of fragmentation in international law.

The last main part of this volume, which contains contributions by Federica Favuzza, Cedric De Koker, Deborah Casalin and Vito Todeschini, provides the reader with novel and original insights as to how IHRL and IHL converge and diverge. Through the lens of a fictional character, Federica Favuzza ascertains whether the right to personal liberty and security is doomed to succumb in times of emergency. Favuzza considers whether and how the norms of other branches of international law come into play, distinguishing among the case of an international armed conflict, that of a non-international armed conflict,

10 N. Boister, *An Introduction to Transnational Criminal Law*, Oxford University Press, Oxford 2012, p. 13.

11 E. van Sliedregt, 'International Criminal Law: Over-studied and Underachieving?' (2016) 29 *Leiden Journal of International Law* 2.

and that of any other public emergency such as terrorism. Cedric De Koker's contribution analyses how the European Court of Human Rights has engaged with IHL in its case law. He addresses the complex legal issues that arise due to this engagement, such as the multifaceted relationship and interaction of the European Convention on Human Rights with the sometimes contradicting norms of IHL. Deborah Casalin's chapter aims to contribute to the body of analysis of the relationship between specific IHL and IHRL norms by examining the rules in these two bodies of law that prohibit arbitrary displacement, and mapping their interaction in situations in which IHL is applicable (i.e. armed conflict and occupation). The last chapter in this volume, written by Vito Todeschini, enquires into how the effectiveness of States' investigations of war crimes committed by their armed forces is to be evaluated. Todeschini proposes paying attention to the relevant standards developed within human rights law, since IHL does not indicate specific criteria for evaluating the effectiveness of an investigation.

Finally, in a short concluding chapter, the editors aim to present some general conclusions that can be drawn from the various chapters.

The Editors
Brussels, November 2017

CONTENTS

ABOUT THE CONTRIBUTORS

Marina Aksenova is a professor of comparative and international criminal law at IE University in Madrid. She previously held positions at iCourts (Centre of Excellence for International Court) at the University of Copenhagen and Institute for Advanced Study at the Central European University. She publishes in the area of international criminal law and international human rights law.

Deborah Casalin is a doctoral researcher in the Law and Development Research Group in the Law Faculty at the University of Antwerp (Prinsstraat 13, 2000 Antwerp, Belgium). She has previously worked as a policy officer/international humanitarian law advisor at CIDSE for the International Committee of the Red Cross, and for a humanitarian organisation in the occupied Palestinian territory.

Mirja Ciesiolka is specialising in the international law of financial crime. She practices at the Bar and holds a PhD in law from the University of Zurich. She is a former research fellow at the Centre for International and Comparative Law at the University of Zurich.

Paul De Hert is a full-time professor at the Vrije Universiteit Brussel (VUB) and an associate professor at Tilburg University. His research focuses, inter alia, on technology and European data protection law; international and European criminal law; fundamental concepts of criminal law and human rights law.

Cedric De Koker is a postdoctoral researcher in the Department of Criminology, Criminal Law and Social Law at Ghent University and is a member of the Institute for International Research on Criminal Policy at Ghent University.

Federica Favuzza is a postdoctoral fellow in international law at the University of Milan '*La Statale*'. She holds a PhD in legal studies (international law concentration) from the same university.

Mathias Holvoet is a senior associate researcher at the Institute for European Studies (IES) and an affiliated researcher at the Fundamental Rights and Constitutionalism (FRC) Research Group. He holds a PhD in international criminal law from the Faculty of Law and Criminology of the Vrije Universiteit Brussel (VUB).

Gerhard Kreutzer is a legal officer at Interpol and holds a PhD from the University of Vienna. Between 2014 and 2017 he was on a temporary assignment to the International Criminal Court, Trial Chambers and from 2005 to 2009, he worked as an assistant legal officer at the Registry of the European Court of Human Rights.

Valentina Milano is an assistant lecturer in international and human rights law at the Faculty of Law at the University of the Balearic Islands. Between 2004 and 2010, she was a human rights officer at the Office of the United Nations High Commissioner for Human Rights, where she was in charge of coordinating the mandate of the UN Special Rapporteur on trafficking in persons.

Patrícia Pinto Soares is a consultant for the United Nations Office on Drugs and Crime and holds a PhD from the European University Institute. She has previously worked, inter alia, as a legal officer in Eurojust and the International Criminal Police Organization (INTERPOL) and was Human Rights Officer in MONUSCO in the Democratic Republic of Congo.

Damien Scalia is a professor in the Faculty of Law and Criminology at the Université libre de Bruxelles. His research focuses on the perception of international criminal justice from the viewpoint of persons tried (acquitted and condemned) by the ICTY and ICTR.

Stefaan Smis is a professor of international and human rights law at the Faculty of Law and Criminology at Vrije Universiteit Brussel (VUB) and Reader in International Law at the School of Law of the University of Westminster.

Vito Todeschini is an associate legal adviser with the International Commission of Jurists, Middle East and North Africa Programme and holds a PhD from Aarhus University. Previously, he was a postdoctoral fellow at the University of Trento.

Amy Weatherburn is a postdoctoral researcher at the Faculty of Law and Criminology at Vrije Universiteit Brussel (VUB), where she has been conducting research on trafficking in human beings for the purpose of labour exploitation. Prior to this, she was Research Assistant at the University of Nottingham Human Rights Law Centre.

PART I

CONVERGENCES AND DIVERGENCES BETWEEN INTERNATIONAL HUMAN RIGHTS LAW AND INTERNATIONAL CRIMINAL LAW *STRICTO SENSU*

CATALYTIC, GAP-FILLING OR RETARDANT EFFECTS OF ICL ON HRL: *QUID JURIS*

Patrícia PINTO SOARES and Gerhard KREUTZER*

1. ICL AND HRL: AS DIFFERENT AS COMPLEMENTARY

For centuries, public international law (PIL) was seen as the legal order regulating the conduct of States and their interaction with other States at an international level. It was only at a relatively late stage that the rights of the

* The views expressed in this chapter are those of the authors alone and should not be associated with, nor do they necessarily reflect the position of, the authors' previous or current employer(s).

individual to be protected from atrocities committed under the command of State authority were regulated (right to war/right in war, under the scope of international humanitarian law (IHL)). To a significant extent, it was with the unprecedented international crisis emerging from World War Two that human rights law (HRL) and international criminal law (ICL) robustly came into being. HRL and ICL are likely to be the two areas of PIL in which the individual's status as an international actor is of central relevance: in HRL as a (potential) victim of misguided State authority and in ICL as a (potential) perpetrator of some of the most severe crimes against mankind.

The HRL project traditionally aimed at protecting individuals against States' abuse, thus limiting the State power. Instead, criminal law was developed to ensure the reach of the State over individuals so as to guarantee order and security.[1] If it is true that HRL consists essentially of a mechanism defining inherent, personal (i.e. inalienable) rights and allocating these rights and resulting freedoms ('*espaces de liberté*') to individuals by balancing potential conflicts between rights, criminal law sets in where some of these freedoms have been violated. From that perspective, criminal law acts as a guarantor so as to ensure that these rights are respected.

With the emergence of ICL, the distinction between HRL and criminal law became blurred. The ICL project was intended to criminalise the most heinous violations of fundamental human rights while at the same time activating the individual responsibility of perpetrators. ICL was therefore seen as a device for the protection and enforcement of human rights, as opposed to being a tool at the disposal of an arbitrary power to be used against individuals. It was then perceived as being more intertwined with HRL than with criminal law. Undoubtedly, ICL and HRL are linked insofar as both are based and built upon the key concept of human dignity.[2] Human rights are a guiding principle in the implementation of ICL: they are an essential component in the ICL procedure (for example, the prominent right to a fair trial). There is also a certain (partial) overlap of objects: ICL (partially) pursues – or in practice reflexively gives effect to the same aims as – HRL, i.e. declaring an act as unlawful, providing just satisfaction/reparation to victims and restoring the balance of interests/*espaces juridiques*/freedoms where severe violations of the most fundamental human rights have taken place. Yet, while one creates a guarantee to be enjoyed, the other creates an individual responsibility.

That being said, ICL and HRL (together and as national criminal laws and IHL) protect human rights in different manners and with different

---

1 W.A. Schabas, 'Criminal Responsibility for Violations of Human Rights' in J. Symonides (ed.), *Human Rights: International Protection, Monitoring, Enforcement*, Ashgate Publishing Ltd, Aldershot 2003, pp. 281–97.

2 D. Robinson, 'The Identity Crisis of International Criminal Law' (2008) 21 *Leiden Journal of International Law* 925, 926–27.

methodological and practical goals. They remain two different branches of law with their own specificities, while sharing some commonalities. Importantly, ICL focuses on individual criminal responsibility and the consequent imposition of punishment on individuals. To do so, individual guilt (and, therefore, intent) needs to be established. HRL is a matter of State responsibility: the State – not a single person – is considered responsible (or not) for a breach of individual rights. As submitted elsewhere, the application of HRL in the realm of ICL had been taking place in a somewhat disarrayed manner,[3] whereby international criminal judges had not fully borne in mind the differences between the rationales of both areas of law, which in turn had caused some fragmentation in ICL and unwarrantedly affected the legitimacy of the system.[4] As then explained, ICL applies mainly to three different normative fields: (i) definition of crimes; (ii) individual liability; and (iii) guarantees of due process. This is not the moment to elaborate on this subject, but it is in respect of the third area that the fundamentals of ICL and HRL are most similar; therefore, it is in this realm that a more direct application and influence of one branch on the other may legitimately take place.[5] It is with this premise in mind that one shall consider the subjects analysed below. Against the same background, it is crucial to ensure that cross-fertilisation efforts between both branches of law follow a methodology that safeguards their distinctive differences so that no additional loopholes are created in the system of international protection of fundamental human rights and the fight against impunity. In other words, both ICL and HRL promote respect for fundamental human rights and endeavour to ensure accountability for those responsible for violations thereof. They do so in different levels – as the main tools they are – in a multi-layered international legal order and, as such, their mutual complementarity is crucial for the effectiveness of the international legal system.

2. ICL AS A VEHICLE FOR BROADENING THE SCOPE OF MATERIAL ENFORCEMENT AND PROTECTION OF HUMAN RIGHTS

ICL gives expression to the most serious violations of human rights in the realm of individual criminal responsibility. The ICL system as a whole widens

---

3 J. Wessel, 'Judicial Policy-Making at the International Criminal Court: An Institutional Guide to Analysing International Adjudication' (2006) 44 *Columbia Journal of Transnational Law* 377, 449; D. Robinson, above n. 2, 926.

4 P. Pinto Soares, 'Tangling Human Rights and International Criminal Law: The Practice of International Tribunals and the Call for "Rationalized" Legal Pluralism' (2012) 23 *Criminal Law Forum* 161.

5 Ibid.

the realm and practical enforcement of HRL. This may be illustrated through specific examples:

i) *Crimes against humanity* first emerged in connection with wartime only (so as to ensure respect for the principle of strict construction) and hence were linked with IHL.[6] Yet, IHL was not enough to deal with the atrocities of World War Two since it outlaws certain conduct when it is undertaken by a war faction against an occupied or adversarial civilian population but not when undertaken by the same power against its own people, as occurred in Nazi Germany. Accordingly, the Nuremberg Charter and the jurisprudence of the Nuremberg Tribunals extended the scope of protection of fundamental human rights. Afterwards, the International Criminal Tribunal for the former Yugoslavia (ICTY), followed by other international tribunals and culminating in the terms of the Rome Statute,[7] advanced this movement by clarifying that crimes against humanity might occur not only in wartime but also in peacetime.[8] It was this shift that opened the way to criminalisation in the international sphere of several additional instances of violation of fundamental human rights. For instance, in *Situation in Libya*, the Pre-Trial Chamber satisfied itself that crimes against humanity had occurred by looking into the administration of the Gaddafi regime before the beginning of civil war in the country. It referred to an organised State apparatus that, inter alia, oppressively breached the freedoms of speech, assembly and association, often culminating in the killing of civilians and the arrest, torture and enforced disappearance of protesters.[9] The Pre-Trial Chamber also noted that such an oppressive regime had successfully operated on grounds of the action of security forces and strict media control that had been designed to keep the regime in power. For the International Criminal Court (ICC), the policy requirement was fulfilled by the plan and actions of the regime to maintain control of the

---

6 See, e.g., International Military Tribunal (IMT), *France et al. v. Goring et al.*, 22 IMT, 203, 13 ILR 203 (1946) 41 *American Journal of International Law* 172.

7 Art. 7 of the Rome Statute.

8 See ICTY: *Prosecutor v. Tadic*, Case No. IT-94—1-A, Judgment, 15.07.1999, para. 249. The Court held that the reference to armed conflict in the Statute of the Tribunal was a jurisdictional pre-condition for it to exercise its mandate, rather than a constitutive element of crimes against humanity. See also the Special Court for Sierra Leone (SCSL): *Prosecutor v. Fofana and Kondewa*, Case No. SCSL, 04.14.T, Judgment, 02.08.2007, para. 111.

9 Situation in the Libyan Arab Jamahiriya: *Decision on the Prosecutor's Application Pursuant to Article 58 as to Muammar Mohammed Abu Minyar Gaddafi, Saif Al-Islam Gaddafi and Abdullah al-Senussi*, 27.06.2011, ICC-01/11-12, para. 19, 24, 28, 33–34. For more recent case law following a similar pattern, see *Prosecutor v. Laurent Gbagbo*, Decision on the confirmation of charges against Laurent Gbagbo, 12.06.2014, ICC-02/11-01/11-656-Red, paras 233–34, 245 and *Prosecutor v. Charles Blé Goudé*, Decision on the Confirmation of Charges, 11.12.2014, ICC-02/11-02/11-186, paras 66, 150 and 157.

State by disrespecting fundamental human rights.[10] It is worth noting that the Security Council referred to the events in Libya as 'gross and systematic violations of human rights, including the repression of peaceful demonstrations'[11] and that the ICC's jurisdiction over the situation in Libya arises pursuant to Resolution 1970/2011, of 26 February 2011, adopted under Chapter VII of the UN Charter.

ii) *Commissions of Inquiry* (CoI) have the potential to assist in the fight against impunity, by collecting information that may be used as, or assist in the gathering of, evidence. Sometimes, CoI are mandated to make findings on international crimes[12] and recommend criminal prosecutions.[13] In this way, it becomes evident how ICL may be a vehicle for the material enforcement of human rights, specifically by attributing individual criminal responsibility for violations thereof. In light of the human rights-based focus of the mandate of the Human Rights Council, the competence of CoI established thereby to make findings on ICL has been challenged. That notwithstanding, CoI have justified their jurisdiction to make findings on international crimes on the ground that they are enforcement mechanisms of IHL and HRL.[14] It is, however, important to note in this regard that CoI with an accountability mandate have resorted to ICL to qualify the conduct examined, but not the mode of criminal liability. Even in respect of the definition of the criminal offence, CoI have used more flexible approaches, which are at odds with, for example, the principle of strict construction that is typical of ICL and essential for purposes of the right to a fair trial. Furthermore, despite claiming to resort to the Rome Statute, some CoI failed to consider the policy requirement – in Article 7(2)(a) of the Rome Statute – when assessing whether crimes against humanity had been committed.[15] Not only may this lead to fragmentation in ICL; it means that

10 Ibid.: Situation in the Libyan Arab Jamahiriya.

11 UN Security Council Resolution 1970/2011, of 26 February 2011.

12 E.g. Mission to the Syrian Arab Republic to Investigate Alleged Violations of International Human Rights Law, Human Rights Council Resolution S-16/1, 04.05.2011. It enquired into, inter alia, the use of prohibited weapons as well as crimes against humanity.

13 CoI have been established with the following functions: (i) information (i.e. aiming at providing an independent account of the facts in dispute); (ii) alert (i.e. intending not only to inform but also to alert regarding threats to international peace and security and serious violations of human rights, and incentivise proper response from the international community) (e.g. UN Fact Finding Mission established by the UN GA on 11.10.1963); (iii) accountability (envisaging the assessment and recommendation of possible avenues for the enforcement of accountability) (e.g. International Commission of Inquiry on Libya, established by Resolution of the Human Rights Council S-15/1 of 25.02.2011).

14 L. van den Herik and C. Harwood, 'Sharing the Law: The Appeal of International Criminal Law for International Commissions of Inquiry', *Grotius Centre Working Paper Series* 2014/016-ICL, 13–14.

15 See, e.g., August 2012 Report of the Syria Commission, UN Doc A/HRC/21/50, 16.08.12, Annex II, paras 48–50. See ibid., 17.

> international criminal tribunals must be careful when using the findings of CoI, as they can be used as a basis for investigation but not immediately taken as evidence. In other words, there cannot be an automatic transposition of the outcome of CoI into the realm of ICL. Conversely, for, at least, a matter of credibility and legitimacy – i.e., the conviction that a *dictum* should be respected, acknowledged and/or followed – CoI should endeavour to draw their findings in line with core principles of ICL whenever the latter is resorted to. That notwithstanding, a certain flexibility is welcome and should be recognised when CoI display their mandates, given that they do not have the same power to attribute criminal responsibility in definitive terms as courts do.

HRL mechanisms provide little incentive for States and State representatives to take action against abuses committed by themselves and officials in power (unless one awaits an overturn in politics, which may give rise to concerns of impartiality and political targeting, thus tainting the legitimacy of procedures). ICL provides a back-up mechanism for the enforcement of fundamental human rights *vis-à-vis* the authorities of the State or structured group responsible, where States are genuinely unwilling or unable to carry out the investigation or prosecution.[16] Furthermore, by qualifying a crime as an international one, a full range of possibilities arise that are usually not available at the domestic level (for example, prosecution before an international tribunal, universal jurisdiction, *aut dedere aut judicare*, no statute of limitations and immunities and no defence of superior orders).

Indeed, it is worth mentioning that several human rights treaties (such as the International Covenant on Civil and Political Rights (ICCPR), the European Convention on Human Rights (ECHR) and the American Convention on Human Rights (ACHR)) resort to institutes of ICL and require States parties to abide thereby. This is the case, for instance, with the obligation to assert jurisdiction and criminalise certain criminal conduct. The relevant treaty bodies are often mandated to monitor compliance with such obligations, thus bestowing upon these structures enhanced watchdog powers. In line with this view, a recent study has revealed how the Inter-American Court of Human Rights has been monitoring prosecutions of international crimes in approximately 51 cases in 15 States. Pursuant to the Court's orders, States have, inter alia, opened a number of criminal investigations and bypassed statutes of limitations. At least 39 prosecutions initiated pursuant to the Court's orders are reported to have culminated in convictions.[17]

---

16 See, e.g., J.W. Davis, 'From Crimes Against Humanity to Human Rights Crimes' (2012) 18 *New England Journal of International and Comparative Law* 225, 226–27.

17 A. Huneeus, 'International Criminal Law by Other Means: The Quasi-Criminal Jurisdiction of the Human Rights Courts' (2013) 107 *American Journal of International Law* 1, 1–2.

3. ICL AS AN ADDITIONAL VECTOR OF RAISING AWARENESS OF HUMAN RIGHTS AND FURTHER EMPOWERMENT OF HRL

As previously explained, *Situation in Libya* and the approach taken by the ICC illustrate how ICL can work as the louder voice of HRL. For all the gravity of the conduct that falls under the scope of ICL, there is inevitably a strong emotional message in the ICL discourse that is unlikely to pass unnoticed. Grounding an assessment on 'crimes against humanity' also on breaches of the freedoms of speech, assembly and association enhances the momentum of the whole HRL system.

Likewise, it is by meeting the threshold of ICL that human rights violations are translated into the responsibility to protect (R2P) doctrine and the potential (at least in principle) it entails by recalling the moral, political and arguably legal responsibility of the international community (here including the UN organs) to take action (preventive, repressive or constructive) and condemning the State where violations are being committed.[18] Such actions are authoritative because they are backed up by the legitimate use and application of ICL.

When discussing the ICL's potential for empowerment of HRL, the chapter will inevitably come to note the discrepancy between the ICL's frequent reference to HRL and the somewhat reserved approach that HRL holds in readiness for ICL. The European Court of Human Rights' (ECtHR's) jurisprudence dealing with ICL is surprisingly limited: most cases with an ICL nexus concern mere references to the ICL tribunals' legal framework in the comparative law part of the judgment[19] – at times, without any visible signs of these provisions being used in the analysis part.[20] However, there are instances in which the ECtHR would have recourse to ICL for the purpose of defining legal terms and concepts[21] (and one out of many authorities for) identifying international legal standards or common

[18] L. van den Herik and C. Harwood, above n. 14, 9, 11 *et seq.*; G. Evans, *The Responsibility to Protect: Ending Mass Atrocity Crimes Once and for All*, Brookings Institution, Washington 2008; A. Oxford, *International Authority and the Responsibility to Protect*, Cambridge University Press, Cambridge 2011; A. Clapham, 'Human Rights and International Criminal Law', *SSRN*, <http://papers.ssrn.com/sol3/papers.cfm?abstract_id=2596659>, 6–7, accessed 14.11.2016.

[19] *Kafkaris v. Cyprus* [GC], no. 21906/04, §75–76, ECHR 2008; *Aslakhanova and Others v. Russia*, nos 2944/06, 8300/07, 50184/07, 332/08 and 42509/10, §62–63, ECHR 2012.

[20] *Babar Ahmad and Others v. United Kingdom*, nos 24027/07, 11949/08, 36742/08, 66911/09 and 67354/09, §140, ECHR 2012; *Harkins and Edwards v. United Kingdom*, nos 9146/07 and 32650/07, §64, ECHR 2012.

[21] *MC v. Bulgaria*, no. 39272/98, §§102–107 and 162, ECHR 2003-XII; (definition of 'rape' with the help of ICTY jurisprudence); *Rantsev v. Cyprus and Russia*, no. 25965/04, §280, ECHR 2010 (regarding the definition of 'slavery or servitude').

international practice.[22] Besides, ICL proved a valuable asset in Article 7 ECHR cases, assisting the Court to establish the foreseeability of crime.[23] In at least two cases the ECtHR relied on (historical) facts as established by international courts and tribunals – interestingly, without further ascertaining their reliability and accuracy.[24] The ICL's hitherto-limited assistance as called upon by the ECtHR could be linked to the novel character of ICL and the inherent lead time for relevant cases to be brought before the Strasbourg Court. In addition, its genealogy (ICL derives from and continuously draws upon IHL and HRL, as well as national criminal law)[25] may explain the enhanced need for judges in The Hague to have recourse to HRL. This is not the case for their counterparts in Strasbourg, as they watch over the respect for and the implementation of human rights – a self-standing body of law that does not require incursions by ICL for its due implementation. This unequal reliance of ICL on HRL makes them an unbalanced duo, and there are chances, as with odd couples in general, that that discrepancy will further accentuate with the passing of the years.

4. ICL: NARROWING THE SCOPE OF APPLICATION OF FUNDAMENTAL HUMAN RIGHTS?

In resorting again to crimes against humanity as an illustrative example, one realises that the definition thereof as provided in the Rome Statute requires that the specific criminal conduct must be performed in order to further a 'State or organizational policy'. This reference to the State or organisational policy may make us think of influences of HRL (which indeed aims to protect the individual from abuses of the State). One could thus consider that this constitutive element of the crime requires that the involvement of the State or a State-like organisation be determined. In line with this view, the policy requirement makes the burden of proof more demanding and consequently it might somehow narrow the enforcement of human rights through this

---

22 *Khoroshenko v. Russia* [GC], no. 41418/04, §142–43, ECHR 2015 (ICL's stance on ban on long-term visit of life prisoners); *Ahorugeze v. Sweden*, no. 37075/09, ECHR 2011 (standard established by the International Criminal Tribunal for Rwanda (ICTR) for transfers/extraditions to Rwanda); *Al-Adsani v. United Kingdom* [GC], no. 35763/97, §60–61, ECHR 2001-XI (prohibition of torture has achieved the status of a peremptory norm).

23 *Korbely v. Hungary* [GC], no. 9174/02, §70, ECHR 2008; *Jorgic v. Germany*, no. 74613/01, §89, ECHR 2007-III, *Šimšić v. Bosnia and Herzegovina*, no. 51552/10, §§22–25, *Vasiliauskas v. Lithuania* [GC], no. 35343/05, §§153–91, ECHR 2015.

24 *Mago and Others v. Bosnia and Herzegovina*, nos 12959/05, 19724/05, 47860/06, 8367/08, 9872/09 and 11706/09, §7, ECHR 2012; *Đokić v. Bosnia and Herzegovina*, no. 6518/04, §§60–61, ECHR 2010.

25 A. Cassese, P. Gaeta, L. Baig, M. Fan, C. Gosnell and A. Whiting, *Cassesse's International Criminal Law*, 3rd ed., Oxford University Press, Oxford 2013, pp. 3–5.

specific crime. In a similar sense, it has been argued that international crimes create a hierarchy in human rights whereby only those whose violation amounts to genocide, crimes against humanity and war crimes are a kind of first-class human rights.[26] However, it is submitted that this is not the case. ICL, HRL, IHL and national criminal laws all work – in one way or another – for the sake and protection of human rights. Each has its specific tools and scope of application. ICL is to be considered an *ultima ratio* branch of law: called upon only in relation to the most serious crimes and when other legal systems are not available to sanction outlawed conduct. The policy requirement is one of the contextual elements that makes, for example, a murder, abduction or rape a matter of concern of international law and not only domestic criminal law. This does not mean that it is less serious or demands less attention. Simply, it does not fall under the *chapeau* of ICL: its sanctioning belongs to another system.

Moreover, the very concept of human rights as being universal, inalienable and indivisible rights deriving from an individual's *conditio humana* is squarely in contradiction with such a hierarchical approach. Just as academics were able to identify 'absolute rights' among the extensive body of human rights and fundamental freedoms, their attempt to 'rank' some of these guarantees 'on top' of others was in no way meant to limit the scope of these rights. They merely conferred to these guarantees an additional layer of quality without derogating from the validity of ordinary (i.e. non-absolute) rights.

5. INTERNATIONAL CRIMINAL INVESTIGATIONS AND PROSECUTIONS: A THREAT TO WELL-ESTABLISHED HUMAN RIGHTS?

The seriousness of crimes under international law, the risk that they pose to the international community and the eagerness (and sometimes the pressure) speedily to identify perpetrators and hold them responsible may lead to unwarranted derogations of fundamental human rights, which have considerable negative impact on the whole structure of HRL. In 2014, two Guantanamo Bay detainees won their respective cases against Poland before the ECtHR. Both applicants claimed to have been held at a CIA 'black site' in Poland, where they were kept in secret detention for six and nine months respectively, without sound legal basis or review and with no contact with family. As per the submissions, Poland knowingly and intentionally allowed the CIA to transfer the applicants to Guantanamo Bay, and thus into a jurisdiction where there existed a real risk of further ill treatment and incommunicado detention and no assurances persisted

26 A. Clapham, above n. 18, 7 and accompanying references.

of compliance with the right to a fair trial. In view of the available evidence, the ECtHR held Poland responsible for breaches of, inter alia, Articles 3 (prohibition of torture and inhuman and degrading treatment), 5 (right to liberty and security), 8 (right to respect for private and family life), 13 (right to an effective remedy) and 6 (right to a fair trial) ECHR.[27]

Still related to the fight against terrorism, following the large-scale terrorist attacks in the region of Paris on 13 November 2015, the French Government declared a state of emergency in the country.[28] On 24 November 2015, France filed a formal notice of derogation from the ECHR with the Secretary-General of the Council of Europe, as per Article 15 ECHR. The implications of the declaration of emergency and the scope of the derogation from the ECHR have been criticised. On one hand, it has been pointed out that the state of emergency and the extensive powers accorded to police and intelligence forces have been used in relation to matters other than terrorism, such as to curb climate change protests in Paris.[29] Human Rights Watch has denounced the breach of civil liberties.[30] Furthermore, the derogation notice appears to have been extremely vague, simply stating that some of the emergency measures adopted 'may involve a derogation from the obligations' enshrined in the ECHR without elaborating on the measures that would or could imply derogation and the extent to which such measures were strictly necessary to respond to the critical situation existing in France. In this regard, it is important to note that Article 15(1) ECHR establishes:

> In time of war or other public emergency threatening the life of the nation any High Contracting Party may take measures derogating from its obligations under this Convention to the *extent strictly required by the exigencies of the situation*, provided that such measures are not inconsistent with its other obligations under international law (emphasis added).

---

27 *Al Nashiri v. Poland*, no. 28761/11, ECHR 2014; *Husayn (Abu Zubaydah) v. Poland*, no. 7511/13, ECHR 2014. In a similar sense, see *El-Masri v. Former Yugoslav Republic of Macedonia*, no. 39639/09, ECHR 2013; and *Nasr and Ghali v. Italy*, no. 44883/09, ECHR 2016.

28 Decree No. 2015-1475 of 14.11.2015, applying Law 55-385 of 03.04.1955.

29 Under the new law, the Minister of Interior may, inter alia, place under house arrest – without prior judicial authorisation or oversight – anyone who there are *serious reasons* to believe poses a threat to public order and security. The Interior Minister and the prefect may also order searches without a judicial warrant, at any time and place that is frequented by a person against whom there are *serious reasons* to believe he or she poses a threat to public order and security. Authorities conducting the searches may access and copy digital data saved on electronic devices on the premises searched. The law provides no guarantee to limit the use or disclosure of such material, namely in situations where the searches revealed no wrongdoing.

30 HRW, *France: New Emergency Powers Threaten Rights: Parliament should ensure new powers not misused*, 24.11.2015, available at <https://www.hrw.org/news/2015/11/24/france-new-emergency-powers-threaten-rights> accessed 14.11.2016.

In addition, paragraph 2 reads as follows:

> No derogation from Article 2, except in respect of deaths resulting from lawful acts of war, or *from Articles* 3, 4 (paragraph 1) and 7 shall be made under this provision (emphasis added).

In this regard, reality has shown that the averred fight against terrorism has often been accompanied by serious derogations from fundamental rights, especially violations of the prohibition of torture and inhuman and degrading treatment (Article 3 ECHR). Breaches of fundamental human rights resulting from the over-reaching powers derived from the declaration of a state of emergency are likely to be challenged before both French courts and the ECtHR. Developments at this level will shed light on the exact impact of the state of emergency in France on HRL. Importantly, the jurisprudence of the ECtHR is demanding in respect of derogations of human rights. In *Aksoy v. Turkey*, the ECtHR acknowledged the dangers of terrorism and the threat to the community posed thereby; however, it was not persuaded that the exigencies of the situation required the holding of the applicant (suspected of involvement in terrorist offences) in detention and incommunicado for 14 days or more, without access to a judge.[31]

Certainly, one may argue that such intrusive powers are the result of extraordinary circumstances or threats and, hence, a necessary consequence to guarantee the wellbeing of the people and the security and life of the State. This chapter does not intend to delve into the merits of this subject but rather to highlight that, whatever the reasons, there is a risk that, in order to facilitate investigations into the most serious crimes that shock the conscience of humanity, one may be taking a worrying approach *vis-à-vis* human rights and all the achievements in this realm. One does not need to speculate on the future: rather, the restrictive policies following the terrorist attacks in the United States on 11 September 2001 are illustrative of the dangers at stake.[32] In addition – and

---

31 *Aksoy v. Turkey*, no. 21987/93, ECHR 1996. See also *Demir v. Turkey*, no. 71/1997/855/1062-1064, ECHR 2006.

32 In the *Kadi* case, the ECJ ruled that the re-examination procedure established by the UN Sanctions Committee manifestly did not assure judicial protection for the following reasons: (i) the essentially diplomatic and intergovernmental nature of the Committee; (ii) the lack of opportunity for requesting parties to assert their rights during the procedure; (iii) lack of communication to requesting parties of the reasons for their appearance on the list or, at least, restricted access to their data. See Joint Cases C-402/05 P and C-415/05 P, *Yassin Abdullah Kadi and Al Barakaat International Foundation v. Council of the European Union and Commission of the European Communities* ECLI:EU:C:2008:461. The UN Special Rapporteur on the Promotion and Protection of Human Rights and Fundamental Freedoms While Countering Terrorism stated, in respect of the UN Sanctions Committee, that '[a]t a minimum, the standards required to ensure a fair hearing must include the right of an individual to be informed of the measures taken and to know the case against him or her as soon as, and to the extent possible, without thwarting the purpose of the sanctions regimes;

paradoxically – it might be the case that the specifics of this approach to the war on terrorism may open the way to very serious crimes: for instance, by allowing or condoning waterboarding as a justified technique of interrogation, even if only limited to 'ticking bomb' scenarios.[33]

From a different, though related, perspective, the various instances of witness intimidation in proceedings before the ICC reveal that perhaps the international community demands too much from victims of international crimes without having yet developed a capable system of protection. *Situation in Kenya* and its encompassing cases reveal regrettable incidents that, far from being the exception, led to unnecessary anguish and grief for witnesses and victims, including intolerable cases of witness interference, such as reported threats of physical attacks and psychological pressure by third parties, including governments.[34]

6. THE ICC AND THE RIGHT TO A FAIR TRIAL: 'HOLIER THAN THE POPE'?

Any impartial analysis of the effects of ICL on HRL will necessarily entail an assessment of the international criminal tribunals' jurisprudence.

The aim of the present analysis is to assess the level of human rights protection afforded to individuals in international criminal procedure and determine the possible impact of ICL jurisprudence on HRL. For reasons of brevity, it will be confined to a representative number of fair trial aspects.

---

the right to be heard within a reasonable time by the relevant decision-making body; the right to effective review by a competent and independent review mechanism; the right to counsel with respect to all proceedings; and the right to an effective remedy'. See Statement by M. Scheinin, Special Rapporteur on the Promotion and Protection of Human Rights and Fundamental Freedoms While Countering Terrorism, 63rd session of the General Assembly, Third Committee, Item 64(b), 22.10.2008, 6. He further held that '... so long as there is no independent review of the listings at the United Nations level, there must be access to domestic judicial review of any implementing measure. A person subject to such measures must be informed of the measures taken and to know the case against him or her, and to be able to be heard within a reasonable time by the relevant decision-making body' (ibid., 5).

33 A. Dershowitz, 'Democrats and Waterboarding', *Wall Street Journal*, 07.11.2007, <http://www.wsj.com/articles/SB119439827396084663> accessed 14.11.2016.

34 The most emblematic example of this situation is likely to be materialised in the dropping of the charges before the ICC against Mr Uhuru Kenyatta, President of Kenya. The ICC Prosecutor, Mrs Fatou Bensouda, accused the Kenyan Government of threatening and intimidating potential witnesses to the extent that the available evidence did not permit any outcome other than the withdrawal of charges (though with no prejudice to the possibility of bringing a new case, should additional evidence become available). See Statement of the Prosecutor of the International Criminal Court, Fatou Bensouda, on the withdrawal of charges against Mr. Uhuru Muigai Kenyatta, 05.12.2014, <https://www.icc-cpi.int/en_menus/icc/press%20and%20media/press%20releases/Pages/otp-statement-05-12-2014-2.aspx> accessed 14.11.2016.

Far from being exhaustive, it seeks to examine the overall compliance of the ICC law and practice with the applicable international standards, and notably the ones developed under the regime of the ECHR.

The fair trial principle is a central pillar of the Rome Statute;[35] numerous references testify to its importance in proceedings before the ICC,[36] which is also demonstrated by the Court's (inherent) authority to stay proceedings in cases of serious violations of the principle.[37]

6.1. EQUALITY OF ARMS

The equality of arms principle lies at the heart of a fair trial. While lawmakers have refrained from adopting specific regulations,[38] emerging practice attests to the ICC's commitment to protect the equality of arms principle in a real and effective manner.[39]

On numerous occasions, the defence has invoked the equality of arms principle by alleging lack of access to relevant and admissible evidence due to non-cooperation by domestic authorities.[40] Article 57(3)(b) of the Rome

---

35 Arts 21(3), 61(6), 66, 74, 64(2), 67(1), 68(1) and (5) and 55 of the Rome Statute.

36 ICC, *Situation in the Democratic Republic of Congo, Appeals Chamber, Judgment on the Prosecutor's Application for Extraordinary Review of Pre-Trial Chamber I's 31 March 2006 Decision Denying Leave to Appeal*, ICC-01/04-168, para 11, 13.07.2006: 'the term "fair" in the context of [...] the Statute is associated with the norms of a fair trial, the attributes of which are an inseverable part of the corresponding human right, [...] making its interpretation and application subject to internationally recognized human rights; equally stipulating that the principles of a fair trial are not confined to trial proceedings, but extend to pre-trial proceedings and the investigation of crime'.

37 ICC, *Prosecutor v. Thomas Lubanga Dyilo, Judgment on the Appeal of Mr. Thomas Lubanga Dyilo against the Decision on the Defence Challenge to the Jurisdiction of the Court pursuant to Article 19 (2) (a) of the Statute of 3 October 2006*, 14.12.2006, ICC-01/04-01/06 (OA 4), para. 39.

38 See, however, Art. 67(1) of the Rome Statute 'in full equality', Art. 69(3) of the Statute read in conjunction with Arts 64 and 67(e) (presentation of evidence), Arts 61(3), 64(3)(c) and 67(2) of the Statute and Rules 76, 77, 78, 84 and 121 of the Rules of Procedure and Evidence.

39 ICC, *Prosecutor v. Thomas Lubanga Dyilo, Decision on defence's request to obtain French transcripts*, ICC-01/04-01/06-1091, 14.12.2007, para 18; see also *Situation in Uganda, Decision on Prosecutor's Application for leave to Appeal in Part Pre-Trial Chamber II's Decision on the Prosecutor's Applications for Warrants of Arrest under Article 58*, ICC-02/04-01/05-20-US-Exp, 19.08.2005, para. 30; *Prosecutor v. Thomas Lubanga Dyilo, Décision sur la demande d'autorisation d'appel de la Defense relative à la transmission des Demandes de participation des victimes*, ICC-01/04-01/06-672, 06.11.2006, 7; *Prosecutor v. Germain Katanga and Mathieu Ngudjolo Chui, Decision on the Prosecutor's Bar Table Motions*, ICC-01/04-01/07-2635, 17.12.2010, para 16; and *Decision on the disclosure of evidentiary material relating to the Prosecutor's site visit to Bogoro on 28,29 and 31 March 2009* (ICC-01/04-01/07-1305, 1345, 1360, 1401, 1412 and 1456), 09.10.2009, ICC-01/04-01/07-1515-Corr, para. 68.

40 ICC, *Prosecutor v. Germain Katanga and Mathieu Ngudjolo Chui, Revised Request for Co-operation*, ICC-01/04-01/07-406-Conf-Exp; *Prosecutor v. Abdallah Banda Abakaer*

Statute bestows upon the defence a procedural right to seek assistance from the Pre-Trial Chamber (including re the issuance of orders and requests for cooperation addressed to States and intergovernmental organisations) in order to ease its investigation process. Chambers have consistently granted such requests,[41] (implicitly) confirming earlier jurisprudence by the ICTY that held that, in the context of ICL, the principle of equality of arms must be given a more liberal interpretation than that normally upheld with regard to proceedings before domestic courts.[42] This approach goes way beyond the requirements established by the ECtHR, which suggests that the principle of equality of arms is not applicable to conditions outside the control of a court.[43]

In addition, substantial participatory rights have been afforded to victims, giving them an opportunity to express their views and concerns.[44] The ICC thus considerably broadened the scope of the equality of arms principle *ratione personae* as defined by the ECtHR.[45]

Nourain and Saleh Mohammed Jerbo Jamus, Defence Application pursuant to Article 57(3)(b) of the Statute for an order for the preparation and transmission of a cooperation request to the Government of the Republic of the Sudan, 17.11.2010, ICC-02/05-03/09-95.

41 ICC, *Prosecutor v. Germain Katanga and Mathieu Ngudjolo Chui, Decision on the Defence's Application pursuant to Article 57(3)(b) of the Statute to Seek Cooperation of the Democratic Republic of Congo (DRC)*, ICC-01/04-01/07-444, 25.04.2008; as for decisions granting the approach (in principle) while rejecting the specific request: see *Prosecutor v. Abdallah Banda Abakaer Nourain and Saleh Mohammed Jerbo Jamus, Decision on Defence Application pursuant to articles 57(3)(b) and 64(6)(a) of the Statute for an order for the preparation and transmission of a cooperation request to the Government of the Republic of Sudan*, ICC-02/05-03/09-169, 02.07.2011 (rejecting the request for lack of specificity); *Prosecutor v. Callixte Mbarushimana, Decision on the Defence Request for and order for State Cooperation Pursuant to Article 57(3)(b) of the Rome Statute*, ICC-01/04-01/10-85, 24.03.2011; *The Prosecutor v. Abdallah Banda Abakaer Nourain and Saleh Mohammed Jerbo Jamus, Decision on Defence Application pursuant to Articles 57(3)(b) & 64(6)(a) of the Statute for an order for the preparation and transmission of a cooperation request to the African Union*, ICC-02/05-03/09-170, 01.07.2011.

42 ICTY, *Prosecutor v. Duko Tadic*, Judgement, IT-94-1-A, 15.07.1999, para. 48, noting that the ICCPR remained silent on this specific question and that international tribunals had no choice but to rely on the cooperation of States.

43 *Kaufman v. Belgium*, no. 10938/84, ECHR 1986, Decisions and Reports (DR) 50, 98; *Neumeister v. Austria*, 27 June 1968, Series A, no. 8; *Bendenoun v. France*, 24 February 1994, Series A, no. 284; *Dombo Beheer BV v. The Netherlands*, 27 October 1993, Series A, no. 274, as referred to in para 49 *Prosecutor v. Duko Tadic*, IT-94-1-A, above n. 42.

44 M. Fedorova, *The Principle of Equality of Arms in International Criminal Law*, School of Human Rights Research Series, Vol 55, Intersentia, Antwerp 2012, 424 with accompanying references: 'Thus, victims have the right to notification and to attend all public and closed hearings, have access to both public and confidential filings, are allowed to question witnesses, to make submissions orally and in writing on various issues as well as opening and closing statements, and introduce and challenge evidence.'

45 *Foucher v. France*, Reports of Judgments and Decisions, §34, ECHR, 1997-II, 1997; *Bulut v. Austria*, Reports of Judgments and Decisions, ECHR 1996-II, 1996; *Bobek v. Poland*, no. 68761/01, §56, ECHR 17 July 2007. The victims' ability to lead and challenge evidence

6.2. REASONING OF JUDICIAL DECISIONS

The ICC's legal framework has duly integrated this principle at various stages of the proceedings[46] and some case law has emerged on the necessity for reasoned opinions when rendering decisions or judgments.[47]

The ICC's practice reveals a rather verbose approach. Chambers habitually attach great importance to adequate reasoning, providing parties and participants with a fair amount of information as to how they reached their conclusions.[48] Common questions of a procedural nature are often dealt with in an overly exhaustive manner.[49] Pre-Trial Chambers have been criticised for the fact that confirmation of charges decisions pursuant to Article 61(7) consistently exceeded the 100-page benchmark, 'although these decision[s] [are] not even

has exposed them to criticism alleging that they would act as a 'second prosecutor'. See the Dissenting Opinion of Judge Pikis in: *Prosecutor v. Thomas Lubanga Dyilo*, Appeals Chamber, *Judgment on the appeals of the Prosecutor and the Defence against Trial Chamber I's Decision on Victims' Participation of 18 January 2008*, 11.07.2008, ICC-01/04-01/06-1432, para 4. See also *Prosecutor v. Lubanga Dyilo*, Appeals Chamber, *Decision of the Appeals Chamber on the Joint Application of Victims a/0001/06 to a/0003/06 and a/0105/06 concerning the 'Directions and Decision of the Appeals Chamber' of 2 February 2007*, 13.06.2007, ICC-01/04-01/06-925, para 19.

46 Arts 74(5), 83(4) and 72(7)(a)(ii) of the Rome Statute; Rules 50(5), 64(2), 108(1), 110(1), 135(2), 139(2), 159(2), and 224(2) of the Rules of Procedure and Evidence; Reg. 20(2) of the Regulations of the Court.

47 ICC, *Prosecutor v. Saif Al-Islam Gaddafi and Abdullah Al-Senussi*, Appeals Chamber, *Judgment on the appeal of Libya against the decision of Pre-Trial Chamber I of 31 May 2013 entitled 'Decision on the admissibility of the case against Saif Al-Islam Gaddafi'*, ICC-01/11-01/11-547-Red, 21.05.2014, para 207 with further references. See also Judge Ušacka's Dissenting Opinion in *Prosecutor v. Laurent Koudou Gbagbo*, Appeals Chamber, *Judgment on the appeal of Mr Laurent Koudou Gbagbo against the decision of Pre-Trial Chamber I of 13 July 2012 entitled 'Decision on the "Requête de la Défense demandant la mise en liberté provisoire du président Gbagbo"'* ICC-02/11-01/11-278-Red, 26.10.2012, paras 12–14; *Prosecutor v. Thomas Lubanga Dyilo*, Appeals Chamber, *Judgment on the appeal of Mr Thomas Lubanga Dyilo against his conviction*, ICC-01/04-01/06-3121-Red, 01.12.2014, para. 178, with further references.

48 ICC, *Situation in the Republic of Kenya, Decision Pursuant to Article 15 of the Rome Statute on the Authorisation of an Investigation into the Situation in the Republic of Kenya*, 31.03.2010, ICC-01/09-19-Corr.

49 ICC, *Situation in the Central African Republic, Decision on the Interim Release of Jean-Pierre Bemba Gombo and Convening Hearings with the Kingdom of Belgium, the Republic of Portugal, the Republic of France, the Federal Republic of Germany, the Italian Republic, and the Republic of South Africa*, ICC-01/05-01/08-475, 14.08.2009; *Decision on the Prosecutor's Application for Warrants of Arrest, Article 58*, ICC-01/04-01/07-520-Anx2, 10.02.2006; *Prosecutor v. Jean-Pierre Bemba Gombo, Decision on the Admissibility and Abuse of Process Challenges*, ICC-01/04-02/06-785-Red, 18.08.2005; *Prosecutor v. William Samoei Ruto and Joshua Arap Sang, Decision on Prosecutor's Application for Witness Summonses and resulting Request for State Party Cooperation*, ICC-01/09-01/11-1274-Corr2, 17.04.2014.

renewable on appeal'.[50] One notes also the first generation of judgments pursuant to Article 74 of the Statute, which extend to more than 600 pages each.[51]

One may question the need to delve into a detailed analysis of what are, arguably, not always highly relevant matters.[52] Excessive reasoning could be perceived as being suspiciously lengthy, thereby undermining the credibility and authority of the decision.[53] In addition, lengthy reasoning may unnecessarily open new questions for litigation which otherwise would not come under dispute. Be that as it may, it is safe to say that ICC judges, just as their counterparts at the ICTY, fully meet – and frequently exceed – the requirement for reasoning of judicial decisions.

6.3. RIGHT TO A PUBLIC HEARING

The principle of publicity includes the right to an oral hearing and the accused's presence at trial as well as the public pronouncement of judgments. The ICC – as have international courts and tribunals in general – has operated a policy that allows the largest possible number of observers to follow the trial either by physical attendance at the place of the hearing or by video link. It is noteworthy

---

50 C. Safferling, *International Criminal Procedure*, Oxford University Press, Oxford 2012, 337, with further reference to M. Miraglia, 'Admissibility of Evidence, Standard of Proof, and Nature of the Decision in the ICC Confirmation of Charges in Lubanga' (2008) 6 *Journal of International Criminal Justice* 489, 500, alleging that such 'extreme reasoning' could negatively influence the perception of the trial judges.

51 624 pages in the case of *Prosecutor v. Thomas Lubanga Dyilo*, Judgment pursuant to Article 74 of the Statute, ICC-01/04-01/06-2842; 660 pages in the case *Prosecutor v. Germain Katanga*, Judgment pursuant to Article 74 of the Statute, ICC-01/04-01/07-3436-tENG, excluding separate opinions, Annexes and Decisions on the Sentence pursuant to Article 76 of the Statute. Note, however, the considerably shorter judgment in *Prosecutor v. Jean-Pierre Bemba Gombo*, Judgment pursuant to Article 74 of the Statute, ICC-01/05-01/08-3343 (364 pages). The aforementioned decisions squarely contrast with the ECtHR's settled jurisprudence, requiring that only the *essential issues* of a case be addressed in a decision (*Boldea v. Romania*, no. 1997/02, §30, 15 February 2007; *Van de Hurk v. The Netherlands*, §61, 19 April 1994, Series A no. 288).

52 See, for instance, the pertinent observation by Judge Tarfusser in his Separate Opinion to the Decision on the confirmation of charges in the Abu Garda case: *Prosecutor v. Bahar Idriss Abu Garda, Decision on the Confirmation of Charges*, ICC-02/05-02/09-243-Red, 08.02.2010, Separate Opinion, Judge Tarfusser, para 9. See also the critical comment in *Stoitchkova*, International Criminal Court (notes) in (2010) 28(3) *Netherlands Quarterly of Human Rights*, 475.

53 N.H.B. Jorgensen and A. Zahar, 'Deliberation, Dissent, Judgment' in G. Sluiter, H. Friman, S. Linton, S. Zappalà and S. Vasiliev, *International Criminal Procedure: Principles and Rules*, Oxford University Press, Oxford 2014, 1167: 'too much detail is counterproductive. The 689-page trial judgment in [the ICTY-case] of Hadžihasanović and Kubura case was considered excessively long (or long-winded) by the Appeals Chamber [...] with the problem being] the prolixity of the judgment rather than the number of pages per se'.

that transmission of hearings via the internet ('live stream') and (by implication) the use of photographs/screenshots is authorised, whereas many domestic jurisdictions do not allow for such practice.[54] While this is mainly due to the enhanced attention that ICC trials will receive from the public, the ICC's law and practice go way beyond what is legally required from the perspective of the ECHR.[55]

Further, the ICC legal framework does not allow for trials to be conducted in the absence of the accused. Only where the defendant is removed from the proceedings on the ground that he has repeatedly and continually disrupted them, may trials *in absentia* be permitted under Article 64 of the Statute. Without entering into discussion of the appropriateness and practicability of trials *in absentia* before international courts and tribunals in general,[56] and the ICC in particular,[57] suffice it to say that the current legal framework involves a regime that is, by far, more defence-friendly than that proposed by the ECtHR.[58] This becomes apparent in cases where a suspect deliberately eludes capture.

---

54 For Germany, see §169 Satz 2 *Gerichtsverfassungsgesetz* stipulating a general prohibition of audio and video recordings in the courtroom. Regarding France, see Art. 38*ter de la loi du 29 juillet 1881 sur la liberté de la presse* containing a similar provision. The underlying rationale of these legislative barriers is closely linked to the protection of the right to private life of the parties and participants in the trial (in particular the accused, witnesses and others) who shall be shielded against possible additional mental stress resulting from their presence in the courtroom. In addition it is submitted that said provisions are meant to thwart possible encroachments on the public order in courtroom and eventual interferences with the truth finding process (Zeder, 'Medienrecht im Spannungsfeld zwischen Meinungsfreiheit und Persönlichkeitsschutz', *Österreichische Juristenzeitung* 2011, 17).

55 *Sutter v. Switzerland*, 22 February 1984, Series A no. 74; *Grabenwarter*, Europäische Menschenrechtskonvention, 316 with further references.

56 For a detailed analysis of legislation and practice of the ICTY, ICTR and Special Tribunal for Lebanon (STL), see G.J. Shaw, 'Convicting Inhumanity in Absentia: Holding Trials in Absentia at the International Criminal Court' (2012) 44 *George Washington International Law Review* 107.

57 See the most recent developments in the *Ruto and Kenyatta* cases, including the adoption of Rule 134*quater* and Ruto's conditional excuse from presence at trial on the basis of foresaid provision in (*Prosecutor v. William Samoei Ruto and Joshua Arap Sang, Decision on Mr Ruto's Request for Excusal from Continuous Presence at Trial*, ICC-01/09-01/11-777, 18.06.2013) in M.H. Zakerhossein and A.-M. De Brouwer, 'Diverse Approaches to Total and Partial *In Absentia* Trials by International Criminal Tribunals' (2015) 26 *Criminal Law Forum* 181, 224, concluding that the presence at trial is a right of the accused, which (i) prohibits the holding of *in absentia* trials, and (ii) an obligation upon the accused, which obliges him to be present at trial, even though he waives his right to be present. Specifically, '[t]he accused is not allowed to be absent at trial by waiving his right, unless the Court accepts his request. And also, the Court it is not allowed to hold an in absentia trial unless the accused explicitly waives his right to be present'. For the historical coming into being of this regime, see J. Crawford, 'The ILC's Draft Statute for an International Criminal Court' (1994) 88 *American Journal of International Law* 141.

58 *Colozza v. Italy*, 1985, §§27–29, Series A no. 89; *Sejdovic v. Italy* [GC], no. 56581/00, §82, ECHR *Reports of Judgments and Decisions* 2006-II with further reference to, inter alia,

While the ECtHR would, subject to stringent conditions, allow proceeding with a prosecution,[59] the Rome Statute still prevents such a situation from happening before the ICC.

Lastly, under Article 6 ECHR, judgment is to be pronounced publicly. However, the Strasbourg organs abstained from adopting a literal approach and considered that means other than reading out in full may be compatible with Article 6, as long as they are amenable to scrutiny of the judiciary by the public with a view to safeguarding the right to a fair trial.[60] ICC judgments are not only publicly pronounced but systematically read out in open court.[61] Again, the ICC not only conforms to the minimum requirements of the ECHR but, in fact, surpasses the requisite standards under the Convention.[62]

6.4. RIGHT TO REMAIN SILENT AND NOT TO INCRIMINATE ONESELF

The relevant provisions in the Statute[63] explicitly state that silence is not to be a consideration in the determination of guilt or innocence of the accused[64] (contrary to the views of the ECtHR, which merely requires that 'a conviction must not be *solely or mainly* based on the accused's silence or on a refusal to answer questions or to give evidence himself').[65] In addition, the prosecution's consistent practice of informing all persons questioned – including under

FCB v. Italy, 1991, §33, Series A no. 208-B; and *Belziuk v. Poland*, 25 March 1998, §37, *Reports of Judgments and Decisions* 1998-II. For the even less stringent requirements applying to appeal proceedings, see *Hermi v. Italy* [GC], no. 18114/02, §60, ECHR, *Reports of Judgments and Decisions* 2006-XII and *Fejde v. Sweden*, 1991, §31, Series A no. 212-C.

59 *Medenica v. Switzerland*, no. 20491/92, §55, ECHR; *Sejdovic v. Italy* [GC], no. 56581/00, §§82–83 ECHR, Reports 2006-II.

60 Such means include deposition in the court registry and publication in an official collection of judgments. See *Pretto and Others v. Italy*, 1983, §27, Series A no. 71; *Sutter v. Switzerland*, 22 February 1984, §33, Series A no. 74.

61 Although the delivery of judgments in open court is commonly limited to essential parts, see the recent hearing in *Prosecutor v. Jean-Pierre Bemba Gombo*, in which a summary of the judgment was read out in the presence of the accused and his defence team (Press release of 14 March 2016 ICC-CPI-20160314-MA198 'Judgment in Bemba case to be delivered on 21 March 2016: Practical information').

62 *Sutter v. Switzerland*, 22 February 1984, §33, Series A no. 74; *Campbell and Fell v. United Kingdom*, 28 June 1984, §91, Series A no. 80.

63 Arts 55(2)(b) and 67(g) of the Rome Statute. Said provisions need to be read in combination with the relevant provisions stipulating the presumption of innocence (Arts 66 and 67(i) of the Rome Statute).

64 K. de Meester, K. Pitcher, R. Rastan and G. Sluiter, 'Investigation, Coercive Measures, Arrest and Surrender' in G. Sluiter, H. Friman, S. Linton, S. Zappalà and S. Vasiliev, above n. 53, 235, observing that the 'ICC Statute offers greater protection than the ad hoc Tribunals and the SCSL.'

65 *Murray v. United Kingdom*, 28 October 1994, §47, Series A no. 300-A.

Article 55(2) – that their evidence may be used in subsequent proceedings has become firmly established in Regulation 40(f) of the Regulations of the Office of the Prosecutor.[66] Again, such a caveat informing the accused or suspect that his or her statement may be used in evidence at trial goes beyond what is required by the Strasbourg jurisprudence.

The right not to incriminate oneself[67] is 'the corollary of the right to remain silent, both of which are intimately tied to the presumption of innocence'.[68] Contrary to international human rights standards,[69] including the jurisprudence of the ECtHR ('incriminate himself' and 'self-incrimination'),[70] Article 67 of the Statute is not limited to 'testimony against oneself', suggesting that the accused may refuse *any* testimony, even if it might be argued that it could or would be 'in favour' of the accused.[71] It remains doubtful whether the fathers of the Rome Statute had intended such an excessive level of protection.

6.5. RIGHT TO LEGAL ASSISTANCE

Articles 55(2) and 67(d) of the Rome Statute guarantee that proceedings against an accused person will not take place without adequate representation of the case for the defence.[72] However, while Article 6(3)(c) ECHR leaves it to the accused to assert his rights under the Convention, Articles 55(2)(c) and 67(d) of the Statute both require that the suspect or accused be officially informed of his rights to receive legal assistance and 'to have legal assistance assigned by the Court in any case where the interests of justice so require, and without payment if the accused lacks sufficient means to pay for it'.

As to the right to free legal assistance (legal aid), the ICC's legal framework applies a higher threshold than that of the ECHR[73] and limits the accused's or

66 K. de Meester, K. Pitcher, R. Rastan and G. Sluiter, above n. 64, 234.

67 As per Arts 55(1)(a) and 67(1)(g) of the Rome Statute.

68 ICC, *Prosecutor v. Germain Katanga and Mathieu Ngudjolo Chui, Decision on the implementation of regulation 55 of the Regulations of the Court and severing the charges against the accused persons*, ICC-01/04-01/07-3319-tENG/FRA, 21.11.2012, para. 48.

69 Art. 14 ICCPR.

70 *Funke v. France*, 25 February 1993, §44, Series A no. 256-A; *Saunders v. United Kingdom*, 17 December 1996, §60, *Reports of Judgments and Decisions* 1996-VI; *John Murray v. United Kingdom*, 8 February 1996, §45, *Reports of Judgments and Decisions* 1996-I.

71 W. Schabas, *The International Criminal Court: a Commentary on the Rome Statute* (2010), 813, as cited in J.P. Pérez-León Acevedo and B. Elberling, 'Article 67(1)(g) – Applicable Law, The Rome Statute' in M. Klamberg (ed.), *The Commentary on the Law of the International Criminal Court*, <www.casematrixnetwork.org/cmn-knowledge-hub/icc-commentary-clicc> accessed 14.11.2016.

72 See also Art. 6(3)(c) ECHR.

73 *Meftah and Others v. France* [GC], nos 32911/96, 35237/97 and 34595/97, ECHR 2002, *Reports of Judgments and Decisions* 2002-VII; *Croissant v. Germany*, 1992, Series A no. 237-B; *Lagerblom v. Sweden*, no. 26891/95, 2003; *Pakelli v. Germany*, 25 April 1983, Series A no. 64.

suspect's choice to counsel who meet clearly defined requirements as to their previous experience, their expertise, languages skills and others.[74]

The ICC's lenient regime on the right to defend oneself is further accentuated by the lack of distinction between Article 70 and Article 5 offences as regards the right to legal aid.[75] Therefore, thresholds higher than usual (i.e. by reference to the ECHR) apply to the right to legal assistance, providing for an enhanced level of protection for the defence.

6.6. RIGHT TO BE INFORMED PROMPTLY ABOUT CHARGES

Article 67(1)(a) of the Statute[76] is said to be framed in a more defence-friendly manner, as it refers not only to the nature and cause of the charge (see Article 6 of the ECHR) but also to its *content*. Taken together with the Statute's thorough disclosure regime, these provisions arguably indicate the desire of the Rome Conference to have the accused benefit from a level of information that goes well beyond the threshold set by domestic justice systems and endorsed by international human rights tribunals as being acceptable.[77]

Such observations are confirmed by the ICC's burgeoning jurisprudence as to which type of information must be made available: for example, a 'readable version of the part of the arrest warrant that refers to the case against him'[78] or 'all public documents in the record of the [...] situation, which [...] includes non-redacted versions, public redacted versions, or web-site announcements of

---

74 Rule 22 of the Rules of Procedure and Evidence and Regulation 67 *et seq* of the Regulations of the Court. In addition, at the ICC and other international and hybrid criminal courts – so as to guarantee effective representation – there is a trend aimed at aligning the qualifications of the accused person's assigned counsel to those of an equivalent position in the prosecution side. See J.P. Pérez-León Acevedo and B. Elberling, above n. 71, with further references.

75 ICC, *Prosecutor v. Jean-Pierre Bemba Gombo, Aimé Kilolo Musamba, Jean-Jacques Mangenda Kabongo, Fidèle babala Wandu and Narcisse Arido*, ICC-01/05-01/13-955, 21.05.2015, paras 34 and 35. Although the seriousness of the offence, severity of the penalty at stake, and the complexity or personal situation for Art. 70 cases are not nearly comparable with the ones in Art. 5 offences, Trial Chamber VII cogently noted that the relevant provisions, Arts 55(2)(c) and 67(1) of the Rome Statute, do not make apparent any distinction between the two types of offences. Therefore, they do not support the argument that there is inevitably a difference in the accused's entitlement to legal aid in Art. 5 and Art. 70 proceedings. See, by contrast, *Quaranta v. Switzerland*, 1991, §33, Series A no. 205; *Pakelli v. Germany*, 1983, §34, Series A no. 64; *Granger v. United Kingdom*, 1990, §46, Series A no. 174.

76 For equivalent provisions guaranteeing the accused's access to the relevant information for the preparation of his defence, see further Arts 55(2)(a), 61(3) and 67(2) of the Rome Statute.

77 W. Schabas, 'Article 67' in O. Triffterer and K. Ambos, *The Rome Statute of the International Criminal Court: A Commentary*, 3rd ed., Hart Publishing, Oxford, Nomos/Baden Baden 2016, 20.

78 ICC, *Prosecutor v. Thomas Lubanga Dyilo, Decision concerning Pre-Trial Chamber I's Decision of 10 February 2006 and the Incorporation of Documents into the Record of the Case against Mr Thomas Lubanga Dyilo*, ICC-01/04-01/06-8-US-Corr, 24.02.2006, 2, para 7.

all decisions issued by [the competent] Pre-Trial Chamber'.[79] However, none of this is required, from the EtCHR's point of view.[80]

6.7. PRESUMPTION OF INNOCENCE

Article 66(1) of the Statute replicates the general precept as couched in regional and global human rights treaties.[81] However, by explicitly ruling out any reversal of the burden of proof, Article 67(1)(i) goes beyond most human rights norms.[82] The ECtHR, for example, allows for reversals within certain limits.[83] Indeed, an absolute reverse onus prohibition appears to be problematic in certain instances, such as defence pleas of lack of mental capacity.

6.8. THE LANGUAGE REQUIREMENT

The ICC's legal framework[84] tracks, for the most part, the conventional international law and jurisprudence: first and foremost, the ECtHR's case law.[85]

---

79 ICC: *Prosecutor v. Thomas Lubanga Dyilo, Decision on the Defence Request for Unrestriced Access to the Entire File of the Situation in the Democratic Republic of the Congo*, ICC-01/04-01/06-103, 17.05.2006, 3, para 4.

80 Art. 6(3)(a) ECHR does not impose any specific formal requirement as to the manner in which the accused is to be informed of the nature and cause of the accusation against him. See *Pélissier and Sassi v. France* [GC], no. 25444/94, §53, ECHR, 1999, *Reports of Judgments and Decisions* 1999-II with further reference to *Kamasinski v. Austria*, 1989, 36–37, §79 Series A no. 168.

81 See, for instance, Art. 6(2) ECHR or Art. 14(2) ICCPR. According to B. ELBERLING, above n. 71, Arts 55(2)(b) (right to silence) and 67(1)(i) (prohibition of burden of proof or onus of rebuttal) of the Rome Statute are commonly considered to be corollaries to this maxim.

82 W. SCHABAS, above n. 77, 23.

83 *Falk v. The Netherlands* (dec.), no. 66273/01, ECHR 2004, *Reports of Judgments and Decisions* 2004-XI; *Salabiaku v. France*, 7 October 1988, §§26–28, Series A no. 141-A; *Janosevic v. Sweden*, no. 34619/97, §100, *Reports of Judgments and Decisions* 2002-VII; *Radio France and Others v. France*, no. 53984/00, §24, *Reports of Judgments and Decisions* 2004-II. See J.P. PÉREZ-LEÓN ACEVEDO and B. ELBERLING, above n. 71, with reference to W. SCHABAS, *The International Criminal Court: a Commentary on the Rome Statute*, Oxford University Press, Oxford 2010, 784–85. For a critical discussion of the allegedly excessive scope of this principle in the Rome Statute in respect of Defence pleas of lack of mental capacity, see W. SCHABAS, above n. 77, 20–21.

84 Arts 67(1)(a) and 55(c) of the Rome Statute.

85 ICC, *Prosecutor v. Thomas Lubanga Dyilo, Decision on the Requests of the Defence of 3 and 4 July 2006*, ICC-01/04-01/06-268, 04.08.2006, 6; *Prosecutor v. Germain Katanga, Decision on the Defence Request Concerning Languages*, ICC-01/04-01/07-127, 21.12.2007, paras 5–6 and 30 (no right to choose the language); *Prosecutor v. Jean-Pierre Bemba Gombo, Decision on the Defence's Request Related to Language Issues in the Proceedings*, ICC-01/05-01/08-307, 04.12.2008, paras 13 and 15 ('fully understands and speaks' applies only to the accused and not his defence counsel); *Prosecutor v. Germain Katanga, Judgment on the appeal of Mr Germain Katanga against the decision of Pre-Trial Chamber I entitled 'Decision on the Defence Request*

However, one notes at least three instances in which the Court has substantially deviated from the Strasbourg jurisprudence, affording the accused a considerably higher standard of protection.

In *Katanga*, the Appeals Chamber found that the standard of 'fully understands and speaks', as set out in Article 67(1)(a) and (f), meant that 'he or she is completely fluent in the language in ordinary, nontechnical conversation; it is not required that he or she has an understanding as if he or she were trained as a lawyer or judicial officer',[86] concluding that 'the standard applicable under the Statute is high – higher, for example, than that applicable under the European Convention on Human Rights and the ICCPR'.[87]

Secondly, by authorising not only the interpretation of oral statements made at the trial hearing but also the (almost systematic) translation of documents presented to the Court in addition to the translation of documents, the Statute afforded the accused significantly higher protection than that in ordinary human rights treaties. The Chambers have frequently ordered the Registrar to make available, free of any cost, an interpreter to assist the accused and the defence team with documents of the case that were available in only one of the Court's working languages.[88]

Lastly, in *Bemba*, the Pre-Trial Chamber stated that the defendant does not have an absolute right to have all documents translated into a language that he fully understands and speaks.[89] Rather, the accused is to be provided

---

Concerning Languages', ICC-01/04-01/07-522, 27.05.2008, paras 36–48 (admissibility of a request for interpretation into a language other than the official languages of the Court).

86 ICC, *Prosecutor v. Germain Katanga, Judgment on the appeal of Mr Germain Katanga against the decision of Pre-Trial Chamber I entitled 'Decision on the Defence Request Concerning Languages'*, ICC-01/04-01/07-522, 27.05.2008, paras 36–48, 61.

87 Ibid., paras 51–55.

88 ICC, *Prosecutor v. Thomas Lubanga Dyilo, Decision on the Requests of the Defence of 3 and 4 July 2006*, ICC-01/04-01/06-268, 04.08.2006, pp. 5–6. See also *Prosecutor v. Jean-Pierre Bemba Gombo, Decision on the Defence's Request Related to Language Issues in the Proceedings*, ICC-01/05-01/08-307, 04.12.2008, para 11, whereby Pre-Trial Chamber II granted assistance of an interpreter '*without any limitations*'; and para. 16. See further *Prosecutor v. Germain Katanga, Decision on the Defence Request Concerning Languages*, ICC-01/04-01/07-127, 21.12.2007; *Prosecutor v. Mathieu Ngudjolo Chui, Decision on the Defence Request concerning time limits*, ICC-01/04-02/07-45, 27.02.2008; *Prosecutor v. Germain Katanga, Decision on the Defence for Mathieu Ngudjolo Chui's Request concerning translation of documents*, ICC-01/04-01/07-477, 15.05.2008, in which the Single Judge ordered the Registry to arrange for a mechanism which allowed the accused to have the assistance of the interpreter assigned to him at a much shorter notice than the 24 hours anticipated in an earlier decision. See *Prosecutor v. Germain Katanga and Mathieu Ngudjolo Chui, Decision Implementing the Appeals Chamber Judgment concerning Languages*, ICC-01/04-01/07-539, 02.06.2008, paras 13–16, whereby the Single Judge confined the assistance by an interpreter to the hearings as the defence request was limited to interpretation in the courtroom.

89 ICC, *Prosecutor v. Jean-Pierre Bemba Gombo, Decision on the Defence's Request Related to Language Issues in the Proceedings*, ICC-01/05-01/08-307, 04.12.2008, para. 11; *Prosecutor v. Thomas Lubanga Dyilo, Decision on the Requests of the Defence of 3 and 4 July 2006*, ICC-01/04-01/06-268, 04.08.2006.

with a written translation of such documents as inform him in detail of the nature, cause and content of the charges brought against him, namely: (a) the prosecutor's application for a warrant of arrest and the Chamber's decision thereon; (b) the document containing the charges and the list of evidence, as well as any amendment thereto; and (c) (in compliance with Rule 76(3) of the Rules of Procedure and Evidence), the statements of prosecution witnesses.[90] Again, the ICC clearly goes beyond the settled case law of the ECtHR, which limits translations to the indictment,[91] going as far as accepting oral translations if this allows the accused to prepare his defence.[92]

Far from being an exhaustive assessment of the law and practice of the ICC, there is reason to believe that the Court not only satisfies but far exceeds the requisite level of protection of the accused's right to a fair trial. When compared with the requirements under Article 6 of the ECHR, it is safe to say that the ICC acts 'holier than the Pope'. That is not to say that the Court's human rights record is without blemish. The ongoing discussion surrounding the length of proceedings[93] and the (potential) tensions between the right to a public hearing and protective measures ordered under Article 68 of the Rome Statute[94] indicates that there is still room for improvement. However, this does not belie the fact that the vast majority of fair trial rights are meticulously observed and, as has been shown, frequently exceeded – very occasionally reaching the point of overkill.[95] As mentioned above, there was also an inherent risk of fragmentation of HRL, were international tribunals to apply certain procedural rights in a manner

90 Ibid. See also the subsequent jurisprudence following this approach in *Prosecutor v. Jean-Pierre Bemba, Decision on the Defence's Request Related to Language Issues in the Proceedings*, ICC-01/05-01/08-307, 04.12.2008, para 9; *Prosecutor v. Thomas Lubanga Dyilo, Decision on the Requests of the Defence of 3 and 4 July 2006*, ICC-01/04-01/06-268, 04.08.2006, 5; *Prosecutor v. Germain Katanga, Decision on the Defence Request Concerning Languages*, ICC-01/04-01/07-127, 21.12.2007, paras 40–41; *Prosecutor v. Callixte Mbarushimana, Decision on the 'Prosecution's request for the assessment of the English proficiency of Callixte Mbarushimana'*, ICC-01/04-01/10-145, 12.05.2011, p. 8; *Prosecutor v. Germain Katanga, Decision on the Defence for Mathieu Ngudjolo Chui's Request concerning translation of documents*, ICC-01/04-01/07-477, 15.05.2008, 3; *Prosecutor v. Abdallah Banda Abakaer Nourain and Saleh Mohammed Jerbo Jamus, Reasons for the Order on translation of witness statements* (ICC-02/05-03/09-199) *and additional instructions on translation*, ICC-02/05-03/09-214, 12.09.2011.

91 *Kamasinski v. Austria*, 1989, §79, Series A no. 168; *Hermi v. Italy* [GC], no. 18114/02, §68, ECHR, *Reports of Judgments and Decisions* 2006-XII.

92 *Kamasinski v. Austria*, ibid., §81; *Husain v. Italy* (dec.), no. 18913/03, ECHR, *Reports of Judgments and Decisions* 2005-III.

93 G. Acquaviva, N. Combs, M. Heikkilä, S. Linton, Y. McDermott and S. Vasiliev, 'Trial Process' in G. Sluiter, H. Friman, S. Linton, S. Zappalà and S. Vasiliev above n. 53, 770 ('general duty to ensure the right to a fair and expeditious trial'). See also W. Schabas, above n. 77, 25–26.

94 W. Schabas, above n. 71, 825.

95 Concerning the risks of excessive reasoning, see above section 6.2. Regarding the absolute prohibition of the reverse onus of proof, see above section 6.7.

inconsistent with the well-consolidated jurisprudence of the most authoritative human rights bodies.

The ICC's defence-friendly approach results from a combination of the Court's generous legal framework[96] and its benign interpretation by the judiciary, which is arguably linked to the specificities of ICL and, in particular, the seriousness of the charges,[97] the complexity of the case,[98] the porosity of the Rome Statute[99] and a permissive approach towards victims and witnesses.[100] Moreover, the high-profile nature of the cases, which attract public interest, constant scrutiny by academia and the public at large, requires an increased level of publicity and transparency. Additional factors to consider when endeavouring to understand the genesis of this approach might be the ICC's role-model function for the prosecution of serious international crimes, calling for exemplary performance by all actors, and a generation of judges and lawyers who, by virtue of their education and practice, became particularly receptive to the protection of the rights of individuals.

While it might be difficult to measure the concrete impact of the Court's jurisprudence on HRL,[101] it is worth noting that the ICC not only imports and applies pre-existing human rights standards but actively adopts and refines these principles for the purposes of proceedings before the Court. That is to say that the ICC (together with other international criminal tribunals) is somehow developing its HRL microcosm. In this sense, one could conceptualise the specific sub-structure of HRL as being a distinctive one, and thus different from, for instance, regional and national HRL systems.

96 For the preparatory works of Art. 67, see W. Schabas, above n. 71, 793–94, suggesting that Art. 14 ICCPR was the starting point of the discussions, but that the minimum guarantees of Art. 14 were considerably enlarged during the negotiation of the Rome Statute.

97 ICC, *Prosecutor v. Jean-Pierre Bemba Gombo, Aimé Kilolo Musamba, Jean-Jacques Mangenda Kabongo, Fidèle babala Wandu and Narcisse Arido*, ICC-01/05-01/13-955, 25.05.2015, paras 34–35. See also *Quaranta v. Switzerland*, 1991, §33, Series A no. 205, suggesting a more generous approach towards granting legal assistance in serious cases.

98 Requiring a more flexible approach on the equality of arms, the reasoning, the language requirement and others.

99 While being current practice in ICL, the voluminous and painstakingly detailed analysis is partly linked to the Rome Statute's gaping lacunae regarding most basic issues of procedural law and the merits, which need to be filled in by jurisprudence following a laborious case-by-case approach. The foregoing aspect is exacerbated by the Court's public exposure, making each and every procedural step susceptible to external scrutiny and potential criticism from the media, observers, academic commentators and the public at large. This requires a traceable and transparent decision-making process, enabling the public to understand the verdict that has been given. In addition, the reasoned decision requirement constitutes a vital safeguard against arbitrariness.

100 On extending the equality of arms principle to victims, see above section 6.1.

101 See above section 3 for an analysis of the ECtHR's jurisprudence on ICL-related matters.

7. CONCLUSION

ICL appears to be the polarised mirror of HRL, reflecting into the arena of individual criminal responsibility. It allows enhanced possibilities of enforcement of human rights and permits the establishment of individual guilt for violations thereof. In turn, HRL emerges as the springboard for ICL legitimately to expand its reach in the effort of closing the impunity gap. This complementary relationship is thus welcoming as well as a resourceful and powerful tool in ensuring and promoting respect for fundamental human rights. Such a dynamic interplay is furthermore legitimate, given the teleological bridge between the two branches of law: protection of individual human rights. That notwithstanding, due care must be given to exercises and efforts of cross-fertilisation between both areas of law, since – while sharing some goals and core principles – they are permeated by distinctive rationales, rules, objectives, methodologies and axiological substrates.

USE OF HUMAN RIGHTS IN INTERNATIONAL CRIMINAL LAW: INFLUENCE OR APPEARANCES OF LEGITIMACY?

Damien SCALIA

1. INTRODUCTION

The complex relations between human rights and criminal law range from rejection and respect to influence and disunity. The tortuous interaction between both bodies of law fascinates many authors. For instance, van de Kerchove has questioned whether human rights should be considered as the shield or the sword of criminal law.[1] The relationship of international criminal law (ICL) with human rights law (HRL) is no exception to the rule. Indeed, at the international

[1] Y. CARTUYVELS, H. DUMONT, F. OST, M. VAN DE KERCHOVE and S. VAN DROOGHENBROECK, *Les droits de l'homme, bouclier ou épée du droit pénal?*, FUSL, Brussels 2007.

level, a true 'judicial dialogue' has been developed between international criminal courts on the one hand, and human rights protection bodies on the other hand,[2] such as the European Court of Human Rights (ECtHR). The relation between the two corpuses of law, and especially the recourse to international human rights law (IHRL) by international criminal courts, is very complex given that abundant so-called cross-fertilisation is taking place between both branches of law. In this chapter, only the recourse to IHRL by international criminal tribunals and courts will be analysed.

This chapter proposes analysing this recourse along three axes. First, ICL can be analysed as a repressive form of human rights: the purpose of ICL in prosecuting some international crimes is to condemn massive violations of human rights. Consequently, IHRL is used in order better to interpret elements of definition of international crimes. Secondly, human rights can be understood as an important source of law allowing the development of international criminal procedure. Indeed, the Strasbourg case law, for example, has clearly influenced the International Criminal Tribunals (ICTs) for both the former Yugoslavia and Rwanda (respectively ICTY and ICTR), in the interpretation of rights of the accused. Thirdly, the reference to HRL could be analysed as a means of legitimising ICL, especially related to what Cassese has called the 'universal values legitimacy'.[3]

Following the lines of these three axes, this chapter will be divided into three parts. First, the chapter will present how ICL as an enforcement mechanism of human rights makes use of IHRL, more specifically to define and interpret certain crimes, such as crimes against humanity (see below section 3). Then, some cases in which international criminal tribunals and courts will be presented, taking into consideration HRL in order to determine rights of the accused (see below section 4). Finally, the chapter will demonstrate that, in certain circumstances, recourse to HRL is (mis)used as a legitimation tool (see below section 5). Before these three parts are developed, some opening remarks will be provided (see below section 2).

2. PRELIMINARY REMARKS

Before analysing specific issues raised in the introduction, some general remarks are necessary.

---

2 T. Mariniello and P. Lobba, 'The Cross-fertilisation Rhetoric in Question: Use and Abuse of the European Court's Jurisprudence by ICTs' (2015) 84 *Nordic Journal of International Law* 363.

3 A. Cassese, 'The Legitimacy of International Criminal Tribunals and the Current Prospects of International Criminal Justice' (2012) 25 *Leiden Journal of International Law* 491, 492.

First, human rights are not explicitly mentioned in the Statutes of International Criminal Tribunals. Nevertheless, on many occasions these tribunals make reference to the jurisprudence of regional courts in the area of human rights or use HRL in their decisions.[4] As Cassese has written, qualifying as '*sauvage*' (in French) the approach taken by the ICTs when referring to sources of law:

> it is obvious that this 'wild' approach tends to place the law stemming from outside an international criminal jurisdiction [...] on the same level as the law applicable to that jurisdiction: the International Criminal Tribunal refers to or applies domestic case law or case law from the European Court [of Human Rights] in the same way as its own jurisprudence or that of other international criminal jurisdictions.[5]

On the contrary, the Statute of the International Criminal Court (ICC) explicitly mentions IHRL in the article regulating the applicable law before the Court. Article 21(3) of the Rome Statute refers to 'internationally recognized human rights' as those that can serve in the interpretation and application of other sources of law that are found in the same article.[6] In this context, they are not referred to as applicable law but as a framework for interpreting and applying the law.[7] In fact, whatever source of law the Court refers to under Article 21, it has to do so in consistence with 'internationally recognized human rights'.

Notwithstanding this provision, the ICC has stated that it is not a universal court of human rights. Indeed, in the case of *Saif Al-Islam Gaddafi*, the Judges

4 *Prosecutor v. Tadić* IT-95-9 Judgment Appeals Chamber (ICTY, 2 October 1995), para. 45; *Prosecutor v. Furundžija* IT-95-17/1 Judgment Trial Chamber (ICTY, 10 December 1998), para. 183; G. Gaggioli, *L'influence mutuelle entre les droits de l'homme et le droit international humanitaire à la lumière du droit à la vie*, Pédone, Paris 2013.

5 The author's translation from A. Cassese, 'L'influence de la CEDH sur l'activité des Tribunaux pénaux internationaux' in A. Cassese and M. Delmas-Marty (eds), *Crimes internationaux et Juridictions internationals*, PUF, Paris 2002, p. 149.

6 '1. The Court shall apply: (a) In the first place, this Statute, Elements of Crimes and its Rules of Procedure and Evidence; (b) In the second place, where appropriate, applicable treaties and the principles and rules of international law, including the established principles of the international law of armed conflict; (c) Failing that, general principles of law derived by the Court from national laws of legal systems of the world including, as appropriate, the national laws of States that would normally exercise jurisdiction over the crime, provided that those principles are not inconsistent with this Statute and with international law and internationally recognized norms and standards.
2. The Court may apply principles and rules of law as interpreted in its previous decisions.
3. The application and interpretation of law pursuant to this article must be consistent with internationally recognized human rights, and be without any adverse distinction founded on grounds such as gender as defined in article 7, paragraph 3, age, race, colour, language, religion or belief, political or other opinion, national, ethnic or social origin, wealth, birth or other status.'

7 I. Caracciolo, 'Applicable Law' in F. Lattanzi and W. Schabas (eds), *Essays on the Rome Statute of the International Criminal Court*, Ripa Fagnano Alto (AQ), Il Sirente 1999, pp. 211, 228.

of the Appeals Chamber answered a crucial question related to the respect of human rights as an element to be taken into account to evaluate the admissibility of a case. Since the establishment of the ICC and the writing of Article 17 of the Rome Statute, authors have discussed the status of human rights in relation to the complementarity principle.[8] It is disputed whether the Court should analyse the respect of human rights to declare a case admissible before it. Judges stated that 'the Court was not established to be an international court of human rights, sitting in judgment over domestic legal systems to ensure that they are compliant with international standards of human rights'.[9] This statement reaffirms the character of the ICC as a criminal court. The Court based its reasoning especially on the *travaux préparatoires* of the Rome Statute:

1) For a case to be admissible under Article 17(2)(c) it must be shown that the proceedings were not or are not being conducted independently or impartially and that the proceedings were or are being conducted in a manner which, in the circumstances, is inconsistent with an intent to bring the person concerned to justice.
2) Taking into account the text, context, object and purpose of the provision, this determination is not one that involves an assessment of whether the due process rights of a suspect have been breached per se. In particular, the concept of proceedings 'being conducted in a manner which, in the circumstances, is inconsistent with an intent to bring the person concerned to justice' should generally be understood as referring to proceedings which will lead to a suspect evading justice, in the sense of not appropriately being tried genuinely to establish his or her criminal responsibility, in the equivalent of sham proceedings that are concerned with that person's protection.
3) However, there may be circumstances, depending on the facts of the individual case, whereby violations of the rights of the suspect are so egregious that the proceedings can no longer be regarded as being capable of providing any genuine form of justice to the suspect so that they should be deemed, in those circumstances, to be 'inconsistent with an intent to bring that person to justice'.[10]

---

8 For example, E. Fry, 'Between Show Trials and Sham Prosecutions: The Rome Statute's Potential Effect on Domestic Due Process Protections' (2012) *Criminal Law Forum* 35; B. Bernard, *Juger et juger encore les crimes internationaux, Etude du principe* ne bis in idem, Bruxelles, Bruylant 2014.

9 *Prosecutor v. Saif Al-Islam Gaddafi and Abdullah Al-Senussi* ICC-01/11-01/11-565 Judgment on the appeal of Mr Abdullah Al-Senussi against the decision of Pre-Trial Chamber I of 11 October 2013, entitled 'Decision on the admissibility of the case against Abdullah Al-Senussi' (ICC, 24 July 2014), paras 219 et 221–30.

10 Ibid., para 230.

The Court thus clarifies that the non-respect of human rights can be taken into consideration only if its purpose is to not bring a person to justice. As further clarified by Mégret and Giles Samson, 'the litmus test is not whether the right to a fair trial has been violated in itself, but whether the degree to which it has been violated is such that one cannot realistically say that there has been a trial at all, thus revealing an unwillingness or inability'.[11] Given that such cases will arguably remain the exception rather than the rule, the ICC can indeed not be considered as a supranational court of human rights that scrutinises the respect of human rights by national courts and tribunals. While the ICC pays respect to these rights in its procedures and trials, what is happening at the domestic level is of no concern to the Court if this is not an obstacle in the fight against impunity. If it were otherwise, the Court would not meet its objectives and could overstep its boundaries.

3. USE OF HUMAN RIGHTS LAW TO INTERPRET CRIMES

IHRL occupies a particular place as a source for substantive ICL.[12] Even if it is not problematic *in se* for Judges of the international criminal jurisdictions to refer to this legal body, it would not be judicious if they simply transposed every rule of IHRL. As stated by the ICTY Trial Chamber in the *Kunarac* case:

> In attempting to define an offence under international humanitarian law, the Trial Chamber must be mindful of the specificity of this body of law. In particular, when referring to definitions which have been given in the context of human rights law, the Trial Chamber will have to consider two crucial structural differences between these two bodies of law: (i) First, the role and position of the state as an actor is completely different in both regimes. Human rights law is essentially born out of the abuses of the state over its citizens and out of the need to protect the latter from state-organised or state-sponsored violence. Humanitarian law aims at placing restraints on the conduct of warfare so as to diminish its effects on the victims of the hostilities. In the human rights context, the state is the ultimate guarantor of the rights protected and has both duties and a responsibility for the observance of those rights. In the event that the State violates those rights or fails in its responsibility to protect the rights, it can be called to account and asked to take appropriate measures to put an end to the infringements. In the field of international humanitarian law, and in particular in the context of international

---

11 Fr Mégret and M. Giles Samson, 'Holding the Line on Complementarity in Libya: the Case for Tolerating Flawed Domestic Trials' (2013) 11 *Journal of International Criminal Justice* 571, 585.

12 G. Gaggioli, above n. 4, p. 206 *et seq*.

> prosecutions, the role of the state is, when it comes to accountability, peripheral. Individual criminal responsibility for violation of international humanitarian law does not depend on the participation of the State and, conversely, its participation in the commission of the offence is no defence to the perpetrator. Moreover, international humanitarian law purports to apply equally to and expressly bind all parties to the armed conflict whereas, in contrast, human rights law generally applies to only one party, namely the State involved, and its agents [...] (ii) Secondly, that part of international criminal law applied by the Tribunal is a penal law regime. It sets one party, the prosecutor, against another, the defendant. In the field of international human rights, the respondent is the state. Structurally, this has been expressed by the fact that human rights law establishes lists of protected rights whereas international criminal law establishes lists of offences. The Trial Chamber is therefore wary not to embrace too quickly and too easily concepts and notions developed in a different legal context. The Trial Chamber is of the view that notions developed in the field of human rights can be transposed in international humanitarian law only if they take into consideration the specificities of the latter body of law.[13]

Nevertheless, in many cases, Judges of the ICTs and the ICC have made appropriate use of IHRL in order to interpret crimes. In this context of interpreting crimes, HRL enabled the Judges to define more precisely the specific crime of torture or inhuman and degrading treatment (especially in the context of war crimes but also as crime against humanity) (see below section 3.1). It also contributes to a more precise and complete interpretation of certain other individual acts considered as 'crimes against humanity' (crimes against humanity are closer to human rights violations than they are to other crimes: war crimes or genocide, for example) (see below section 3.2).[14]

3.1. TORTURE OR INHUMAN AND DEGRADING TREATMENT

In a number of cases, the ICTY refers to HRL in order to define 'cruel, inhuman or degrading treatment'.[15] In the *Aleksovski* case, for example, in making reference to the jurisprudence of the ECtHR and to the Convention against Torture and Other Cruel, Inhuman and Degrading Treatment, Judges of the Trial Chamber of the ICTY reaffirmed the existing definition in HRL and transposed

---

13 *Prosecutor v. Kunarac* IT-96-23 et 23/1 Judgment Trial Chamber (ICTY, 22 February 2001), paras. 470–71.

14 P. Currat, *Les crimes contre l'humanité dans le statut de la Cour pénale internationale*, Schulthess, Genève 2006, p. 746.

15 *Prosecutor v. Delalić* IT-96-21 Judgment Trial Chamber (ICTY, 16 November 1998), para. 462; *Prosecutor v. Blagojević* IT-02-60 Judgment Trial Chamber (ICTY, 17 January 2005), para. 587.

it into ICL. The Judges decided that 'it is also instructive to recount the general definition of the term "inhuman treatment" propounded by the ECHR, which to date is the only human rights monitoring body that defines the term'.[16] Here, the reference helps to define a protected interest as well as to define the essential criteria necessary to determine the objective element of the crime.[17]

Similarly, the Judges of the ICTY referred to IHRL to define 'torture', which is not defined by the Statutes of the ICTY or international humanitarian law.[18] According to Maculan, the concept of torture represents 'a relevant intersection point among international human rights law, international criminal law and also international humanitarian law'.[19] The Convention against Torture and other Cruel, Inhuman or Degrading Treatment or Punishment defines torture by three main elements: severity of pain or suffering caused by the act, the public official requirement and the specific purposes pursued by perpetrators.[20] In parallel, the European Court has traditionally defined torture principally by the first element. It is beyond the scope of this chapter to discuss in detail the evolution of the case law of both the ECtHR and the UN Committee against Torture case law and how they approximated over time.[21] It is, however, worth mentioning that, according to Maculan, the influence of ECtHR case law in the jurisprudence of the ad hoc tribunals 'has caused three main effects: (1) The gradual abandoning of the public official requirement; (2) The development of distinctive criteria between torture and inhuman treatment (…); (3) The determination of a severity threshold for an act to amount to torture'.[22]

In the same vein, the Judges of the ICTY used HRL in order to consider rape an act of torture.[23] In the context of rape, the Judges interpreted the notion of torture as having a broader definition than any other existing definition of torture existing in international human rights instruments.[24] In this perspective, the Judges of the ICTY make recourse to the jurisprudence

---

16 *Prosecutor v. Aleksovski* IT-95-14/1 Judgment Trial Chamber (ICTY, 25 June 1999), para. 53.

17 A. Cassese, above n. 5, p. 149.

18 *Prosecutor v. Krnojelac* IT-97-25 Judgment Trial Chamber (ICTY, 15 March 2002), para. 181; *Prosecutor v. Kvocka* IT-98-30/1 Judgment Trial Chamber (ICTY, 2 November 2001), para. 142; *Prosecutor v. Kunarac*, above n. 13, para. 466.

19 E. Maculan, 'Judicial Definition of Torture as a Paradigm of Cross-fertilisation: Combining Harmonisation and Expansion' (2015) 84 *Nordic Journal of International Law* 456.

20 Art. 1 of the Convention against Torture 1984.

21 N.S. Rodley, 'The Definition(s) of Torture in International Law' (2002) 55 *Current Legal Problems* 467.

22 E, Maculan, above n. 19, 472–73.

23 *Prosecutor v. Furundžija*, above n. 4, para. 159. This decision will be reaffirmed in a number of judgments: *Prosecutor v. Delalić*, above n. 15, paras. 481–493; *Prosecutor v. Kvocka*, above n. 18, para. 145; *Prosecutor v. Kunarac*, above n. 13, para. 437.

24 A. Cassese, above n. 5, pp. 177–178.

of human rights bodies.[25] In the *Čelibići* judgment, the Judges referred to the case law of ECtHR and the Inter-American Commission on Human Rights[26] in stating the following:

> The European precedent allows the TC to confirm, first, that the infliction of an especially severe pain or suffering amounts to torture, as opposed to other forms of ill-treatment, and that rape, due to its inherent gravity, undoubtedly reaches this threshold. Secondly, it suggests that it is hardly imaginable that a rape inflicted by a person acting in official capacity, mostly on a victim who is under detention, does not involve at least one of the prohibited purposes of torture (including punishment, intimidation, or obtaining information). Following these considerations, the Trial Chamber asserts that such scenario is 'inherent in situations of armed conflict'. In other words, it implies that a rape committed by public official in a context of armed conflict amounts to torture.[27]

3.2. CRIMES AGAINST HUMANITY

Referring to IHRL also allows for other violations of HRL to be defined – specifically those that amount to crimes against humanity. In this regard, the Judges of the ICTY as well as those of the ICTR have employed IHRL in many cases. First, in the *Kunarac* case, the Judges of the ICTY referred to a number of international texts on HRL in order to define the abolition of slavery (the Universal Declaration of Human Rights (UDHR) of 1948, the ICCPR, the ECHR, the Inter-American Convention on Human Rights of 1968 and the African Charter on Human and Peoples' Rights of 1981).[28] Secondly, in the *Simić* case, the Judges referred to human rights in order to define imprisonment as crimes against humanity[29] and also to define inhumane acts mentioned in Article 5 of the Statute of the ICTY.[30]

Moreover, to draw the contours of the crime of persecution as a crime against humanity,[31] which was not defined by the Statutes of the ICTs, judges are required to resort to IHRL in order to delimit the specific acts that fall under the scope of this crime. In the *Simić* case, the Judges stated that 'persecution may

---

25 *Prosecutor v. Furundžija*, above n. 4, paras 160–63. The same reasoning has been followed by the ICTR: *Prosecutor v. Akayesu* ICTR-96-4-T Judgment Trial Chamber (ICTR, 2 September 1998), para. 593.

26 *Prosecutor v. Delalić*, above n. 15, paras 481–93.

27 E. Maculan, above n. 19, 456–71.

28 *Prosecutor v. Kunarac*, above n. 13, para. 533.

29 *Prosecutor v. Krnojelac*, above n. 18, para. 109.

30 *Prosecutor v. Simić* IT-95-9 Judgment Trial Chamber (ICTY, 17 October 2003), para. 48; *Prosecutor v. Stakić* IT-97-24 Judgment Trial Chamber (ICTY, 31 July 2003), para. 720.

31 For an analysis of this crime, see: O. Quirrico, 'La persécution devant les tribunaux pénaux internationaux' 2010 *Les Dossiers du Grihl* <http://dossiersgrihl.revues.org/3894> accessed 18.03.2016.

encompass acts which are listed in the Statute, as well as acts which are not listed in the Statute'.[32] In the same vein, the ICTR decided that:

> it has resulted from international customary law that the crime of persecution can encompass acts that are contained in sub-categories of crimes against humanity – whether they are murder or deportation – as long as they have been motivated by discriminatory reasons. Persecution can also encompass other diverse acts of discrimination that are not enumerated elsewhere in the Statute but which concern grave attacks of the rights of the individual.[33]

Moreover, in the *Kupreskić* case, the Trial Chamber of the ICTY pursued the same reasoning:

> drawing upon the various provisions of these texts it proves possible to identify a set of fundamental rights appertaining to any human being, the gross infringement of which may amount, depending on the surrounding circumstances, to a crime against humanity. Persecution consists of a severe attack on those rights, and aims to exclude a person from society on discriminatory grounds. The Trial Chamber therefore defines persecution as the gross or blatant denial, on discriminatory grounds, of a fundamental right, laid down in international customary or treaty law, reaching the same level of gravity as the other acts prohibited in Article 5.[34]

Under this case law, various acts have been included in the crime of persecution, such as: retaliations,[35] forced labour,[36] destruction of property,[37] illegal arrest, unlawful imprisonment,[38] murder, extermination and torture[39] and terrorisation.[40] In brief: 'de manière générale, le tribunal a considéré que toute violation grave de droits considérés comme indérogeables par les droits de l'Homme était susceptible d'être qualifiée de persécutions' ['in general, the court held that any serious violation of rights considered as inalienable by human rights could be described as persecution'].[41]

---

32 *Prosecutor v. Simić*, above n. 30, para. 48.

33 *Prosecutor v. Semanza* ICTR-97-20 Judgment and Sentence Trial Chamber (ICTR, 15 May 2003), para. 349.

34 *Prosecutor v. Kupreskić* IT-95-16 Judgment Trial Chamber (ICTY, 14 January 2000), paras 619–21.

35 Ibid., para. 529.

36 *Prosecutor v. Krnojelac* IT-97-25 Judgment Appeals Chamber (ICTY, 17 September 2003), para. 200; *Prosecutor v. Simić*, above n. 30, para. 84.

37 *Prosecutor v. Kupreskić*, above n. 34, para. 631.

38 *Prosecutor v. Simić*, above n. 30, para. 60.

39 *Prosecutor v. Kordić* and *Čerkez* IT-95-14/2 Judgment Appeals Chamber (ICTY, 17 December 2004), para. 106; *Prosecutor v. Blaskić* IT-95-14 Judgment Appeals Chamber (ICTY, 29 July 2004), paras 136 and 143; *Prosecutor v. Blaskić* IT-95-14 Judgment Trial Chamber (ICTY, 3 March 2000), para. 220.

40 *Prosecutor v. Blagojević*, above n. 15, para. 592.

41 G. Gaggioli, above n. 4, p. 226, quoting *Prosecutor v. Blaskić*, above n. 39, para. 220. Translated by the author.

4. RIGHTS OF THE ACCUSED

As stated by Cassese, the ICTs' recourse to human rights is also straightforward in the context of the rights of the accused.[42] In order to illustrate such reliance on HRL by the ICTs in this area, the following matters will be discussed: the general principles of criminal law (see below section 4.1), the right to liberty (see below section 4.2) and the right to a fair trial (see below section 4.3).

4.1. GENERAL PRINCIPLES OF CRIMINAL LAW

In many cases, reference is made to HRL in order to define the principle of legality of crimes and penalties.[43] Judges of the international criminal jurisdictions use both international conventions and case law from the ECtHR and of the Inter-American Court of Human Rights (IACtHR) to define this principle: 'while the Statute of the International Tribunal lists offences over which the International Tribunal has jurisdiction, the Tribunal may enter convictions only where it is satisfied that the offence is proscribed under customary international law at the time of its commission'.[44] Despite the lip service that is paid to the legality principle, it does not appear to have been fully respected by the ICTs – at least in relation to the principle of legality of penalties, as will be argued below.[45]

Furthermore, the Judges of the ICTY have made reference to the principle of *stare decisis* by making reference to HRL. In the *Aleksovski* case, the Appeals Chamber referred to the jurisprudence of the ECtHR and stated that while it was 'not strictly bound, it would normally follow its previous decisions and would only depart from them if there were "cogent reasons"'.[46]

4.2. RIGHT TO LIBERTY

The ICTY and the ICC have repeatedly referred to IHRL in order to interpret the definition of the right to liberty. In the *Dokmanović* case, the Trial Chamber of the ICTY used human rights first to define the terms 'arrest'

---

42 A. Cassese, above n. 5, pp. 150–51.

43 *Prosecutor v. Blaskić*, above n. 39, para. 141.

44 Ibid.

45 D. Scalia, *Du principe de légalité des peines en droit international pénal*, Bruylant, Brussels 2011.

46 *Prosecutor v. Aleksovski* IT-95-14/1-A Judgment Appeals Chamber (ICTY, 24 March 2000), para. 95.

and 'detention'.[47] It also used the ECHR and the ICCPR to define what 'ruse' means in the context of arrest.[48] Having interpreted different jurisdictions' decisions on the matter, the Judges concluded that no violation of human rights had occurred in the arrest of Mr Dokmanović, even if he had been arrested while he believed he would be meeting a representative from the ICTY Prosecutor's office to discuss the possibility of standing witness.

Furthermore, the Judges of the ICTY made reference to HRL as it relates to liberty, stating that pre-trial detention should be the exception and not the rule.[49] They added that the 'detention of an accused on the basis of a reasonable suspicion that the accused committed the crime or crimes charged is in accordance with jurisprudence under the European Convention for the Protection of Human Rights and Fundamental Freedoms'.[50] They defined that 'having a "reasonable suspicion" presupposes the existence of facts or information which would satisfy an objective observer that the person concerned may have committed the offence'.[51]

In two cases, the ICC made reference to international and European HRL in order to define what constitutes a violation of the right to liberty. In the *Bemba* case, the Pre-trial Chamber III referred to the jurisprudence of the ECtHR in order to confirm the rule that 'when dealing with the right to liberty, one should bear in mind the fundamental principle that deprivation of liberty should be an exception and not a rule'.[52] In the *Lubanga* case, the Judges of the ICC referred to HRL in order to interpret 'reasonable suspicion'[53] that allows a person to be kept imprisoned prior to the Court's judgments. In all cases, the references made to human rights allowed for continued imprisonment of the accused.

4.3. RIGHT TO A FAIR TRIAL

Finally, numerous references to IHRL can be found to interpret the definitions of 'fair trial' and 'due process'. In the *Delalić* case, the ICTY Judges referred to

47 *Prosecutor v. Dokmanović* IT-95-13a Décision relative à la requête aux fins de mise en liberté déposée par l'accusé Slavko Dokmanović Trial Chamber (ICTY, 22 October 1997), paras 27–28. In this decision, Judges made references to human rights (ECHR and ICCPR) to define the term 'law' (para. 60).

48 Ibid., paras 64–67.

49 *Prosecutor v. Delalić* IT-96-21 Decision on the Motion for Provisional Release Filed by the Accused Zelnil Delalić Trial Chamber (ICTY, 25 September 1996), para. 19.

50 Ibid., §21.

51 Ibid., §22.

52 *Prosecutor v. Bemba* ICC-01/05-01/08 Decision on Application for Interim Release Pre-Trial Chamber III (ICC, 16 December 2008), para. 31.

53 *Prosecutor v. Lubanga* ICC-01/04-01/06-8-Corr Decision on the Prosecutor's Application for a warrant of arrest, Article 58 Pre-Trial Chamber I (ICC, 10 February 2006), Annex I to decision issued on 24 February 2006, paras 11–12.

the ICCPR and the ECHR to decide that the defence would have to inform the Prosecutor of the names of the witnesses it intended to call to trial, at least seven days before their hearing.[54] The Judges of the ICTY have also made reference to the jurisprudence of the European Commission and the ECtHR in order to define the power of Judges to limit the number of witnesses (making reference to Article 6(3) of the ECHR).[55] In the same vein, in the decision of 19 September 1997, the Judges of the ICTY stated that 'article 42 du Statut énonce les dispositions essentielles du droit à un interrogatoire équitable comme prévu à l'article 6(3)(c) de la CEDH'.[56] In addition, they decided that the absence of a lawyer at police interrogation stage violates Article 18 of the Statute and Article 42 of the RPE. They added that the latter, Article 42, is a *mutatis mutandis* adaptation of Article 6(3) of the ECHR and of Article 14(3) of the ICCPR.[57] Finally, the right to protection from self-incrimination is also discussed in the *Delalić* case, in referring to the jurisprudence of the ECtHR.[58]

In the context of the right to fair trial, the Judges in the *Blaskić* case consistently referred to IHRL when defining the right of the accused to be informed of the charges and the accusations being made against him. Noting this right (Article 6(3) of the ECHR and Article 14(3)(a) of the ICCPR),[59] the Judges decided that the indictment required only some modifications.[60] Regarding the same question, the ICTR also made reference to regional and international conventions on the protection of human rights in the *Semanza* case.[61] The ICTR decided, notably, that a delay of 18 days without being informed of the charges brought against the accused is a violation of human rights that would necessitate proportionate redress for the accused.[62]

---

54 *Prosecutor v. Delalić* IT-96-21 Decision on the Prosecution's motion for an order Requiring advance disclosure of Witnesses by the Defence Trial Chamber (ICTY, 4 February 1998), para. 22.

55 *Prosecutor v. Delalić* IT-96-21 Decision on the Motion of the Joint Request of the Accused Persons Regarding the Presentation of Evidence, dated 24 May 1998 Trial Chamber (ICTY, 12 June 1998), paras 34–48.

56 A. Cassese, above n. 5, pp. 166–67.

57 *Prosecutor v. Delalić* IT-96-21 Decision on Zdravko Mucić's Motion for the Exclusion of Evidence Trial Chamber (ICTY, 2 September 1997), paras 48–60.

58 *Prosecutor v. Delalić* IT-96-21 Decision on the Prosecution's Oral Requests for the Admission of Exhibit 155 into Evidence and for an Order to Compel the Accused, Zdravko Mucic, to Provide a Handwriting Sample Trial Chamber (ICTY, 19 January 1998), paras 45–46 and Disposition.

59 *Prosecutor v. Blaskić* IT-95-14 Decision on the defence Motion to dismiss the Indictment based upon Defects in the Form thereof (Vagueness/Lack of adequate Notice of Charges) Trial Chamber (ICTY, 4 April 1997), paras 12–16.

60 Ibid., Disposition.

61 *Prosecutor v. Semanza* ICTR-97-20-A Decision Appeals Chamber (ICTR, 31 May 2000), para. 78.

62 Ibid., para. 87. In the case of Barayagwiza, the same Tribunal decided, basing their decision on the ECHR, that a maximum period of time of 24 hours before the arrest of the accused

In addition, the ICTR and ICC Judges have made references to human rights of the accused to choose his legal counsel freely,[63] as well as when it is necessary to reconcile the rights of the accused with those of witnesses[64] when, for example, the ICC provided 'that under the jurisprudence of the European Court of Human Rights a guilty verdict may not be founded solely on the evidence of anonymous witnesses'.[65]

While the aforementioned uses of HRL by international criminal jurisdictions are appropriate, the following section will clarify how, in certain circumstances, it has been misused.

5. MISUSE OF HUMAN RIGHTS LAW

In order to demonstrate the misuse of references to HRL by the ICTs and other mechanisms, two symptomatic ways in which this misuse occurs will be analysed: first, at times, the ICTs and other mechanisms of ICL (such as the Mechanism for the International Criminal Tribunal (MICT)) recognise the applicability of a human right without respecting it in practice (see below section 5.1). In other instances, the recourse to HRL merely served to legitimise a decision. In such instances, Judges referred only to certain decisions of ECtHR (for example) to support their position without providing meticulous analysis as to how HRL applies to the question at issue (see below section 5.2).

5.1. PAYING LIP SERVICE TO HUMAN RIGHTS LAW WITHOUT RESPECTING IT IN PRACTICE

According to Article 7 of the ECHR, the *nulla poena sine lege* principle states that: '[A penalty shall not be imposed that is heavier] than the one that was applicable at the time the criminal offence was committed.' This principle is also

---

and informing them of charges against them does not violate the human rights of the accused (*Prosecutor v. Barayagwiza* ICTR-97-19-AR72 Judgment Appeals Chamber (ICTR, 3 November 1999), para. 84).

63 *Prosecutor v. Kambanda* ICTR 97-23-A Judgment Appeals Chamber (ICTR, 19 October 2000), para. 33. In this decision, Judges quote another judgment with the same conclusion: *Prosecutor v. Ntakirutimana* ICTR-96-10-T and ICTR-96-17-T Decision on the Motions of the Accused for Replacement of Assigned Counsel Trial Chamber (ICTR, 11 June 1997), pp. 2 *et seq.*

64 *Prosecutor v. Delalić* IT-96-21 Decision on the Motions by the Prosecution for Protective Measures for the Prosecution Witnesses Pseudonymed 'B' through to 'M' Trial Chamber (ICTY, 28 April 1997), paras 34–55. This decision answers the argument from the Accusation to protect the witnesses, victims of sexual abuse.

65 *Prosecutor v. Lubanga* ICC-01/04-01/06 Decision on Victims' participation Pre-Trial Chamber (ICC, 18 January 2008), para. 78.

enshrined in Article 11(2) of the UDHR and Article 15 of the ICCPR. With regard to sentences, the ECtHR has confirmed that: 'the notion of the legality of a sentence implies not only that the sentence has a legal basis but that the law itself fulfils the conditions of accessibility and foreseeability'.[66]

The principle is defined by material criteria: the quality, the accessibility and the foreseeability of the law.[67] The quality of the law implies clear and precise formulation.[68] These criteria are not absolute and have to be interpreted by 'appropriate legal advice',[69] allowing individuals 'to assess, to a degree that is reasonable in the circumstances, the consequences which a given action may entail'.[70] Precision and clarity must be appreciated within the global context of the text concerned. A vague provision can become more precise when read jointly with other provisions of the same law.[71] The criterion of accessibility has been explained as follows:

> the law must be adequately accessible: the citizen must be able to have an indication that is adequate in the circumstances of the legal rules applicable to a given case ... a norm cannot be regarded as a 'law' unless it is formulated with sufficient precision to enable the citizen to regulate his conduct: he must be able – if need be with appropriate advice – to foresee, to a degree that is reasonable in the circumstances, the consequences which a given action may entail.[72]

Moreover, the law has to be foreseeable: people must be able 'to foresee, to a degree that is reasonable in the circumstances, the consequences which a given action may entail'.[73] In fact, these criteria have to be analysed by converse implication: unreasonable, unexpected and surprising elements cannot satisfy the foreseeability criteria.[74] Finally, it is important to highlight that the 'law' – the cornerstone of the *nulla poena sine lege* principle – encompasses both the *lex scripta* and the law in a more general sense, including case law.

The recognition of applicability of the principle of legality related to sentencing in the international criminal context is confirmed both by the Rome Statute of the ICC and the ICTs. The *nulla poena sine lege* principle is recognised under Article 23 of the Rome Statute as well as in the emerging case law of

---

66 *Gragnic v. France*, App. no. 15312 (EurCommHR, Report, 29 June 1994), para. 32.
67 *Sunday Times v. United Kingdom*, App. no. 6538/74 ECHR 1979, para. 49.
68 *Kokkinakis v. Greece*, App. no. 14307/88 ECHR 1993, para. 52.
69 *Sunday Times*, above n. 67, para. 40.
70 *Cantoni v. France*, App. no. 17862/91 ECHR 1996, para. 35.
71 *G v. Liechtenstein*, App. no. 10980/84 (EurCommHR, 30 October 1984).
72 *Sunday Times*, above n. 67, para. 49.
73 *Cantoni*, above n. 71, 35; *Sunday Times*, above n. 67, para. 49.
74 D. Zerouki, *La légalité criminelle, Enrichissement de la conception formelle par une conception matérielle*, Lyon, Université Jean Moulin, 2001, p. 311.

the Court.[75] Even if the ICTs' statutes do not enshrine the principle of legality related to sentencing, they have recognised the applicability of the principle.[76] In order to do so, abundant reference is made to HRL in a number of cases in order to clarify the principle.[77] In this context, the Judges of the various international criminal jurisdictions have used both international conventions and case law from the ECtHR and the ACtHR to define the principle.[78] Despite this recognition, in practice the *nulla poena sine lege* principle seems to be violated routinely.[79]

Within ICTY and ICTR jurisprudence, the principle of legality of sentences is arguably not strictly respected. First, the Statutes of the ICTY and the ICTR mention only one penalty (i.e. life imprisonment) for all crimes; this does not respect the requirements of the principle of legality of sentences as presented earlier. It should be noted that the ICTY and ICTR Statutes, seemingly in an attempt to address concerns in relation to the principle of legality in respect to sentencing, ask the sentencing chamber to have recourse to the general practice regarding prison sentences in the courts of the former Yugoslavia and Rwanda, respectively.[80] However, Judges have stated that this provision is only indicative.[81] Secondly, the lack of respect for the *nulla poena sine lege* principle is also noticeable in the area of aggravating and mitigating circumstances, as trial chambers have considerable discretion in determining which circumstances they wish to consider.[82] Indeed, the mitigating and aggravating circumstances that may be taken into account are not exhaustively listed in the Statutes or the RPE of the ICTY and the ICTR. As an example, the good morals of the accused prior to the conflict have at times been taken into account as mitigating

---

75 *Prosecutor v. Germain Katanga* ICC-01/04-01/07 Decision on Sentence pursuant to Article 76 of the Statute Trial Chamber (ICC, 23 May 2014), para. 39.

76 *Prosecutor v. Blagojević*, above n. 15, para. 625; *Prosecutor v. Tadić* IT-94-1-T and IT-94-1 Abis Judgment in Sentencing Appeals Appeals Chamber (ICTY, 26 January 2000), Separate Opinion of Judge Cassese, paras 4 *et seq.*; *Prosecutor v. Erdemović* IT-96-22 Sentencing Judgment Trial Chamber (ICTY, 29 November 1996), para. 38.

77 *Prosecutor v. Blaskić*, above n. 39, para. 141.

78 Ibid.

79 D. Scalia, above n. 45.

80 Art. 24(1) ICTY Statute and Art. 23(1) ICTR Statute.

81 *Prosecutor v. Popović et al.* IT-05-88-T Judgment Trial Chamber (ICTY, 10 June 2010), para. 2142; *Prosecutor v. Milutinović et al.* IT-05-87-T Judgment Trial Chamber (ICTY, 26 February 2009), para. 1160; *Prosecutor v. Stakić* IT-97-24-A Judgment Appeals Chamber (ICTY, 22 March 2006), para. 398.

82 *Prosecutor v. Naletilić and Martinović* IT-98-34-T Judgment Trial Chamber (ICTY, 31 March 2003), para. 742. For an extensive quantitative analysis of sentencing data in the case law of the ICTY and ICTR, see S. D'Ascoli, *Sentencing in International Criminal Law: The UN ad hoc Tribunals and Future Perspectives for ICC*, Hart Publishing, Oxford 2011. This problem has not been resolved by the Appeal Chamber (see D. Scalia, above n. 45).

circumstances and other times as aggravating circumstances, while in other cases they are deemed to be irrelevant.[83]

The Rome Statute seems to be more in accordance with the principle of *nulla poena sine lege*. For instance, it contains a fixed term of imprisonment, with a maximum of 30 years. However, no specific sentence is provided for the different crimes. Articles 77 and 78 of the Rome Statute, together with Rule 145 of the RPE, provide an extensive list of aggravating and mitigating circumstances that should be taken into consideration when pronouncing penalties. Nevertheless, the list of criteria that Judges have to take into account is non-exhaustive; this is especially problematic for aggravating circumstances, for which the last provision states that 'other circumstances which, although not enumerated above, by virtue of their nature are similar to those mentioned could be taken into consideration'. Regarding the criteria of the definition of the *nulla poena sine lege* principle, this list is problematic. Indeed, the circumstances that the court could be take into consideration are not foreseeable for an accused.

Thus, the criteria identified by the ECtHR to define the principle of legality of penalties are not complied with by the ICTY and ICTR Statutes and are not strictly observed by the founding instruments of the ICC. The foreseeability, as well as the quality and the accessibility, of law are not strictly respected. The ICTs and the Court, therefore, do not seem to comply with the principle of the legality of sentences. Recourse to the principle seems to be made merely to legitimise the sentences which have been pronounced.

5.2. PROVIDING LEGITIMATION BY REFERENCE TO HUMAN RIGHTS LAW

In order to demonstrate that recourse to human rights by the ICTs or the ICC sometimes serves unfair purposes and allows them to legitimise decisions that, in fact, disrespect human rights, a recent case concerning an early release issued by the MICT will be discussed.

According to long-term jurisprudence established by the MICT, early release can be requested and is generally accepted after the execution of two-thirds of a sentence of imprisonment. The President of the MICT is required to take into consideration various elements in order to issue the early release: potential rehabilitation, the gravity of the crimes and cooperation with the Prosecutor of the prisoner. Recently, the MICT made a decision in the case of *Galić*,

[83] *Prosecutor v. Jean Bosco Barayagwiza et al.* ICTR-99-52-A Judgment Appeals Chamber (ICTR, 28 November 2007), para. 1069; *Prosecutor v. Plavsić* IT-00-39&40/1-S Judgment Trial Chamber (ICTY, 27 February 2003); *Prosecutor v. Tadić* IT-94-1-T Sentencing Judgment Trial Chamber (ICTY, 14 July 1997), para. 59.

an individual sentenced to life imprisonment. He was arrested in 1999, sentenced in 2003 to 20 years' imprisonment, and, in 2009, to life imprisonment by the Appeals Chamber of the ICTY. He is currently serving his sentence in Germany. According to the decision in the *Galić* case, it was unclear how to calculate two-thirds of life imprisonment. Indeed, in the constituent texts of the ICTY (in contrast to the ICC Statute, which states that, after 25 years of imprisonment, early release can be requested), there are no guidelines for such a situation and no case law has addressed the issue to date.

In order to answer this question, the President of the MICT issued a decision on 23 June 2015.[84] It was accompanied by a decision explaining the reasons for the refusal of early release.[85] In his explanation, the President of MICT began (as expected) by dismissing in one sentence the possibility of application of German law that allows the early release, after 25 years' imprisonment, of a person sentenced to life. The President accepted the principle that persons sentenced to life imprisonment are entitled to early release, which is justified by the principle of individualisation of punishment recognised under international standards of human rights.[86]

Consequently, the President answered the question as to when an individual condemned to life imprisonment is entitled to ask for early release. The MICT Prosecutor offered to translate the sentence of life imprisonment into time corresponding to the maximum sentence imposed by international or internationalised criminal courts: he referred to the sentence against Charles Taylor, issued by the Special Court for Sierra Leone, i.e. 52 years.[87] The MICT President rejected this interpretation. After making an inventory of IHRL, he concluded that there was no international consensus about potential early release or review of a prison sentence.

This conclusion seems to be incorrect: the ICC Statute or the relatively established jurisprudence of the ECtHR accepts this term after 25 years.[88] In order to reject this apparent consensus under international law, the President of the MICT based his reasoning solely on the recent *Bodein v. France* judgment

84 *Prosecutor v. Galić* MICT-14-83.ES, Version publique de la décision du 5 décembre 2014 relative à la libération de Stanislav Galić qui sera motivée ultérieurement (MICT, 23 June 2015).

85 *Prosecutor v. Galić* MICT-14-83.ES, Reasons for the President's Decision to Deny the early Release of Stanislav Galić and Decision on Prosecution Motion President (MICT, 23 June 2015).

86 Ibid., paras 20–25.

87 Ibid., para. 26.

88 Indeed, Art. 110 of the Rome Statute of ICC states that 'when the person has served two thirds of the sentence, or 25 years in the case of life imprisonment, the Court shall review the sentence to determine whether it should be reduced'. Moreover, the ECtHR has accepted, for a long time, the fact that after 25 years of imprisonment, there is an obligation to review the sentence.

of the ECtHR, which is still to be upheld by the Grand Chamber. In the latter, the Strasbourg Court accepted a period longer than 25 years in order to review a sentence of life imprisonment. However, in citing this case law, the President of the MICT seems to have disregarded that the ECtHR decision was based on a French national law that applied in the *Bodein* case, while in the same decision he rejected the German national law. Thus, to refuse the early release of Galić, the President of the MICT did indeed use HRL – but his decision relied only on a single decision and ran contrary to what important authorities on the matter prescribed. The casting aside of these authorities regarding the question at issue demonstrates the misapplication and misuse of HRL, in this case by the President of the MICT.

At the end of his decision, the President of the MICT sided with the Prosecutor's proposal but based on the longest sentence imposed by the ICTY, i.e. 45 years.[89] He concluded that a person sentenced to life imprisonment was eligible for early release after two-thirds of 45 years, i.e. 30 years' imprisonment. It is apparent that the President of the MICT used human rights at his discretion. His purpose seemed to be not to respect HRL but rather to legitimise the decision that he would have liked to achieve.

6. CONCLUSION

One could state that, according to Judge Shahabuddeen quoting the EComHR: '"The exceptional character of criminal proceedings involving war crimes committed during WWII renders, in the Commission's opinion, inapplicable the principles developed in the case law of the Commission and the Court of Human Rights in connection with cases involving criminal offences" (…) the application of principles has to take account of the peculiarities and difficulties of (the present case)'.[90] The Trial Chamber stated the same approach in the *Tadić* case: 'The interpretations of Article 6 of the ECHR […] by the European Court of Human Rights are meant to apply to ordinary criminal and, for Article 6(1), civil adjudications. By contrast, the International Tribunal is adjudicating crimes which are considered so horrific as to warrant universal jurisdiction. The International Tribunal is, in certain respects, comparable to a military tribunal, which often has limited rights of due process and more lenient rules of evidence'.[91] Nevertheless, this approach seems to be founded on

89 *Prosecutor v. Galić*, above n. 85, para. 35.

90 *Prosecutor v. Kovačević* IT-97-24-AR73 Individual Opinion of Judge Shahabuddeen (ICTY, 2 July 1998), para. 4.

91 *Prosecutor v. Tadić* IT-94-1 Decision on the Prosecutor's Motion requesting Protective Measures for Victims and Witnesses Trial Chamber (ICTY, 10 August 1995), para. 28.

a moralistic approach that cannot be accepted in ICL: principles of criminal law (as the legality principle) and human rights have to be respected by Judges even if the crimes are considered so horrific. Moreover, contrary to Article 6, referred to previously, in the case of the legality principle (Article 7 of the ECHR) no derogation is accepted by IHRL.[92]

As was discussed, IHRL and ICL have developed complex relations. While the former is of use for the latter in order to interpret founding instruments of criminal courts, it is also misused in order to legitimise decisions. The use of IHRL runs in two directions: sometimes, it serves to substantiate decisions touching upon on human rights issues, in other instances, the recourse to human rights is (mis)used only to justify a decision in defiance of established authorities on the matter. In this instance, HRL appears to be used as a legitimation tool. And, according to Lordon, legitimacy is so polysemous that it might be interpreted as a doubtful, circular and empty concept.[93] The (mis)use of HRL seems to be driven by mere opportunism.

92 See Art. 15 ECHR.

93 F. Lordon, 'La légitimité n'existe pas. Éléments pour une théorie des institutions' (2007) *Cahiers d'économie politique* 2, 53, 135, 150–53.

THE FUTURE OF THE INTERNATIONAL CRIMINAL COURT: A NON-HUMAN RIGHTS BODY?

Marina AKSENOVA

1. INTRODUCTION

Discussion about the interaction between human rights law (HRL) and international criminal law (ICL) is gaining momentum in scholarly circles.[1] This is not unexpected. Human rights issues are continuously lurking in the background of international criminal trials. It is difficult to imagine international criminal justice without its HRL component – legal guarantees afforded to different parties in the process as well as principles underlying substantive offences in international law. The Rome Statute of the International Criminal Court (ICC) expressly requires that the legal sources used by the

[1] E.g. E. SCHMID, *Taking Economic, Social and Cultural Rights Seriously in International Criminal Law*, Cambridge University Press, Cambridge 2015; P. LOBBA and T. MARINIELLO, 'The Cross-fertilisation Rhetoric in Question: Use and Abuse of the European Court's Jurisprudence by International Criminal Tribunals' (2015) 84 *Nordic Journal of International Law*, 363–69; J. GENUESS, 'Obstacles to Cross-fertilisation: The International Criminal Tribunals' "Unique Context" and the Flexibility of the European Court of Human Rights' Case Law' (2015) 84 *Nordic Journal of International Law*, 404–27; S. VASILIEV, 'International Criminal Tribunals in the Shadow of Strasbourg and Politics of Cross-fertilisation' (2015) 84 *Nordic Journal of International Law*, 371–403; R. CRYER, 'ESIL-International Human Rights Law Symposium: International Criminal Law and International Human Rights Law' EJIL Talk, <http://www.ejiltalk.org/esil-international-human-rights-law-symposium-international-criminal-law-and-international-human-rights-law/> accessed 15.03.2016.

Court must be interpreted consistently with internationally recognised human rights standards.[2] The relevance of HRL for international criminal trials seems to be implicitly acknowledged, but is rarely studied or analysed systematically.[3]

However, can one equate the ICC to a human rights body? To what extent does its mission converge with the mandate of its regional human rights counterparts – the European Court of Human Rights (ECtHR) and the Inter-American Court of Human Rights (IACtHR) – in upholding and reinforcing human rights? Vasiliev has argued that there exists a strong normative pull to ensure the tribunals' (and presumably the ICC's) conformity with HRL. It results in an informal hierarchy, in which deference to human rights courts is seen as an aspect of good judging.[4] This tendency stems from a concern shared by both sets of courts to protect human rights from abuses as well as to ensure fair administration of criminal justice. Informal supremacy of human rights case law – or 'the asymmetry of influence' – is the result of the uneven mutual substantive relevance of the two disciplines reinforced by the expectation that the ad hoc tribunals would treat human rights jurisprudence with deference – a belief internalised by international judges.[5] Vasiliev has acknowledged the links between ICL and IHRL, but has argued against the normative rhetoric of 'cross-fertilisation' – widely accepted in scholarly circles – as it misconstrues the tribunals' engagement with the regional human rights courts and is incapable of enhancing human rights compliance by the ad hoc tribunals.[6]

This chapter continues this line of discourse by invoking an empirical example evidencing the limitations that the ICC faces when incorporating human rights norms in its judicial reasoning. It critically examines the pronouncement of the *Al Senussi* Appeals Chamber that the ICC was not established as an international court of human rights designed to adjudicate on the internal functioning of the domestic legal systems of States in relation to due process guarantees.[7] The appellate Judges reinforced the view previously voiced by the Pre-Trial Chamber: Mr Al Senussi's lack of access to defence counsel during

2 Art. 21(3) Rome Statute.

3 Lobba and Mariniello argue that 'scholarly research has thus far fallen short of developing a systematic approach to the appraisal of the interactions between human rights bodies and international criminal tribunals': P. Lobba and T. Mariniello, above n. 1, 364; see also S. Vasiliev, above n. 1, 364.

4 S. Vasiliev, above n. 1, 373.

5 Ibid., 374–78.

6 This is for reasons of the horizontal character of transjudicial communication, the pluralistic nature of human rights, and judicial autonomy of international courts and tribunals: ibid., 384 *et seq*.

7 *Prosecutor v. Saif Al-Islam Gaddafi and Abdullah Al-Senussi* (ICC-01/11-01/11 OA 4), Judgment on the appeal of Mr Abdullah Al-Senussi against the decision of Pre-Trial Chamber I of 11 October 2013 entitled 'Decision on the admissibility of the case against Abdullah Al-Senussi' (24 July 2014), ('*Al Senussi* Appeal Judgment'), para. 219.

investigation proceedings in Libya in the context of the fragile security situation in the country does not render the case admissible before the ICC. This position is consonant with the one voiced in the *Kony* admissibility proceedings whereby the Appeals Chamber refuted the defence's argument that a suspect is entitled to legal representation in admissibility proceedings. The Judges ruled that such a right exists only *at trial* and in respect of persons appearing before the Court, as opposed to those for whom the arrest warrant has been issued.[8]

This stance could be contrasted with the *Katanga* case, in which Judges ruled that the accused is entitled to a level of human rights protection *higher* than that guaranteed under the European Convention on Human Rights (ECHR) or the International Covenant on Civil and Political Rights (ICCPR). The matter concerned the extent of the accused's language competence that was required to meet the threshold of Article 67(1)(a) and (f) of the Rome Statute. These provisions guarantee that the accused is properly informed about the charges against them and receive legal assistance in the language that they *fully* understand and *speak*.[9] The ECHR and the ICCPR stop short of this comprehensive standard, guaranteeing protection in the language that the person charged with a criminal offence understands.[10] Admittedly, this ruling concerned the rights of persons before the ICC Pre-Trial Chamber, rather than the situation of the suspects singled out for domestic prosecutions and examined in the context of the admissibility proceedings.

There are at least two explanations for the above contradiction. The most obvious one is explicitly suggested by the Judges in *Al Senussi* and *Kony*: the scope of the human rights protection guaranteed by the ICC depends on the stage of the proceedings and the exact role of the person seeking protection (suspect or accused). This compartmentalisation differs from the predominant approach of the ECtHR in assessing individual due process guarantees against the notion of the overall fairness of the proceedings.[11] In *Al-Khawaja and Tahery*, the ECtHR evaluated the relationship between the general fair trial

---

8 *Prosecutor v. Joseph Kony et al.* (ICC-02/04-01/05 OA 3), 'Judgment on the appeal of the Defence against the "Decision on the admissibility of the case under article 19 (1) of the Statute" of 10 March 2009' (16 September 2009) ('*Kony* Appeal Judgment'), paras 64–66.

9 *Prosecutor v. Germain Katanga* (01/04-01/07 (OA 3), Judgment on the appeal of Mr. Germain Katanga against the decision of Pre-Trial Chamber I entitled 'Decision on the Defence Request Concerning Languages', (27 May 2008) ('*Katanga* Languages Judgment'), paras 62–63.

10 Arts 6(3) ECHR and 14(3) ICCPR.

11 P. Lemmens, 'The right to a fair trial and its multiple manifestations: Article 6(1) ECHR' in E. Brems and J. Gerards, *Shaping Rights in the ECHR: The Role of the European Court of Human Rights in Determining the Scope of Human Rights*, Cambridge University Press, Cambridge 2015, p. 312. Art. 6(1) of the ECHR stipulates: 'In the determination of his civil rights and obligations or of any criminal charge against him, everyone is entitled to a fair and public hearing within a reasonable time by an independent and impartial tribunal established by law.'

requirements under Article 6(1) of the ECHR and the specific guarantees for persons charged with a criminal offence under Article 6(3). It held that the latter are 'specific aspects of the right to a fair hearing set forth in paragraph 1' and 'the Court's primary concern under Article 6(1) is to evaluate the *overall* fairness of the criminal proceedings' (emphasis added).[12]

The second possible explanation for diverging approaches to human rights protection on a case-by-case basis at the ICC could be the *nature* of the rights at stake and the role of the *party* seeking protection. Is it possible that victims' rights receive a higher degree of protection at the ICC than those of other parties? The Rome Statute reserves a prominent role for victims in proceedings before the ICC. The Preamble makes an emotional call to ensure the recognition of suffering of 'victims of unimaginable atrocities that deeply shock the conscience of humanity'. In *Lubanga*, the ICC upheld the centrality of victim-related concerns by holding:

> The Statute and the Rules introduce a system of reparations that reflects a growing recognition in international criminal law that there is a need to go beyond the notion of punitive justice, towards a solution which is more inclusive, encourages participation and recognizes the need to provide effective remedies for victims.[13]

Participation of victims in proceedings at the ICC alongside the accused may potentially create situations whereby conflicting sets of rights are at stake. In such circumstances, it is unavoidable for the Judges or the prosecution to have to make choices prioritising one set of rights over the other or, in the alternative, to devise a strategy reconciling the two positions. For example, in her separate and dissenting opinion to the *Lubanga* judgment, Judge Odio Benito argued that it is incumbent on the ICC to regard the interests of victims and, as a result, provide comprehensive legal definitions that go beyond the circumstances of each individual case. She referred to the elements of the crime of enlisting and conscripting the use of children under the age of 15 not directly relevant to the case at issue and claimed:

> [...] In the present case, the statutory provisions are meant to protect the life and personal integrity of children under the age of 15. It would thus be impermissible for a Chamber to decline to enter a comprehensive legal definition of a crime and leave it open to a case-by-case analysis or to the limited scope of the charges brought against the accused. [...][14]

---

12 *Al-Khawaja and Tahery* v. *United Kingdom*, ECHR (GC), 15 December 2011, para. 118 (emphasis added).

13 *Lubanga* Reparations Decision, para. 177.

14 *Prosecutor v. Thomas Lubanga Dyilo*, ICC-01/04-01/06, Separate and Dissenting Opinion of Judge Odio Benito to the Trial Chamber I, Judgment pursuant Article 74 of the Statute, 14 March 2012 ('Separate and Dissenting Opinion of Judge Odio Benito'), para. 7.

This view seems to extend the powers of the Trial Chamber beyond those envisaged in Article 64(2) of the Rome Statute.[15] The overly expansive legal definitions are at odds with the rights of the accused – in particular, their right to be informed about the charges, to have adequate time for preparation and to be tried without delay.[16]

Diverging degrees of protection of human rights could be explained not only by the party seeking protection but also by the nature of rights at stake. The unique context in which international criminal courts and tribunals operate requires reinterpretation and re-adjustment of certain fair trial guarantees as compared with their application in the domestic law context.[17] For example, the need for a speedy trial must be balanced against the complexity of mass atrocities cases; the exclusionary rule must contain room for manoeuvre to accommodate, in some instances, evidence obtained from an illegal source. This is due to the difficulty of collecting evidence in the wake of war and the gravity of the crimes in question.[18] The 'uniqueness' rhetoric should not be overstated, however. Indeed, the context matters in interpreting human rights, but international criminal courts and tribunals are still criminal courts in the way in which they are designed and operate. What is more important, human rights jurisprudence is often fact driven and case specific, leaving enough flexibility for its adoption by other disciplines and courts.[19]

This chapter argues neither for nor against more intensive dialogue between ICL and IHRL, but rather examines their intrinsic qualities using the example of *Al Senussi* against the background of the principle of complementarity, which is at the core of the case.

The chapter largely supports previously voiced concern in academic circles about the lack of 'grammar'[20] in the process of cross-fertilisation barring its objective assessment as proper or erroneous.[21] With the view of the existing gap in methodology, the chapter advances the third type of explanation as to why the degree of human rights protection differs from case to case and from right to right. This explanation is rooted in the nature of judicial or prosecutorial discretion. It is maintained that discretion is an essential tool 'moderating' human rights guarantees in an international criminal process. Discretion is

15 Art. 64(2) reads as follows: 'The Trial Chamber shall ensure that a trial is fair and expeditious and is conducted with full respect for the rights of the accused and due regard for the protection of victims and witnesses.'
16 Art. 67(1)(a)–(c) of the Rome Statute.
17 M. Damaska, 'Reflections on Fairness in International Criminal Justice' (2012) 10(3) *Journal of International Criminal Justice*, 611–20.
18 Ibid.
19 J. Genuess, above n. 1, 405.
20 P. Lobba and T. Mariniello (eds), above n. 1.
21 Ibid., 365.

largely subjective and accounts for particular circumstances of the case, thus shaping the argument by tilting it into a certain direction within legal boundaries set by the Rome Statute and the Rules of Procedure and Evidence (RPE).

The second part of the chapter explores the place of HRL within the architecture of the ICC. Section 3 discusses in detail the nature of arguments underlying the *Al Senussi* admissibility judgment.[22] The aim is to examine the 'compartmentalisation' thesis, whereby human rights issues get a lesser degree of exposure before the commencement of trial. The final part argues that discretion is the primary vehicle behind the human rights discourse at the ICC.

2. PLACE OF HUMAN RIGHTS LAW WITHIN THE ICC ARCHITECTURE

There are a number of ways in which HRL affects international criminal trials. First, HRL informs the procedure at the ICC. The Rome Statute comprises 128 articles that regulate not only substantive issues such as sentencing or elements of crimes but also the conduct of proceedings at different stages. For example, Article 40 of the Rome Statute is dedicated in its entirety to the independence of Judges. It requires that judges are independent in the performance of their functions, shall not engage in activity likely to interfere with these functions or affect confidence in their independence, and shall devote their full time to judging, not engaging in any other professional occupation. This provision regulates judicial activity so as to ensure the overall fairness of the criminal process. It also eliminates obvious impediments to the exercise of judicial discretion.

Secondly, one of the defining features of the Rome Statute is the explicit requirement enshrined in Article 21(3) of the Rome Statute to interpret applicable law in a manner consistent with internationally recognised human rights. This provision reflected the rise of the human rights consciousness characteristic of the time of the adoption of the Rome Statute. Early case law of the ICC repeatedly referenced this article.[23] Its potential is immense, for it opens the door to expanding assurances contained in other provisions of the Statute.[24]

---

22 *Al Senussi* Appeal Judgment; *Prosecutor v. Saif Al-Islam Gaddafi and Abdullah Al-Senussi* (ICC-01/11-01/11), 'Decision on the admissibility of the case against Abdullah Al-Senussi' (11 October 2013), ('*Al Senussi* Pre-Trial Decision').

23 W. Schabas, *The International Criminal Court: A Commentary on the Rome Statute*, Oxford University Press, Oxford 2010, pp. 398–99.

24 Ibid.

Early on, the Appeals Chamber stressed that *every* article of the Rome Statute has to be interpreted and applied in accordance with Article 21(3).[25] This leads to the conclusion that HRL is relevant for both procedural and substantive crime provisions of the Rome Statute. For example, in defining the crime of recruiting children, the *Lubanga* Trial Chamber referred to, inter alia, the Convention on the Rights of the Child.[26]

Thirdly, HRL underpins specific guarantees afforded to different parties in the process. Article 67 of the Rome Statute contains a list of fair trial guarantees for the accused, which is not only richer in detail than its analogues in the statutes of the ad hoc tribunals but also extends the scope of rights traditionally protected by human rights courts.[27] The presumption of innocence is hosted by a separate provision (Article 66) and so are the rights of persons during the investigations (Article 55). Article 75 of the Rome Statute instructs the Court to develop principles of reparations to the victims. Article 54 lists duties and powers of the Prosecutor with respect to investigations, including the duty fully to respect the rights of persons arising under the Statute.[28] Finally, Article 68 regulates victim participation in the proceedings and ensures, among other things, their wellbeing, dignity and privacy.

Fourthly, HRL serves as a source of customary law before the ad hoc tribunals and, less so, at the ICC.[29] For example, the International Criminal Tribunal for the Former Yugoslavia (ICTY) relied in its early jurisprudence on international treaty rules on human rights banning torture to expand its subject matter jurisdiction and define the parameters of this offence in ICL.[30] In this case, treaty provisions corroborated customary status of the rule in question. The Special Court for Sierra Leone referred to the jurisprudence of the IACtHR when declaring without effect the Lomé Peace Accords, granting absolute pardon to all combatants for anything done by them in pursuit of

25 *Situation in the Democratic Republic of the Congo* ICC-01/04-168 OA3, Judgment on the Prosecutor's Application for Extraordinary Review of Pre-Trial Chamber I's 31 March 2006 Decision Denying Leave to Appeal, AC (13 July 2006), para. 38.

26 *Prosecutor v. Lubanga* (ICC-01/04-01/06-2842) Judgment pursuant to Article 74 of the Statute, TC (14 March 2012) para. 604.

27 L. Gradoni, 'General Framework of International Criminal Procedure' in G. Sluiter et al. (eds) *International Criminal Procedure: Principles and Rules*, Oxford University Press, Oxford 2012, p. 76.

28 Art. 54(1)(c) of the Rome Statute.

29 Art. 21 of the Rome Statute establishes the hierarchy of sources at the ICC, giving express priority to the Court's constituent documents. Art. 21(1)(b) of the Rome Statute acknowledges as a source of law at the ICC '[i]n the second place, where appropriate, applicable treaties and the principles and rules of international law, including the established principles of the international law of armed conflict.'

30 *Prosecutor v. Furundžija*, ICTY Case No. IT-95-17/1-T, Trial Judgment, 10 December 1998, paras 143 *et seq.*

their objectives.[31] The Inter-American Commission on Human Rights declared amnesty laws of El Salvador, Uruguay and Argentina to be incompatible with the American Convention on Human Rights because they deprive victims of their right to an effective investigation and prosecution.[32] The IACtHR continued striking down blanket amnesties for the same reason, thereby solidifying the customary status of the prohibition of absolute amnesties for core international crimes.[33]

The feature of HRL as an 'informant' of ICL is particularly relevant for categories of crimes not yet comprehensively codified in treaty law, such as crimes against humanity.[34] In this instance, HRL serves a normative foundation for the whole category of international offences. The logic of human rights both underlies the definitions of various elements of crimes against humanity and justifies their existence as a general category. The special character of crimes against humanity stems from their role as a guardian against the most egregious human rights abuses committed by either State or non-State actors when the State is unable or unwilling to stop the violence. The legal criteria that they are perpetrated as a part of a widespread or systematic attack against civilian population establishes a certain level of severity required for triggering the feeling of collective repulsion across borders.[35] The Rome Statute of the ICC expressly requires that crimes against humanity be committed in furtherance of a state or organisational policy.[36] The majority in the ICC *Kenya* case interpreted 'organization' broadly, as a group with 'the capability to perform acts which infringe on basic human values'.[37] HRL also informs specific types of crimes against humanity. For example, the *Tadić* Trial Chamber explained that 'persecution'-type crimes against humanity (as opposed to

---

31 *Kallon and Kamara*, Appeal Decision, 13 March 2004, para. 84; *Prosecutor v. Kondewa*, Case No. SCSL-2004-14-AR72(E), Decision on lack of jurisdiction/abuse of process: amnesty provided by the Lomé Accord, Separate Opinion of Justice Robertson, (25 May 2004), paras 30 *et seq.*

32 IACHR Report 26/92, Case 10.287, *Las Hojas Massacre* (El Salvador), 24 September 1992; IACHR Report 29/92, Cases 10.029, 10.036, 10.145, 10.305, 10.372, 10.373, and 10.375, Uruguay, 2 October 1992; Report 28/92, Cases 10.147, 10.181, 10.240, 10.262, 10.309, and 10.311, Argentina, 2 October 1992.

33 E.g. *Barrios Altos v. Peru*, 2001 Inter-Am. Ct. H.R. (ser. C) No. 75, 42 (14 March 2001), paras 41 *et seq.*

34 R. Cryer, above n. 1. The International Law Commission (ILC) is currently preparing a Draft Convention on Crimes Against Humanity. See ILC Report on the work of the 66thsession (2014), UN DOC A/69/10, chapter XIV, sect. A.1.

35 See, e.g., D. Luban, 'Beyond Moral Minimalism: Response to Crimes Against Humanity' (2006) 20 *Ethics and International Affairs.*

36 Art. 7(2)(a) of the Rome Statute.

37 Situation in the Republic of Kenya, Case No. ICC-01/09, Decision Pursuant to Article 15 of the Rome Statute on the Authorization of an Investigation into the Situation in the Republic of Kenya ('Kenya Decision'), para. 92.

the 'murder' type) imply some form of discrimination that results in an infringement of an individual's fundamental rights.[38]

Lastly, it is essential to acknowledge the importance of human rights bodies in the fact-finding work of the ICC. The recent report issued by the Office of the Prosecutor in relation to violence allegedly committed following the *coup d'état* in Honduras in June 2009 (Honduras Report) finding lack of a reasonable basis to proceed to investigation stage relied almost exclusively on the sources assembled by the human rights agencies – the Inter-American Commission on Human Rights, the UN Office of the High Commissioner for Human Rights, and other UN agencies, various reports from domestic civil society organisations and international non-governmental organisations including, Human Rights Watch, the International Federation for Human Rights, and Amnesty International.[39] The Honduras Report is particularly salient for present discussion because it distinguishes (on the basis of the evidence collected by the human rights bodies) between crimes against humanity and widespread human rights violations that do not reach the threshold of conduct captured by the relevant provision of the Rome Statute.[40]

3. CASE STUDY: *AL SENUSSI* ADMISSIBILITY PROCEEDINGS

The situation in Libya has been referred to the ICC by the UN Security Council in February 2011, following reports about murders and persecutions of civilians taking part in demonstrations in the weeks preceding the fall of the Gaddafi regime.[41] Four months later, the Pre-Trial Chamber issued three arrest warrants against the former Prime Minster, Muammar Mohammed Abu Minyar Gaddafi; his son, Saif Al-Islam Gaddafi; and the former head of the Libyan military intelligence, Abdullah Al-Senussi.[42] The case against Muammar Gaddafi was later terminated due to his death, while the other two cases proceeded to the admissibility stage. Libya insisted on trying both individuals domestically.

The Rome Statute upholds the primacy of States in handling cases. Thus, a case comes within the purview of the Court only if the crimes are of sufficient gravity and the country in question is 'unwilling or unable genuinely to

38 *Prosecutor v. Tadić*, ICTY Case No. IT-94-1-T, Trial Judgment, 7 May 1997 ('*Tadic* Trial Judgment'), para. 697.

39 Situation in Honduras, Article 5 Report, October 2015, <http://www.icc-cpi.int/iccdocs/otp/SAS-HON-Article_5_Report-Oct2015-ENG.PDF>, para 40.

40 Ibid., para. 16.

41 UN SC Resolution 1970, 26 February 2011.

42 On 22 November 2011, Pre-Trial Chamber I formally terminated the case against Muammar Gaddafi due to his death.

carry out the investigation or prosecution'.[43] It is important that the offences allegedly prosecuted and investigated at a national level cover substantially the same conduct as those charged by the ICC, while legal characterisation of the underlying incidents matters less.[44] The State is 'unwilling' if it initiates the proceedings with unjustified delay or with the purpose of shielding the person concerned from criminal responsibility or fails to conduct the proceedings independently or impartially – all of which signals lack of intent to bring the person concerned to justice.[45]

The Pre-Trial Chamber in *Al Senussi* assessed both whether Libya was investigating the 'same case' and whether it was not 'unable and unwilling'. The Pre-Trial Chamber unanimously rendered the case inadmissible.[46] This is in contrast with the connected case against Saif Al-Islam Gaddafi, which was found to be admissible before the ICC on the ground that Libya had not been investigating the same case.[47] Mr Al Senussi's defence team attempted to draw parallels between the two cases by pointing to a contradiction between the findings in the *Al Senussi* and *Gaddafi* cases.[48] The Appeals Chamber in *Al Senussi* refuted this argument by claiming that the case is distinct from *Gaddafi* because it had attracted more evidence and its scope had been more limited, both geographically and temporarily.[49]

Putting the 'same case' issue aside, the bulk of the arguments furnished by Mr Al Senussi's defence team and, to a certain extent, the representatives for victims, rested on major human rights concerns, including the lack of legal representation. Their overarching position, heavily supported by human rights jurisprudence, was that the case must be tried at the ICC because Libya could not guarantee the due process rights of the suspect, rendering the country unable or unwilling. The nature of these objections brought human rights issues into the focus and prompted first the Pre-Trial Chamber and then the Appeals Chamber to consider the extent to which the ICC is ready to engage with the issue of the suspect's fair trial guarantees at the domestic level.

Raising human rights concerns as an obstacle to the domestic handling of the case was not an unexpected move: the RPE provide that unwillingness

---

43 Art. 17(1) of the Rome Statute.

44 *Al Senussi* Appeal Judgment, para. 119.

45 Art. 17(2) of the Rome Statute.

46 *Prosecutor v. Saif Al-Islam Gaddafi and Abdullah Al-Senussi* (ICC-01/11-01/11-466-Red.) Decision on the admissibility of the case against Abdullah Al-Senussi of Pre-Trial Chamber I of 11 October 2013 ('*Al-Senussi* Pre-Trial Decision'), para. 311.

47 *Prosecutor v. Saif Al-Islam Gaddafi and Abdullah Al-Senussi* (ICC-01/11-01/11 OA 4), Judgment on the appeal of Libya against the decision of Pre-Trial Chamber I of 31 May 2013 entitled 'Decision on the admissibility of the case against Saif Al-Islam Gaddafi' ('*Gaddafi* Appeal Judgment') (21 May 2014), para. 213.

48 *Al-Senussi* Appeal Judgment, para. 93.

49 Ibid., paras 95–96.

of the State may be assessed in the light of evidence pertaining to national courts compatibility with internationally recognised human rights standards.[50] The *chapeau* of Article 17(2) prescribes that, in determining unwillingness, the Court must have regard to the principles of due process recognised by international law, and subparagraph (c) of the same provision ensures that domestic proceedings are conducted independently and impartially.[51] Moreover, Article 55(2)(c) of the Rome Statute expressly grants the right to legal assistance to persons questioned during investigation by national authorities. Therefore, the normative framework of the ICC allowed certain room to manoeuvre when it came to assessing Libya's unwillingness in the light of the lack of legal representation and other procedural shortcomings.

Kevin Heller has suggested that plain reading of Article 17, and in particular subparagraph (c), does not support what he refers to as the 'due process thesis', or the possibility to declare a case admissible to the ICC in instances when national jurisdiction cannot guarantee due process rights for the accused. He argued that the due process aspects of Article 17 only come into play in situations in which domestic legal systems make it difficult to convict the accused, indicating lack of intent, rather than when national law makes it easy to convict an individual.[52] Heller bases this conclusion mainly on the fact that the requirements of Article 17(2)(c) are conjunctive, and not disjunctive: unwillingness is established if '[t]he proceedings were not or are not being conducted independently or impartially, *and* they were or are being conducted in a manner which, in the circumstances, is inconsistent with an intent to bring the person concerned to justice' (emphasis added).[53] Therefore, it is not enough that domestic proceedings are not impartial or independent to render a case admissible to the ICC; they must also be aimed at shielding an individual from justice. Heller further noted that the *chapeau* of Article 17(2), containing the requirement of due process, is not an independent clause and is subordinated to the specific provisions that follow.[54]

Heller then concluded that the meaning of the provision is clear following textual interpretation, rendering recourse to *travaux préparatoires* unnecessary. He nonetheless provided a few comments related to the drafting history of Article 17(2). In support of his general argument, he pointed to the express rejection of Italy's proposal of including in the definition of 'unwillingness' the absence of national due process guarantees as a ground for admissibility.[55]

50 Rule 51 of the Rules of Evidence and Procedure. See also W. Schabas, above n. 23, p. 345.

51 Representatives for both the victims and the defence made arguments to that effect: *Al-Senussi* Appeal Judgment, paras 204–10.

52 K. Heller, 'The Shadow Side of Complementarity: The Effect of Article 17 of the Rome Statute on National Due Process' (2006) 17 *Criminal Law Forum* 255–80.

53 Ibid., 261; Art. 17(2)(c) of the Rome Statute (emphasis added).

54 K. Heller, above n. 52, 262.

55 Ibid., 271–72.

There is clear merit in reading Article 17 in accordance with grammar rules and attempting to discern the meaning that the drafters intended to give it. This chapter contends, however, that a plain reading of Article 17 does not automatically lead to the denial of the 'due process' thesis and leaves enough wiggle room for ruling on admissibility in instances when national law makes it easier *or* harder to convict an individual.[56] Suggesting otherwise would make subparagraph (c) redundant as it becomes nearly identical to subparagraph (a), which provides that unwillingness occurs when '[t]he proceedings were or are being undertaken or the national decision was made for the purpose of shielding the person concerned from criminal responsibility for crimes within the jurisdiction of the Court referred to in article 5'.[57] Since both clauses discuss lack of intent to bring those responsible to justice, the subtle difference seems to lie in the extra guarantee of independence and impartiality enshrined in subparagraph (c). If impartiality and independence assessment is reserved exclusively for situations in which an individual may escape justice, it is difficult to justify the existence of subparagraph (c) as an independent clause, for mere addition of 'impartiality and independence' to the wording of subparagraph (a) would suffice. The conclusion that follows is that the provisions on admissibility as formulated in the Rome Statute are at the very least unclear with respect to the level of human rights protection they grant to suspects or any other parties to domestic proceedings. The other provisions of the Rome Statute and the RPE expressly upholding human rights and due process guarantees do not dispel this ambiguity.

Articles of the Rome Statute not dealing with human rights directly but embodying the Court's core operational principles also provide contextual backing to the idea of the existence of some form of due process thesis within the complementarity framework. Take, for example, the provision banning immunities for State officials with respect to crimes falling under the ICC radar.[58] Article 27 of the Rome Statute calls for equal application of the Statute to *all* persons regardless of their capacity. Its rationale is preventing impunity in cases in which immunity shields high-level functionaries from criminal responsibility. Requiring the State to introduce procedural safeguards to prevent those in power from enjoying immunity and enable equal application of the values enshrined in the Rome Statute to *all*, while simultaneously overlooking

56 See also E. Fry, 'Between Show Trials and Sham Prosecutions: The Rome Statute's Potential Effect on Domestic Due Process Protections' (2012) 23(1–3) *Criminal Law Forum*, 35, 42.

57 Art. 17(2)(a) of the Rome Statute.

58 Art. 27(1) of the Rome Statute of the ICC: 'This Statute shall apply equally to all persons without any distinction based on official capacity. In particular, official capacity as a Head of State or Government, a member of a Government or parliament, an elected representative or a government official shall in no case exempt a person from criminal responsibility under this Statute, nor shall it, in and of itself, constitute a ground for reduction of sentence.'

proceedings designed to convict in flagrant violation of the principles of fairness and equality of arms, contradicts the letter and spirit of the Rome Statute. Speedy trials with a predetermined outcome would most likely target the very same persons who previously held power and who would, in theory, otherwise benefit from immunity. Why, then, would the Rome Statute call on States to abandon protection for high-ranking perpetrators of mass atrocities, while leaving room for them to be (mis)treated during the subsequent domestic proceedings? This would be a tilt in the opposite direction, distorting the idea of equality of application of the Statute to all perpetrators irrespective of their position. Why would the Rome Statute advocate for equal application of its provisions to *all* in one article and simultaneously allow for the violation of the same principle in another?

Finally, if one takes a closer look at the negotiating history of the complementarity provision, it becomes clear that it is the result of a carefully crafted compromise, as many delegations were unhappy with the article – often for different reasons.[59] Some delegations worried about the lack of objectivity in the ICC's assessment of a State's unwillingness and its unfettered discretion in this regard. The initial solution was to add an element of objectivity by introducing the phrase 'in accordance with the principles of due process recognized by international law' to the third aspect of unwillingness dealing with lack of impartial and independent proceedings – a natural place for this supplement. The level of objectivity resulting from this amendment still kept some States dissatisfied. As a result, the final deal that gained support and was included in the Rome Statute was to add the phrase 'having regard to the principles of due process recognized by international law' to the *chapeau* of the paragraph on unwillingness.[60] This solution implies, first, the States' concern about the ICC's possible interference in their respective investigations and trials, and, secondly, the delegates' agreement on a 'due process' test as an acceptable objective criterion of the ICC's assessment of national proceedings.

Returning to the *Al Senussi* case, it is essential to note up front that, in assessing the arguments put before it, the Appeals Chamber only determined whether the Pre-Trial Chamber's approach was 'so unfair and unreasonable as to constitute an abuse of discretion'.[61] This consideration effectively

59 J.T. Holmes, 'The Principle of Complementarity' in R.S. Lee (ed.), *The International Criminal Court: The Making of the Rome Statute: Issues, Negotiations, Results*, Kluwer Law International, Leiden 1999, p. 52.

60 Ibid., pp. 53–54.

61 *Al-Senussi* Appeal Judgment, para. 79. See also *Gaddafi* Appeal Judgment, para. 146; *Prosecutor v. William Samoei Ruto et al.*, Judgment on the appeal of the Prosecutor against the decision of Trial Chamber V(a) of 18 June entitled 'Decision on Mr Ruto's Request for Excusal from Continuous Presence at Trial', 25 October 2013, ICC-01/09-01/11-1066 (OA 5), para. 60.

limited the scope of the analysis of the Appellate Judges. For example, the argument that no *ex parte* material should have been used to the detriment of the defence was dismissed precisely on this ground. The Appeals Chamber ruled that there was no abuse of discretion by the lower instance because the purpose of the admissibility proceedings was to establish whether Libya was investigating the same case and not to determine the criminal responsibility of the suspect.[62]

The main claim of the defence was that the Pre-Trial Chamber abused its discretion in finding that Libya was not unwilling and unable genuinely to carry out the proceedings.[63] One of the central points of contention during the pre-trial proceedings was the lack of legal representation for the suspect during the investigations in Libya.[64] The Pre-Trial Chamber concluded that thatdid not render Libya unwilling, since it was caused by the objective security situation on the ground. This, however, did not imply that Libya would be unable to provide legal representation in future judicial proceedings. Moreover, Libya was not unable because it obtained the suspect held in its custody and the security situation still allowed the local authority to collect evidence.[65] The defence team disputed this assessment before the Appellate Panel, pointing to a number of shortcomings in the local criminal justice system.[66]

The defence specifically highlighted that the Pre-Trial Chamber should not have proceeded with determining admissibility of the case when Mr Al Senussi did not have an opportunity to instruct his international counsel. The defence also emphasised Mr Al Senussi's lack of domestic legal representation during the proceedings in Libya. The Appeals Chamber dismissed the former argument, upholding the discretion of the Pre-Trial Chamber to determine the scope of the participatory rights of the suspect in the proceedings. Reference was made to the largely procedural provision of the RPE that enables the Chamber to determine the modalities of the proceedings concerning jurisdiction or admissibility.[67] The Appellate Judges drew a line between *any* suspect and a suspect either surrendered to the Court or appearing before it. Only the latter category benefited from participatory rights and other guarantees, while the rights of the former group were left to the discretion of the Pre-Trial Chamber.[68] The Appeals Chamber also rejected the later assertion regarding the lack of domestic legal representation. It acknowledged that this issue might become fatal in the case.

---

62 *Al-Senussi* Appeal Judgment, para. 79.
63 Ibid., para. 124.
64 *Al-Senussi* Pre-Trial Decision, para. 230.
65 Ibid., paras 292, 304–06.
66 *Al-Senussi* Appeal Judgment, para. 131.
67 Art. 58(2) of the RPE; ibid., para. 150.
68 *Al-Senussi* Appeal Judgment, paras 146–47.

However, it was not Libya's unwillingness that prevented the appointment of legal counsel in domestic proceedings but rather the security situation in the country.[69]

The Appeals Chamber dismissed as speculative other arguments by the defence concerning Libya's lack of independent judiciary threatening the accused with death penalty and a pre-determined outcome.[70] The Judges also failed to find Libya's inability to conduct investigations and prosecutions despite the claims that the country's authorities do not exercise full control over the detention centres and fail to ensure proper witness protection.[71]

The Judges were left with a difficult choice in light of the express provisions of the Rome Statute guaranteeing due process rights.[72] Arguably, the legal framework allowed for deciding the issue of admissibility both ways. It is noteworthy that the Judges did not reject up front the incompatibility of the due process concerns raised by the defence with the framework of the admissibility proceedings. The reasoning of the Appellate Panel was more nuanced and rested on two related but separate grounds: the nature of admissibility proceedings *and* the severity of violation. Generally speaking, the Judges dismissed due process claims as resulting from an incorrect understanding of the role of the suspect in the admissibility proceedings.[73] They invoked the reasoning, voiced in one of the previous cases, that human rights jurisprudence is of limited value in admissibility proceedings because the nature of these proceedings is not to accommodate a mechanism for individual complaints about human rights violations.[74] However, stopping at this conclusion would have rendered guarantees implicit in the Rome Statute futile.

Therefore, the Appeals Chamber introduced the second, more specific, ground for rejecting due process claims – insufficient severity of the violation at stake. The Chamber made a normative determination as to the qualitative aspect of the violation of Mr Al Senussi's rights and the impact of this violation on the admissibility proceedings. The Appeals Chamber held that the purpose of admissibility proceedings is not to rule on human rights matters; therefore the violation must be 'so egregious that the proceedings can no longer be regarded as being capable of providing any genuine form of justice to the accused'.[75]

---

69 *Al-Senussi* Pre-Trial Decision, para. 292, *Al-Senussi* Appeal Judgment, paras 181 and 189.

70 *Al-Senussi* Appeal Judgment, paras 244 and 256.

71 Ibid., paras 287 and 295.

72 *Cf.* K. Heller, above n. 52.

73 *Al-Senussi* Appeal Judgment, para. 145.

74 Ibid., para. 169. See also *Kony* Appeal Judgment, para. 66.

75 *Al-Senussi* Appeal Judgment, paras 190, 229 and 230. See also F. Mégret, 'What Sort of Global Justice is "International Criminal Justice"?' (2015) 13 *Journal of International Criminal Justice*, 77–96.

In the subsequent rather apologetic paragraph the Judges acknowledged that they did not wish to downplay the importance of legal counsel in the present case, but that the nature of violation did not reach the required threshold.

Introducing the qualitative aspect of the violation that may or may not render a State in question unwilling is a controversial solution.[76] The Appeals Chamber further clarified that references to due process, independence and impartiality in Article 17(2) of the Rome Statute refer primarily to situations in which the suspect may evade justice as a result of the State not being willing genuinely to investigate and prosecute.[77] The violations of the rights of the suspect *per se* are not sufficient for finding unwillingness, and accepting otherwise would bring the ICC very close to a human rights court overseeing domestic jurisdictions, which is inconsistent with the intentions of Article 17.[78] Through this reasoning, the Judges endorsed a softer version of Heller's argument:[79] they chose not to turn a blind eye to the violations, while simultaneously acknowledging the subordinate status of due process concerns at the stage of the admissibility proceedings.

The Appeals Chamber position resonates with the 'moderate due process' thesis advanced by Elinor Fry in 2012. Fry assessed the degree of human rights protection implicit in the complementarity regime and came to the conclusion that interpreting the Article 17 due process provision as only preventing abuse of the criminal process to the advantage of the accused goes against the generally accepted principle of international law that trials must be fair.[80] She built her argument largely on the need for objective assessment of unwillingness – the issue that drew consensus during the negotiations of Article 17 of the Rome Statute and that served as a rationale for the inclusion of the due process clause and the word 'genuinely' in Article 17.[81]

Fry concluded that focusing on procedure rather than result (conviction or acquittal) is a way to introduce objectivity in the assessment of unwillingness.[82] While it is unrealistic to demand full compliance with all fair trial guarantees in the context of complementarity analysis, it is possible to focus on *basic* fair trial rights having potential to render the case admissible to the ICC.[83] The Appeals Chamber in *Al Senussi* did not elaborate on the list of basic or core fair trial

76 *Al-Senussi* Appeal Judgment, para. 191.
77 Ibid., para. 218.
78 Ibid., paras 219–20.
79 K. Heller, above n. 52.
80 E. Fry, above n. 56, 46.
81 Ibid., 49. See also International Criminal Court Office of the Prosecutor, 'An Informal Expert Paper: The Principle of Complementarity in Practice' (2003) <http://www.icc-cpi.int/iccdocs/doc/doc654724.pdf>, accessed 20.08.2016.
82 E. Fry, above n. 56, 49.
83 Ibid., 52.

guarantees impacting the admissibility assessment but rather focused on the qualitative aspect of the violation, namely its severity. The underlying logic is nonetheless similar, namely examining the modalities of domestic proceedings at hand against the backdrop of competing demands.

4. DISCRETION AS A VEHICLE BEHIND HUMAN RIGHTS CONSIDERATIONS

All three explanations regarding the varying degrees of human rights protection at the ICC mentioned in the introductory part of this chapter hold true in the *Al Senussi* case. First, the Judges explicitly admitted that the stage of the proceedings is crucial in determining the scope of due process guarantees afforded to Mr Al Senussi. In particular, they stressed that his status as a suspect in domestic proceedings, rather than the accused appearing *before* the ICC, effectively limits the scope of due process rights afforded to him. This is in stark contrast with the approach of the ECtHR in providing an evaluation of fairness of the entire proceedings when determining whether there existed a breach of the right to a fair trial.[84] At the same time, the early stage of the proceedings did not *per se* render these rights inapplicable in the present case. Rather, the issue was identified as being within the discretion of the Judges deciding on admissibility. The Appeals Chamber exercised this discretion and assessed whether the violation at stake was of sufficient gravity to declare Libya's unwillingness or inability genuinely to prosecute the case.

The second explanation as to the divergent level of human rights protection at the ICC related to the rights holders at stake. The *Al Senussi* Appeals Chamber implicitly acknowledged the relevance of this consideration by stating that references to due process, impartiality and independence in Article 17(2) of the Rome Statute refer *primarily* to situations in which the suspect may evade justice. Presumably, comparison is being made with instances in which a suspect faces trial but his rights are violated. The same statement may also be interpreted as implying the possibility of higher degree of scrutiny of the national criminal justice system in situations in which interests other than those of the suspect are at stake. For instance, victims' right to justice may call for more detailed examination of the willingness and ability of domestic actors to produce the desired result. The idea that victims' rights play a significant role in the assessment of the admissibility criteria by the ICC underlies one of the main

84 A. Mowbray, *European Convention on Human Rights*, Oxford University Press, Oxford 2012, p. 427; R. Spano, 'Universality or Diversity of Human Rights? Strasbourg in the Age of Subsidiarity' (2014) 14 *Human Rights Law Review*, 494.

distinctions between international criminal trials and human rights proceedings: the former must ensure fairness to all parties appearing or represented (victims, international community and prosecution), while the latter only deals with protecting the interests of an individual against the abuses by the State.[85] HRL is characterised by a high level of abstraction. This feature gives the ECtHR the flexibility to adjust universally recognised principles to the facts of the case, while allowing States a certain margin of appreciation in complying with their obligations flowing from the European Convention on Human Rights.[86] The rulings of the ECtHR aspire to an *erga omnes* status but often fail to reach this recognition,[87] which could be partially explained by the difficulty of applying the reasoning designed for one unique situation to another distinct set of facts.

This distinction between the two disciplines implies that the Judges sitting in international criminal trials balance conflicting interests of different stakeholders in the process, as opposed to human rights Judges focusing primarily on the dichotomy of State versus individual. The overall fairness of an international criminal trial thus becomes a matter of a *compromise* reached by virtue of maximising human rights protection for all those involved in the light of the circumstances of the case. As a rule, ICL judgments do not purport to be universally binding, as their primary focus is still on the participants in a given criminal trial.[88]

Assessment of the specific circumstances includes giving weight to policy concerns and pragmatic limitations inherent to ICL. Judicial discretion allows for this delicate balancing exercise to take place. This tool is particularly relevant in the absence of an effective methodology for transplanting HRL into the ICL plane.[89] High abstraction of human rights norms enables criminal law judges to exercise their discretion, with maximum sensitivity being given to the context. Article 21(3) of the Rome Statute provides an additional motive to engage creatively with HRL as it invites the Court to interpret its sources in a manner consistent with internationally recognised human rights.

It is not incidental that both the Statutes of the ad hoc tribunals and the Rome Statute have specific provisions directed at Judges and requiring them to ensure that a trial is fair and expeditious, and is conducted with full respect for the

---

85 S. Trechsel, 'Rights in Criminal Proceedings under the ECHR and the ICTY Statute – a Precarious Comparison' in B. Swaart *et al.* (eds), *The Legacy of the International Criminal Tribunal for the Former Yugoslavia*, Oxford University Press, Oxford 2011, p. 154. See also R. Cryer, above n. 1.

86 J. Genuess, above n. 1, 415.

87 Ibid.

88 In matters concerning humanity as a whole, however, international criminal proceedings may result in highly authoritative pronouncements reflecting customary international law.

89 J. Genuess, above n. 1.

rights of the accused and due regard for the protection of victims and witnesses.[90] These provisions are *lex generalis* and they create a general framework for the exercise of judicial discretion. Specific concerns are then viewed through the prism of this rule. This is not to suggest that judicial discretion is not implicit in other provisions of the Rome Statute. For example, Article 69(4) reads as follows:

> The Court may rule on the relevance or admissibility of any evidence, taking into account, inter alia, the probative value of the evidence and any prejudice that such evidence may cause to a fair trial or to a fair evaluation of the testimony of a witness, in accordance with the Rules of Procedure and Evidence.

The Judges are thus equipped with discretion to reject implicated evidentiary materials. They measure the probative value of the evidence against the possible prejudice that the admission of the evidence may cause to a fair trial.[91] This provision was the basis for the Chamber's refusal to admit into evidence recordings of an interview between the witness and investigators of the Office of the Prosecutor in the *Ruto* case. In this instance, the Judges were not convinced that a witness's waiver of the right to the presence of counsel was truly voluntary in the light of investigators' failure to record their initial contact with the witness and then rushing him through the waiver during the interview.[92] Judicial discretion is therefore a powerful tool for defining the scope of rights afforded to different parties.

The specificity of indictments at the ICTY is a good example of the measure of control resting with the Judges. Jordash and Coughlan note that, for a long time, the predominant approach of the ad hoc tribunals was to require a lesser degree of particularity of the indictments compared with that in domestic proceedings. The Judges left unchallenged the prosecution's justification that the massive scale of crimes at stake makes it impracticable to require a higher degree of specificity.[93] For a long time, the efficiency of prosecutorial strategies underlying this statement did not provoke judicial scrutiny. This complacency

---

90 Art. 20(1) of the ICTY/R Statutes; Art. 19(1) of the ICTR Statute; Art. 64(2) of the Rome Statute.

91 *Prosecutor v. William Samoei Ruto and Mr Joshua Arap Sang*, Reasons for the Decision on Admission of Certain Evidence Connected to Witness [REDACTED], rendered on [REDACTED], ICC-01/09-01/11, T. Ch (V)(a), 16 December 2014, para. 43.

92 Ibid., para. 40.

93 W. Jordash and J. Coughlan, 'The Right to be Informed of the Nature and Cause of the Charges: A Potentially Formidable Jurisprudential Legacy' in S. Darcy and J. Powderly (eds), *Judicial Creativity at the International Criminal Tribunals*, Oxford University Press, Oxford 2010, p. 289, citing *Prosecutor v. Kvocka*, Trial Chamber Decision on Defence Preliminary Motion on Form of Indictment, IT-97-25-PT (11 February 2000), para. 37.

resulted in a gap between the right of the accused to be informed about the charges against him and a practical implementation of this right.[94]

The *Al Senussi* case is a vivid example of the immense role that judicial discretion plays at the ICC. The legislative framework of the Rome Statute, with its extensive references to due process guarantees, arguably allowed for deciding the case both ways. It rested with the Judges to rule on the degree of compliance with HRL norms required from Libya. In doing so, they had to take into account not only the rights of the suspect, but also a number of other factors including the importance of vesting trust in the local judiciary by upholding the principle of complementarity, the security situation in Libya and possible difficulties in apprehending the suspect. At this juncture, the Judges could either prioritise due process guarantees for the suspect and align themselves with the position of the ECtHR or give more weight to other considerations. The ECtHR views the denial of access to lawyers at the early stages of proceedings, including police interrogation, as a violation of the right to fair trial and, in particular, the right to legal representation that is guaranteed by the ECHR.[95]

The exercise of discretion in *Al Senussi* resulted in a compromise. The Judges recognised the violation of Mr Al Senussi's right to legal representation, but then conceded that this factor alone did not render the case admissible to the ICC. At the same time, due process concerns were not entirely neglected or rendered irrelevant in the admissibility proceedings. The Appeals Chamber upheld the qualitative distinction between any violation of the due process rights and violation so severe that it blocks any genuine form of justice at the domestic level.

5. CONCLUSION

This chapter sought to identify the place of human rights guarantees within the framework of the Rome Statute of the ICC, with reference to its complementarity regime. HRL plays a crucial role in the development of the substantive and procedural body of ICL. Close cooperation of these two disciplines does not rule out the possibility of conflicts, however. They arise primarily out of the divergent purposes and architecture of the two fields of law: ICL concerns itself with an individual accused and borrows heavily from domestic criminal law, while HRL is premised on the idea of State responsibility *vis-à-vis* an individual and, despite its aspirational focus and characteristic teleological methods of interpretation, incorporates more features of classical international law.

---

94 Art. 21(4)(a) of the ICTY Statute; W. Jordash and J. Coughlan, above n. 93, 290.

95 *John Murray v. United Kingdom*, App. no. 18731/91, 8 February 1996, para. 66; *Salduz v. Turkey*, App. no. 36391/02, 27 November 2008, para. 52.

The *Al Senussi* case demonstrated a collision between human rights concerns and other considerations implicit in the framework of the ICC. The Rome Statute appears to be of limited value in resolving these types of conflict because it is written in the spirit of HRL and thus does not adopt a position on the hierarchy of values to be endorsed in specific cases. As a result, many of its provisions contain references to due process guarantees, some of which are unrealistic to achieve because of the constraints imposed by international trials. *Al Senussi* does not offer an instant solution to this problem, but rather provides hints as to *how* the practice of the ICC intends to approach the matter, namely through the exercise of judicial discretion. While it is true that Article 17 of the Rome Statute is very restrictive when it comes to assessing a country's level of compliance with due process at the stage of admissibility proceedings, it is clear that the Judges did not rule out the possibility of seizing over the matter should the severity of violations reach a certain threshold. This reasoning points to the importance of the circumstances of the case in each instance and highlights the power vested in international Judges by virtue of their ability to exercise discretion.

PART II

CONVERGENCES AND DIVERGENCES BETWEEN INTERNATIONAL HUMAN RIGHTS LAW AND TRANSNATIONAL CRIMINAL LAW

STRENGTHENING ACTION TO END FORCED LABOUR: THE ILO FORCED LABOUR PROTOCOL AND STATES' POSITIVE HUMAN RIGHTS OBLIGATIONS

Amy WEATHERBURN*

1. INTRODUCTION

The adoption of the International Labour Organization Protocol of 2014 to the Forced Labour Convention, 1930 (No. P029) (the ILO Protocol) and the accompanying Forced Labour (Supplementary Measures) Recommendation

* This chapter takes into account the status of the law as of 1 December 2016.

2014 (No. 203) (the Recommendation)[1] reinforces the need for a strengthened legal framework to address the existence, globally, of significant implementation gaps in combating forced labour. The 2012 ILO Global Estimate of Forced Labour states that 20.9 million people are victims of forced labour. Three-quarters of labour exploitation occurs in productive activities such as agriculture, domestic work, construction, fisheries and manufacturing, and the remainder involves commercial sexual exploitation.[2]

Section 2 of this chapter will outline the principal elements of the ILO forced labour framework aimed at tackling forced labour, as well as beginning to establish the convergence with international human rights law (IHRL) from a historical perspective. Section 3 of the chapter will determine the convergence of forced labour and the positive human rights obligations on States.[3] An examination of the HRL jurisprudence will illustrate growing acceptance that States have a duty to protect against non-State human rights abuses within their territory and/or jurisdiction. An estimated 90 per cent of forced labour today occurs in the 'private economy', therefore perpetrators are non-State actors not accountable for violations of human rights.[4] Taking this figure into account, this chapter will suggest that the suppression of forced labour therefore necessitates preventive action by States who are bound by the ILO forced labour conventions[5] and positive human rights obligations.

In section 4 of this chapter, the ILO Protocol and its accompanying Recommendation will be introduced by outlining the rationale that led up to the drafting process of the ILO Protocol and some of its main features, while taking into account the contemporary context in which forced labour occurs. Finally, section 5 of this chapter will outline the measures that can be implemented to strengthen action to end forced labour. Particular focus will be placed upon the application of positive human rights obligations, as developed by human rights jurisprudence in the context of human trafficking, when operationalising the measures outlined by the ILO Protocol, including the provision of strong victim protection measures, appropriate and accessible justice and compensation mechanisms. Furthermore, this chapter will examine the need for a robust

---

1 International Labour Organization (ILO), ILO Protocol of 2014 to the Forced Labour Convention 1930 (P029); ILO Forced Labour (Supplementary Measures) Recommendation 2014 (No. 203).

2 ILO Global Estimate of Forced Labour 2012: Results and Methodology, 1 June 2012.

3 *Rantsev v. Cyprus and Russia*, no. 25965/04, ECHR 2010; Guiding Principles on Business and Human Rights: Implementing the United Nations 'Protect, Respect and Remedy' Framework (A/HRC/17/31); OHCHR, Recommended Principles and Guidelines on Human Rights and Human Trafficking (2002).

4 ILO Global Estimate of Forced Labour 2012: Results and Methodology, 1 June 2012, 13; ILO Profits and Poverty: The Economics of Forced Labour, 20 May 2014, 7.

5 ILO Forced Labour Convention 1930 (No. 29); ILO Abolition of Forced Labour Convention 1957 (No. 105).

enforcement response, such as a strengthened role for labour inspectorates in the identification of victims of forced labour. Finally, building upon established networks in the context of combating human trafficking, the chapter will outline the importance of broadening international and regional policy and cooperation frameworks.

Overall, this chapter will consider the role of IHRL in strengthening and facilitating actions to end forced labour in order to achieve the newly adopted ILO Protocol's aim of a modern approach to addressing forced labour. The normative framework that human rights offers is crucial as it 'offers legal and political space for the disenfranchised to begin to claim these needs as rights, and thereby bring the scope of state responsibility into sharper focus'.[6] For instance, the strength of the human rights framework can be seen in the prohibition of slavery, servitude and forced or compulsory labour in Article 8 of the International Covenant on Civil and Political Rights (ICCPR),[7] which is stronger than previous instruments as it can be enforced through its reporting mechanism and individual petition system.[8]

In particular, the principal object of enquiry will be to determine the extent to which adherence to positive human rights obligations may ensure that a comprehensive and effective response is adopted, addressing prevention, prosecution and victim protection within the broader framework of promoting decent work.

2. THE ILO FORCED LABOUR FRAMEWORK AND ITS HISTORICAL INTERACTION WITH INTERNATIONAL HUMAN RIGHTS LAW

Forced labour was defined in the ILO Forced Labour Convention 1930 (No. 29) as: 'all work or service which is exacted from any person under the menace of any penalty and for which the said person has not offered himself voluntarily'.[9] It must be noted that although the prohibition on forced or compulsory labour is recognised as a fundamental right, it is not a *jus cogens* norm, as it is possible for States to derogate from it – unlike the provisions of slavery and servitude

6 J. Chuang, 'Beyond a Snapshot: Preventing Human Trafficking in the Global Economy' (2006) 13(1) *Indiana Journal of Global Legal Studies* 137, 157.

7 International Covenant on Civil and Political Rights (1966).

8 A. Edwards, 'Trafficking in Human Beings: At the Intersection of Criminal Justice, Human Rights, Asylum/Migration and Labor' (2007–08) *Denver Journal of International Law and Policy* 36, 26.

9 ILO Forced Labour Convention 1930 (No. 29).

that are non-derogable.[10] The circumstances in which the prohibition of forced or compulsory labour may be derogated from include: (i) any work or service required of a person who is under detention in consequence of a lawful order of a court, or of a person during conditional release from such detention; (ii) any service of a military character; (iii) any service exacted in cases of emergency or calamity threatening the life or wellbeing of the community; and (iv) any work or service that forms part of normal civil obligations.[11] Subsequent IHRL treaties have also affirmed the aforementioned 'negative' definitions that permit the ongoing use of forced or compulsory labour in certain situations, both internationally and regionally.[12]

Further, the 1930 Convention merely required States to undertake the suppression of the use of forced or compulsory labour in all its forms within the shortest possible period.[13] This gap was addressed by the supplementary ILO Abolition of Forced Labour Convention 1957 (No. 105), which states that it is mandatory for all ILO Member States to take effective measures to secure the immediate and complete abolition of forced or compulsory labour,[14] even where such forced labour might fall under the exceptions enumerated in the 1930 Convention.[15] The 1957 Convention elaborates upon the circumstances where forced or compulsory labour must be abolished: (a) as a means of political coercion; (b) as a method economic development; (c) as a means of labour discipline; (d) as a punishment for strikes; (e) as a means of discrimination.[16]

The ILO has determined a number of forced labour indicators whereby the presence of a single indicator in a given situation may, in some cases, imply

10 R. Piotrowicz, 'States' Obligations under Human Rights Law towards Victims of Trafficking in Human Beings: Positive Developments in Positive Obligations' (2008) 24(2) *International Journal of Refugee Law* 181, 183; A. Gallagher, 'Human Rights and Human Trafficking: Quagmire or Firm Ground? A Response to James Hathaway' (2009) 49 *Virginia Journal of International Law* 789, 807.

11 ILO Forced Labour Convention 1930 (No. 29), Art. 2(2).

12 International Covenant on Civil and Political Rights 1966, Art. 8(3)(c); European Convention for the Protection of Human Rights and Fundamental Freedoms 1950, Art. 4(3); International Convention on the Protection of the Rights of All Migrant Workers and Members of Their Families 1990, Art. 11(4); American Convention on Human Rights 1978, Art. 6(3); European Charter of Fundamental Rights 2000, Art. 5(2). NB the latter does not explicitly state the exceptions to the prohibition of forced labour, however, the Charter commentary states that the prohibition on forced or compulsory labour in Art. 5(2) is thus guaranteed in the same way as in ECHR, Art. 4(2) and must be understood in light of the 'negative' definitions contained in ECHR, Art. 4(3). EU Network of Independent Experts on Fundamental Rights, *Commentary on the Charter of Fundamental Rights of the European Union*, 2006, 57.

13 ILO Forced Labour Convention 1930 (No. 29), Art. 1(1).

14 ILO Abolition of Forced Labour Convention 1957 (No. 105), Art. 2.

15 J. Allain, *Slavery in International Law. Of Human Exploitation and Trafficking*, Martinus Nijhoff Publishers, Leiden 2013, 239.

16 ILO Abolition of Forced Labour Convention 1957 (No. 105), Art. 1(a)–(e).

the existence of forced labour worthy of investigation. The ILO forced labour indicators are: abuse of vulnerability, deception, restriction of movement, isolation, physical and sexual violence, intimidation and threats, retention of identity documents, withholding of wages, debt bondage, abusive working and living conditions and excessive overtime.[17]

Reinforcing the aforementioned legal framework is the ILO Decent Work Agenda, a policy initiative that finds its normative foundation in Article 7 of the International Covenant on Economic, Social and Cultural Rights (ICESCR) 1966. The ILO Decent Work Agenda affirms the right of everyone to the enjoyment of just and favourable conditions of work, including fair and equal remuneration, decent living, safe and healthy working conditions, equal opportunity for everyone and rest, leisure and reasonable limitation of working hours and periodic holidays with pay, as well as remuneration for public holidays.[18]

General Comment 18 of the Committee on Economic, Social and Cultural Rights defines 'decent work' as:

> work that respects the fundamental rights of the human person as well as the rights of workers in terms of conditions of work safety and remuneration. It also provides an income allowing workers to support themselves and their families as highlighted in Article 7 of the Covenant. These fundamental rights also include respect for the physical and mental integrity of the worker in the exercise of his/her employment.[19]

As outlined above, the ILO policy and legal framework regarding forced labour and, more broadly, the fulfilment of the Decent Work Agenda are composed of a number of instruments, policies and declarations that seek to apply the core labour standards within ILO Member States. As can be deduced from the above introduction, the ILO initiatives have embedded a fundamental rights perspective that builds upon the provisions of key international human rights instruments. This convergence between the ILO and international HRL is also evident in the ILO Declaration on fundamental principles and rights at work 1998.[20] Here, ILO Member States pledged their commitment to core human rights standards reinforcing the respect and promotion of four key categories of principles and rights: (i) freedom of association and the effective recognition of the right to collective bargaining; (ii) the elimination of forced or compulsory labour; (iii) the abolition of child labour; and (iv) the elimination

---

17 ILO Indicators of Forced labour (2009).

18 International Covenant on Economic, Social and Cultural Rights 1966, Art. 7.

19 General Comment No. 18, The Right to Work, Committee on Economic, Social and Cultural Rights, E/C.12/Gc/18, 6 February 2006. para. 7.

20 D. Maul, 'ILO and Globalisation of Human Rights' in S.L. Hoffmann (ed.), *Human Rights in the 20th Century*, Cambridge University Press, Cambridge 2011, 319.

of discrimination in respect of employment and occupation.[21] It is important to note, for the purposes of the present chapter, that all ILO Member States are bound to promote and to realise these core labour rights by reporting on progress in implementation, regardless of their level of economic advancement.[22]

Nowadays, there is no doubt that the core labour standards articulated by the ILO instruments and the decent work agenda are intrinsically linked to the international human rights legal regime. Despite recognition today of the ILO Forced Labour Convention 1930 as a human rights instrument, it is important to note that the Convention pre-dates the development of the international human rights framework. Indeed, Maul correctly asserts that while the universal human rights regime was taking shape, the ILO had already articulated an extensive collection of international agreements or international labour standards that covered a range of issues, including: minimum age regulation, wages, working hours, invalidity insurance and unemployment provision. Thus, in 1945, when the ILO became the first specialised UN agency, it was possible to implement a working mechanism but formalise the principles so as to be binding under international law.[23] To this end, for Maul, the integration and promotion of human rights principles allowed the ILO to extend its influence and to broaden its remit into other areas related to labour and social policy.[24] For Kolben, the shift towards a human rights discourse was also strategic, so that use could be made of the hegemonic status of human rights discourse and the relative effectiveness of some human rights advocacy strategies.[25]

Nevertheless, the legal validity and convergence of the ILO forced labour framework with the IHRL regime can be demonstrated by the continued use and reference to the ILO legal definition of forced labour. For instance, as previously mentioned, the legal definition of 'forced labour' has been adopted, in an almost identical manner,[26] in many international and regional human rights instruments.[27] Further, in addition to international and regional human rights law adopting the ILO forced labour framework, it is worth noting the emergence

21 ILO Declaration on Fundamental Principles and Rights at Work, Adopted by the International Labour Conference at its Eighty-sixth Session, Geneva, 18 June 1998 <http://www.ilo.org/declaration/thedeclaration/textdeclaration/lang--en/index.htm> accessed 02.11.2015.

22 K. Kolben, 'Labor Rights as Human Rights' (2010) 50 *Virginia Journal of International Law* 449, 484.

23 D. Maul, above n. 20, 303.

24 Ibid., 305.

25 K. Kolben, above n. 22, 451.

26 N. McGeehan, 'Misunderstood and Neglected: The Marginalization of Slavery in International Law' (2012) 16(3) *International Journal of Human Rights* 436, 437.

27 International Covenant on Civil and Political Rights 1966, Art. 8(3); European Convention for the Protection of Human Rights and Fundamental Freedoms 1950, Art. 4(2); International Convention on the Protection of the Rights of All Migrant Workers and Members of Their Families 1990, Art. 11(2); American Convention on Human Rights 1978; Art. 5(2), European Charter of Fundamental Rights 2000, Art. 6(2).

of scholarly discussion regarding the categorisation of labour rights as human rights.[28] Although not the focus of the present chapter, such a categorisation shows the interaction between these two types of law and, most significantly, as will be seen in the next section, the acceptance of positive obligations on States in relation to labour rights. The latter is of significance when considering the interaction of the human rights framework with a new Protocol and Recommendation that strongly advocate a human rights approach. Furthermore, effective implementation of new ILO instruments will, according to the author, heavily rely upon States' positive obligations to tackle a phenomenon whereby the primary role of international law is to secure State prohibitions but, instead, requires due diligence and preventative measures, to combat an issue firmly situated in the private economy.

3. FORCED LABOUR AND THE POSITIVE HUMAN RIGHTS OBLIGATIONS ON STATES

Taking into account the influence of the international human rights regime thus far on combatting forced labour, the following section will briefly introduce a significant development in IHRL that will have considerable impact upon the ILO's approach to eradicating forced labour as advocated in the ILO Protocol: the positive human rights obligations on States to combat forced labour.

3.1. THE ROLE OF NON-STATE ACTORS

The development of the positive obligations discourse has emerged following increased recognition of the role played by non-State actors in the violation of human rights. Traditionally, the rationale behind the development of the IHRL regime was that any harm resulting from an act or omission by a State could be considered a violation resulting in the State being held accountable for the failure to protect the human rights of all persons within its jurisdiction.[29]

This development in the context of IHRL is extremely pertinent to the current understanding of the scope and scale of forced labour globally. In 2005, the ILO

---

28 See K. Kolben, above n. 22, 451; J. Todres, 'Human Rights, Labour, and the Prevention of Human Trafficking: A Response to a Labour Paradigm for Human Trafficking' (2013) 60 *UCLA Law Review Discourse* 144; E. Albin, 'Human Rights and the Multiple Dimensions of Precarious Work' (2012) 34 *Comparative Labour Law and Policy Journal* 193; J. Pope, 'A Free Labor Approach to Human Trafficking' (2010) 158 *University of Pennsylvania Law Review* 1849.

29 R. Piotrowicz, 'The Legal Nature of Trafficking in Human Beings' (2010) 4 *Intercultural Human Rights Law Review* 175, 191–92.

Special Action Programme to Combat Forced Labour refined the forced labour definition, specifying three main categories of forced labour, namely (a) forced labour imposed by the State; (b) forced labour imposed by private agents for commercial sexual exploitation; and (c) forced labour imposed by private agents for economic exploitation.[30] Thus, by doing so, the key role of non-State actors in the promulgation of forced labour was identified and brought to the fore of all ILO measures aimed at combating forced labour.

3.2. THE DUTY TO PROTECT

Taking into account the converging recognition in both IHRL and the ILO regime of the role of non-State actors, it is necessary to determine the extent to which a State is accountable for the actions of private individuals in the context of forced labour.[31] Crucially, in this regard, an obligation on States that requires the implementation of a duty of protection has emerged whereby a State implements an appropriate and enforceable legal framework aimed at preventing prohibited practices, such as forced labour.[32] In essence, the duty on the State constitutes a 'responsibility to regulate, and prevent, the actions of others, including criminals, failure in which will lead the State to be in breach of its human rights obligations'.[33] Therefore, in the context of the ILO Protocol, States have a duty to promote and facilitate the suppression of forced labour.

The use of positive obligations as a means of fulfilling the State's duty to protect was reaffirmed in General Comment No. 31 of the United Nations Human Rights Committee. The General Comment outlines the Nature of the General Legal Obligation on States Parties to the International Covenant on Civil and Political Rights (1966) and, more pertinently for the present chapter, to Article 8 of the ICCPR on the prohibition of slavery, servitude and forced labour:

> The ... obligations are binding on States [Parties] and do not, as such, have direct horizontal effect as a matter of international law ... However the positive obligations on States Parties to ensure Covenant rights will only be fully discharged if individuals are protected by the State, not just against violations of Covenant rights by its agents,

30 ILO, 'A Global Alliance Against Forced Labour: Global Report under the Follow-up to the ILO Declaration on Fundamental Principles and Rights at Work', International Labour Office, 2005, 10.

31 M. Eriksson, 'The Prevention of Human Trafficking – Regulating Domestic Criminal Legislation through the European Convention on Human Rights' (2013) 82 *Nordic Journal of international Law* 339, 343.

32 R. Piotrowicz, above n. 29, 191–92.

33 R. Piotrowicz, above n. 10, 186.

> but also against acts committed by private persons or entities that would impair the enjoyment of Covenant rights in so far as they are amenable to application between private persons or entities.[34]

The due diligence principle is also of relevance when determining the exact scope of a State's duty to protect. It is important to note the obligation of States, according to the due diligence principle, to protect the rights of workers from other countries to decent working conditions from being violated by employers. However, this obligation is not absolute, as it is not an obligation of result but of means and of best endeavour.[35] The due diligence principle therefore focuses strongly on the preventative measures that can be developed to interrupt the prohibited practice – in this case, forced labour. Such measures could incorporate 'a broad range of activities from training of personnel working in the justice system, information campaigns to the public, to the adoption of a specific legislative framework'.[36]

In the context of human trafficking, the 'prohibition on slavery and servitude [and forced labour] has been called a "paradigmatic example" of a State's obligation to protect against non-State interference with human rights. The relevance of international human rights law to situations in which the State is not the immediate agent of harm is a key issue when it comes to identifying precise legal obligations and responsibilities of States'.[37] For States to determine the exact scope of their duty to protect from the actions of non-State actors there are a number of key documents that provide guidance on the nature of the States' positive obligations. For instance, the duty on States to address the role of non-State actors in human trafficking – a process that can lead to labour exploitation or forced labour – was reinforced by the Office of the High Commissioner for Human Rights, Recommended Principles and Guidelines on Human Rights and Human Trafficking (2002). Principle 12 affirms the need for States to 'effectively investigate, prosecute and adjudicate trafficking, including its component acts and related conduct, whether committed by governmental or by non-State actors'.[38] Furthermore, the international community has increasingly accepted

---

34 Human Rights Committee, General Comment 31, Nature of the General Legal Obligation on States Parties to the Covenant, para. 8, UN Doc. CCPR/C/21/Rev.1/Add.13 (2004).

35 European Union Agency for Fundamental Rights, Severe labour exploitation: workers moving within or into the European Union States' obligations and victims' rights, June 2015, 25 <http://fra.europa.eu/sites/default/files/fra-2015-severe-labour-exploitation_en.pdf> accessed 01.02.2016.

36 R. Piotrowicz, above n. 10, 345.

37 A. Gallagher, 'Using International Human Rights Law to Better Protect Victims of Human Trafficking: the Prohibitions on Slavery, Servitude, Forced Labour and Debt Bondage' in L.N. Sadat and M.P. Scarf (eds), *The Theory and Practice of International Criminal Law: Essays in Honour of M. Cherif Bassiouni*, Martinus Nijhoff, Leiden 2008, 397–430.

38 OHCHR, Recommended Principles and Guidelines on Human Rights and Human Trafficking (2002).

that multinational corporations have a role and responsibility in respecting human rights and ensuring that they face the legal consequences of human rights violations.[39] This has been affirmed by the Guiding Principles on Business and Human Rights: Implementing the United Nations 'Protect, Respect and Remedy' Framework (2011).[40] Consequently, States are operationalising action plans and measures to ensure that corporations address forced labour in their supply chain.[41]

3.3. THE PROHIBITION OF FORCED LABOUR AND POSITIVE OBLIGATIONS ON STATES

Building upon the duty to protect that is articulated in international law, this chapter will now consider the role of the European Court of Human Rights' (the Court's) jurisprudence in the development of this doctrine, including the determination of the exact extent and scope of the duty on States to suppress the use of forced labour under the scope of Article 4 of the European Convention on Human Rights (ECHR), which prohibits slavery, servitude and forced and compulsory labour.[42] It must be noted that the positive obligations discussed here are directly applicable to Council of Europe Member States but, nevertheless, in the light of limited international jurisprudence in relation to the prohibition of forced labour, may also be persuasive in ILO Member States that are not bound by the ECHR. Estimates of the prevalence of forced labour in Europe suggest that millions of persons are being subjected to indecent working conditions,[43]

---

39 R. Steinhardt, 'Corporate Responsibility and the International Law of Human Rights: The New Lex Mercatoria' in P. Alston (ed.), *Non-State Actors and Human Rights*, Oxford University Press, Oxford 2005, 177–227.

40 United Nations, Guiding Principles on Business and Human Rights: Implementing the United Nations 'Protect, Respect and Remedy' Framework (2011/A/HRC/17/31).

41 See case study of UK and Brazil in A. Feasley, 'Deploying Disclosure Laws to Eliminate Forced Labour: Supply Chain Transparency Efforts of Brazil and the United States of America' (2015) 5 *Anti-Trafficking Review* 30.

42 A. Mowbray, *The Development of Positive Obligations under the European Convention on Human Rights by the European Court of Human Rights*, Hart Publishing, Oxford 2004; A. Mowbray, *Cases and Materials on the European Convention on Human Rights*, Oxford University Press, Oxford 2007, 229–41. D. Harris, M. O'Boyle, E. Bates and C. Buckley, *Law of the European Convention on Human Rights*, 3rd ed, Oxford University Press, Oxford 2014, 284–86; B. Andrees and P. Belser (eds), *Forced Labor: Coercion and Exploitation in the Private Economy*, Leinne Reinner Publisher, New York 2009, 133.

43 ILO Global Estimate of Forced Labour 2012: Results and Methodology, 1 June 2012, 15; ILO Profits and Poverty: The Economics of Forced Labour, 20 May 2014, 7. Developed Economies and European Union account for 1.5 million (7%), while countries of Central, South-Eastern and Eastern Europe (CSEE) and the Commonwealth of Independent States (CIS) have 1.6 million (7%).

including many non-EU nationals.[44] In particular, it is important to note the transnational nature of forced labour and the importance of cross-border action, most significantly through cooperation between States (both Council of Europe Member States and non-Member States) in preventing, investigating and prosecuting labour exploitation and providing protection to victims.

Before moving forward, two points must be noted: first, very few cases have been brought before the Court under Article 4;[45] and, secondly, where such cases have been considered by the Court, they have been particularly in relation to cases of trafficking in human beings, rather than the practices explicitly prescribed in Article 4, i.e. slavery, servitude and forced and compulsory labour.[46] This latter point has critiqued by Stoyanova, who contests that the lack of engagement by the Court on the issue of ensuring 'that States must adopt the specific labels of slavery, servitude and forced labour in their domestic law' fails to acknowledge the necessity of a clear national perspective when it comes to these prohibited practices.[47] For Stoyanova, the jurisprudential emphasis on human trafficking impacts upon not only the certainty of criminal law, but also developments regarding the interpretation of these violations in IHRL. This discussion is crucial to the present chapter, particularly in relation to the role that the ILO Protocol plays in addressing implementation gaps in the suppression of forced labour. By engaging with the ILO Protocol, to what extent will States re-engage with the issue of forced labour, separate from the human trafficking paradigm, where the main emphasis would be on a labour market approach rather than

---

44 EUROSTAT, Trafficking in Human Beings, 2015 edition, pp. 11, 35 and 38. The 2nd edition of the EUROSTAT Trafficking in Human Beings reported that the top five non-EU countries of citizenship of registered victims were: Nigeria, Brazil, China, Vietnam and Russia [NB these figures include victims of trafficking for all forms of exploitation, including sexual exploitation and removal of organs].

45 *Siliadin v. France*, no. 73316/01, ECHR 2005; *Rantsev v. Cyprus and Russia*, no. 25965/04, ECHR 2010; *CN v. UK*, no. 4239/08, ECHR 2012; *CN and V v. France*, no. 67724/09, ECHR 2012; *LE v. Greece*, no.71545/12, ECHR 2016; *J. and Others v. Austria*, no. 58216/12, ECHR 2017; *Chowdury and others v. Greece*, no. 21884/15, ECHR 2017.

46 For further examination of the Court's handling of Art. 4, see J. Allain, 'Rantsev v Cyprus and Russia: The European Court of Human Rights and Trafficking as Slavery' (2010) 10(3) *Human Rights Law Review* 546; H. Cullen, 'Siliadin v France: Positive Obligations under Article 4 of the European Convention on Human Rights' (2006) 6 (30) *Human Rights Law Review* 585; D. Keane, 'Abolitionist in Heart but Not in Action: Slavery, Servitude and the Status of Article 4 ECHR in Irish Law' (2013) 50 *Irish Jurist* 166; A. Nicholson, 'Reflections on Siliadin v France: Slavery and Legal Definition,' (2010) 14(5) *International Journal of Human Rights*, 705; V. Stoyanova, 'Article 4 of the ECHR and the Obligation of Criminalizing Slavery, Servitude, Forced Labour and Human Trafficking' (2014) 3(2) *Cambridge Journal of International and Comparative Law* 407; V. Stoyanova, 'Dancing on the Borders of Article 4: Human Trafficking and the European Court of Human Rights in the Rantsev Case,' (2012) 30(2) *Netherlands Quarterly of Human Rights* 164.

47 V. Stoyanova, 'Article 4 of the ECHR and the Obligation of Criminalizing Slavery, Servitude, Forced Labour and Human Trafficking' (2014) 3(2) *Cambridge Journal of International and Comparative Law* 407, 426.

the criminal justice approach adopted by the Palermo Protocol and other major trafficking instruments? Only time will tell the real impact of the ILO Protocol, but it is nevertheless something to bear in mind.

Acknowledging the shortcomings of the Article 4 jurisprudence, in general, this chapter will nevertheless build upon the positive obligations on States that have been articulated by the Court in the context of human trafficking. Such a discussion will be positioned with a view to the implementation of the ILO Protocol measures and the extent to which positive human rights obligations may be employed in an interpretative manner to the provisions of the ILO Protocol.

In *Siliadin v. France*,[48] the Court identified the positive dimension for the practical and effective protection of the human rights and fundamental freedoms of the individual that are prescribed by Article 4. More specifically, the Court held that a State is required to regulate and prevent the actions of non-State actors that may violate Article 4, through the penalisation and effective prosecution of any practice that falls within the scope of the prohibited practices.[49] Following on from the initial recognition of positive obligations in *Siliadin*, the Court articulated the following positive obligations in *Rantsev v. Cyprus and Russia*,[50] namely: (i) a positive obligation to establish an appropriate legislative and administrative framework;[51] (ii) a procedural

48 The applicant was a Togolese national who, at the age of 15, came to Paris in January 1994. Upon arrival, Mrs D, her benefactor, told her that she would have her immigration status regularised and education arranged; in exchange, she would conduct domestic tasks until her airfare had been repaid. At this time, her passport was confiscated. In October 1994, the applicant was temporarily moved to Mr and Mrs B, friends of Mrs D, to assist with domestic tasks and provide childcare. The temporary nature of the role became more permanent once Mrs B had another child. Following this, the applicant was made to work from 7.30am to 10.30pm with no days off. She slept on a mattress on the floor of the children's bedroom and wore old clothes. In 1998, the case was brought to the attention of the authorities after the applicant informed a neighbour of her situation, who contacted the Committee Against Modern Slavery.

49 *Siliadin v. France*, above n. 45, para. 112.

50 The applicant's daughter, Ms Rantseva, arrived in March 2001 on an artiste visa, which granted her a temporary work permit until June 2001 to work as an artiste in the cabaret club owned by XA and managed by MA. After working for three days, on 19 March 2001, MA employees informed him that the applicant had left her accommodation and wished to return to Russia. MA informed the immigration office that she had abandoned her place of work and residence and requested that she be expelled from Cyprus, so that he could bring in a replacement. The authorities, however, did not include her name in the list of persons wanted by the police. On 28 March 2001, MA was informed that Ms Rantseva had been seen in another cabaret club. As a result, MA contacted the police and requested that she be arrested. MA went to the cabaret club and presented Ms Rantseva to the local police, where the duty officers could not find any record of the complaint made by MA on 19 March, therefore MA was requested to collect Ms Rantseva from the police station, whereupon she was taken to an apartment owned by MA. The following morning, Ms Rantseva was found dead in the street. She had attempted to leave the room she was in via the balcony: police found a bedspread tied around the balcony's railing.

51 *Rantsev v. Cyprus and Russia*, above n. 45, para. 283.

obligation to investigate trafficking where a real and immediate risk is known to the authorities;[52] and (iii) a positive obligation to take protective measures.[53] In 2012, the Court, in *CN and V v. France*,[54] reiterated that 'States are required to put in place a legislative and administrative framework that prohibits and punishes forced or compulsory labour, servitude and slavery',[55] an obligation that was once again emphasised in *CN v. United Kingdom*,[56] noting the UK's failure to enact domestic law provisions specifically criminalising the

---

52 Ibid., para. 288.

53 Ibid., para. 287.

54 The applicants (CN and V) were two sisters. They were French nationals, born in Burundi. Following the death of their parents as a result of the civil war in Burundi, the applicants arrived in France in 1994 and 1995 respectively, under the guardianship and custody of their aunt and uncle (Mr and Mrs M). The applicants were accommodated in the basement and required to do domestic tasks and look after Mr and Mrs M's children, including their disabled son. The applicants also alleged that they had been accommodated in conditions contrary to human dignity, were not allowed to eat with the family and were subjected to verbal and physical abuse. The situation of the applicants had been brought to the attention of the authorities in 1995, but an investigation by a child protection team led to no further action being taken. In January 1999, the situation of the applicants was once again brought to the attention of the authorities by an organisation called Enfance et Partage, in this instance, the Public Prosecutor's Office. The applicants also ran away and were accommodated by the organisation, which had raised the alarm with authorities.

55 *CN and V v. France*, above n. 45, para. 105.

56 The applicant, CN, arrived in the UK in 2002 from Uganda, to escape sexual violence, and had been facilitated by her relative, S, who lived in London and obtained a false passport and visa for her. Upon her arrival, these documents were confiscated. From 2003, CN worked as a live-in carer for an elderly Iraqi couple (Mr and Mrs K), where she was to be available 24 hours a day and had one afternoon per month off. CN's wages were sent to M, who then passed a percentage on to S, and CN herself would only ever receive a small amount. CN was threatened by S with denunciation to the authorities if she were to disclose her situation. CN went to a local bank in August 2006 in order to have her situation brought to the attention of the police. Following health problems (including a diagnosis of HIV and psychosis), CN applied for asylum, which was rejected on the grounds that the applicant could access protection in Uganda to prevent further sexually motivated attacks and that she could have tried to escape from S earlier. An appeal was dismissed on the basis that the court found CN's credibility and account of her situation implausible. In April 2007, her solicitor requested that the police investigate her case. However the outcome, communicated in September 2007, was that there was no evidence of trafficking for domestic servitude and none to substantiate that the applicant had been trafficked into the UK. In December 2008, the applicant was assessed by the Poppy Project, which provided housing and support to trafficked persons, which concluded that her situation raised five of the ILO forced labour indicators, including her movement restricted to her workplace, the withholding of wages and debt-bondage, retention and confiscation of identity document and threats of denunciation to authorities. Despite the assessment of the Poppy Project, the police on two further occasions in February 2009 and August 2009, reiterated that there was no evidence that would support 'exploitation of any kind', as defined in s. 4 of the Asylum and Immigration Act 2004 on trafficking, as her case did not appear to constitute an offence of trafficking for the purpose of exploitation, and that they were not aware of any specific offence of forced labour or servitude in English criminal law that would apply to the facts of the case.

conduct prohibited by Article 4.[57] Accordingly, in the latter case, the Court also reiterated the need for States to conduct an effective investigation into alleged abuses where complaints give rise to a reasonable suspicion of exploitation that amounts to the prohibited practices in Article 4.[58] The case of *LE v. Greece*[59] affirmed the positive obligations developed thus far when ruling that the Greek authorities failed to take effective operational measures – as evidenced by an unreasonable delay in granting victim status to the applicant[60] – and to conduct an effective police investigation and judicial proceedings,[61] including a lack of international cooperation with Nigerian authorities.[62] In contrast, the Court ruled in favour of the Austrian authorities in *J. and Others v. Austria*[63] as it was held that the investigations into alleged exploitation

---

57 *CN v. UK*, above n. 45, paras 77 and 81.

58 D. Harris, M. O'Boyle, E. Bates and C. Buckley, above n. 42, 285; *CN v. UK*, above n. 45, para. 72.

59 In 2004, the applicant, LE, a Nigerian national, entered Greece, accompanied by KA. KA had allegedly promised LE employment in bars and nightclubs. Upon arrival, LE owed 40,000 euros to KA, who confiscated her passport and forced her into prostitution for approximately two years. During this time, LE was arrested three times for breaching the laws on prostitution and on entry and residence of aliens in Greece. On each occasion, she was acquitted. In November 2006, while in detention pending deportation, LE filed a criminal complaint against KA and his partner DJ for forced prostitution and claimed that she was a victim of human trafficking. LE was supported by Nea Zoi (an NGO that specialised in providing material and psychological support for women forced into prostitution). The prosecutor at the Athens Criminal Court rejected the claim. In January 2007, the applicant requested a re-examination of her complaint, stating that important evidence had not been included, such as the testimony provided by Nea Zoi. The request for re-examination was successful and the prosecutor did bring criminal proceedings against KA and DJ for human trafficking, as well as officially recognising LE as a victim of human trafficking, thus leading to the suspension of her deportation order. KA could not be located and thus was not prosecuted. DJ was arrested and prosecuted and was eventually found not guilty as it was determined that she was not KA's accomplice, but rather another of his victims who had been sexually exploited.

60 *LE v. Greece*, above n. 45, paras 73–78.

61 Ibid., para. 82.

62 Ibid., para. 85.

63 This case concerned the Austrian authorities' investigation into an allegation of human trafficking. The applicants, two Filipino nationals, who had gone to work as maids or au pairs the United Arab Emirates, alleged that their employers had taken their passports away from them and exploited them. They claimed that this treatment had continued during a short stay in Vienna where their employers had taken them and where they had eventually managed to escape. Following a criminal complaint filed by the applicants against their employers in Austria, the authorities found that they did not have jurisdiction over the alleged offences committed abroad and decided to discontinue the investigation into the applicants' case concerning the events in Austria. The applicants maintained that they had been subjected to forced labour and human trafficking, and that the Austrian authorities had failed to carry out an effective and exhaustive investigation into their allegations. They argued in particular that what had happened to them in Austria could not be viewed in isolation, and that the Austrian authorities had a duty under international law to also investigate those events which had occurred abroad. The Court, finding that the Austrian authorities had complied with their

and the support offered to victims was sufficient to discharge them of any obligations in this regard.[64] Arguably, the last case of the Court is of most relevance to the prohibition of forced labour.[65] In *Chowdury and others v. Greece*[66] the Greek authorities were found to have not sufficiently discharged their positive obligations with regards to the strawberry cultivation in the region of Manolada. Crucially, however, it must be noted that the Court's assessment of positive obligations in the context of forced labour was grounded in the positive obligations imposed by the Council of Europe Convention on Action against Trafficking in Human Beings.[67] It remains to be seen what role the ILO Protocol's emphasis on positive obligations will have in future jurisprudence, but arguably the provisions discussed in section 5 of this chapter will offer an additional legal foundation to enforce the prohibition of forced labour.

duty to protect the applicants as (potential) victims of human trafficking, held that there had been no violation of Article 4 (prohibition of forced labour) and no violation of Article 3 (prohibition of inhuman or degrading treatment) of the Convention. *J. and Others v. Austria*, no. 58216/12, ECHR 2017.

64 The Court concluded that the authorities had taken all steps which could have reasonably been expected in the situation. The applicants, supported by a government-funded NGO, had been interviewed by specially trained police officers, had been granted residence and work permits in order to regularise their stay in Austria, and a personal data disclosure ban had been imposed for their protection (paras 110–111). Moreover, the investigation into the applicants' allegations about their stay in Vienna was sufficient and the authorities' resulting assessment, given the facts of the case and the evidence available, was reasonable (para. 112). Any further steps in the case – such as confronting the applicants' employers – would not have had any reasonable prospect of success, as no mutual legal assistance agreement existed between Austria and the United Arab Emirates, and as the applicants had only turned to the police approximately one year after the events in question, when their employers had long left the country (para. 117).

65 Although not of relevance to the present chapter, the Court provided further elaboration of the concept of forced labour by affirming that forced labour does not require a restriction of freedom of movement distinguishing it from servitude, whereby an individual would be in a situation of total exclusion (paras 99 and 125).

66 The facts relate to 42 Bangladeshi nationals with undocumented status who worked on a strawberry farm in Manolada, Greece. The employers of the farm promised the workers wages of 22 euros for seven hours' labour and 3 euros for each hour of overtime, less 3 euros for food. They worked in plastic greenhouses picking strawberries every day from 7 a.m. until 7 p.m. under the supervision of armed guards. They lived in makeshift tents of cardboard boxes and nylon without running water and toilets. They were warned by their employers that they would only receive their salaries if they continued to work for them. After striking several times in order to receive their wages a further group of Bangladeshi nationals were recruited to work in the fields. Fearing that the wages of those recruited for the 2012–2013 season would not be paid, 100–150 of the workers demanded their salaries from their employers. They were subsequently shot at by an armed guard, who seriously injured several of the workers. *Chowdury and others v. Greece* above n. 45.

67 *Chowdury and others v. Greece*, above n. 45, para. 104.

What has become clear from this jurisprudence is that 'full compliance with article 4 therefore requires positive acts by the State to discourage and penalise slavery, servitude and forced labour'.[68] However, positive obligations on States are not absolute in nature and restrictions are permissible as long as their necessity is demonstrated, the measures are proportionate to the pursuance of legitimate aims in order to ensure continuous and effective protection and the restrictions do not impair the essence of [the] right.[69] The non-absolute nature of positive obligations has been affirmed by the Court, which stated that an obligation must not impose 'an impossible or disproportionate burden on the authorities'.[70] Despite this limitation, the development of positive obligations demonstrates that these legal provisions require more than the mere prohibition of the practices outlined in the treaties:[71] they also positively oblige States' law to discourage and prevent enslavement, forced labour and servitude perpetrated by non-State actors, as well as to protect those at immediate risk.[72] The latter is of crucial importance when it comes to making the law practical and effective, rather than theoretical and illusory.

The relevance of these positive obligations on States to the prohibition, suppression and prevention of forced labour has been recognised by Piotrowicz, who states that the jurisprudence affirms 'a requirement for States to ensure fair treatment of workers'.[73] Bearing this mind, it is important to situate any discussion of the positive obligations on States arising from the severe labour exploitation of individuals by non-State actors in the current context of the global labour market. First of all, many of the economic sectors that are of relevance to the forced labour discourse have been subject to increased deregulation and privatisation that significantly impacts upon the protection of employment rights.[74] Secondly, the erosion of workers' rights, coupled with the flexibility of the labour market, has led to an increased precarity and subsequent vulnerability to labour exploitation.[75] Taking into account the contemporary context of the global labour market, the current chapter will consider how the ILO made provision for these characteristics when developing the parameters of the ILO Protocol measures aimed at supressing forced labour.

---

68 R. Piotrowicz, above n. 10, 187.

69 Human Rights Committee, General Comment 31, Nature of the General Legal Obligation on States Parties to the Covenant, para. 6, U.N. Doc. CCPR/C/21/Rev.1/Add.13 (2004).

70 *Rantsev v. Russia and Cyprus* above n. 45, para. 287.

71 H. Cullen, above n. 46, 588.

72 R. Piotrowicz, above n. 10, 183 and 187.

73 Ibid.,186.

74 C. Robinson, 'Claiming Space for Labour Rights within the United Kingdom Modern Slavery Crusade' (2015) 5 *Anti-Trafficking Review* 133.

75 H. Lewis *et al.*, *Precarious Lives: Forced Labour, Exploitation and Asylum*, Policy Press, Bristol 2015.

4. INTRODUCING THE ILO PROTOCOL TO THE FORCED LABOUR CONVENTION

Despite the broad reach of the ILO Forced Labour Conventions and the measures taken by ILO Member States, there has been recognition at an international level of 'an added value in the adoption of supplementary measures to address the significant implementation gaps remaining in order effectively to eradicate forced labour in all its forms'.[76] Recognition of the need for supplementary measures became the foundation of the drafting process of the newly adopted ILO Protocol. A particular focus on the prevention of forced labour, in light of changes in the global labour market, led to a number of measures being prioritised, such as the preventative role of labour inspectorates and the need for better coordination with law enforcement agencies. The drafting process also adopted a victim-centred approach, with measures aimed at securing victim protection, including: compensation, better identification and appropriate measures to protect all victims and suspected victims of forced labour, whether they have been trafficked or not.[77]

Another key factor acknowledged in the drafting process was the recognition of the shift in the contemporary context in which forced labour occurs, namely that an estimated 90 per cent of all forced labour victims are exploited by private individuals in the informal economy, outside of the rule of law.[78] Consequently, the drafting process of the ILO Protocol had to ensure that the definition stayed abreast of the contemporary social and historical context, in which forced labour is no longer a State-sponsored (colonial) activity but mainly a form of exploitation by private actors in a global labour market economy.[79]

At the 103rd Session of the International Labour Conference (2014), a new, legally binding ILO Protocol was adopted, accompanied by a Recommendation on the supplementary measures for the effective suppression of forced labour: ILO Protocol of 2014 to the Forced Labour Convention 1930 (No. P029) and

---

76 ILO (2013) Strengthening action to end forced labour – Report I, 16 July 2013, 4.

77 Conclusions adopted by the Tripartite Meeting of Experts on Forced Labour and Trafficking for Labour Exploitation (Geneva, 11–15 February 2013), paras 11–14; ILO (2014) Strengthening action to end forced labour – Report IV (2a), 27 March 2014, 1.

78 Report for discussion at the Tripartite Meeting of Experts concerning the possible adoption of an ILO instrument to supplement the Forced Labour Convention, 1930 (No. 29) – Geneva, 11–15 February 2013, 1; Conclusions adopted by the Tripartite Meeting of Experts on Forced Labour and Trafficking for Labour Exploitation (Geneva, 11–15 February 2013); ILO (2013a) Strengthening action to end forced labour – Report I, 16 July 2013, 1; J. Allain, above n. 15, 204.

79 N. Ollus, 'Regulating Forced Labour and Combating Human Trafficking: the Relevance of Historical Definitions in a Contemporary Perspective' (2015) 63(5) *Crime Law and Social Change* 221, 229; P. Kotiswaran, 'ILO Protocol at the Crossroads: Rethinking Anti-trafficking Law from an Indian Labour Law Perspective' (2015) 4 *Anti-trafficking Review* 33.

Forced Labour (Supplementary Measures) Recommendation 2014 (No. 203).[80] The adoption of the ILO Protocol seeks to achieve the effective and sustained suppression of forced or compulsory labour.[81] The promulgation of the new ILO instruments demonstrates recognition by the international community that forced labour still requires extensive legal and political attention in order to eradicate its practice. Since its adoption, the ILO Protocol came into force on 9 November 2016, and has been ratified by 22 States.[82]

The ILO Protocol introduces a number of significant measures that are aimed at the prevention of forced labour for *all* workers, including migrant workers, in *all* economic sectors. The principal focus of the ILO Protocol is on the enforcement of legislation and strengthening of labour inspection.[83] All measures taken by ILO Member States must be presented in a national policy and action plan that will be developed in consultation and in coordination with employers' and workers' organisations.[84]

The ILO Protocol also strengthens the protection of victims by reinforcing the need to implement effective measures for their identification, release, protection, recovery and rehabilitation, in addition to other forms of assistance and support.[85] ILO Member States must also secure access to remedies for all victims,[86] and ensure that competent authorities are entitled not to prosecute victims for unlawful activities that they have been compelled to commit.[87]

The ILO Protocol is supported by a detailed Recommendation, which develops the exact parameters of the measures to be taken by Member States to ensure that they fully comply with their legal obligations for the effective and sustained suppression of forced or compulsory labour. The Recommendation reiterates the preventative tone of the ILO Protocol, outlining in detail the measures that a State should take to ensure adequate protection and compensation for victims of forced labour, to enforce forced labour legislation and to strengthen international cooperation.[88]

As noted in section 3, the role of private actors in the persistence of forced or compulsory labour globally means that States must take a proactive approach that complies with the positive obligations imposed upon them by

80 ILO Forced Labour Protocol 2014 (PO29): The prevention measures in the ILO Protocol include the creation of national action plans (Art. 1), the strengthening of labour laws and labour inspections (Art. 2(c)), the requirement on governments to support due diligence by businesses to eradicate forced labour (Art. 2(e)) and to take measures to identify, release, and provide assistance to forced labour victims (Art. 3).

81 ILO Forced Labour (Supplementary Measures) Recommendation 2014 (No. 203).

82 Ratifications of P029 – Protocol of 2014 to the Forced Labour Convention, 1930.

83 ILO Forced Labour Protocol 2014 (PO29), Art. 2(c).

84 Ibid., Art. 1.

85 Ibid., Art. 3.

86 Ibid., Art. 4(1).

87 Ibid., Art. 4(2).

88 ILO Forced Labour (Supplementary Measures) Recommendation 2014 (No. 203).

the international human rights legal framework. This is most noteworthy in relation to the ILO's emphasis on prevention in the newly adopted ILO Protocol. For instance, careful consideration of the ILO Protocol and accompanying Recommendation clearly demonstrates the need for affirmative action on the part of States in order to fulfil their legal obligation to 'suppress the use of forced or compulsory labour in all its forms'[89] in order 'to prevent and eliminate its use, to provide to victims protection and access to appropriate and effective remedies, such as compensation, and to sanction the perpetrators of forced or compulsory labour'.[90]

5. STRENGTHENING ACTION TO END FORCED LABOUR

In order to achieve the newly adopted ILO Protocol's aim of a modern approach to addressing forced labour, this section of the chapter will consider the role of IHRL in strengthening and facilitating actions to end it. A key observation, relevant not just to this section but also to the chapter overall, is the ILO's adoption of a rights-based approach in its core business.[91] Such an approach is illustrative of convergence with human rights that provides a normative conceptual framework based on international human rights standards and that is operationally directed to promoting and protecting human rights.[92] By acknowledging the added value of such a human rights framework, this chapter will now consider the extent to which adherence to positive human rights obligations ensures that a comprehensive and effective response is adopted, addressing prevention, prosecution and victim protection within the broader framework of promoting decent work.

This chapter asserts that the effective operationalisation of the ILO Protocol and Recommendation will be facilitated by the enforcement of and adherence to States' positive human rights obligations (see above section 3). The development of positive obligations in this context, particularly at a European level, has focused significantly on the scope and situation of human trafficking for all forms of exploitation – an approach that has favoured the criminal justice approach for combating violations that fall within the remit of human trafficking, including slavery, forced labour and servitude.[93]

89 ILO Forced Labour Convention 1930 (No. 29), Art. 1(1).
90 ILO Forced Labour Protocol 2014 (PO29), Art. 1.
91 ILO, *International labour migration. A rights-based approach*, 2010.
92 Office of the High Commissioner of Human Rights, Human Rights and Human Trafficking Fact Sheet No. 34, 2014, 8.
93 H. Cullen, above n. 46, 590.

Costello states that '[…] positive human rights obligations aim to ensure that human rights violations do not happen in the first place, they identify how the regulatory environment should be developed to avoid forced labour, taking measures to ensure the threshold of forced labour is not crossed. […] Indeed, the newly agreed ILO Protocol embodies precisely this preventative ethos'.[94] This chapter contends that the shift towards a labour rights perspective in the ILO Forced Labour framework will be able to build upon the positive obligations developed as part of the human trafficking discourse and will facilitate a holistic approach to suppressing forced labour that places its central focus on prevention and protection.

The remainder of this chapter will examine a selection of these measures and determine the extent to which the application of positive human rights obligations will assist in their effective operationalisation: (i) the provision of strong victim protection measures, including appropriate and accessible justice and compensation mechanisms; (ii) a robust enforcement response, including strengthened labour inspections; and (iii) broad international and regional policy and cooperation frameworks. Finally, the chapter will reflect upon a few issues for future consideration the resolution of which will depend significantly upon national level political engagement with the ratification and implementation of the ILO Protocol.

5.1. PROVISION OF STRONG VICTIM PROTECTION MEASURES

The ILO Protocol emphasises the importance of strong victim measures and the need for States to identify, release, protect, support and assist the recovery and rehabilitation of victims of forced or compulsory labour.[95] This protection must be extended to all victims of forced or compulsory labour, irrespective of their presence or legal status in the national territory[96] and must ensure the non-prosecution of victims for their involvement in unlawful activities that they are compelled to undertake as a direct consequence of their forced or compulsory labour.[97]

The preventative nature of the protection measures is further outlined in the Recommendation, which places an emphasis on the need to eliminate abuses and fraudulent practices by labour recruiters and employment agencies. ILO Member States must implement measures that eliminate the charging

94 C. Costello, 'Migrants and Forced Labour: a Labour Law Response' in A. Bogg *et al.* (eds), *The Autonomy of Labour Law*, Hart Publishing, Oxford 2015, 220.

95 ILO Forced Labour Protocol 2014 (PO29), Art. 3.

96 Ibid., Art. 4(1).

97 Ibid., Art. 4(2).

of recruitment fees to workers; require transparent contracts that clearly explain terms of employment and conditions of work; establish adequate and accessible complaint mechanisms; impose adequate penalties; and regulate or license these services.[98] Further, States must address workers' vulnerability and susceptibility to forced labour. The ILO Protocol states that efforts should be made to conduct targeted awareness-raising campaigns regarding employment rights and implement training programmes for at-risk populations to increase their employability and earning potential.[99] Further, it is vital that States address the non-fulfilment of economic, social and cultural rights by securing access to employment, food, health care, shelter and education.[100]

The implementation of the victim protection measures outlined in the ILO Protocol can be reinforced by the positive obligations on States to take protective measures, as outlined by the European Court of Human Rights in *Rantsev*. This requires a State to take 'operational measures to protect victims or potential victims of trafficking' in circumstances in which State authorities know, or should have known, that 'an identified person had been or was at real and immediate risk'.[101] The operational measures suggested in the *Rantsev* case, such as training law enforcement officers in identification factors, would also be relevant to the need to suppress forced labour as outlined by the ILO Protocol and Recommendation, including training of relevant authorities.[102] In *J. and Others v. Austria*, the obligation was sufficiently discharged as the potential victims were interviewed by specially trained police officers.[103]

The ILO Protocol also provides for access to remedies, and in particular the need to provide access to appropriate and effective remedies, such as compensation.[104] In this regard, the Article 4 jurisprudence highlights the need for the administrative and legal framework to consider the availability of remedies for victims of forced labour. In *CN v. UK*, the Court held that an individual must be afforded practical and effective protection against treatment falling within the scope of Article 4 of the Convention, thus reaffirming the Court's findings in *Siliadin* and *Rantsev*.[105] Therefore, the legislative provisions must be broad enough to ensure that authorities are able to investigate and penalise

98 ILO Forced Labour (Supplementary Measures) Recommendation 2014 (No. 203), [8].

99 Ibid., [4].

100 R. Pati, 'States' Positive Obligations with Respect to Human Trafficking: The European Court of Human Rights Breaks New Ground in Rantsev v. Cyprus & Russia' (2011) 29 *Boston University International Law Journal* 135.

101 *Rantsev v. Cyprus and Russia*, above n. 45, para. 286.

102 Ibid., para. 296; ILO Forced Labour (Supplementary Measures) Recommendation 2014 (No. 203), [13].

103 *J. and Others v. Austria*, above n. 45, para. 110.

104 ILO Forced Labour Protocol 2014 (PO29), Art. 4(1).

105 *Siliadin v. France*, above n. 45, paras 121 and 148; *Rantsev v. Cyprus and Russia*, above n. 45, para. 284.

all situations that could lead to the prohibited treatment and therefore provide victims who had suffered such treatment the ability to access remedies.[106] In this regard, the Recommendation elaborates upon the type of personal and material damage that should be compensated for, including unpaid wages and statutory contributions for social security benefits.[107] However, one shortcoming of the final ILO Protocol is that, despite the emphasis on compensation for victims, it is mentioned as a potential remedy rather than as a required remedy.[108] Furthermore, draft recommendations for governments to establish victim compensation funds were not included in the final text.[109]

5.2. ROBUST ENFORCEMENT RESPONSE

The ILO Protocol places the enforcement emphasis on the role of labour inspectorates. The provisions, therefore, explicitly focus upon strengthening the prevalence of labour inspections when taking action to ensure the enforcement of legislation relevant to the prevention of forced labour.[110] Labour inspectors are in the front line when dealing with issues of labour exploitation in the workplace, as they are the main mechanism for ensuring respect for international labour standards through the enforcement of domestic employment law.[111]

Historically, as Allain outlines, labour inspection has been a central mandate of the ILO. However, the renewed focus on the role of labour law and labour inspectorates is a positive development, as it facilitates a shift away from the dominant criminal justice approach that has been the main focus of most national responses to forced labour, under the guise of anti-human trafficking legislation. To this end, the ILO Protocol and Recommendation place an emphasis upon the need to secure the mandate, resources and training of labour inspection services, to allow them to enforce the law effectively and cooperate with other organisations concerned in the prevention and protection of victims of forced or compulsory labour. In order for these changes to be effective, it will be important for all actors to have additional guidance in the form of operational indicators that can assist the better identification of victims.[112]

One channel for identifying potential victims of forced labour is to target the economic sectors in which labour exploitation is most prevalent. The 2012

106 *CN v. UK*, above n. 45, para. 76.

107 ILO Forced Labour (Supplementary Measures) Recommendation 2014 (No. 203), [12].

108 Human Rights Watch, *Global Treaty to Protect Forced Labor Victims Adopted*, 11 June 2014 <https://www.hrw.org/news/2014/06/11/global-treaty-protect-forced-labor-victims-adopted> accessed 02.11.2014.

109 Ibid.

110 ILO Forced Labour Protocol 2014 (PO29), Art. 2(c)(ii).

111 J. Allain, above n. 15, 207.

112 ILO Forced Labour (Supplementary Measures) Recommendation 2014 (No. 203), [13].

ILO Global Estimate of Forced Labour demonstrates that 75 per cent of victims who are subject to forced or compulsory labour are engaged in 'low-skilled, low-technology and labour-intensive'[113] activities such as agriculture, domestic work, construction, fisheries and manufacturing, and the remainder in commercial sexual exploitation.[114] One of the key features of these economic sectors is the lack of regulation.[115] Furthermore, it must be noted that a lack of political will to adequately resource the inspection and monitoring of these economic sectors creates difficulties.[116] Nevertheless, the prominence of strengthening labour inspection in the ILO Protocol suggests an acceptance by the international community of the link between widespread labour abuses and severe labour exploitation, and the need to address this through a labour lens.[117]

It is clear that the international community is aware of the economic sectors most affected, as evidenced above. The procedural obligations outlined by the court in *Rantsev*, and reinforced in *CN v. UK*, emphasised the need to investigate forced labour, where there is a credible suspicion of real and immediate risk of forced labour.[118] In *Chowdury*, the authorities, both nationally and locally were well aware of the situation of irregular migrant workers in the region and in the agricultural sector, however, no measures were adopted to sufficiently protect the workers from the abuses they endured. Thus, the Court found the Greek authorities to have failed to uphold their obligation to put in place operational measures that sought to prevent human trafficking and protect victims.[119]

Notwithstanding, the European Court of Human Rights has emphasised that 'the existence of useful detection and reporting mechanisms are fundamental to the effective implementation of the relevant criminal laws'.[120] Within the scope of the ILO Protocol, this procedural obligation could be conferred upon the role of labour inspections, where they would be required to ensure that the legislative framework is enforced, thereby regulating recruitment and employment agencies to ensure that they are licensed, do not charge recruitment fees and

113 B. Andres and P. Belser, 'Introduction', above n. 42, 2.

114 ILO Global Estimate of Forced Labour 2012: Results and Methodology, 1 June 2012.

115 B. Anderson and J. O'Connell Davidson, *Is trafficking in human beings demand driven? A multi-country pilot study, International Organisation for Migration – Migration Research Series*, 2003, 44.

116 B. Andres and P. Belser, 'Strengthening Labor Market Governance against Forced Labor' in B. Andres and P. Belser (eds), above n. 42, 115.

117 M. Ford, 'Trade Unions, Forced Labour and Human Trafficking' (2015) 5 *Anti-Trafficking Review* 11.

118 *Rantsev v. Cyprus and Russia*, above n. 45, paras 301–06; *CN v. UK*, above n. 45, para. 71.

119 *Chowdury and others v. Greece*, above n. 45, paras 110–115.

120 *Juppala v. Finland*, no. 18620/03, ECHR, 2008, para. 42; *O'Keefe v. Ireland*, no. 35810/09, ECHR, 2014, para. 148; *TM and CM v. Republic of Moldova*, no. 26608/11, ECHR, 2014, para. 46.

provide transparent contracts that clearly explain terms of employment and conditions of work.[121] The operationalisation of the procedural obligation will serve a dual role, not only in prevention of forced labour but also in protection of forced labour victims. By including investigations by labour inspectorates within the scope of this obligation, a duty would be placed on States to ensure that these economic sectors, where vulnerability to forced labour is high, are subjected to rigorous and robust labour inspections to ensure that victims are identified and provided with support and assistance. This was supported by the findings of the FRA research into severe forms of labour exploitation, which found that inspection and reporting services for implementing and monitoring standards of decent work fulfil a crucial function.[122]

5.3. BROAD INTERNATIONAL AND REGIONAL POLICY AND COOPERATION FRAMEWORKS

Forced labour is an issue of global concern and must be addressed at an international level. There are a number of transnational elements that will require international and regional policy and cooperation when implementing measures that tackle forced labour, including the complex nature of supply chains, the impact of globalisation on the labour market, the demand for cheap labour and the poor socio-economic conditions that make individuals vulnerable to labour exploitation.

The ILO Protocol addresses this issue by requiring all Members to cooperate with each other to ensure the prevention and elimination of all forms of forced or compulsory labour.[123] This issue has not been addressed directly by the Court in the context of the positive obligations on States; however, the *Rantsev* case did refer to the obligations on States to implement international cooperation and coordination in relation to prevention, victim assistance and protection, and criminal measures.[124] In the context of forced labour, the principal methods of cooperation have been further developed in the Recommendation. States will be expected to mobilise resources for national action programmes and international technical cooperation and assistance; provide mutual legal assistance; prevent forced or compulsory labour by diplomatic personnel; and provide mutual

121 ILO Forced Labour (Supplementary Measures) Recommendation 2014 (No. 203), [8].

122 European Union Agency for Fundamental Rights, Severe labour exploitation: workers moving within or into the European Union States' obligations and victims' rights, June 2015, 26 <http://fra.europa.eu/sites/default/files/fra-2015-severe-labour-exploitation_en.pdf> accessed 01.02.2016.

123 ILO Forced Labour Protocol 2014 (PO29), Art. 5.

124 *Rantsev v. Cyprus and Russia*, above n. 45, paras 154, 155 and 158.

technical assistance.[125] From an IHRL perspective, and based upon the Court's Article 4 jurisprudence, States are under a positive obligation to fulfil a duty to cooperate with States in cases in which events may happen outside of a State's own territory.[126]

However, it will be important for such cooperation to build on lessons learned from previous cooperation agreements and frameworks, particularly in relation to trafficking in human beings for labour exploitation. In addition to having clearly drafted agreements that contain specific and concrete measures, it will be essential, for sufficient funding and political will, to ensure that they are effectively implemented.[127]

5.4. FUTURE CONSIDERATIONS

As has been noted, there are many strengths of the ILO Protocol, as it constitutes 'a legally binding ILO Protocol, which provides a baseline of minimum standards globally – a critical advance in an increasingly interconnected world'.[128] However, there are a number of issues for future consideration. For instance, whilst the ILO Protocol has now entered into force, it is not yet widely ratified.[129] It will therefore be essential for Member States to implement the legal obligations effectively at a national level, requiring clear legislation and operational guidance. This is an issue that has been noted more generally regarding the ratification and operationalisation of ILO Conventions, notably where 'specific provisions in national law are too vague or entirely absent'.[130]

Operationalisation may well be particularly complex for certain ILO Member States who must abide by other regional legal obligations, such as European Union Member States who are bound by EU law. Consequently, the implications of the positive obligations outlined in this chapter may have an impact on these ILO Member States due to the complexity of the issue of forced labour. In particular, effective operationalisation of the measures in the ILO Protocol will require significant harmonisation with other areas of EU law, such as immigration law,

---

125 ILO Forced Labour (Supplementary Measures) Recommendation 2014 (No. 203), [14].

126 R. Pati, 'States' Positive Obligations with Respect to Human Trafficking: The European Court of Human Rights Breaks New Ground in Rantsev v. Cyprus & Russia' (2011) 29 *Boston University International Law Journal* 131.

127 B. Andres and P. Belser, above n. 42, 114.

128 N. Varia, EU: Show leadership to end forced labour, 1 May 2014 <http://euobserver.com/opinion/123963> accessed 02.11.2015.

129 Ratifications of P029 – Protocol of 2014 to the Forced Labour Convention, 1930 <http://www.ilo.org/dyn/normlex/en/f?p=1000:11300:0::NO:11300:P11300_INSTRUMENT_ID:3174672> accessed 02.11.2015.

130 B. Andres and P. Belser, above n. 42, 115–16.

labour law and criminal law.[131] For instance, the ILO Protocol measures regarding the need to sanction perpetrators of forced labour (Article 1(1)) and the provision of remedies, including compensation (Article 4(1)) must be harmonised with the requirements of EU Directive 2009/52/EC, providing for minimum standards on sanctions and measures against employers of illegally staying third-country nationals to implement mechanisms to ensure that third-country nationals can claim any outstanding remuneration from their employers (Article 6) and that the employment of persons in particularly exploitative conditions must be criminalised (Article 9).[132]

Furthermore, this chapter has posited that the operationalisation of the ILO Protocol can be facilitated by the enforcement of positive obligations under IHRL. In particular, the relevance of this pertains to the requirement on States 'to comply with their obligations under international law by observing their duty to protect, promote, facilitate and fulfil applicable human rights'.[133] However, the enforcement of both the ILO Protocol's measures and the positive human rights obligations must be reviewed and monitored to determine the extent to which the core labour standards are being applied. Once again, the convergence between the two bodies of law is prominent in relation to the monitoring and review process.

One method of review is the ILO supervisory mechanism, the ILO Committee of Experts on the Application of the Conventions and Recommendations. However, ILO review is only applicable to States that have ratified ILO Conventions and, furthermore, the lack of provision for sanctions in the ILO supervisory mechanism may put into question the extent to which the ILO Protocol will really carry weight.[134] Further, Allain notes that the ILO supervisory committee has not always adhered to its terms of reference, 'to examine from a purely legal point of view to what extent the countries, which have ratified the Convention on forced labour give effect to their national legislation and practices to the obligations deriving therefrom'. Conversely, the Committee has in fact 'facilitated and legitimised an expansive reading of the

131 H. Askola, 'Article 5 – Prohibition of Slavery and Forced Labour', in S. Peers *et al.* (eds), *The EU Charter of Fundamental Rights: A Commentary*, Hart Publishing, Oxford 2011, 101–19.

132 European Parliament and Council Directive 2009/52/EC of 18 June 2009 providing for minimum standards on sanctions and measures against employers of illegally staying third-country nationals [2009] OJ L168/24.

133 R. Pati, 'States' Positive Obligations with Respect to Human Trafficking: The European Court of Human Rights Breaks New Ground in Rantsev v. Cyprus & Russia' (2011) 29 *Boston University International Law Journal* 141.

134 P. Alston, 'Facing Up to the Complexities of the ILO's Core Labour Standards Agenda' (2005) 16(3) *European Journal of International Law* 467.

exception, thus allowing for the wider use of forced or compulsory labour'[135] by being 'willing to accept the various moves of States to widen the exception and thus narrow the prohibition against forced or compulsory labour',[136] In light of the limitations of the ILO supervisory mechanism, the gap-filling role of IHRL could play a part; as the UN treaty body monitoring mechanism and the human rights judicial mechanisms may also review States parties' implementation of core labour standards.

6. CONCLUSION

This chapter has shown that the ILO Protocol and accompanying Recommendation provide great detail regarding the possible measures that States could take to ensure that progress is made with regard to the eradication of forced labour.

Above all, the shift towards a labour approach by the ILO Protocol demonstrates international communities' willingness to ensure that all victims of forced labour are provided with protection, support and assistance, whether they have been victims of human trafficking or not. Nevertheless, it is necessary to recognise that swift operationalisation may be hampered by States who are required to implement these standards at a national level. For instance, the UK Explanatory Memorandum states that no new legislative activity is required to implement the provisions of the ILO Protocol, as the UK is bound by the ILO Convention.[137] This conviction is questionable, as the national referral mechanism (NRM) is not yet fully enforced to include all victims of forced labour who are not victims of human trafficking for labour exploitation, thus limiting their access to justice and protection. Additionally, the principal labour inspectorate system is not yet mandated to cover all economic sectors, and all workers, including irregular migrant workers. The reaction of the UK to the adoption of the ILO Protocol illustrates that there remains an onus on States themselves to abide by the obligations and to implement the measures promulgated by the ILO Protocol.

With this in mind, it will be vital that employers' and workers' organisations play a significant role in the implementation process with ILO Member States, as envisaged by Article 6 of the ILO Protocol. In particular, such third-party actors will be required actively to participate in the development, coordination,

---

135 J. Allain, *Slavery in international law of human exploitation and trafficking*, above n. 15, 213.

136 Ibid., 246.

137 UK Home Office Explanatory Memorandum on the Protocol of 2014 to the Forced Labour Convention 1930 <https://www.gov.uk/government/uploads/system/uploads/attachment_data/file/401981/EM__Cm_9008.pdf> accessed 03.11.2015.

implementation, monitoring and evaluation of national policies and action plans aimed at the effective and sustained suppression of forced or compulsory labour in all its forms, through prevention, protection and access to remedies, such as compensation of victims, and the sanctioning of perpetrators.[138] In essence, this will require significant galvanisation of a 'global grassroots movement'[139] against forced labour.

138 ILO Forced Labour (Supplementary Measures) Recommendation 2014 (No. 203), [1].

139 Z. Muskat-Gorska, 'Will the new ILO Protocol and Recommendation make a difference?', DemandAT Blog, October 2014 <http://demandat.eu/blog/will-new-ilo-ILO Protocol-and-recommendation-make-difference> accessed 03.11.2015.

THE INTERNATIONAL LAW OF HUMAN TRAFFICKING: AT THE FOREFRONT OF THE CONVERGENCE BETWEEN TRANSNATIONAL CRIMINAL LAW AND INTERNATIONAL HUMAN RIGHTS LAW?

Valentina MILANO

1. INTRODUCTION

Is human trafficking foremost a heinous crime, requiring concerted action against organised criminal networks? Or is it primarily a grave human rights violation, in which the protection of victims must be the utmost priority? Human trafficking is about one person appropriating the labour, freedom and dignity of another person. It is about slavery, forced labour, debt bondage, forced marriage, organ removal and the commercial sexual exploitation of mostly women and children.[1] Traditionally, human trafficking activities have been exclusively categorised as crimes and tackled with law enforcement strategies focused on criminalisation and punishment. Now that agreement seems to have been reached that trafficking is also a human rights issue and that a certain degree of complementarity between a criminal and a human rights law approach is utterly needed, important divergences persist on the degree of convergence required and on whether and how this complementarity should be translated into clear and coherent international law commitments. In the meantime, trafficking continues to flourish as a low-risk, high-profit activity for criminals,[2] where millions of women, men and children continue to be exploited all around the word.

Human trafficking lies at the intersection of international human rights law (IHRL) and transnational criminal law (TCL).[3] It is certainly a criminal activity, often perpetrated by transnational organised groups and involving the illegal crossing of borders and the use of violence and corruption to carry out illegal activities. A criminal justice or 'law and order' response is undoubtedly required. From the international law perspective, criminal justice matters are dealt with by TCL, which promotes 'the indirect suppression by international law, through domestic penal law, of criminal activities that have actual or potential trans-boundaries effects'.[4] As opposed to international criminal law (ICL) *stricto sensu*, where the penal proscription is international, the so-called crime control conventions, the typical TCL instrument, establish 'prohibition regimes'[5] which are

1 A. Gallagher, *The International Law of Human Trafficking*, Cambridge University Press, Cambridge 2010, p. 5. For recent data on human trafficking, see UNODC, *Global Report on Trafficking in Persons*, New York, 2016 (UNODC Global Report 2016).

2 UNODC *Global Report on Trafficking in Persons*, New York 2014, p. 1; and UNODC Global Report 2016, p. 51 and 57.

3 Human trafficking is, to a lesser extent, also a matter for international labour law and refugee/migrant law. However, an analysis of these approaches goes beyond the limits of this chapter. On this topic, see A. Edwards, 'Traffic In Human Beings: At the Intersection of Criminal Justice, Human Rights, Asylum/Migration and Labor' (2007) 36(1) *Denver Journal of International Law & Policy* 9, 9–53; and E.M. Bruch, 'Models Wanted: The Search for an Effective Response to Human Trafficking' (2004) 40(1) *Stanford Journal of International Law* 1, 1–45.

4 N. Boister, 'Transnational Criminal Law?' (2003) 14(5) *European Journal of International Law* 953, 955.

5 E.A. Nadelman, 'Global Prohibition Regimes: The Evolution of Norms in International Society' (1990) 44(4) *International Organization* 479.

to be implemented at national level, mainly through adapting national criminal law in order to 'minimize or eliminate the potential havens from which certain crimes can be committed and to which criminals can flee to escape prosecution and punishment'.[6]

But human trafficking is also a human rights issue – a severe and multifaceted one in which various human rights violations occur at different stages of the trafficking cycle. First, trafficking frequently finds its origins in situations in which human rights violations are widespread: root causes of trafficking include poverty, discrimination, violence and insecurity linked to armed conflict or climate change. Secondly, persons who become trafficked suffer from a wide range of violations of their fundamental rights, which often include the right not to be held in slavery or servitude, the right to freedom from forced labour, the right to life, the right to freedom from violence and discrimination based on gender, race and other grounds, the right to liberty and security of the person, the right to be free from torture and cruel, inhuman or degrading treatment, the right to privacy and the right to just and favourable conditions of employment.[7] Thirdly, trafficked persons who escape their situation are typically subject to human rights violations at the hands of governments, i.e. to re-victimisation. Traditional criminal law responses tend to treat them as irregular migrants, giving priority to detention, prosecution and expulsion of trafficking victims in violation of their basic rights, including their right to be free from arbitrary detention, the right to *non-refoulement*, the right to life and the right to access to effective remedies.[8] Alternatively, they are treated as 'disposable witnesses' who deserve protection only to the extent that they may be useful to trafficking investigations and prosecutions.

Yet, the responses of these two bodies of law to the human trafficking phenomenon remained fully separated during the whole 20th century, with discouraging results. On the one hand, the five trafficking-specific treaties adopted during the last century focused heavily on the criminalisation and prosecution of trafficking, omitting any consideration relating to victims' rights.[9] The consequences for victims in terms of lack of protection have been

---

6 Ibid., 481. On the development of transnational criminal law as a separate category of international law, see N. Boister, above n. 4, 953–76; and generally N. Boister and R.J. Currie, *Routledge Handbook of Transnational Criminal Law*, Routledge, London and New York 2015.

7 See United Nations Human Rights Council (UNHRC) 'Report of the Special Rapporteur on trafficking in persons' (2009) UN Doc A/HRC/10/16, para. 44.

8 Ibid.

9 These treaties are: the International Agreement for the Suppression of the 'White Slave Traffic' (adopted 4 May 1904, entered into force 18 July 1905) 1 LNTS 83; International Convention for the Suppression of White Slave Traffic (adopted 4 May 1910, entered into force 8 August 1912) 20 *United Kingdom Treaty Series* Cd. 6326; International Convention for the Suppression of the Traffic in Women and Children (adopted 30 September 1921,

devastating.[10] Also, its failure in terms of traffickers' prosecution was patent. On the other hand, while TCL dominated the scene, IHRL remained almost silent. Apart from two limited prohibitions directed specifically at women and children,[11] IHRL did not include a general prohibition of human trafficking. Certainly, the combined action of different IHRL provisions relevant to trafficking, such as those on slavery, practices similar to slavery, forced labour, torture, gender and racial discrimination and refugees/asylum, ultimately ended up conforming a prohibition that covered the broad range of human rights violations relevant to this phenomenon. However, such a fragmented and unclear regulation – a 'patchwork tapestry that has yet to connect all the dots or to fill all the gaps'[12] – has proven ineffective. It is all but user friendly: it lacks clarity, both for rights-holders and duty-bearers. Only more recently have human rights monitoring bodies started seriously engaging with trafficking and shedding light on individual rights and States' obligations in this area. From the perspective of users, the 20th century certainly marks the failure of IHRL to address human trafficking as a human rights abuse.[13]

In this context, the adoption in 2000 of the United Nations (UN) Protocol to Prevent, Suppress and Punish Trafficking in Persons[14] (Palermo Protocol) marks a partial but significant change of course. The adoption of the Protocol resulted in a collision, but also a first reticent convergence, between these two branches of law. A few years later, European countries went a step further into that process, with the adoption of the Council of Europe Anti-Trafficking Convention (2005)[15] and, thereafter, the European Union Anti-Trafficking Directive (2011).[16]

---

entered into force 15 June 1922) 9 LNTS 415; International Convention for the Suppression of the Traffic of Women of Full Age (adopted 30 September 1921, entered into force 24 August 1934) 150 LNTS 431; Convention for the Suppression of the Traffic in Persons and of the Exploitation of the Prostitution of Others (adopted 21 March 1950, entered into force 25 July 1951) 96 UNTS 271. On these anti-trafficking conventions, see J. Allain, *Slavery in International Law. Of Human Exploitation and Trafficking*, Martinus Nijhoff Publishers, Leiden/Boston 2013, pp. 340–54; and E. Decaux, *Les formes contemporaines de l'esclavage*, Martinus Nijhoff Publishers, Leiden/Boston 2009, pp. 97–103 and 148–54.

10 See UNHRC, 'Report of the Special Rapporteur on violence against women' (2000) UN Doc E/CN.4/2000/68 (Special Rapporteur on violence against women 2000), paras 22, 24 and 25.

11 Art. 6 of the Convention on the Elimination of All Forms of Discrimination against Women (adopted 18 December 1979, entered into force 3 September 1981) 1249 UNTS 13 (CEDAW), and Art. 35 of the Convention on the Rights of the Child (adopted 20 November 1989, entered into force 2 September 1990) 1577 UNTS 3 (CRC).

12 A. Edwards, above n. 3, 10.

13 On this point, see E.M. Bruch, above n. 3, 11.

14 Protocol to Prevent, Suppress and Punish Trafficking in Persons, Especially Women and Children, supplementing the United Nations Convention against Transnational Organized Crime (adopted 15 November 2000, entered into force 25 December 2003) 2237 UNTS 319.

15 Council of Europe Convention on Action against Trafficking in Human Beings (adopted 3 May 2005, entered into force 1 February 2008) (European Anti-trafficking Convention).

16 Directive 2011/36/EU of the European Parliament and of the Council on preventing and combating trafficking in human beings and protecting its victims, and replacing Council

Both provide examples of an enhanced degree of integration between the criminal and human rights-based approach. This chapter explores the extent to which IHRL is permeating the TCL response to human trafficking, and vice versa. The distinctive ways in which these two bodies of law coexist in the Palermo Protocol and in the more recent European instruments are analysed, and observations are made in terms of convergence and divergence of their approaches: are they fundamentally distinct, in terms of norms but also of monitoring mechanisms? To what extent are they mutually reinforcing? What are their main gap-filling and guiding effects? Lastly, this chapter examines whether TCL, and even national criminal law, is in a process of transformation under the influence of IHRL, and vice versa. To conclude, the author explores whether the human rights-based approach provides a suitable theoretical framework for the integration of different bodies of international law.[17]

2. INTEGRATION AT THE UNIVERSAL LEVEL

2.1. THE PALERMO PROTOCOL

The Palermo Protocol, supplementing the United Nations Convention against Transnational Organized Crime[18] (UNTOC), is the main instrument regulating human trafficking at the universal level. At the outset, the chances of succeeding in integrating human rights elements into this instrument were not at all clear. Negotiations were taking place in the UN Commission on Crime Prevention and Criminal Justice in Vienna, clearly in charge of TCL issues. Despite the active participation of numerous human rights governmental and non-governmental organisations, many delegates dismissed the idea that trafficking was a human rights issue. As the representative of the UN High Commissioner for Human Rights in the negotiations reports, a senior member of one of the

---

Framework Decision 2002/629/JHA (adopted on.5 April 2011), [2011] OJ 15.4.2011, L 101/1 (European Anti-trafficking Directive).

17 On the issue of fragmentation of international law into different specialised regimes or bodies of law, see International Law Commission (ILC), 'Fragmentation of International Law: Difficulties Arising from the Diversification and Expansion of International Law' (2006), Report of the Study Group of the International Law Commission (UN Doc A/CN.4/L.682) (ILC Report on Fragmentation of International Law). See also M. Young (ed.), *Regime Interaction in International Law: Facing Fragmentation*, Cambridge University Press, Cambridge 2012; T. Broude and S. Yuval (eds), *Multi-Sourced Equivalent Norms in International Law*, Hart Publishing, Oxford 2011; and R. Huesa Vinaixa and K. Wellens, *L'influence des sources sur l'unité et la fragmentation du droit international*, Bruylant, Brussels 2006.

18 United Nations Convention against Transnational Organized Crime (adopted 15 November 2000, entered into force 29 September 2003) 2225 UNTS 209 (UNTOC).

leading delegations was dismissive of the efforts to integrate human rights into the Protocol, affirming: 'This is not like torture. [...]. We governments are not the villains here. Traffickers are just criminals. We can't be responsive of what they are doing'.[19] This statement clearly encapsulates some of the difficulties that lie at the heart of the efforts aiming at the integration of two considerably distinct branches of international law. In this context, the Palermo Protocol is the first anti-trafficking treaty that attempts to reconcile these opposing approaches. While the result is clearly unbalanced, a limited degree of integration of IHRL is to be found mainly in two aspects: the definition of trafficking and the purposes of the Convention.

The Protocol contains the first internationally agreed definition of 'trafficking'. While this achievement is fundamental in terms of establishing a common ground for inter-state cooperation, it is also a considerable success from a human rights perspective, as the definition covers a broad range of victims – women, men and children – and of exploitative situations: not only sexual exploitation but also forced labour, slavery, servitude and practices similar to slavery (two concepts that coincide since they refer to the same practices) and organ removal. While previous TCL anti-trafficking treaties typically focused exclusively on women and children and on exploitation solely related to prostitution, this definition reflects the reality of contemporary forms of exploitation and enables to reach many more potential victims. However, both States[20] and scholars[21] have pointed to ambiguities surrounding some core concepts of the definition – such as 'abuse of a position of vulnerability' or 'exploitation' – that have prompted their use to support expansive definitions of trafficking, with a negative impact on the

19 A. Gallagher, above n. 1, p. 5.

20 In October 2010, the Conference of the Parties (CoP) to UNTOC welcomed the recommendation of its Working Group (WG) on Trafficking in Persons (Open-ended Interim Working Group on the Protocol to Prevent, Suppress and Punish Trafficking in Persons, Especially Women and Children, established by decision 4/4 (2008) of the CoP) that the Secretariat should prepare, in consultation with States parties, Issue Papers to clarify key concepts of the human trafficking definition, on subjects such as consent, harbouring, receipt and transport: abuse of a position of vulnerability; exploitation; and transnationality (UN Doc. CTOC/COP/2010/17, 2 December 2010, Resolution 5/2: 'Implementation of the Protocol to Prevent, Suppress and Punish Trafficking in Persons, Especially Women and Children, supplementing the United Nations Convention against Transnational Organized Crime', para. 5). Three of these Issue Papers have been published so far, on 'abuse of a position of vulnerability and other "means" within the definition of trafficking in persons' (2012), 'the role of "consent"'(2014) and 'the concept of "exploitation"' (2015) respectively.

21 See, e.g., J. Chuang, 'Exploitation Creep and the Unmaking of Human Trafficking Law' (2014) 108 *American Journal of International Law* 606, 606–49; A. Gallagher, 'Two Cheers for the Trafficking Protocol' (2015) 4 *Anti-Trafficking Review* 14, 29–31; P. Kotiswaran, 'Feminist Approaches to Criminal Law' in M.D. Dubber and T. Hörnle, *The Oxford Handbook of Criminal Law*, Oxford University Press, Oxford 2014, p. 75.

certainty principle in criminal law and the risk of complicating and diluting national efforts in the fight against the worst forms of trafficking.

The other novelty lies in the fact that the need to protect the human rights of trafficked persons is included for the first time in the purposes of an anti-trafficking treaty. The three main purposes of the Protocol are to prevent and combat trafficking in persons, to protect and assist the victims of trafficking, and to promote cooperation among States Parties.[22] The inclusion of these purposes reflects a major progress: the acceptance by a TCL instrument of the so-called 'Three Ps' framework (prevention, protection and prosecution), which is rooted in IHRL. At the outset, this represents a fundamental switch in terms of TCL, since the previous treaty adopted a much narrower focus, which could be referred to as 'One P and a half': a heavy focus on prosecution and, to a limited extent, on prevention. However, a deeper look at the Protocol shows that the adoption of the 'Three Ps' framework is more a statement of principle than an actual commitment: when it comes to substantive provisions, human rights protection is addressed in only a marginal way. Only few provisions on protection are of a mandatory nature.[23]

For instance, under Article 6(3), States parties 'shall consider' implementing measures to provide for the physical, psychological and social recovery of victims of trafficking in persons. The consequence of this non-mandatory wording is that States that fail to provide victims with access to a shelter or medical care, or with information about their rights in a language they understand, would not breach any obligation under the Palermo Protocol. While the provisions relating to criminal justice are mandatory, the non-mandatory nature of a substantial part of the protection and assistance provisions has been criticised both by scholars[24] and by UN organisations and bodies.[25] Finally, the Protocol is silent on a number of key issues in terms of protection: how victims of trafficking are to be identified, and the status of victims who were compelled to commit

22 Art. 2 of the Palermo Protocol.

23 See 'The Legislative Guide for the Implementation of the Protocol to Prevent, Suppress and Punish Trafficking in Persons, especially Women and Children' (2004), para. 49, which lists the Protocol's requirements to be considered mandatory in terms of victims' rights.

24 See, e.g., T. Obokata, 'Human Trafficking' in N. Boister and R.J. Currie, above n. 6, pp. 177–78; E.M. Bruch, above n. 3, 21; A. Gallagher, above n. 1, p. 336.

25 See United Nations, 'Travaux préparatoires of the negotiations for the elaboration of the United Nations Convention against Transnational Organized Crime and the Protocols thereto' (2006), p. 368. See also Special Rapporteur on violence against women 2000, above n. 10, 7; and the 'Note by the Office of the High Commissioner for Human Rights, the Office of the High Commissioner for Refugees, the United Nations Children's Fund and the International Organization for Migration on the Draft Protocols Concerning Migrant Smuggling and Trafficking in Persons' (2000) A/AC.254/27, 2000 and A/AC.254/27/Corr.1 (Inter-agency Submission), 3, para. 7.

'trafficking related offences' (including irregular entry into a country, prostitution or criminal activities such as theft).[26]

In terms of prevention, while the need to address root causes of trafficking is addressed, it is formulated in very general terms, making it difficult for States both to implement it and to be held accountable for it. On the contrary, the criminalisation, prosecution and international cooperation provisions are to be praised. They are very detailed, of a mandatory nature and provide a comprehensive set of tools for enhancing criminal responses to trafficking both nationally and internationally.

The lack of mechanisms to promote States' accountability under the Protocol, which reflects a feature common to all TCL treaties,[27] displays another major weakness of this instrument from a human rights perspective. While the Conference of the Parties to UNTOC (CoP) 'may establish such supplemental review mechanism as it deems appropriate',[28] past intents have been unsuccessful. Discussions have been ongoing for many years on the establishment of an effective review mechanism.[29] While a group of States – led by European States – called for an expert-based mechanism open to civil society participation, another group of States only supported the idea of a closed-doors, non-expert intergovernmental process. Some consensus was reached at the eighth session of the CoP held in 2016. States decided to develop specific procedures and rules for a review mechanism due to be adopted by the CoP at its ninth session in 2018, following a number of agreed principles.[30] Regrettably, the agreed principles reflect the majority position in favour of a strictly intergovernmental process to

26 On the non-punishment of trafficking victims for offences related to their status, see R.W. Piotrowicz and L. Sorrentino, 'Human Trafficking and the Emergence of the Non-Punishment Principle' (2016) 16(4) *Human Rights Law Review* 669, 669–99; M. Jovanovic, 'The Principle of Non-Punishment of Victims of Trafficking in Human Beings' (2017) 1 *Journal of Trafficking and Human Exploitation* 41, 41–76.

27 According to Duran and Chin, 'Efforts to establish consequences for a State's non-compliance with its treaty obligations have not been very successful. [...]. In short, in the area of transnational criminal law, there are very few real consequences for a State's non-compliance with its obligations under a treaty it has ratified': Y. Duran and V. Chin, 'Implementation of transnational criminal law' in N. Boister and R.J. Currie, above n. 6, pp. 442–43.

28 Art. 32(4) of UNTOC.

29 At the request of the Extended Bureau of the CoP, Italy has been conducting informal consultations on this topic: see 'Food for thought on the establishment of a mechanism to review the implementation of the United Nations Convention against Transnational Organized Crime and the Protocols thereto' (2014) Non-Paper by Italy, CTOC/COP/2014/CRP.3. See also the draft resolution tabled by Austria, France, Italy and Mexico, *Strengthening the implementation of the United Nations Convention against Transnational Organized Crime and the Protocols thereto*, CTOC/COP/2014/L.4/Rev.2.

30 Conference of the Parties to UNTOC, Resolution 8/2, 2016, para. 3, in *Report of the Conference of the Parties to the United Nations Convention against Transnational Organized Crime on its eighth session*, CTOC/COP/2016/15, p. 10.

be conducted within the framework of the existing Working Groups: the idea of an independent, expert-based mechanism has been discarded and the active participation of civil society organisations is mentioned as a mere possibility.

The only mechanism that exists to date is the Working Group (WG) on Trafficking in Persons, established in 2008.[31] It is, however, an intergovernmental body mandated to undertake only general reviews on the implementation of UNTOC and its Protocols. Even if at its next session the CoP will most likely mandate it with the country-based review mechanism referred to above, the mentioned weaknesses will significantly compromise the effectiveness and potential added-value of this mechanism.[32]

Another weakness relates to the limited scope of State responsibility under TCL, in line with the traditional concept of international law as an intra-State and State-centric system. As has been rightly pointed out, 'a major drawback to the law enforcement perspective [...] is that it only penalizes individual offenders. It does not address the role of the state or government officials in committing or tolerating trafficking'.[33] State responsibility may in principle only be found in relation to States' failure to comply with the criminalisation and judicial cooperation provisions of the Protocol. The much more important issue of States' responsibility for participating in or tolerating trafficking, or for failing to protect individuals from the action of traffickers, is not addressed under the Palermo Protocol.[34] Finally, under that same State-centric logic, no mechanism is established for individuals to bring complaints internationally against States for failure to comply with the Protocol.

Lastly, similar concerns can be raised in terms of transparency and participation. The engagement with civil society is generally weak. The Protocol requires States to cooperate with non-governmental organisations (NGOs) in limited areas and only 'in appropriate cases'.[35] Similarly, NGOs' participation in the works of the CoP is limited to plenary sessions, while they are excluded from participation in the WG on Trafficking in Persons' meetings, where substantive issues are discussed. Under the Palermo Protocol, there is indeed very little role to play for victims – and the non-governmental organisations that represent them – as rights-holders.

In conclusion, the Palermo Protocol remains a predominantly State-centric instrument that regulates trafficking from a State-to-State perspective, in line with other TCL treaties, failing to consider human rights concerns and

31 See above n. 20.

32 A. Gallagher, 'Human Rights and the New UN Protocols on Trafficking and Migrant Smuggling: A Preliminary Analysis' (2001) 23 *Human Rights Quarterly* 975, 1004, and, more recently, A. Gallagher, above n. 21, 22–23.

33 E.M. Bruch, above n. 3, 21.

34 Ibid.

35 Art. 6(3); see also Art. 9(3).

individuals as addressees of both primary and secondary norms. Now, the extent to which these limitations can be adequately addressed through the parallel application of international human rights norms will be explored.

2.2. INTERNATIONAL HUMAN RIGHTS LAW

Since the adoption of the Palermo Protocol in 2000, the need to add a human rights perspective to the fight against trafficking in persons has been articulated not only by UN treaty bodies and special procedures[36] but also by the General Assembly[37] and the Human Rights Council.[38] Clearly, the lack of integration of a human rights perspective into the international and national anti-trafficking legal response was identified as an issue of concern. Since its failed intent to integrate stronger human rights standards into the Palermo Protocol, IHRL has clearly taken action to fill existing gaps from the 'outside'. To a considerable extent, it has succeeded in this endeavour. This effort has materialised fundamentally in two different ways. On the one hand, with the adoption of a specialised soft law instrument on human rights and human trafficking, and, on the other hand, with the increasing engagement of human rights bodies with this issue. In both contexts, the due diligence standard[39] has been recognised as key in order to identify the extent to which IHRL creates state obligations in relation to human trafficking.[40]

---

36 See, e.g., UN Committee on Economic, Social and Cultural Rights 'Concluding observations: Germany' (2001), para. 25 and 43; UN Human Rights Committee 'Concluding observations: Czech Republic' (2001) CCPR/CO/72/CZE, para. 13; More recently, see UN Human Rights Committee 'Concluding observations: Barbados' (2007) CCPR/C/BRB/CO/3 para. 8; and UN Committee on the Elimination of Discrimination against Women 'Concluding Observations: Brazil' (2007) CEDAW/C/BRA/CO/6, para. 24. See further the UNHRC 'Report of the Special Rapporteur on trafficking in persons', A/HRC/10/16, para. 44 and the conclusions and recommendations at 25–27; and United Nations Commission on Human Rights (UNCHR) 'Report of the Special Rapporteur on trafficking in persons', E/CN.4/2005/71, paras 10–11 and 55–57.

37 See, e.g., United Nations General Assembly (UNGA) Res 63/156 (18.12.2008) UN Doc A/RES/63/156, UNGA Res 61/144 (19.12.2006) UN Doc A/RES/61/144, UNGA Res 59/166 (10.02.2005) UN Doc A/RES/59/166, UNGA Res 58/137 (22.12.2003) UN Doc A/RES/58/137 and UNGA Res 55/67 (31.01.2001) UN Doc A/RES/55/67.

38 See, e.g., UNCHR resolution 2000/44 (20.04.2000) UN Doc E/CN.4/RES/2000/44, para. 8; and UNHRC resolution 11/3 (17.06.2009) UN Doc A/HRC/RES/11/3, para. 1.

39 While the standard of due diligence developed in the field of diplomatic protection in relation to the duty of States to exercise due diligence in preventing and punishing harmful behaviours by non-State actors against foreigners, it later became a central element of IHRL in relation to States' 'due diligence' or 'positive' obligations to protect any individual from the acts of non-State actors.

40 See, e.g., the UNHRC 'Report of the Special Rapporteur on trafficking in persons', A/70/260, 2015, which analyses the implications of the due diligence standard in the area of human trafficking.

2.2.1. *Recommended Principles and Guidelines on Human Rights and Human Trafficking*

In 2002, OHCHR developed a set of principles and guidelines on human rights and human trafficking (Trafficking Principles and Guidelines).[41] In addition to the need to fill the gaps left by the Palermo Protocol, it is also argued that the Trafficking Principles and Guidelines respond to a weakness inherent to the human rights system that has already been referred to: the lack of clarity and indirect nature of international human rights standards applicable to trafficking. It that sense, there was a need to provide order and clarity within IHRL in order to afford all users, both rights-holders and duty-bearers, guidance on how human rights standards are directly applicable to a criminal activity as complex as human trafficking, mostly perpetrated by non-State actors.

Importantly, this soft law instrument went a step further and spelled out what is referred to as a 'human rights-based approach to trafficking'. Under that approach, IHRL not only provides a range of substantive standards, but also a conceptual and methodological framework for integrating human rights into legal and policy responses by other branches of law. As opposed to TCL, it puts the individual at the centre of all efforts to combat trafficking and affirms the primacy of human rights norms,[42] calling for a convergence of other branches of law under the overall guiding effect of human rights standards, as the Commentary to this instrument makes clear:

> Prioritizing human rights does not mean that other objectives or approaches are to be considered unimportant or invalid. For example, States remain entitled to develop strong criminal justice responses to trafficking. In fact, the Commentary identifies a number of specific obligations in this regard [...]. States also remain free, within the constraints imposed by international law, to develop migration strategies that seek to address trafficking. However, at each step of every response, the human rights impact of that step and of the overall response must be considered and monitored. The ultimate objective of responses to trafficking should be to protect individuals from trafficking-related violations of their human rights and to provide assistance when such violations are not – or cannot be – prevented.[43]

The Guidelines' declared purpose is to 'promote and facilitate the integration of a human rights perspective into national, regional and international

---

41 Recommended Principles and Guidelines on Human Rights and Human Trafficking, in UNCHR 'Report of the United Nations High Commissioner for Human Rights to the Economic and Social Council' (2002) E/2002/68/Add.1.

42 Principle 1.

43 OHCHR, 'Commentary to the Recommended Principles and Guidelines on Human Rights and Human Trafficking' (2010) HR/PUB/10/2 (Commentary to the Recommended Principles and Guidelines), 51.

anti-trafficking laws, policies and interventions'.[44] Via this instrument, IHRL clearly spells out its intention to integrate and influence other areas of law, in order to fill gaps in terms of human rights protection but also to exercise an overall guiding effect, by influencing the perspective taken to conceive, implement and evaluate legal and policy anti-trafficking responses.

The human rights-based approach (HRBA), which was first developed in the field of international development cooperation,[45] has two main components: a substantive and a methodological one. Applied to trafficking, the HRBA under its substantive component adopts the 'Three Ps' framework and develops it in a significantly more balanced way than the Palermo Protocol, recalling that 'States have a responsibility under international law to act with due diligence to prevent trafficking, to investigate and prosecute traffickers and to assist and protect trafficked persons'.[46] In terms of prevention, it requires addressing the root causes of this phenomenon, whereby a considerable part of State efforts should be geared towards removing the human rights violations that cause human trafficking in the first place, but also towards reducing demand for trafficking, raising awareness both among particularly vulnerable groups and the general public and eradicating public-sector involvement into trafficking. In terms of protection, this approach requires that priority be given to protecting and supporting individuals who have been trafficked. Key requirements in this regard are that States refrain from practices that infringe victims' rights,[47] that they provide protection and assistance[48] and that they guarantee a safe and preferably voluntary return,[49] in which specific rights are to be accorded to children.[50] Thirdly, the criminal justice response remains a crucial component of the anti-trafficking response.[51] It must, however, be addressed in a fundamentally different manner than under TCL: through integrating the rights of victims to participation, protection, assistance and redress at all stages of criminal justice interventions.

Turning to the second aspect, the HRBA provides a methodological framework that provides guidance on how to design, implement and evaluate anti-trafficking responses. In short, interventions should: (1) be directed towards identifying rights-holders and duty-bearers and towards strengthening

---

44 Ibid., 15.
45 See OHCHR, 'Frequently Asked Questions on a Human Rights-based Approach to International Development Cooperation' (2006) HR/PUB/06/8; see also United Nations Development Group, 'United Nations Agencies Statement of Common Understanding on the Human Rights Based Approach to Development Cooperation' (2003).
46 Principle 2.
47 Principle 7.
48 Principles 8 and 9 and related Guidelines.
49 Principle 11.
50 Principle 10 and related Guidelines.
51 Principles 12–17.

their capacity to secure their rights and meet their obligations respectively; and (2) be guided by core principles and standards derived from IHRL: equality and non-discrimination, universality of all rights, participation, accountability and the rule of law.[52] What are some of the practical implications of this methodological approach? For instance, the accountability principle requires strengthening accountability mechanisms, judicial, quasi-judicial and administrative, while the participation principles requires ensuring that relevant stakeholders (victims, civil society organisations etc.) be allowed actively to participate in anti-trafficking programming, for them to have 'genuine ownership and control'[53] over these policies. Participation and accountability, as all other core principles, are an objective as well as a means: they should be included as policy objectives but also as a procedural requirement to be integrated in decision-making processes at both national and international levels.[54]

Since their adoption, the Trafficking Principles and Guidelines have been referred to as an essential tool for integrating human rights law into anti-trafficking policies, including by the General Assembly.[55] Importantly, the WG on Trafficking in Persons established by the CoP refers to it as an instrument that was 'produced to support the implementation of the Trafficking in Persons Protocol', encouraging States parties to make better use of it.[56] It also adds: 'With regard to developing a comprehensive, multidimensional response to trafficking in persons, States parties should apply a victim-centred approach, with full respect for the human rights of victims of such trafficking.'[57] If this position is considered as manifesting a 'subsequent practice between the parties' regarding the interpretation of the Protocol under Article 31(3) of the Vienna Convention on the Law of Treaties (VCLT), this would be a key element in order to establish the extent to which States parties have a duty to adopt a HRBA when interpreting and implementing the Protocol.[58] However, this hypothesis may be seriously

---

52 For a detailed analysis of the human rights-based approach to trafficking, see the 'Commentary to the Recommended Principles and Guidelines', in particular the introduction to this concept at 49–51.

53 See OHCHR, above n. 45, 26.

54 See Guideline 1, paras 2, 7 and 8.

55 See, e.g., UNGA Res 68/192 (18.12.2013) UN Doc A/RES/68/192, as follows: 'Stressing the need to promote and protect the rights of victims of trafficking in persons and to reintegrate victims into the community, including by taking into account, where appropriate, the Recommended Principles and Guidelines on Human Rights and Human Trafficking [...]': Preamble, Recital 20. This same wording is also to be found in UNGA Res 70/179 (17.12.2015) UN Doc A/RES/70/179, Preamble, Recital 23.

56 CoP to UNTOC, Report of the Working Group on Trafficking in Persons, CTOC/COP/WG.4/2010/6, 17.02.2010, para. 8.

57 Ibid., para. 9.

58 In the context of its ongoing work on the issue of 'Subsequent agreement and subsequent practice in relation to the interpretation of treaties', the ILC upholds that 'decisions of Conferences of States Parties may embody under certain circumstances subsequent

undermined by what appears to be a decreasing engagement of the CoP with the WG's recommendations. Worryingly, while, in its Resolution 5/2 of 2010 devoted to human trafficking, the CoP welcomes the recommendations adopted up to that time by the WG, in 2012 the CoP fails to adopt a specific resolution on trafficking and, in its final report of the session, only welcomes the activities and debates of the WG.[59] Finally, in 2014 and 2016, the CoP does not take any position on the WG's recommendations: it only decides that the WG should continue its work and, in the summary of its deliberations, merely indicates that many States welcomed the recommendations of the WG.[60]

2.2.2. Human Rights Bodies

In the last two decades, both UN treaty bodies and special procedures have increasingly addressed States' obligations in relation to human trafficking, clarifying the extent to which this phenomenon constitutes a human rights violation. While in some cases it has been considered a violation of the prohibition of trafficking as such, in many others it has been addressed as a violation of other rights, such as the prohibition of slavery, servitude and forced labour, the prohibition of violence against women or the prohibition of torture. Also, their role has been relevant in confirming the existence and scope of 'positive obligations' or 'due diligence obligations', which were initially identified by the European Court of Human Rights (ECtHR) as requiring States to provide 'practical and effective protection'[61] even 'in the sphere of the relations of individuals between themselves'.[62]

Following the way paved by the ECtHR, the Inter-American Court of Human Rights (IACtHR) stated in its first case that Article 1 of the American Convention on Human Rights requires States Parties not only to 'respect' but also to 'guarantee' the rights recognised in the Convention.[63] Thus 'the State is obligated to prevent, investigate and punish human rights violations',[64] but this obligation is not limited to State conduct:

> An illegal act which violates human rights and which is initially not directly imputable to a State (for example, because it is the act of a private person or because the person responsible has not been identified) can lead to international responsibility of the State,

agreements under Art. 31(3)(a), and give rise to subsequent practice under Art. 31(3)(b), or to other subsequent practice under Art. 32 if they do not reflect agreement of the parties': ILC Report, A/69/10, 2014, chap. VII, para. 76(23).

59 CoP to UNTOC, Report on its sixth session (2012), CTOC/COP/2012/15, p. 6.

60 CoP to UNTOC, Report on its seventh session (2014), CTOC/COP/2014/13, pp. 5 and 28, and Report on its eighth session (2016), CTOC/COP/2016/15, p. 33.

61 *X and Y v. Netherlands*, no. 8978/80, ECHR, judgment of 26 March 1985, para. 23.

62 Ibid., para. 30.

63 *Velasquez Rodriguez v. Honduras*, IACtHR, judgment of 29 July 1988, para. 164.

64 Ibid., para. 172.

not because of the act itself, but because of the lack of due diligence to prevent the violation or to respond to it as required by the Convention.[65]

In this context, UN treaty bodies have played a considerable role in developing this concept and describing how it is applicable to trafficking. In 1992, the Committee on the Elimination of Discrimination against Women (CEDAW) adopted General Recommendation n. 19 on 'Violence against women', which refers to trafficking as a practice that is incompatible with the equal enjoyment of rights by women, since it puts them at special risk of violence and abuse.[66] It then underscores that 'States may be responsible for private acts if they fail to act with due diligence to prevent violations of rights or to investigate and punish acts of violence, and for providing compensation'.[67] General Recommendation n. 28, adopted in 2010, reaffirms this principle, adding that 'appropriate measures States parties are obliged to take include the regulation of the activities of private actors in regard to education, employment and health policies and practices, working conditions and work standards [...]'.[68] In a number of decisions taken on individual complaints relating to the domestic violence – the death of women at the hands of their husbands or of girls at the hands of their fathers –, the Committee reaffirmed the central importance of the obligation to act in accordance with the due diligence standard in order effectively to prevent violence against women as a particularly serious manifestation of discrimination against women, and elaborates on the measures that States should adopt to that effect.[69] Also, CEDAW addresses human trafficking obligations extensively in its concluding observations to States.[70]

---

65 Ibid. For an analysis of human rights due diligence, see R. Pisillo Mazzeschi, 'Responsabilité de l'Etat pour violation des obligations positives relatives aux droits de l'homme' (2008) 333 *Recueil des Cours de l'Académie de Droit International* 175, 175–506; V. Waisman, 'Human Trafficking: State Obligations to Protect Victims' Rights, the Current Framework and a New Due Diligence Standard' (2010) 33 *Hastings International & Comparative Law Review* 385; G. Khrystova, 'State Positive Obligations and Due Diligence in Human Rights Domestic Violence Perspective' (2014) 1(5) *European Political and Law Discourse* 109; and A. Gallagher, above n. 1, pp. 235–51.

66 CEDAW, General Recommendation n. 19 (1992) UN Doc A/47/38, para. 14.

67 Ibid., para. 9.

68 CEDAW, General Recommendation n. 28 (2010) UN Doc CEDAW/C/2010/47/GC.2, para. 13.

69 See *Goekce v. Austria*, communication 5/2005 (2007) CEDAW/C/39/D/5/2005, paras 12.1.1–12.3; *Yildirim v. Austria*, communication 6/2005 (2007) CEDAW/C/39/D/6/2005, paras 12.1.1–12.3: and, more recently, *González Carreño v. Spain*, comunication 47/2012 (2014) CEDAW/C/58/D/47/2012, paras 9.9 and 11. Also, of particular interest is the dissenting opinion by three members of the Committee to the inadmissibility decision in the *Zhen Zhen Zheng case* on the failure to provide asylum based on allegations of trafficking, where the three members elaborate on the State due diligence obligation to provide specific protection and assistance to women who are potential victims of trafficking; *Zhen Zhen Zheng v. Netherlands*, communication 15/2007 (2007) CEDAW/C/42/D/15/2007, individual opinion, para. 8.

70 See CEDAW, 'Concluding observations on Pakistan' (2013) UN Doc CEDAW/C/PAK/CO/4, para. 14; CEDAW, 'Concluding observations on Mexico' (2012) UN Doc CEDAW/C/MEX/CO/7-8,

Even if trafficking is not explicitly mentioned in Article 8 of the International Covenant on Civil and Political Rights[71] which prohibits slavery, servitude and forced labour, the Human Rights Committee has formally stated that, under that article, States should report on their efforts to eliminate trafficking,[72] thus recognising that the prohibition of trafficking falls under the scope of Article 8. The Committee also clarified the scope of States' positive obligations in relation to all rights enshrined in the Covenant.[73] The Committee on Torture reached the same conclusion in General Comment n. 2, where it recalls that it has applied the due diligence duty to trafficking cases:

> Since the failure of the State to exercise due diligence to intervene, to stop, sanction and provide remedies to victims of torture facilitates and enables non-State actors to commit acts impermissible under the Convention with impunity, the State's indifference or inaction provides a form of encouragement and/or de facto permission. The Committee has applied this principle to States parties' failure to prevent and protect victims from gender-based violence, such as rape, domestic violence, female genital mutilation, and trafficking.[74]

A number of recent Concluding Observations issued by other treaty monitoring bodies, for example the CRC[75] and CMW,[76] include recommendations to States that reflect a due diligence duty and a HRBA to trafficking. Similarly, reports by the Special Rapporteur on trafficking, both thematic and country specific,[77] provide in-depth guidance to both rights-holders and duty-bearers on how IHRL rights and obligations are relevant to trafficking. Of particular relevance is the latest report by the Special Rapporteur on trafficking, entirely devoted to examining the relevance of the due diligence standard in the area of human trafficking and its implications in terms of human rights obligations.[78]

---

para. 12; CEDAW, 'Concluding observations on India' (2010) UN Doc CEDAW/C/IND/CO/SP.1, paras 12–19.

71 International Covenant on Civil and Political Rights (adopted 16 December 1966, entered into force 23 March 1976) 999 UNTS 13971.

72 Human Rights Committee (HRC), General Comment n. 28 (2000) UN Doc CCPR/C/21/Rev.1/Add.10, para. 12.

73 HRC, General Comment n. 31 (2004) UN Doc CCPR/C/21/Rev.1/Add.13, para. 8.

74 Committee on Torture (CAT), General Comment n. 2 (2008), UN Doc CAT/C/GC/2, para. 18.

75 See, for instance, CRC, 'Concluding Observations on Liberia' (2012) UN Doc CRC/C/LBR/CO/2-4, paras 81 and 82; and CRC, 'Concluding Observations on Albania' (2012) UN Doc CRC/C/ALB/CO/2-4, paras 81, 82 and 83.

76 See, for instance, CMW, 'Concluding Observations on Mexico' (2011) UN Doc CMW/C/MEX/CO/2, paras 41, 42, 49 and 50.

77 Country reports are available at <http://www.ohchr.org/EN/Issues/Trafficking/Pages/visits.aspx>. Thematic reports on issues such as measures to discourage demand or effective remedies for trafficking victims, are available at <http://www.ohchr.org/EN/Issues/Trafficking/Pages/Annual.aspx>, accessed 19.03.2018.

78 UNHRC, 'Report of the Special Rapporteur on trafficking in persons', above n. 40.

2.2.3. *The 2014 Protocol to the ILO Forced Labour Convention*

While the 2014 Protocol to the ILO Forced Labour Convention[79] was adopted in order to clarify the scope of States' obligations on the elimination of forced labour, it also applies to trafficking in persons for the purpose of labour exploitation.[80] This protocol deserves a brief mention, as it strikes a very different balance between the 'Three Ps' than the Palermo Protocol: indeed, it establishes broad prevention and protection obligations as mandatory requirements, in order to complement the old 1930 convention framework that, similarly to 20th-century anti-trafficking conventions, was based predominantly on criminal law measures.

In affirming that 'measures of prevention, protection, and remedies, such as compensation and rehabilitation, are necessary to achieve the effective and sustained suppression of forced or compulsory labour', it establishes the duty to adopt 'effective measures for the identification, release, protection, recovery and rehabilitation of all victims of forced or compulsory labour, as well as the provision of other forms of assistance and support'.[81] It also requires States to ensure that national authorities are entitled not to prosecute or sanction victims for unlawful activities they were compelled to commit, and to guarantee to victims, irrespective of their presence or status in the territory, access to effective remedies.[82] While this Protocol addresses some of the main shortcomings of the Palermo Protocol, it comes as a confirmation that the need to integrate a human rights perspective into the anti-trafficking international legal framework is also increasingly being recognised at the universal level. However, this recognition is still weak as, four years after the adoption of the Protocol, only 22 States have ratified it, of which 15 are European States that were already bound by this approach under European law.

3. INTEGRATION AT THE EUROPEAN LEVEL

3.1. THE COUNCIL OF EUROPE ANTI-TRAFFICKING CONVENTION

Dissatisfied with the approach adopted in the Palermo Protocol, Member States of the Council of Europe embarked on the negotiation of a regional

79 Protocol of 2014 to the Forced Labour Convention of 1930 (adopted 11 June 2014, entered into force 9 November 2016), n. P029.

80 Art. 1(3).

81 Art. 3.

82 Art. 4. On this Protocol, see L. Swepston, 'Trafficking and Forced Labour: Filling in the Gaps with the Adoption of the Supplementary ILO Standards, 2014', in P. Kotiswaran (Ed.), *Revisiting the Law and Governance of Trafficking, Forced Labour and Modern Slavery*, Cambridge University Press, Cambridge 2017, pp. 395–421.

anti-trafficking treaty 'geared towards the protection of victims' rights and the respect for human rights, and aiming at a proper balance between matters concerning human rights and prosecution'.[83] The intention to complement the Palermo Protocol with a convention strongly focused on the protection of victims' rights was clear from the beginning.[84] The European Trafficking Convention, adopted in 2005, is widely considered to be the most advanced and comprehensive treaty currently addressing human trafficking.

3.1.1. *The Three Ps*

The main three purposes of the Convention reflect the by then well-established 'Three Ps' framework: to prevent trafficking, to protect the human rights of victims, and to prosecute trafficking effectively.[85] A key added value of the Convention is the recognition that human trafficking constitutes a violation of human rights and an offence to the dignity and integrity of the human being.[86] In this context, the Convention includes a comprehensive framework for the protection and assistance of victims, including, on the appropriate identification of victims,[87] the provision of assistance irrespective of the fact that they agree to act as witnesses,[88] the granting of a reflection period of at least 30 days in which victims cannot be forcibly returned,[89] a framework for the granting of residence permits[90] and a broad range of assistance requirements.[91] Also, the Convention recognises the importance of avoiding criminalisation of victims of trafficking.[92]

In terms of prevention, the Convention sets out a broad range of measures and requires States to adopt a HRBA in their development, implementation and assessment.[93] Among others, it calls upon States to undertake research, training and education activities,[94] to enable migration to take place legally[95] and details a

---

83 Council of Europe, Steering Committee for Equality between Women and Men, 'Feasibility Study for a Convention of the Council of Europe on Trafficking in Human Beings', Doc. DG-11 (2002), p. 5. See also 'Explanatory Report on the Council of Europe Convention on Action against Trafficking in Human Beings' (2005), Annex to the Convention (European Trafficking Convention Explanatory Report), para. 29.

84 European Trafficking Convention Explanatory Report, para. 30. See also Art. 39 of the Convention.

85 Art. 1(1).

86 Recital 3 of the Preamble.

87 Art. 11(1) and (2).

88 Art. 12(6).

89 Art. 13.

90 Art. 14.

91 Art. 12(1).

92 Art. 26.

93 Art. 5(3).

94 Art. 5(2).

95 Art. 5(4).

set of measures that States shall adopt in order to discourage demand.[96] In terms of criminal justice, the adoption of a human rights focus has not been made at the expenses of the criminal justice and border control aspects of trafficking, since the two chapters devoted to these issues include a comprehensive range of obligations that are almost identical to those in the Palermo Protocol, with some important extensions.[97]

3.1.2. Accountability and Participation

Another key aspect of the Convention is that, for the first time, an advanced monitoring mechanism with features that are distinctive of IHRL is included in a human trafficking specialised treaty. The Group of Experts on action against trafficking in human beings (GRETA), established under the Convention, undertakes country evaluation rounds in which each State's performance is assessed, including through country visits and ample participation by civil society organisations. Country reports are particularly detailed and thorough in their analysis, providing a very useful tool for the assessment of the degree of implementation of States' obligations under the Convention. Indeed, they are more exhaustive than UN human rights bodies' reports. However, in comparison with UN bodies, GRETA lacks the capacity to receive individual complaints. Nevertheless, this weakness may potentially be outweighed by the role the ECtHR has started assuming in ruling on human trafficking cases.

Indeed, the ECtHR has done so in 2010 in *Rantsev*,[98] a landmark case in which the Court has, for the first time, found a State party responsible for a failure to comply with its obligations arising under the ECHR[99] in relation to human trafficking. While Cyprus and Russia were not directly responsible for the exploitation and death of Ms Rantseva, a young Russian woman trafficked to Cyprus, they were nevertheless found responsible for violating their positive obligations in relation to human trafficking. Despite the fact that Article 4 of the ECHR, on the prohibition of slavery, servitude and forced labour, does not refer to human trafficking, the Court stated that, since the ECHR is a living instrument that must be interpreted in the light of present-day conditions:[100]

> trafficking itself, within the meaning of Article 3(a) of the Palermo Protocol and Article 4(a) of the [European] Anti-Trafficking Convention, falls within the scope of Article 4 of the Convention.[101]

---

96 Art. 6.
97 A. Gallagher, above n. 1, pp. 121–22.
98 *Rantsev v. Cyprus and Russia*, no. 25965/04, ECHR, judgment of 7 January 2010 (*Rantsev*).
99 Convention for the Protection of Human Rights and Fundamental Freedoms (European Convention on Human Rights, as amended) (ECHR).
100 *Rantsev*, above n. 98, para. 277.
101 Ibid., para. 282.

While a judgment by the Court stating that trafficking violated the Convention is especially welcome, the reasoning followed by the Court in *Rantsev* lacks clarity and coherence. First, it states that trafficking 'is based on the exercise of powers attaching to the right of ownership', which amounts to saying that trafficking is a form of slavery, an arbitrary limitation when one considers that the trafficking definition encompasses many other practices different from slavery. Yet, immediately after the Court states that trafficking itself violates Article 4, without the need to ascertain whether it constitutes slavery, servitude or forced labour. Here, in sharp contradiction with its previous assertion, it expands the scope of Article 4 beyond its textual boundaries, to make it applicable to all other forms of exploitation included in the definition of trafficking.[102] But can the Court safely assert that all forms of trafficking, including trafficking for organ removal, fall within the scope of Article 4? Indeed, instead of clarifying the links between trafficking and the conduct prohibited under Article 4, the Court simply 'avoided the issue by declining to say precisely how trafficking of human beings is a violation of article 4'.[103] This part of the Court's reasoning fails to promote legal certainty and brings with it questions regarding the understanding by the Court of what human trafficking actually is.[104] In its subsequent judgments on human trafficking, the Court fails to bring in further elements of clarification.[105] It is only in *Chowdury and others v. Greece*[106] that the ECtHR establishes a link between human trafficking and forced labour. However, even in this judgment, a clear explanation of how trafficking relates to forced labour is not provided, while a tendency to assimilate the two concepts prevails.[107]

Despite these weaknesses in the *Rantsev* judgment, it is undeniable that the consequences that the Court attaches to this finding are indeed significant when identifying the scope of States' anti-trafficking obligations. While, in a previous case on Article 4 in which it found France responsible for violating its positive obligations under the prohibition on servitude and forced labour, the Court focused exclusively on its failure to adopt an appropriate criminal

---

102 See J. Allain, 'Rantsev v Cyprus and Russia: The European Court of Human Rights and Trafficking as Slavery' (2010) 10(3) *Human Rights Law Review* 546, 555.

103 R. Piotrowicz, 'Statess' Obligations under Human Rights Law towards Victims of Trafficking in Human Beings: Positive Developments in Positive Obligations' (2012) 26(2) *International Journal of Refugee Law* 181, 196.

104 In this context, Jean Allain questions the 'very narrow understanding of trafficking' by the Court and the 'very ability of the Court to adjudicate over issues emanating from Article 4 of the ECHR', in J. Allain, above n. 102, 546 and 557.

105 See *L.E. v. Greece*, no. 71545/12, ECHR, judgment of 21 January 2016 (*L.E.*). On this judgment, see V. Milano, 'The European Court of Human Rights' Case Law on Human Trafficking in Light of L.E. v. Greece: a Disturbing Setback?' (2016) 17(4) *Human Rights Law Review* 701, 709.

106 *Chowdury and others v. Greece*, no. 21884/15, ECHR, judgment of 30 March 2017 (*Chowdury*).

107 For an analysis of this aspect of the judgment, in light of the rest of the ECtHR's human trafficking case law, see V. Milano, 'Uncovering labour exploitation: lights and shadows of the latest European Court of Human Rights' case law on human trafficking' (2017) 21 *Spanish Yearbook of International Law* 83, 83–94.

law framework to deter and punish the relevant conducts,[108] in *Rantsev* it went further and endorsed a much broader concept of positive obligations in relation to trafficking,[109] based on the 'Three Ps' framework:

> The Court observes that the Palermo Protocol and the Anti-Trafficking Convention refer to the need for a comprehensive approach to combat trafficking which includes measures to prevent trafficking and to protect victims, in addition to measures to punish traffickers. It is clear from the provisions of these two instruments that the Contracting States, including almost all of the member States of the Council of Europe, have formed the view that only a combination of measures addressing all three aspects can be effective in the fight against trafficking [...]. Accordingly, the duty to penalise and prosecute trafficking is only one aspect of member States' general undertaking to combat trafficking. The extent of the positive obligations arising under Article 4 must be considered within this broader context.[110]

Therefore, in addition to criminal law measures to punish traffickers, States are required to 'put in place adequate measures regulating businesses often used as a cover for human trafficking' and that 'a State's immigration rules must address relevant concerns relating to encouragement, facilitation or tolerance of trafficking'.[111] In addition, States shall adopt measures to remove individuals from situations of risk in which they are 'aware, or ought to have been aware, of circumstances giving rise to a credible suspicion that an identified individual had been, or was at real and immediate risk of being, trafficked or exploited'.[112] It thus applies to a human trafficking case its well-established theory of foreseeable risk – also referred to as the 'Osman test' – that describes the circumstances under which the Court considers that a State has failed in its positive – or due diligence – obligations.[113] However, a difference in wording appears to reveal an increase in the level of diligence required from States in this context: while, in *Osman*,[114] the Court required that authorities knew or ought to have known of the 'existence' of a real and immediate risk to the individual in order for the duty to take protective measures to be triggered, what is required in *Rantsev* is awareness of 'circumstances giving rise to a credible suspicion' of

---

108 *Siliadin v. France*, no. 73316/01, ECHR, judgment of 26 July 2005 (*Siliadin*).

109 For an analysis of the *Rantsev* judgment and the scope of States' positive obligations in relation to human trafficking under human rights law, see R. Piotrowicz, above n. 103, 181–201.

110 *Rantsev*, above n. 98, para. 285.

111 Ibid., para. 284.

112 Ibid., para. 286.

113 For a critical appraisal of the '*Osman* test' and its development in the recent case law of the ECtHR and the IACtHR, see F.C. Ebert and R.I. Sijniensky, 'Preventing Violations of the Right to Life in the European and Inter-American Systems: From the Osman Test to a Coherent Doctrine on Risk Prevention?' (2015) 15(2) *Human Rights Law Review* 343, 343–68.

114 *Osman v. UK*, no. 23452/94, ECHR, judgment of 28 October 1998, para. 116.

that risk. In the opinion of the author, this more flexible concept is rightly aimed at addressing the specific features of human trafficking, in which States – claiming their ignorance – too often fail to take action with regard to individual situations that respond to well-known trafficking patterns. Finally, the Court interpreted the duty to investigate human rights violations as including the obligation not only to investigate events occurring in their own territory but also to cooperate with authorities of other States where trafficking offences have taken place.[115]

Regrettably, in its subsequent judgments the Court has largely failed to consolidate this broad understanding of States' positive obligations, showing a worrying regressive trend on a number of important aspects. In particular on States' duties to establish a legal and administrative framework to prevent and criminalise trafficking and to protect its victims, but also to a certain extent in relation to States' duties to take operational measures to protect victims and to investigate and prosecute trafficking offences.[116]

In sum, in the framework of the European human rights system, the European continent is in principle well equipped to address human trafficking from a holistic and human rights-based perspective: it has the most advanced anti-trafficking convention, an expert monitoring body that conducts in-depth country reviews, and a human rights court that has – even with significant limitations – paved the way to an emerging case law that might adequately complement GRETA's focus on States' broad duties in the area of trafficking. Hopefully, this framework will be used to its full potential. For this to happen, the ECtHR should improve its capacity to truly engage with a human rights-based approach to trafficking as required under European law.

3.2. THE EUROPEAN ANTI-TRAFFICKING DIRECTIVE

A similar development also materialised within the European Union (EU), but through a lengthier process and with different results on a number of issues. Two years after the Palermo Protocol, the EU adopted a Framework Decision on human trafficking[117] that was supposed to go 'considerably further than the UN Protocol on trafficking in persons'.[118] However, the final text focused almost exclusively on establishing standards for a common criminal law framework. It was only in 2011 that the EU changed its approach with the adoption of Directive 2011/36/EU, in which the protection and recognition of the human

[115] *Rantsev*, above n. 98, para. 289.

[116] See V. Milano, above n. 105, 709–27; V. Milano, above n. 107, 95–115.

[117] Council Framework Decision of 19 July 2002 on combating trafficking in human beings (2002), 2002/629/JHA, OJ L203, 1–4.

[118] European Commission, 'EU urges Higher priority on Trafficking in Women and Children', Press release IP/01/325, 07.03.2001.

rights of trafficking victims becomes a central focus in the fight against what is defined as 'a serious crime' and 'a gross violation of fundamental rights'.[119]

With the adoption of Directive 2011/36/EU, the EU declares embracing 'an integrated, holistic, and human rights approach to the fight against trafficking in human beings'.[120] The Directive is also structured around the 'Three Ps' framework. However, the way in which the three aspects are integrated is different compared with that in the European Convention. Overall, a tendency to prioritise a criminal law focus is apparent. First, the granting of a reflection period to victims of trafficking who have been identified remains conditional upon the victim's cooperation in criminal proceedings. On this aspect, criminal and human rights law have failed to converge. Secondly, prevention aspects are covered in a rather more succinct way, with a single provision devoted to them. Thirdly, accountability mechanisms established under the Directive are sensibly weaker. On the one hand, no country-based international review mechanism such as GRETA is established – only a coordination body: the EU Anti-Trafficking Coordinator. However, in order to address this weakness, the EU will most probably rely on evaluation work done by GRETA, as confirmed by the Council of the European Union in its call to the European Commission to make full use of GRETA's evaluation reports, in order to avoid unnecessary duplication.[121] On the other hand, victims who find themselves under the jurisdiction of both the EU Directive and the European Trafficking Convention will find it more beneficial to rely on the Convention in order to claim their rights, not only because its provisions provide a broader spectrum of guarantees in terms of victims' rights, but also because, upon exhaustion of domestic remedies, they could directly challenge States' violations before the ECtHR, while the EU system does not allow individuals to bring cases on States' infringements of EU law before the Court of Justice of the European Union (CJEU).[122]

Overall, the commitment to a holistic HRBA to trafficking is weaker at the EU level than in the context of the Council of Europe, which indeed creates a certain perplexity in light of the fact that these two systems are closely linked in terms of human rights protection requirements.[123]

119 Recital 1 of the Directive's Preamble.

120 Recital 7 of the Directive's Preamble.

121 Group of Experts on Action against Trafficking in Human Beings (GRETA), 'Third general report' (2003), 5. See also Recital 9 of the Directive's Preamble.

122 The two mechanisms that may allow an individual to get a CJEU ruling against a State for an infringement of EU law are indirect: an individual can either inform the European Commission of a possible infringement, where the Commission will decide whether to bring an action before the Court against that State for failure to fulfil EU obligations, or seize national courts exhorting them to refer the issue to the CJEU under the preliminary ruling procedure.

123 For an analysis of the post-Lisbon different layers of fundamental rights in the EU and their relationship, see W. Weiss, 'Human Rights in the EU: Rethinking the Role of the European Convention on Human Rights After Lisbon' (2011) 7 *European Constitutional Law Review* 64, 64–95.

4. CONCLUSIONS ON THE INTERACTION BETWEEN INTERNATIONAL HUMAN RIGHTS LAW AND TRANSNATIONAL CRIMINAL LAW

4.1. CONVERGENCE AND GAP-FILLING EFFECTS

Eighteen years ago, the process of convergence between IHRL and TCL started with the adoption of the Palermo Protocol. In this short period of time, the international law of human trafficking has changed dramatically. Both at universal and regional level, new instruments, new case law and new monitoring bodies have significantly enhanced the capacity of international law to respond to this phenomenon. The leading roles have been played by IHRL and TCL. More than fifteen years later, what conclusions can be reached on the interaction between these two branches of law?

Progressive convergence between the two is the most significant and positive element. As has just been mentioned, this convergence has generated significant positive developments in a relatively short period of time. In this context, what have been the respective roles of these two branches of law, in particular in complementing each other by filling respective gaps? Undoubtedly, IHRL has had a predominant gap-filling role towards TCL, aimed at addressing a series of long-lasting loopholes in this regime. First and foremost, IHRL fills a particularly significant gap in terms of victims' protection, the area in which TCL has shown its most patent deficiencies. However, it also fills other gaps: it calls for a much stronger response in terms of prevention, showing how human rights violations that constitute the root causes of trafficking should be addressed. Finally, it fills two other important gaps inherent to TCL. First, IHRL promotes State accountability, through constant monitoring by human rights bodies at national, regional and international levels. Also, while TCL reflects the limitations of State responsibility under general international law, 'a law created for states by states within a state-based legal framework',[124] IHRL breaks these rules: it identifies wide-ranging obligations for States, in particular positive or due diligence obligations, that identify the individual as the central beneficiary, and enables individuals to hold States accountable for these obligations before international bodies. Secondly, IHRL promotes civil society participation at national and international levels.

Importantly, these contributions of IHRL are to its own benefit as much as they are to the benefit of TCL's fundamental purpose: the arrest and prosecution of traffickers. Victims are key to criminal investigations: they have first-hand

---

124 R. McCorquodale, 'Impact on State Responsibility' in M. Kamminga and M. Scheinin, *The Impact of Human Rights Law on General International Law*, Oxford University Press, Oxford 2009, p. 254.

knowledge on traffickers' identity, routes and methods. But greater victims' participation in investigations and judicial proceedings is possible only if victims feel adequately protected and assisted and respectfully involved in the process. In sum, IHRL provides significant input for a more holistic and potentially more effective anti-trafficking response. Surely, its main distinctive feature is the central role of the individual, the rights-holder, both as a recipient of human rights protection and as an empowered actor who has a role to play in the investigation and prosecution of traffickers and, more broadly, in terms of participation and accountability mechanisms.

In turn, does TCL also have a gap-filling effect on IHRL? Probably the strongest such effect is to give teeth to the anti-trafficking response in terms of providing effective tools to combat and prosecute crime on the ground, where human rights law lacks these teeth and has been referred to as a 'precious but blunted sword'.[125] While the international human rights system amply demonstrated over many years that, on its own, it was incapable of taking any serious step towards eliminating trafficking and other forms of private exploitation, its convergence – to different extents – with TCL in a number of instruments adopted over the past 15 years has given human rights law new impetus and sharper tools with which to work.[126] Detailed provisions on fundamental issues such as mutual legal assistance, criminal jurisdiction and criminal sanctions or the seizure of traffickers' assets would not have been included under a uniquely human rights instrument. The law enforcement aspects of fighting trafficking are fundamental, both for States and for victims, and TCL's role is essential to advance this cause.

In sum, these two distinct branches are mutually reinforcing.[127] It is therefore fundamental, in terms of international law coherence and efficiency, further to develop this ongoing convergence in order to achieve a holistic and more effective international law response to this phenomenon. In that context, significant differences can be appreciated in the way this convergence is materialising at universal and regional European levels.

At the universal level, the formal integration of these branches into a single instrument, the Palermo Protocol, has been achieved only to a limited extent. In that context, it is argued that a satisfactory degree of convergence is, however, being achieved 'from the outside'. The adoption of the Trafficking Principles and Guidelines and the interpretative work of human rights monitoring bodies both provide guidance on how obligations under IHRL complement the obligations spelled out in the Palermo Protocol. The 2014 Protocol to the ILO Forced Labour Convention comes as a further recognition that, today, international law

125 A. Gallagher, above n. 1, p. 5.
126 Ibid.
127 See T. Obokata, above n. 24, p. 179.

increasingly calls for a 'Three Ps' approach that strikes a proper balance between criminal law and human rights protection aspects.

Undoubtedly, the effective implementation by duty-bearers of this integrated approach is a different issue that depends on a range of factors – not least their political will. However, one of these factors is also legal clarity: the fact that one needs to rely on a fragmented normative framework does not well serve end-users. Understanding the extent to which IHRL is relevant to trafficking is still an excessively cumbersome process for end users, who must refer to a particularly broad array of instruments and mechanisms. In addition, not all States have ratified all instruments, which constitutes an additional shortcoming of this fragmented scenario.

At European level, the clear intention to address the weaknesses of the Protocol has led to the adoption of comprehensive anti-trafficking instruments in which criminal and human rights approaches are included in a much more balanced way. While the EU Directive represents a positive shift towards a more balanced EU anti-trafficking policy, the Council of Europe Convention has achieved a higher degree of convergence between the two disciplines, in terms of both substance and form. In terms of substance, a more adequate balance between matters concerning human rights and prosecution has been achieved. In addition, issues of accountability and participation are quite extensively addressed. In terms of format, both regulatory frameworks are integrated into a single instrument. From a user's perspective, this appears to be a preferable approach: instead of having to come to terms with a highly fragmented landscape, the comprehensive set of rights and obligations applicable to trafficking is clearly spelled out in a single instrument, where both criminal law and human rights law are integrated and conflicting provisions avoided *ab initio*, at least to a certain extent. In addition, accountability and participation mechanisms are readily available through two bodies, as opposed to the vast array of UN mechanisms relevant to trafficking.

4.2. IS TRANSNATIONAL CRIMINAL LAW – AND NATIONAL CRIMINAL LAW – IN A PROCESS OF TRANSFORMATION UNDER THE INFLUENCE OF INTERNATIONAL HUMAN RIGHTS LAW?

4.2.1. Expanding or Narrowing Effect?

Probably the most significant change that national and transnational criminal law have witnessed in the last few decades has been the irruption of the victim into its realm. Victims – traditionally absent – are now increasingly accorded a relevant role under criminal law, not only as witnesses but, most importantly, as victims whose protection and access to effective remedies should be guaranteed.

This significant change has been determined by IHRL, as a direct consequence of its evolution, in particular in relation to positive obligations. As Judge Tulkens very well explains, while human rights law only related to criminal law with a shield function, i.e. a function of neutralising the negative impact of the use or abuse by States of criminal law on individual freedoms, human rights gradually assumed another function: that of a sword that urges States to use criminal law and powers to protect individuals from human rights abuses committed by non-State actors.[128] In Europe, the role of the ECtHR in this process has been significant, as it has called upon States to make use of criminal justice systems to protect the most essential values, such as the right to life, to freedom from torture and to private life,[129] and, more recently, to freedom from servitude and trafficking.[130]

This results in a considerable expanding effect on criminal law. While IHRL traditionally tended to narrow the scope of criminal law, through the emergence of this second function it now expands it. It adds to its principal crime prosecution purpose a second one: the protection of individuals from human rights abuses. However, what remains unclear is whether this expansion also affects TCL or only national criminal law. Indeed, if, under the sword function, 'international human rights law has drawn national criminal law into its ambit',[131] does it mean that it is in fact taking over a number of functions previously assumed by TCL? In other words, the fact that IHRL is directing States in the construction of their domestic criminal law system means that it is performing some of the functions traditionally performed by TCL? While this question remains open, it is suggested that this issue may also be looked at from a different angle: if integration between the two branches reaches its full potential, the dichotomy between the two may be bridged to the point that it cannot be assessed whether TCL or IHRL is carrying out a particular function, as the boundaries between the two have been blurred. This might have happened, for example, with the European Trafficking Convention, in which a clear distinction between the two regimes is not at all obvious. Is it still possible to state whether it is a human rights or a transnational criminal law instrument? In that context, the debate on an expanding or narrowing effect loses relevance, but gives way to one on integration and its adequacy or effectiveness.

---

128 See Françoise Tulkens, who elaborates on this concept initially developed by Christine Van den Wyngaert, in F. Tulkens, 'The Paradoxical Relationship between Criminal Law and Human Rights' (2011) 9(3) *Journal of International Criminal Justice* 577, 577–95.

129 For instance, *A v. UK*, no. 25599/94, ECHR, judgment of 23 November 1998, and *MC v. Bulgaria*, no. 39272/98, ECHR, judgment of 4 December 2003. For a detailed analysis, see M. Eriksson, 'The Prevention of Human Trafficking. Regulating Domestic Criminal Legislation through the European Convention on Human Rights' (2013) 82 *Nordic Journal of International Law* 339, 339–68.

130 *Siliadin*, above n. 108, and *Rantsev*, above n. 98.

131 M. Eriksson, above n. 129, 343.

4.2.2. *Guiding Effect*

Turning to the overall IHRL effect on TCL, the development of a HRBA to trafficking highlights the general guiding effect of IHRL over TCL. Indeed, a HRBA requires that any transnational and national criminal intervention, policy and law should integrate human rights in terms of both objectives to be achieved and processes to be followed.

In sum, the overall guiding effect of human rights law in what is clearly an irreversible convergence process is undeniable. The mentioned changes have taken place under the influence of IHRL and its evolution. Clearly, TCL has not been the driving force of these changes; it has been the recipient. This is certainly due to a fundamental difference between human rights law and criminal law, as highlighted by Trechsel: while 'the most fundamental values of any society are embodied in human rights',[132] 'substantive criminal law does not constitute itself a source of values. [...]. The criminal law is of a purely instrumental character. It constitutes, together with private and administrative law, a means to protect values which have their ultimate source elsewhere, essentially in human rights'.[133] Based on this premise, it may be argued that human rights law is inherently suited to have a guiding effect over other branches of law, as will be explored later. However, the chapter will first turn to the issue of whether TCL may also have an influence on IHRL.

4.3. IS INTERNATIONAL HUMAN RIGHTS LAW IN A PROCESS OF TRANSFORMATION UNDER THE INFLUENCE OF TRANSNATIONAL CRIMINAL LAW?

In what has been referred to as the paradoxical relationship between criminal law and human rights law,[134] these two branches of law are confronting each other under the traditional shield function, while they converge under the sword function where they are called upon to work in a supportive way towards the same goal. Now, it has been argued that the prominent role given to criminal law under this new sword function may carry some risks. First, it may excessively favour the recourse to criminal law, thereby questioning the principle of subsidiarity according to which criminal law should only be used as a tool of last resort.[135] Secondly, the prominent role given to criminal law in protecting human rights 'generally appears to be accompanied by an overall weakening of

---

132 S. Trechsel, 'Comparative Observations on Human Rights and Criminal Law' (2000) 1 *St. Louis-Warsaw Transatlantic Law Journal* 1, 3.

133 Ibid., 5.

134 F. Tulkens, above n. 128, 578.

135 Ibid., 594.

its traditional function as a shield against the threats it poses itself to rights and freedoms'.[136]

Would this expanded role of criminal law have a narrowing effect on IHRL? Would it come at the expenses of human rights law basic guarantees in terms of, for example, fair trial, presumption of innocence or arbitrary detention? Indeed, situations where mandatory detention is imposed in the name of protection have been reported, or where excessive pressure in terms of anti-trafficking prosecution leads to situations where trafficking suspects are convicted without full due process guarantees.[137] These are indeed very serious concerns. In that context, the strengthening of the central and guiding role of IHRL within general international law appears to be the best safeguard in order to combat that risk. The permeation and integration of other branches of international law by human rights law should happen under the firm understanding that the guiding – or prevalent – role of human rights should never be compromised. This leads us to some concluding reflections on the place and role of IHRL under general international law.

4.4. DOES INTERNATIONAL HUMAN RIGHTS LAW PROVIDE A SUITABLE THEORETICAL FRAMEWORK FOR THE INTEGRATION OF DIFFERENT BODIES OF INTERNATIONAL LAW?

It has been described that IHRL has construed a conceptual and methodological framework aimed at achieving integrated legal responses under the umbrella of human rights law, in which other branches of international law – including, but not limited to, TCL – are called upon to integrate existing human rights standards and principles into their legal regime. Why would IHRL be best suited to perform this function as opposed to other branches of international law? Why isn't a criminal law-based approach or a labour law-based approach being debated? Indeed, the HRBA has at least two characteristics that arguably make it a suitable framework for the integration of different bodies of international law.

The first aspect is that a HRBA shows the underlying linkages between different fields of law, by requiring a deep and broad analysis of social phenomena aimed at identifying the root causes of the various human rights abuses involved. A HRBA requires looking at the broader picture and building a response that integrates the promotion of different rights pertaining to distinct fields.

---

136 Ibid., 593.

137 See UNHRC, 'Report of the Special Rapporteur on trafficking in persons' (2012) UN Doc A/HRC/20/18, paras 5, 100 and 101. For an in-depth analysis of this issue, see Global Alliance Against Traffic in Women, 'Collateral Damage. The Impact of Anti-Trafficking Measures on Human Rights around the World' (2007).

In the area of trafficking, for example, such an approach requires addressing the way in which labour laws may promote exploitation, migration policies create opportunities for organised crime, discriminatory laws and practices in the education, health, commercial or tax sector generate gender vulnerabilities to trafficking, or corruption in public administration and the judiciary perpetuates impunity for traffickers. It thus provides a framework for developing a holistic and integrated response across different branches of law that highlights the linkages between human rights violations that are relevant to each of these fields.

As described by the Special Rapporteur on trafficking, 'by requiring a human rights-based approach, due diligence enables States to apply all their international obligations in ways that encourage less compartmentalization and more holistic approaches'.[138] Indeed, it is no coincidence that the concept of a HRBA, first developed in the field of development cooperation, is now employed in such diverse ambits as human trafficking, education,[139] environmental protection,[140] anti-corruption,[141] social services,[142] labour migration,[143] and business management.[144] In terms of the coherence of the overall international law system, the advantage is that it establishes bridges between different branches of law and finds a common language and strategy to address problems that tend to have ramifications in several of these fields.

The second aspect relates to human rights as embodying the fundamental values of human beings. In that context, the debate is closely related to the place of IHRL within general international law and the debate on international constitutionalism.[145] In domestic legal systems, human rights have a higher

138 UNHRC, 'Report of the Special Rapporteur on trafficking in persons', above n. 40, 15.

139 UNICEF/UNESCO, *A Human Rights-Based Approach to Education for All. A framework for the realization of children's right to education and rights within education*, UNICEF, New York 2007.

140 P. Pathak, 'Human Rights Approach to Environmental Protection' (2014) 7(1) *OIDA International Journal of Sustainable Development* 17, 17–24.

141 OHCHR, 'The human rights case against corruption' (2013) HR/NONE/2013/120.

142 J. Ife, *Human Rights and Social Work: Towards Rights-Based Practice*, 3rd ed., Cambridge University Press, New York 2013.

143 International Labour Organization (ILO), *International Labour Migration. A Rights-based Approach*, ILO, Geneva 2010.

144 Business Leaders Initiative on human rights, United Nations Global Compact and OHCHR, *A Guide to Integrating Human Rights into Business Management* (2006).

145 For an overview of leading opinions on this subject matter, see A. Peters, 'Are we Moving towards Constitutionalization of the World Community?' in A. Cassese (ed.), *Realizing Utopia: The Future of International Law*, Oxford University Press, Oxford 2012, pp. 118–35; A. Cassese, 'A Plea for a Global Community Grounded in a Core of Human Rights' in A. Cassese (ed.), ibid., 136–43; J. Klabbers, A. Peters and G. Ulfstein (eds.), *The Constitutionalization of International Law*, Oxford University Press, Oxford 2011; S. Gardbaum, 'Human Rights as International Constitutional Rights' (2008) 19(4) *European Journal of International Law* 749, 749–68; T. Meron, *The Humanization of International Law*, Martinus Nijhoff Publishers, Leiden 2006; R. McCorquodale, 'An Inclusive International Legal System' (2004) 17(3) *Leiden Journal of International Law* 477, 477–504.

rank and are usually embodied in constitutions. At the regional level, the ECtHR consistently considers that Member States' obligations under the ECHR prevail over other international treaty obligations, in light of the 'peremptory character'[146] of the guarantees set out in the Convention, also referred to as a 'constitutional instrument of European public order'.[147] However, at the universal level, recognition of the particular importance and superior status of human rights law has not yet been achieved. Only a very limited sub-set of human rights has been recognised as having *jus cogens* and therefore higher status.

There is undoubtedly something inherently constitutional in the very nature and subject matter of IHRL, in that its primary function is, as it is for human rights law at the national level, to specify limits on what governments can lawfully do to people within their jurisdictions.[148] But this seems to be exactly where the problem lies. To put individual rights at the top of the international legal system, in a higher position, would be a recognition of the shift from the 'private law' model of international law, which exclusively regulates horizontal relations among States based on reciprocity and State interests, to the 'public law' model that also regulates vertical relations between States and individuals, and in which the interests of individuals and communities become central.[149] In other words, it would represent a shift from a contractual to a constitutional paradigm.[150]

It is most likely that international relations between the State and individuals will continue to evolve in the direction of an increasing interaction and that the latter will transfer to the international scene the democratic claims that they have domestically in terms of greater participation and accountability. In that context, the normative framework that is called upon to regulate international relations must be capable of addressing these claims and provide a sense of ownership and respect for individuals and democratic values that is essential for the survival of any society. The ECHR system has placed fundamental rights at the top of the European legal order, empowering individuals to hold States accountable for their inability to fulfil their citizens' rights when accountability mechanisms fail at the national level. The human rights and democratic deficit of the EU was long invoked to discredit its legitimacy: the Charter of Fundamental Rights[151] was eventually adopted as a core element of legitimacy of the EU before its citizens. The permanence and credibility of the international community and its body of law may be put at great risk if a similar effort is not undertaken at the universal

146 *Bosphorus Airways v. Ireland*, no. 45036/98, ECHR, judgment of 30 June 2005, para. 154.
147 *Loizidou v. Turkey*, case 40/1993/435/514, preliminary objections, para. 75.
148 S. Gardbaum, above n. 145, 752.
149 Ibid., 762; and R. Pisillo Mazzeschi, above n. 65, 199–201.
150 S. Gardbaum, above n. 145, 762.
151 Charter of Fundamental Rights of the European Union (adopted 7 December 2000) [2012] OJ C326.

level, in order to put the individual not only at the centre of the efforts to combat trafficking, as has been discussed in this chapter, but more broadly at the centre of the general international legal order, consecrating the move from a 'state-centred' to a 'human-centred' system.

In a recent study, the International Law Association rightly pointed to the fact that the permeation of IHRL through general international law constitutes a quiet revolution that invariably targets international law's most 'statist' features.[152] Criticising the International Law Commission conservative view that regards the VCLT as the answer to any difficulty arising from international law fragmentation,[153] the study concludes that '[i]n the end, human rights rather than the VCLT may be the ultimate unifying factor contributing to the coherence of international law'.[154] Indeed, it should be seen as a priority that the solution to the compartmentalization of international law goes in the direction of its humanisation,[155] of 'promoting the gradual formation of a world community based on a core of universal values',[156] by granting human rights a guiding role that will preserve not only its coherence but also its legitimacy in the eyes of present and future generations.

---

152 International Law Association (ILA), *Final Report on the Impact of International Human Rights Law on General International Law* (2008), Conclusions, para. 8.

153 See ILC Report on Fragmentation of International Law, above n. 17, 15, 248–51, 255; and its addendum 'Draft conclusions of the work of the Study Group' (UN Doc A/CN.4/L.682/Add.1).

154 ILA Report, above n. 152, para. 7.

155 On this concept, see the opinions of judge Cançado Trindade in A.A. Cançado Trindade, *International Law for Humankind, Towards a New Jus Gentium*, 2nd ed., Martinus Nijhoff Publishers, Leiden 2013.

156 A. Cassese, above n. 145, 136.

INTERNATIONAL SECURITY AND FINANCIAL STABILITY: RESOLVING NORM CONFLICTS BETWEEN ANTI-CORRUPTION AND INDIVIDUAL RIGHTS

Mirja Ciesiolka

1. INTRODUCTION AND OVERVIEW

Institutional and systemic corruption in one way or another is an undeniable problem in both Western and developing countries. It plays into the hands of internationally organised crime structures and kleptocratic government regimes. The background, impact and consequences of corruption are as intangible as they are devastating, coming with a serious threat to international security and the integrity of financial systems.[1] Addressing the spread of corruption and so-called white-collar crimes on the international plane is therefore a step that can only be applauded. These efforts inevitably draw controversy in the face of tensions with rights of individuals. Engaging in an open debate on these tensions and the need to effectively uphold and respect civil rights goes without saying, and yet one simple and salient point deserves emphasis: the corruption argument must not be seized upon to silence political competition and diversity. Similarly, the human rights argument must not be seized upon to undermine determined action against corrupt behaviour.

In combating corruption, the United Nations Convention against Corruption (UNCAC)[2] obliges States parties to implement a broad legal programme that goes far beyond previous instruments in both scope and detail. It is the first legally binding global anti-corruption agreement.[3] The measures to be introduced range from international cooperation in anti-corruption efforts such as investigation, prosecution, extradition, seizure and return of misappropriated assets, to the

1 See further S. Chayes, *Thieves of State – Why Corruption Threatens Global Security*, W.W. Norten & Co., New York 2015.

2 United Nations Convention against Corruption 2003 (2349 UNTS 41, No. 42146).

3 For an overview of other international anti-corruption mechanism see J. Wouters, C. Ryngaert and A.S. Cloots, 'The International Legal Framework against Corruption: Achievements and Challenges' (2013) 14 *Melbourne Journal of International Law* 1.

promotion of governance principles such as accountability, transparency, and public and corporate integrity.

Given its far-reaching ambition, the UNCAC opens a field of tension between the security of societies on the one hand and the rights of individuals on the other: aspects of the UNCAC are inconsistent with international obligations on human rights. The chapter therefore explains the legal relationship between the UNCAC and international human rights law (IHRL). It highlights that the UNCAC's aim of containing corruption is an essential element of international peace and security. The tensions between this aim and ensuring the enjoyment of civil and political rights are also a reflection of structural and general problems that come along with the phenomenon of fragmentation in international law.

The relationship between the UNCAC and IHRL gives rise to one of the most urgent problems in a fragmented international legal order: the addressing of norm conflicts between disparate law regimes (*inter*-regime conflicts). The legal practice indicates that such *inter*-regime conflicts tend to arise between international human rights obligations and other legal regimes such as financial security sanctions, trade, investment and immunities. These *inter*-regime relations, as well as the constellation between the UNCAC and human rights, involve methodological challenges: (1) international law does not provide for an explicit rule on resolving *inter*-regime conflicts; (2) the international legal practice does not indicate a coherent manner of dealing with conflicting norms; and (3) the perils of fragmentation add further complexities.

In addressing such *inter*-regime conflicts, this chapter places an emphasis on the principle of systemic integration that finds resonance in Article 31(3)(c) of the Vienna Convention on the Law of Treaties (Vienna Convention). This principle has significant practical relevance as a tool for harmonising conflicting norms of international law by way of harmonious interpretation.

Focusing on the relationship between the UNCAC and IHRL, the chapter finally suggests how norm conflicts between different law regimes of international law can be dealt with practically, by means of systemic integration. It thereby elaborates the legal interaction between anti-corruption law and international human rights.

2. INTERNATIONAL ANTI-CORRUPTION EFFORTS: SECURITY AND FINANCIAL STABILITY

2.1. CORRUPTION AT THE ROOT OF VARIOUS DESTABILISING FACTORS

Corruption has a variety of faces, such as bribes, embezzlement, the siphoning of State funds, money laundering, vote rigging and nepotism, often entailing blatant profiteering. The interplay of corrupt governance with economic and other factors unsettles local populations, paves the way for violent extremism and thereby increases the likelihood of a severe international security event. Low levels of public integrity give rise to destabilising conditions such as unfair competition, inequality and unemployment, which result in economic deterioration. The latter threatens financial sector stability – for example, when banks are pillaged or fraudulent banking practices are widespread. The resulting economic distortions can have destabilising impacts on entire economic ecosystems. Worsening economic and environmental conditions, in turn, put a further strain on the suffering of populations, making them more likely to end up in revolt.[4]

Amid growing concern over these security implications, terrorist financing, transnational organised crime and tax evasion, a series of international initiatives was launched in the late 1990s. These initiatives aimed to address the devastating impact of corruption. For instance, in a resolution the UN General Assembly stressed the seriousness of problems posed by corruption and the links between corruption and other forms of crime. It highlighted that 'corruption may endanger the stability and security of societies, undermine the values of democracy and morality and jeopardise social, economic and political development'.[5] In another resolution, the UN General Assembly noted 'the corrosive effect that corruption has on democracy, development, the rule of law and economic activity'.[6] The UNCAC reflects these concerns and the threat of corruption to the stability and security of States, including fundamental legal as well as social, economic, and political principles.[7] A 2004 report[8] by the High-level Panel on Threats, Challenges and Change, mandated from the then Secretary-General of the UN, defines transnational organised crime as a threat to international security. This is based on the assumption that 'any event or process that leads to … lessening of life chances and undermines States as the basic unit of the international system is a threat to international security'.[9] The report even goes so far as to stress that 'transnational organised crime facilitates many of

4 S. Chayes, above n. 1, pp. 186 *et seq.*

5 UN General Assembly Resolution 51/59, paras 1–2; see further UN General Assembly Resolution 53/176, para. 2.

6 UN General Assembly Resolution 55/61; see further L. Koechlin and M. Sepúlveda Carmona, 'Corruption and Human Rights: Exploring the Connection' in R.I. Rotberg (ed.), *Corruption, Global Security, and World Order*, World Peace Foundation and American Academy of Arts and Sciences, Cambridge, Massachusetts 2009, p. 310.

7 Cf. Preamble to the UNCAC.

8 Report of the High-level Panel on Threats, Challenges and Change, *A more secure world: our shared responsibility*, UN General Assembly document no. A/59/565.

9 Ibid., p. 12; it is, however, a different matter – and often subject to political considerations – what consequences the Security Council infers under its power according to Chapter VII of the UN Charter.

the most serious threats to international peace and security. Corruption, illicit trade and money-laundering contribute to State weakness, impede economic growth and undermine democracy. These activities thus create a permissive environment for civil conflict'.[10] In addition, the same report continues to refer to the UNCAC as one of the instruments to meet the challenges of this threat to international security.[11]

2.2. THE SCOPE, APPROACH AND POTENTIAL IMPACT OF THE UNCAC

The UNCAC provides a multilateral framework for international cooperation. It emphasises that each and every aspect of anti-corruption efforts such as investigation or prosecution of offenders necessitates international cooperation. The UNCAC aims to address corrupt activities in a comprehensive manner that comprises both the public and private level of societies. Therefore, it focuses on criminalisation as well as on preventive measures, provisions on the enhancement of international cooperation, asset recovery and technical assistance, and information exchange. The most significant issue in this regard is laid down in Chapter V of the UNCAC on the return of assets. It specifies how cooperation and assistance are to be rendered, how proceeds of corruption are to be returned to a requesting State and how the legitimate owners are to be considered.

The UNCAC provides various anti-corruption mechanisms. These include, for example: criminalising a large number of bribery and bribery related offences in both the public and private sectors, extensively covering asset recovery, and providing international cooperation for the purpose of prosecution. The breadth of the UNCAC is certainly unparalleled, due to the global quality of the UNCAC and the many offences that it covers.[12] The asset recovery provisions in Chapter V of the UNCAC provide a foundation for international cooperation in this area.[13] Compared with previous anti-corruption instruments, the broad definitions of 'public official', 'foreign public official' and 'official of a public international organisation' ensure the relevance of the UNCAC for the public sector.

---

10 Ibid., pp. 20–21.

11 Ibid., pp. 49–50.

12 O. Brunelle-Quraishi, 'Assessing the Relevancy and Efficacy of the United Nations Convention against Corruption: A Comparative Analysis' (2011) II *Notre Dame Journal of International Law & Comparative Law* 101, 164 *et seq.*

13 Ph. Webb, 'The United Nations Convention Against Corruption' (2005) 8 *Journal of International Economic Law* 191, 228.

The UNCAC, however, suffers from significant weaknesses in its efficacy as an anti-corruption mechanism.[14] For example, the review mechanism for monitoring the implementation of the UNCAC is rather poor[15] and most provisions of the UNCAC are phrased using discretionary terms.[16] The obligations' wordings differ in their strictness. In this regard, the UNCAC contains two main types of obligations: by stating that 'each state party shall adopt' particular measures, many provisions use strict language;[17] in contrast, other provisions contain an obligation to the effect that 'each state party shall consider adopting' particular measures.[18] Most provisions contain the second type of obligation. This wording implies a more discretionary language, as States parties are 'merely' obliged to consider the establishment of particular anti-corruption measures. However, these norms remain, in principle, legal obligations that States parties have to meet.[19] Many terms within the UNCAC's provisions are not defined. For example, it remains unclear how the term 'undue advantage' contained in Articles 15 and 16 UNCAC, which criminalise bribery of officials, is supposed to be defined. Other provisions of the UNCAC include references to adopting legislative measures in accordance with domestic law principles.[20] These obligations are subject to the fundamental principles of each State party. As the definition of what pertains to the fundamental principles is left to States parties, the obligations are, in effect, subject to the (whole) domestic law of each State party. The most provisions contain further qualification as to the strictness of the obligation contained therein. Such norms state, for example, that 'each state party shall consider adopting' particular measures 'where appropriate'.[21] The UNCAC does not define the appropriateness of respective anti-corruption measures; their determination is left to States parties.

---

14 See also ibid., 191–229, pointing out that the UNCAC suffers from basic weaknesses that may prevent it from having a real impact on corrupt behaviour.

15 Cf. R.R. Babu, 'The United Nations Convention Against Corruption: A Critical Overview' Asian African Consultative Organisation, 2006, p. 21 (27); Ph. Webb, above n. 13, 218–22, suggesting that the UNCAC has not shown innovation in this regard: it follows the weakest regional instruments by giving States parties a large degree of leeway to decide whether and how far to incorporate the UNCAC into domestic law.

16 O. Brunelle-Quraishi, above n. 12, 164.

17 For example, Arts 15–17 UNCAC.

18 For example, Arts 18–20 UNCAC; most provisions of the UNCAC contain the second type of obligations. This wording implies a more discretionary or optional language, as States parties are 'merely' obliged to consider the establishment of particular anti-corruption measures. Some authors use this different wording to distinguish between mandatory and non-mandatory provisions: the first type is regarded as mandatory, while the second type is qualified as non-mandatory.

19 O. Brunelle-Quraishi, above n. 12, 125.

20 Cf. Ph. Webb, above n. 13, 206, who criticises that these qualifying clauses provide a potential escape clause for reluctant national legislators.

21 For example, Arts 5(4), 6(1), 7(1), 8(3) and (5), 10, 12(1), 14(1) and 43(1) UNCAC.

The requirement of appropriateness intensifies the discretionary language of these obligations. A mixture of discretionary language and strict language is not unusual within international agreements and is not a weakness *per se*. Open-textured wording and discretionary language are inevitably inherent in multilateral treaties. In negotiating such treaties, States parties aim to accommodate different and often diverging interests. Avoiding explicit language makes an agreement possible: it is a sign of States parties' willingness to align their interests with each other, rather than a sign of disagreement. The UNCAC reflects this aspect of international treaty negotiations; it uses, in general, broader terms and lacks extremely explicit language. The use of broader terms and the absence of specificity provide opportunities for adjustment: these characteristics will allow room to consider a range of external factors, such as future legal and political developments that might concern the interpretation of obligations. The absence of definitions and the resulting ambiguity and broad nature of the language in the text allow for a broader interpretation of the UNCAC.[22] This ambiguity provides the basis for considering other norms. The UNCAC thereby opens the door to balancing controversial relationships with other norms of international law and/or domestic law.

3. THE CONTROVERSIAL RELATIONSHIP BETWEEN SECURITY AND CIVIL RIGHTS: INTERNATIONAL ANTI-CORRUPTION LAW AND CONFLICTING HUMAN RIGHTS

Inconsistencies and conflicting interests with human rights come with legal action relevant to security in areas such as anti-terrorism, crime prevention, sanction regimes, migration and intelligence operations.[23] In seeking to ensure security any kind of initiative or legal action is highly likely to provoke controversy as to civil rights. The extremely specialised human rights regime is therefore the most challenging legal regime as to potential inconsistencies and norm conflicts with the UNCAC: a convention against crime like the UNCAC opens the field of tension between the security of societies on the one hand and rights of individuals on the other.

---

22 O. Brunelle-Quraishi, above n. 12, 133.

23 See the example of tensions between anti-terrorism mechanism and human rights discussed by Lord Hoffmann in *A (FC) and others (FC) (Appellants) v. Secretary of State for the Home Department (Respondent)* and *X (FC) and another (FC) (Appellants) v. Secretary of State for Home Department (Respondent)* [2004] UKHL 56, paras.86 *et seq.*; see also Lady Hale (Deputy President of the UK Supreme Court), Terrorism and Global Security, speech at the 10th Biennial International Conference of International Association of Women Judges, Seoul, South Korea, 12.05.2010.

3.1. THE KEY ROLE OF INTERNATIONAL COOPERATION IN THE FIGHT AGAINST CORRUPTION: THE MAIN DRIVER OF NORM CONFLICTS WITH HUMAN RIGHTS OBLIGATIONS

One of the main reasons for corrupt structures and governance paying off is that the flow of money and revenue streams is being internationally operated.[24] Effective international cooperation in order to curb lucrative revenue streams may therefore be the most promising tool in combating corruption.[25] The UNCAC consists, to a large extent, of measures on international cooperation in the fight against corruption that provide for mutual legal assistance. Legal action in international cooperation is, however, the main driver of norm conflicts with human rights law. These legal uncertainties generate frictions, making effective legal action against criminal offences immensely difficult: it can even amount to letting corrupt behaviour go unpunished. The following examples illustrate such norm conflict situations in mutual legal assistance.

For instance, a State party to the UNCAC is requested by another State party to grant legal assistance by giving effect to a confiscation order issued by the requesting State. Article 54(1)(a) UNCAC obliges the requested State, in principle, to give effect to such an order with respect to property acquired through an offence established according to the UNCAC, on the one hand. On the other hand, the requested State is obliged to guarantee the individual affected by the confiscation order, at least, the right to a fair trial. In addition, the State can be obliged to guarantee rights to the peaceful enjoyment of property (Article 17 UDHR; Article 5(d)(v) CERD; Article 21 ACHR; Article 1 of the First Protocol of 1952 to the ECHR; and Article 14 ACHPR). As the confiscation order is issued by the requesting State, the requested State is confronted with the situation that it has to give effect to the confiscation order without having an opportunity to verify whether the order was issued in compliance with the requested State's obligations on human rights protection. Giving full effect to the obligation derived from Article 54(1)(a) UNCAC could thus violate the requested State's obligations on human rights protection.

In the field of international cooperation, extradition is another illustrating example as to potential norm conflicts with IHRL. A number of human rights obligations are involved when extradition proceedings according to Article 44 UNCAC are being carried out. Human rights may be relevant both at extradition proceedings in the requested State and within the context of criminal proceedings

---

24 See S. Chayes, above n. 1, pp. 213 *et seq.*

25 See also T. Keatinge, 'Ukraine's Own Worst Enemy' <www.foreignaffairs.com>, 31.07.2014, who advocates international cooperation and assistance according to the UNCAC in recovering assets stolen from Ukraine.

in the requesting state. Extradition proceedings could not meet the requirements of the standards of a fair trial. Detention prior to extradition proceedings means a deprivation of liberty (Article 9 ICCPR) and a potential violation of *habeas corpus* rights. When returning to the requesting State, the extradited person could be denied proper access to an effective legal remedy (Article 14 ICCPR) and could be exposed to the application of *ex post facto* law (Article 15 ICCPR). The physical removal of the person to be extradited can affect their rights to family or private life (Article 17 ICCPR).

Measures on uncovering money laundering in the financial sector provide an example of the controversial relationship between the right to privacy and international anti-corruption law. According to Article 14(1)(a) UNCAC, each State party shall institute a comprehensive regulatory and supervisory regime for banks and other financial institutions in order to deter and detect all forms of money laundering. This regime shall emphasise requirements for customer identification, record keeping and the reporting of suspicious transactions. These measures involve personal data of individuals. Preventive measures established according to Article 14(1)(a) UNCAC could therefore affect the right to privacy that is also applied to the processing of personal data.

Article 14(1)(b) UNCAC could interfere with the right to privacy. The right to privacy, for instance as laid down in Article 17 ICCPR, comprises freedom from unwarranted and unreasonable intrusions into activities that society recognises as belonging to the realm of individual autonomy.[26] It also includes the right to control information about oneself. The collection of information about individuals without their consent will interfere with their private life, as will its use, for example, in investigative measures or court proceedings. Examples include measures such as the keeping of secret files.[27] The Human Rights Committee added to the understanding of the right to privacy that gathering and holding of personal information must be regulated by law. Effective measures have to be taken to ensure that information concerning a person's private life does not reach the hands of persons who are not authorised by law to receive, process and use it, and is never used for purposes incompatible with the ICCPR. In addition, individuals should have the right to ascertain whether, and if so what, personal data is stored in automatic data files, and for what purposes. If such files contain incorrect personal data or have been collected or processed contrary to the provisions of the law, every individual should have the right to request its rectification or elimination.[28] The General Data

26 S. Joseph and M. Castan, *The International Covenant on Civil and Political Rights – Cases, Materials, and Commentary*, 3rd ed., Oxford University Press, Oxford 2013, pp. 533–34.

27 Cf. B. Rainey, E. Wicks and C. Ovey, *The European Convention on Human Rights*, 6th ed., Oxford University Press, Oxford 2014, p. 377.

28 Human Rights Committee, General Comment 16, no. 10.

Protection Regulation (GDPR)[29] will intensify the conflict between standards of anti-money laundering and the right to privacy. It brings major changes in the infrastructure of data processing for European Union countries and their cross border data flows. It is therefore relevant to countries that exchange data with European Union countries. The GDPR will significantly strengthen the protection of individuals' rights to personal data protection, reflecting the nature of data protection as a fundamental right for the European Union as laid down in Article 8 of the EU Charter of Fundamental Rights and Article 16 TFEU. The GDPR provides rights such as active consent to the processing of personal data and the right to be forgotten.

These standards are in contrast to Article 14 UNCAC. This provision does not indicate a reflection of data protection standards such as those of Article 17 ICCPR. Moreover, Article 14(1)(b) UNCAC does not specify which customer data should be subject to what kind of identification, record keeping and the reporting of suspicious transactions. There is no specification as to when a payment transaction may qualify as being suspicious. This means that Article 14(1)(a) UNCAC can be understood in a very broad manner, paving the way for the establishment of extensive or systematic measures on data collection and data reporting. Article 14 UNCAC does not explicitly require compliance with Article 17 ICCPR. In addition, pursuant to Article 14(1)(b) UNCAC, States parties shall ensure that authorities in charge of combating money laundering have the ability to cooperate and exchange information at national and international levels; to that end, the establishment of financial intelligence units to serve as a centre for the collection, analysis and dissemination of information regarding potential money laundering shall be considered. Such measures on information exchange and dissemination may increase the danger of frustrating the right to privacy that, as indicated above, includes data protection of individuals: the establishment of intelligence units according to Article 14 UNCAC may intensify adverse effects for privacy rights. 'Information regarding potential money-laundering', as stated in Article 14(1)(b) UNCAC, can be perceived broadly. Personal data of many individuals – perhaps innocent of money laundering – could therefore be affected by the processing of information on 'potential money laundering'. Giving full effect to the obligations contained in Article 14(1) UNCAC will thus lead to a violation of the right to privacy.

---

29 Regulation (EU) 2016/679 of the European Parliament and of the Council of 27 April 2016 on the protection of natural persons with regard to the processing of personal data and on the free movement of such data, and repealing Directive 95/46/EC, OJ L 119, 4 May 2016; see further for the position of the European Commission, COM(2018) 43 final.

3.2. CONSIDERING THE UNIQUE FEATURES OF HUMAN RIGHTS OBLIGATIONS

Two aspects of the conceptual structure of human rights obligations deserve emphasis, as they need to be duly considered when dealing with diverging international obligations. These two aspects distinguish human rights obligations from other international obligations.

Human rights can be claimed by individuals.[30] The human rights law provisions in UN and regional human rights treaties assign rights to individuals and correlative duties to States. Thereby, human rights treaties determine the conduct of States towards individuals. Hence, human rights treaties do not just create reciprocal obligations between States parties. Instead, they establish obligations for States in relation to their treatment of individuals under their jurisdiction.[31] As the Inter-American Court of Human Rights emphasised in its *Effect of Reservations* case:[32]

> modern human rights treaties ... are not multilateral treaties of the traditional type concluded to accomplish the reciprocal exchange of rights for the mutual benefit of the contracting States. Their object and purpose is the protection of the basic rights of individual human beings irrespective of their nationality, both against the State of their nationality and all other contracting States. In concluding these human rights treaties, the States can be deemed to submit themselves to a legal order within which they, for the common good, assume various obligations, not in relation to other States, but towards all individuals within their jurisdiction.

The consequence of the specificity of human rights treaties is recognised in Article 60(5) VCLT. This provision states that the principle according to which the material breach of a treaty by one party authorises the other party to terminate or suspend the agreement does not apply to 'provisions relating to the protection of the human person contained in treaties of a humanitarian character'. Termination or suspension of a treaty in cases of material breach is based on the idea of reciprocity, in which the obligations imposed on one party are set for the benefit of the other parties to the treaty. Article 60(5) VCLT,

---

30 E. Klein, Human Dignity – 'Basis of Human Rights' in H.P. Hestermeyer, *et al.* (eds), *Coexistence, Cooperation and Solidarity*, Nijhoff Publishers, Leiden *et al.* 2012, pp. 437, 443.

31 M. Craven, 'Legal Differentiation and the Concept of the Human Rights Treaty in International Law' (2000) 11 *European Journal of International Law* 489, 513–17; see also B. Çali, 'Specialized Rules of Treaty Interpretation: Human Rights' in D. Hollis (ed.), *The Oxford Guide to Treaties*, Oxford University Press, Oxford 2012, pp. 529 *et seq.*

32 *The Effect of Reservations on the Entry into Force of the ACHR*, Advisory Opinion of 24.09.1982, OC-2/82, series A no. 2, para. 29.

however, takes account of the fact that the beneficiaries of human rights treaties are not the other States parties to the treaty but individuals.[33]

Another important aspect of international human rights obligations is their inherent consideration of human dignity. That consideration provides those obligations with a unique feature that other international obligations do not necessarily have. International human rights documents and treaties refer to human dignity.[34] Both the preambles to the UN Charter and the UDHR affirm, inter alia, 'faith in the dignity and worth of the human person'. These instruments do not state that human rights derive from human dignity. Such a statement can be found, however, in the two Covenants. The preambles to both Covenants express the States parties' recognition that human rights 'derive from the inherent dignity of the human person'. The same phrase is repeated in Article 10(1) ICCPR.[35] The aspect of human dignity recognises the intrinsic worth of the individual that requires that the State should be seen to exist for the sake of the individual human being, and not vice versa.[36]

3.3. FURTHER COMPLEXITIES THROUGH THE DECENTRALISED NATURE OF INTERNATIONAL LAW AND THE PERILS OF FRAGMENTATION

The special nature of human rights obligations and the likelihood of norm conflicts with anti-corruption law provoke the question of the legal relationship between these two regimes. The UNCAC does not specify whether it gives way to competing norms in the event of conflict or whether it prevails. The rather programmatic character of the UNCAC profoundly contrasts with rules providing individual rights. The decentralised structure of international law and the perils of fragmentation give further rise to the question of how to manage such competing legal regimes.

Any new treaty is created within the wider *corpus* of international law, including rules of customary international law, general principles of law and

---

33 Cf. O. De Schutter, *International Human Rights Law*, Cambridge University Press, Cambridge 2010, p. 96; see further Art. 50(1)(b) of the ILC Articles on State Responsibility.

34 For an overview of these references and their content, cf. C. McCrudden, 'Human Dignity and Judicial Interpretation of Human Rights' (2008) 19 *European Journal of International Law* 655, 664–78; see, further, J. Waldron, 'How Law Protects Dignity' (2012) 71 *Cambridge Law Journal* 200.

35 Cf. E. Klein, above n. 30, p. 437.

36 Cf. C. McCrudden, above n. 34, p. 679; A. Cassese, *International Law*, 2nd ed., Oxford University Press, Oxford 2005, p. 397; C. Beyani, 'The Legal Premises for International Protection of Human Rights' in G.S. Goodwin-Gill and S. Talmon (eds), *The Reality of International Law*, Oxford University Press, Oxford 1999, p. 25.

pre-existing treaties.[37] The lack of a general hierarchy in international law and the central role of State consent as to the creation of international law has an important consequence. By concluding a treaty, States can contract out of or deviate from customary international law (other than *jus cogens*) and pre-existing international law of any kind. The pre-existing rule of customary law and – in many cases – the pre-existing treaty rule continue to exist but will be disapplied with respect to the rule or treaty in question.[38]

An analysis of the UNCAC shows that it does not contract out of IHRL.[39] A few norms of the UNCAC even explicitly confirm the relevance of specific human rights obligations, obliging States parties to establish specific anti-corruption measures in accordance with human rights obligations. The UNCAC does not – either implicitly or explicitly – exclude obligations on international human rights protection. However, the question of how conflicting human rights norms should be handled remains. In addition, the perils of fragmentation make the definition of the relationship between international rules on anti-corruption and human rights even more complex.

The international legal order should be viewed from the perspective of bilateral and multilateral States' relations.[40] This perspective and the horizontal structure of international law do not easily lend themselves to the establishment of systemic relations between norms.[41] The development of international law in specialised directions, often under different institutional frameworks, amplifies difficulties in determining relations between legal rules. Much of the action in international law has shifted to functional and specialised regimes.[42] What was once regulated by general public international law is now governed by specialist regimes such as international humanitarian law, international environmental law, human rights law, European Union law, or the law of the World Trade Organization.[43] Such specialised regimes emerge from shifts in legal culture and

37 J. Pauwelyn, 'The Role of Public International Law in the WTO: How far can we go?' (2001) 95 *American Journal of International Law* 535, 536; cf. A. Aust, *Handbook of International Law*, 2nd ed., Cambridge University Press, Cambridge 2010, pp. 8 and 9.

38 See, for instance, *Oil Platforms (Islamic Republic of Iran v. United States of America), Preliminary Objection, I.C.J. Reports 1996*, p. 803 (para. 28); see, e.g., referring to State responsibility, J. Crawford, ILC Special Rapporteur, *Third Report on State Responsibility*, ILC Yearbook (2000), vol. II, p. 3 (para. 420).

39 See, further, M. Ciesiolka, *A Contribution to Norm Conflict Resolution in a Fragmented International Legal Order – The Legal Relationship between the United Nations Convention against Corruption and International Human Rights Law*, Schulthess, Zurich 2015, pp. 49–97.

40 Cf. A. Cassese, *International Law*, 2nd ed., Oxford University Press, Oxford 2005, pp. 5–6.

41 A. Lindroos, 'Addressing Norm Conflicts in a Fragmented Legal System: The doctrine of *Lex Specialis*' (2005) 74 *Nordic Journal of International Law* 27, 28.

42 A. Bodansky and J.R. Crook, 'Symposium: The ILC's State Responsibility Articles – Introduction and Overview' (2002) 96 *American Journal of International Law* 773, 774.

43 B. Simma and D. Pulkowski, 'Of Planets and the Universe: Self-contained Regimes in International Law' (2006) 17 *European Journal of International Law* 483, 485; see, for an early

in response to practical needs of specialisation than as from conscious acts of regime-creation.[44] In addition, such rule systems often function on the basis of divergent sets of rules and a different systemic logic within their respective issue areas. They create seemingly separate norm systems that are unrelated from each other and may also contract out from some of the rules of general international law.[45]

Fragmentation may certainly bring about complexities, and yet international law provides a framework through which relations between different norms of international law can be considered and managed. When making new international law, a crucially important bridge to existing law is the general *corpus* of international law, and in particular the rules on application and interpretation of international law that include the 'tool-box' of the Vienna Convention.[46] Even though the rules of the Convention may certainly not provide a ready-made solution for resolving any kind of conflicting obligations between different treaty regimes or conflicts between treaty regimes and customary international law,[47] it is nevertheless an appropriate point of departure for dealing with the effects of normative fragmentation. These rules apply to any new treaty unless that treaty contracts out of it. In this sense the rules on application and interpretation of international law are a crucial and important element of coherence and unity between different treaty regimes;[48] the Vienna Convention already provides a certain unifying frame for the international treaty practice. When seeking to determine legal relationships, emphasis should therefore be placed on interpretation in accordance with or analogously to the Vienna Convention.[49] At the heart of determining legal relationships is thorough interpretation. An analysis of the UNCAC's content, wording and context shows that its ambiguity – and thus its weakness as an anti-corruption mechanism – provides the basis for balancing conflicting rules of international law.[50]

recognition of international law's tendency to fragmentation, I. Brownlie, 'The Rights of Peoples in Modern International Law' (1985) 9 *Bulletin of the Australian Society of Legal Philosophy* 104, 116.

44 D.H. Joyner and M. Roscini (eds), *Non-proliferation Law as a Special Regime – A Contribution to Fragmentation Theory in International Law*, Cambridge University Press, Cambridge 2012, p. 1.

45 A. Lindroos, above n. 42, p. 28.

46 J. Pauwelyn, 'Bridging Fragmentation and Unity: International Law as a Universe of Inter-Connected Islands' (2003–2004) 25 *Michigan Journal of International Law* 903, 906.

47 Cf. J. Klabbers, 'Conflicting Treaty Provisions' in E. Cannizzaro (ed.), *The Law of Treaties Beyond the Vienna Convention*, Oxford University Press, Oxford 2011, pp. 194 and 205.

48 J. Pauwelyn, above n. 46, 906.

49 Report of the Study Group of the International Law Commission of 13 April 2006 on Fragmentation of International Law: Difficulties Arising from the Diversification and Expansion of International Law, UN General Assembly document no. A/CN.4/L.682 (hereinafter ILC Fragmentation Report), Conclusions, para. 14.

50 See above section 2.2.

4. MANAGING THE COMPETING INTERESTS AND CONFLICTING NORMS IN INTERNATIONAL LAW

4.1. THE ROLE AND POTENTIAL OF TREATY INTERPRETATION AND ARTICLE 31(3)(C) OF THE VIENNA CONVENTION

The Vienna Convention includes no specific rule of application or conflict resolution of customary norms in relation to a particular treaty. It likewise provides no specific rule for addressing conflicting treaty norms between different law regimes (*inter*-regime conflicts). The interactions between two different law regimes should therefore be dealt with as a matter of interpretation under Articles 31 and 32 Vienna Convention. Article 31(3)(c) takes account of the plurality of norms in international law in the context of treaty interpretation. This provision is a codification of customary international law.[51] It requires attention to other rules.[52] The significance of Article 31(3)(c) Vienna Convention was underlined in the decision of the International Court of Justice (ICJ) in *Oil Platforms*,[53] serving as a bridge between rules of a treaty of friendship and the customary international law of armed conflict. The general principle of treaty interpretation expressed in Article 31(3)(c) Vienna Convention is also termed the principle of systemic integration.[54] It is a crucial tool available under international law to reconcile competing or conflicting norms between treaties and rules of customary law and between different treaties. The interpretative mechanism contained in Article 31(3)(c) has been therefore regarded as having a potentially generic application, which could encompass the relationships between different law regimes.[55]

Resolving normative conflicts means putting the norms at issue in a relationship with each other by legal reasoning. In the process of resolving norm conflicts, interpretation of the norms, as well as balancing their underlying interests in the context of aspects such as the intention of the parties, the character of the instruments, and their object and purpose play a significant role. Conflict resolution and interpretation can hardly be distinguished from each other: whether there is a conflict and what can be done with conflicts depend

---

51 *Maritime Dispute (Peru v. Chile), ICJ Reports 2014*, p 3 (para. 57); *Certain Questions of Mutual Assistance in Criminal Matters (Djibouti v. France), ICJ Reports 2008*, p. 177 (para. 112); see H. Thirlway, 'The Law and the Procedure of the International Court of Justice 1960–1989 Supplement, 2006: Part Three' (2006) 77 *British Yearbook of International Law* 1, 19.

52 R. Gardiner, 'The Vienna Convention Rules on Treaty Interpretation' in D. Hollis (ed.), above n. 31, pp. 475, 485.

53 *Oil Platforms (Islamic Republic of Iran v. United States of America), ICJ Reports 2003*, p. 161.

54 C. McLachlan, 'The Principle of Systemic Integration and Article 31(3)(c) of the Vienna Convention' (2005) 54 *International and Comparative Law Quarterly* 279, 280.

55 Cf. Ph. Sands, 'Treaty, Custom and the Cross-fertilization of International Law' (1998) 1 *Yale Human Rights & Development Law Journal* 85, 87.

on the way in which the relevant rules are interpreted. Interpretation does not intervene only once it has already been ascertained that there is a conflict. Rules appear to be compatible or in conflict as a result of interpretation.[56] The principle contained in Article 31(3)(c) Vienna Convention accompanies the process of legal reasoning and deals with the situation in which legal rules external to a given treaty are relevant in its interpretation:[57] The foundation of this principle is that treaties, whatever their subject matter, are predicated for their existence and operation on being part of the international legal order.[58] All treaty provisions establish rights and obligations that exist alongside rights and obligations stipulated by other treaties and rules of customary international law. In principle, no such rights or obligations have priority against each other, and yet their relationship can be approached through a process of reasoning that takes account of the international legal order as a whole.[59] As the ICJ emphasised in its *Namibia* advisory opinion, 'an international instrument has to be interpreted and applied within the framework of the entire legal system prevailing at the time of the interpretation'.[60] The interpretative principle laid down in Article 31(3)(c) can thus operate as an 'intermediary' between a treaty and the international legal order as a whole. Interpretation against the background of international law thereby gives expression to systemic relationships reflecting the plurality of norms. The extrinsic legal materials to be considered in the sense of Article 31(3)(c) include treaties, customary rules or general principles of law. In addition, systemic integration implies legal reasoning in the process of which a fair balance between different norms and law regimes can be provided. Thus, roles for the rule laid down in Article 31(3)(c) Vienna Convention include, at least:[61] (1) interpretative guidance in treaty interpretation (completing the legal picture or filling gaps in a treaty) by reference to customary international law, general principles or other treaties (existent at the time of interpretation); and (2) resolving conflicting obligations, including those arising under different treaties.

4.2. STRIKING A FAIR BALANCE BETWEEN CONFLICTING VALUES AND INTERESTS

In resolving conflicting obligations arising under differently specialised regimes, the principle of systemic integration aims to preserve some degree of coherence

---

56 ILC Fragmentation Report, paras 411 *et seq.*

57 Cf. A. Aust, *Modern Treaty Law and Practice*, 3rd ed., Cambridge University Press, Cambridge 2013, p. 216.

58 C. McLachlan, above n. 54, 280.

59 Cf. ILC Fragmentation Report, para. 414.

60 *Legal Consequences for States of the Continued Presence of South Africa in Namibia (South West Africa) notwithstanding Security Council Resolution 276 (1970), ICJ Reports 1971*, p. 16 (para. 53).

61 Cf. R. Gardiner, *Treaty Interpretation*, Oxford University Press, Oxford 2008, p. 260.

within the international legal order by applying a presumption of compatibility to new treaty obligations.[62] Systemic integration enables a balance to be struck between competing law regimes. This capability is of particular usefulness in resolving apparent (or broad) norm conflicts. It provides no explicit solution for resolving narrow conflicts that mean situations in which a treaty norm unavoidably leads to the breach of another obligation or right.[63] In the case of narrow conflicts it needs to be complemented by techniques that resolve such conflicts by giving precedence to one of the norms. In effect, systemic integration applies as a conflict avoidance technique. It seeks to avert apparent conflicts of norms through harmonious interpretation of rules of international law; thus, it operates before an irreconcilable conflict has arisen. Whether, in the process, a norm conflict is 'resolved' or 'avoided' may be just a matter of definition. In any case, the result is the same: a harmonisation of (potentially) conflicting norms. Interpretative techniques are capable of providing international law with coherence while allowing for a certain flexibility or dynamism in their application.[64] There is neither a fixed theoretical framework of how norm conflicts between different law regimes are to be resolved nor does the legal practice provide for a consistent treatment of these conflicts.[65] Each process of conflict resolution between different law regimes will have to consider the particularities of the norms at issue. It is therefore certainly not possible to constitute a fixed roster of requirements to be fulfilled in the process of norm conflict resolution between different law regimes. The legal practice and the capacity and requirements of Article 31(3)(c) Vienna Convention show, nevertheless, that account is generally to be taken of the following aspects: (1) Article 31(3)(c) is part of the general interpretation process envisaged in Articles 31 and 32: the treaty itself plays a central role. It has to be interpreted in good faith in accordance with its terms in their context and in the light of its object and purpose. If the interpretation shows that the treaty has not contracted out of the conflicting rule, the principle of systemic integration applies and can be described as a presumption of compatibility; (2) this presumption means for *inter*-regime relations that diverging commitments must be harmonised – as far as possible – so that they produce effects that are fully in accordance with existing law; and (3) this process of harmonisation requires that a fair balance has to be struck between the conflicting commitments.

---

62 Cf. *Georges Pinson (France) v. United Mexican States*, 19 Oct. 1928, Recueil des sentences arbitrales, vol. V, p. 327 (422); *Right of Passage over Indian Territory (Portugal v. India), Preliminary objections, I.C.J. Reports 1957*, p. 125 (para. 142); ILC Fragmentation Report, Conclusions, para. 19.

63 Cf. C.J. Borgen, 'Resolving Treaty Conflicts' (2005) 37 *George Washington International Law Review* 573, 639–40.

64 D. French, 'Treaty Interpretation and the Incorporation of Extraneous Legal Rules' (2006) 55 *International and Comparative Law Quarterly* 281, 314.

65 Cf. ILC Fragmentation Report, p. 253; C.J. Borgen, 'Treaty Conflict and Normative Fragmentation' in D. Hollis (ed.), above n. 31, p. 450; D. French, above n. 64, 313–14.

Striking a fair balance between competing norms of different law regimes according to point (3) presupposes, first, a clear recognition of the interests and values embodied in the norms at issue.[66] As Judge Kooijmans, Judge Buergenthal and Judge Higgins put forward in seeking a balance between the conflicting aims of personal immunity and liability for international crimes:[67] 'International law seeks the accommodation of this value [the interest of the community of states to allow certain state officials to act freely on the inter-state level without unwarranted interference] with the fight against impunity, and not the triumph of one norm over the other.' Secondly, the clear recognition of the interests and values underlying the norms at issue provides also the basis for considering one of the major principles of interpretation: the principle of effectiveness. This principle stipulates that particular provisions are to be interpreted so as to give them fullest weight and effect consistent with the normal meaning of the terms and with other parts of the text.[68] Finally, the process of striking a fair balance must not result in a modification of the treaty at issue. In the process of striking a balance between a treaty norm under interpretation and another rule of international law, the temptation to rewrite the treaty – under the guise of interpreting it – should be resisted.[69] As long as this process of legal reasoning and harmonious interpretation leads to a result that is fully in accordance with existing law, there is no need to give precedence to one of the norms.

5. THE INTERACTION BETWEEN INTERNATIONAL ANTI-CORRUPTION LAW AND HUMAN RIGHTS LAW

5.1. NORM CONFLICT BETWEEN DIFFERENT LAW REGIMES

Norm conflicts between international anti-corruption law and IHRL cannot be resolved by simply giving precedence to either of them. The relationship between the UNCAC and IHRL is an example of normative fragmentation in international law: norm conflicts between different regimes. In addressing such conflicts there is a need to resort to techniques of interpretation or coordination

---

66 Cf. J. Dugard and C. Van den Wyngart, 'Reconciling Extradition with Human Rights' (1998) 92 *American Journal of International Law* 187, 188.

67 See their Joint Separate Opinion to *Arrest Warrant of 11 April 2000 (The Democratic Republic of the Congo* v. *Belgium)*, paras 75 and 79.

68 G.G. Fitzmaurice, 'The Law and Procedure of the International Court of Justice: Treaty Interpretation and certain other Treaty Points' (1951) 28 *British Yearbook of International Law* 1, 9.

69 H. Thirlway, 'Treaty Law and the Law of Treaties in Recent Case-Law of the International Court' in M. Craven and M. Fitzmaurice (eds), *Interrogating the Treaty – Essays in the Contemporary Law of Treaties*, Wolf Legal Publishers, Nijmegen 2005, p. 28.

that can avert or otherwise 'draw the sting' from (potential) conflicts.[70] Given the capacity of the principle of systemic integration, this principle is of considerable relevance for the resolution of norm conflicts between the UNCAC and IHRL. As the drivers of norm conflicts can be manifold, it is certainly difficult to present a fixed framework for their resolution. With the considerations on the capacity of Article 31(3)(c) Vienna Convention in mind, it is nonetheless possible to outline some aspects on norm conflict resolution between the UNCAC and international law.

5.2. INTERPRETATIVE MEANS AS RESPONSE TO NORM CONFLICTS: THE TREATY IN THE FIRST PLACE

In consideration of the principle of consent and the legal practice, first resort should always be had to the treaty text in the event that a norm conflict arises. In this regard, an interpretative exercise of the treaty text itself in the sense of Article 31 Vienna Convention will take place.[71] An interpretative analysis of the UNCAC's provisions gives, in a few cases, information on how a particular human rights obligation concerned is to be considered. In these cases an interpretation of the treaty text itself shows that specific human rights obligations are to be considered and are relevant in the interpretation of these UNCAC provisions (for instance, Article 30(4); Article 30(6); or Article 32(2) UNCAC). These UNCAC provisions determine the same legal effect that the principle of systemic integration suggests anyway: they oblige States parties to establish specific anti-corruption measures in accordance with specific human rights obligations. As far as a UNCAC norm is inconsistent with human rights obligations, the latter has to be maintained and not violated.

5.3. THE PRINCIPLE OF SYSTEMIC INTEGRATION

5.3.1. *The Presumption of Compatibility*

In general, the principle of systemic integration nonetheless applies anyway and is especially relevant for provisions that potentially conflict with human rights obligations and do not determine accordance with the latter. The principle of systemic integration can be articulated as a presumption of compatibility with two aspects: (1) that, in entering into anti-corruption obligations, States parties intended not to act inconsistently with generally recognised rules and principles

70 Cf. C.J. Borgen, above n. 65, p. 469.

71 Cf. F. Berman, 'Treaty "Interpretation" in a Judicial Context' (2004) 29 *Yale Journal of International Law* 315, 321.

of international law or with previous treaty obligations – including those on human rights protection; and (2) that a convention such as the UNCAC must be deemed tacitly to refer to general rules of international law for all questions that it does not itself resolve in express terms or in a different way.

Presumption of compatibility is reflected in the *Right of Passage* case, in which the ICJ specified that: 'it is a rule of interpretation that a text emanating from a Government must, in principle, be interpreted as producing and as intended to produce effects in accordance with existing law and not in violation of it'.[72]

5.3.2. *Obligations on Human Rights Protection as Interpretative Background: The 'Party Problem'*

The presumption of compatibility, in principle, comprises human rights obligations derived from customary law, legal principles and human rights treaties. Any anti-corruption treaty is thus to be interpreted and applied in accordance with obligations on human rights protection of customary law and, in principle, human rights treaties. With the latter category the so-called 'party problem' comes into play: the issue of whether a given human rights treaty is 'applicable in the relations between the parties' in the sense of Article 31(3)(c) Vienna Convention.

Two different scenarios may be of practical relevance: (1) the situation in which a State party implements an international anti-corruption rule within its domestic law; and (2) the situation in which two or more States parties to a treaty such as the UNCAC, are involved in the application and interpretation of a norm and different human rights treaties are binding upon those States parties. The first scenario is less of a problem as to what human rights treaties exactly are relevant in the application and interpretation of international anti-corruption rules. As a consequence of the *pacta sunt servanda* principle, the State has to apply the UNCAC in accordance with those human rights treaties that are binding upon that State.

In respect of the second scenario, for example, in a case of legal assistance, a requested State could be obliged under a specific human rights treaty in the light of which the requested State interprets a certain UNCAC measure on international cooperation restrictively; as a consequence, the requested State could refuse legal assistance. The requesting State, however, could argue that not all the parties to the UNCAC are party to the human rights treaty in the light of which the requested State interprets the UNCAC measure on cooperation restrictively; the requesting State could therefore insist that the requested State grant legal assistance. As a convention such as the UNCAC promotes

[72] *Right of Passage over Indian Territory (Portugal v. India), Preliminary objections, ICJ Reports 1957*, p. 125 (para. 142).

international cooperation,[73] the second scenario is of high relevance and arises in connection with measures such as mutual legal assistance[74] or extradition.[75] Regarding the scenario of legal assistance, the UNCAC occasionally provides for a determination on what and whose law is relevant in the application of the UNCAC. For example, Article 46(2) UNCAC states that 'mutual legal assistance shall be afforded to the fullest extent possible under relevant laws, treaties, agreements and arrangements of the requested State Party'. In the application and interpretation of measures on mutual legal assistance pursuant to Article 46 UNCAC, those human rights treaties that are binding upon the requested State are thus relevant. This means that if legal assistance is requested under Article 46 UNCAC, the requested State's restrictive interpretation would be in compliance with the UNCAC.

If the applicable law is not specified in the UNCAC, the 'party problem' arises and involves the following issue:[76] is it necessary that all the parties to the UNCAC are also parties to the human rights treaty relied upon for interpretation purposes, or is it sufficient that the parties between, say, a measure of international cooperation takes place are parties to the human rights treaty relied upon for interpretation purposes? In this regard, emphasis should be placed on the necessity of finding a multilateral context in which reference to human rights treaties – as aids to interpretation as defined by Article 31(3)(c) Vienna Convention – is possible.[77] Regarding human rights treaties as a reference point for interpretation purposes of a specific treaty, it is appropriate to follow the approach that focuses on the presumed common intention of all parties to that treaty under interpretation.[78] According to this approach, it is useful to take into account the extent to which the treaty relied upon for interpretation has been (implicitly) accepted by all States parties of the treaty under interpretation. Actually, all treaties on human rights protection rest on the intention to protect individuals against violations of their internationally guaranteed rights. This intention can serve as an appropriate point of departure to determine whether a given human rights treaty – envisaged as a reference point for interpretation – can be taken to have been accepted or at least tolerated by all parties of the UNCAC. To put it more explicitly: the normative content of the rule to be referred to under Article 31(3)(c) Vienna Convention has to find support in the majority of the relevant international instruments and in the practice of the States that are

---

73 See particularly Arts 43–50 UNCAC.

74 See Art. 46 UNCAC.

75 See Art. 44 UNCAC.

76 For an overview of the 'party problem', see M. Ciesiolka, above n. 39, pp. 164–68.

77 Cf. ILC Fragmentation Report, paras 450 and 471.

78 J. Pauwelyn, *Conflict of Norms in Public International Law – How WTO Law Relates to other Rules of International Law*, Cambridge University Press, Cambridge 2003, p. 261.

parties to a treaty such as the UNCAC.[79] In the above-described second scenario of dispute on legal assistance the decisive question is thus whether the normative content of the rule in the light of which the requested State interpreted the UNCAC measure on cooperation restrictively finds support in the majority of international instruments on human rights protection and in the practice of the States parties to the UNCAC. If this is the case, the restrictive interpretation of the UNCAC measure would be in compliance with Article 31(3)(c) Vienna Convention.

Variety in the interpretation of particular treaty terms among the States parties to the UNCAC would be a reflection of the UNCAC's character as treaty on international cooperation and of legitimate difference due to the plurality of norms in international law. This difference does not have to be necessarily perceived as a threat to the coherence of international law in general; it may be an expression of a pluralist character of international law. As it has been stressed:

> The international legal system is a constructed system and our views of that system may well become a self-fulfilling prophecy. If international legal actors think of the system as fragmented, it may well become so as new obligations are created and enforced without consideration of the coherence of the overall system. However, if international lawyers, judges, and even politicians conceive of the system as pluralist, they are far more likely to leave room for legitimate difference, while recalling the importance of unity in crafting rules, developing procedures, building institutions, or issuing judgments.[80]

5.3.3. Interpretative Guidance: Clarifying the Meaning of Provisions

If the meaning of a term or a phrase contained in an anti-corruption treaty is unclear and concerns interests of individuals, the principle of systemic integration can assist in defining the meaning by reference to applicable human rights standards. As noted earlier, Article 32 UNCAC envisages the protection of witnesses, experts and victims who give testimony concerning offences established according to the UNCAC. The criteria and procedures for such protection have to be defined by taking into account relevant international standards on human rights protection. These include, for instance, the rights to life, liberty and security of persons.[81]

---

79 See the approach of the ECtHR in *Demir and Baykara v. Turkey*, no. 34503/97, paras 85–86, and *National Union of Rail, Maritime and Transport Workers v. UK*, no. 31045/10, para. 76.

80 W.W. Burke-White, 'International Legal Pluralism' (2004) 25 *Michigan Journal of International Law* 963, 979, suggesting that international law is not fragmenting, but rather being transformed into a pluralist system.

81 The protection of witnesses has to be balanced against the rights of the defendant (Art. 32(2) UNCAC); see, for instance, the ECtHR in *Doorson v. Netherlands*, no. 20524/92, para. 70.

5.4. A REASONABLE BALANCE BETWEEN CONFLICTING NORMS

5.4.1. *Open-Textured and Discretionary Wording of the UNCAC*

The presumption of compatibility means, in practice: that when there are multiple possible interpretations of a given provision of the UNCAC, one of which would cause a violation of a human rights obligation, that violative interpretation has to be avoided in favour of one that is not violative of the human rights obligation. In this process, a conflict would be averted.[82] In addition, conflicting norms between the UNCAC and an obligation on human rights protection should be 'rendered compatible' by striking a reasonable balance between the conflicting norms that allows for compliance with all obligations at issue. This presupposes that the application of a UNCAC norm does not unavoidably lead to the breach of a human rights obligation; an unavoidable breach would constitute a narrow conflict. The type of conflict depends upon the relevant parameters of a particular case. The qualification of a conflict can therefore be only subject to a case-by-case analysis. Given the structure and language of the UNCAC's provisions, the conflicts between the Convention and international human rights obligations will be generally rather of a broad (or apparent) type. The most obligations of the UNCAC are phrased using more discretionary language. In addition, the UNCAC includes programmatic provisions that are, by their nature, rather open textured. It lacks extremely explicit language. The UNCAC uses rather broad and general terms, having an aspirational character. This aspirational character also reflects that the UNCAC is intended to achieve a wide margin of appreciation by and among the States parties: the discretionary and broad terminology ensures room to consider other factors and normative standards external to the UNCAC. For instance, Article 52(1) UNCAC obliges States parties to take measures to ensure that financial institutions verify their customers' identity. Article 52(1) UNCAC stipulates further that such enhanced scrutiny shall be 'reasonably designed'. The term 'reasonably' affords flexibility in the mode of implementing Article 52(1) UNCAC for the sake of complying with the requirements of obligations on human rights protection. Another example in this regard is Article 10 UNCAC, according to which each State party shall take measures 'to enhance transparency in its public administration …, where appropriate'. Qualifications such as 'where appropriate' are present in many UNCAC norms that enlist anti-corruption measures to be established, extended, or improved.[83] This open-textured and broad wording allows for a significant flexibility in the mode of interpreting and applying the norms of the

[82] Cf. C.J. Borgen, above n. 63, pp. 459–60.

[83] For instance, Arts 5(4), 6(1), 7(1), 8(3) and (5), 10, 12(1), 14(1) and 43(1) UNCAC.

UNCAC.[84] The norms of the UNCAC can therefore be relatively easily adjusted to conflicting human rights obligations. This broad wording would also allow for taking account of subsequent developments in IHRL. It is therefore rather unlikely that the interpretation or application of a UNCAC provision will lead, unavoidably, to the breach of a human rights obligation. The norm conflicts between the UNCAC and IHRL will be therefore rather of a broad type.

5.4.2. The Principle of Effectiveness

International law seeks the harmonisation of different interests.[85] In this sense, it is said that treaty interpretation is diplomacy – and it is the business of diplomacy to mitigate conflicts.[86] In the process of striking a balance between conflicting norms, a clear recognition of the interests and values embodied in the norms at issue is therefore of high importance. Clear recognition of the interests behind the norms at issue specifies the values to be balanced. In addition, it provides the basis for taking account of one of the major principles of interpretation: the principle of effectiveness.[87] This principle determines that the good faith requirement and the object and purpose of a treaty demand to prefer an interpretation that enables the treaty to have appropriate effects.[88]

The principle of effectiveness has two aspects:[89] (1) it incorporates the maxim that prefers a meaning that ascribes some effect to a term rather than no effect; and (2) it imports a teleological element into treaty interpretation. This aspect is related to the demands of the treaty's objects and purposes that articulate certain interests. In general, the UNCAC is a reflection of the interest of States in the suppression of corrupt activities for the purpose of ensuring the security and stability of States and a contribution to the maintenance of international security. This interest includes the aims of establishing and maintaining a framework of

---

84 Cf., e.g., the ECtHR in *Nada v. Switzerland*, no. 10593/08, para. 178, in which the wording 'where appropriate' in Security Council Resolution 1390(2002) was qualified as having 'the effect of affording the national authorities a certain flexibility in the mode of implementation of the resolution' for the sake of meeting the requirements of the ECHR.

85 Cf. C. Rousseau, 'De la Compatibilité des normes juridiques contradictoires dans l'ordre international' (1932) 39 *Revue Générale de Droit International Public* 133, 153, who states that 'dérogation, abrogation, ce sont là des formules trop absolues, dont s'accommode mal l'ordre juridique international, plus soucieux d'harmoniser que d'exclure, d'adapter que de détruire. ... lorsqu'il est en présence de deux accords de volontés divergents, il doit être tout naturellement porté à rechercher leur coordination plutôt qu'à consacrer leur antagonisme'.

86 ILC Fragmentation Report, para. 37.

87 Cf. G.G. Fitzmaurice, 'The Law and Procedure of the International Court of Justice' (1951) 28 *British Yearbook of International Law* 1, 9.

88 ILC, Draft Articles on the Law of Treaties with Commentaries, ILC Yearbook (1966), vol. II, p. 187 (219).

89 R. Gardiner, 'The Vienna Convention Rules on Treaty Interpretation' in D. Hollis (ed.), above n. 31, p. 496; see, further, H. Lauterpacht, *The Development of International Law by the International Court*, Stevens & Sons, London 1958, pp. 227–30.

anti-corruption measures and of international cooperation in the fight against corruption. In addition, it encompasses the aims of preserving or regaining confidence in adherence to the law and the functioning of the justice systems of States as well as the fight against impunity, which are, for instance, reflected in the UNCAC's mechanisms on legal assistance, asset recovery and extradition. It is the accommodation of this interest with the protection of individuals against violations of their internationally guaranteed rights that has to be sought and not the 'technical' triumph of human rights law over the UNCAC or vice versa.

5.4.3. The Principle of Effectiveness and Striking a Balance between Conflicting Norms

Striking a balance between conflicting norms inevitably involves the question of the normative weight to be given to particular rights and obligations. In general, this normative weight can be argued only on a case-by-case basis.[90] In this connection, care should be taken that the different obligations at stake are being considered according to the needs of their character. As aforementioned, the UNCAC has a rather programmatic character. Its provisions fundamentally contrast with provisions providing individual rights. Unlike other rule complexes in international law, human rights treaties do not merely protect the reciprocal interest of other signatory States, but the rights of non-parties, namely individual rights-holders.[91] This special characteristic requires that human rights treaties are interpreted in a manner sufficiently favourable to the effective protection of individual rights.[92] Balancing different law regimes by way of systemic integration is indeed an instrument to be used in a responsible and pertinent way.[93] In addition, there are no specific rules for dealing with conflicts between two regimes.[94] Systemic integration of such *inter*-regime relations should therefore be based upon a process of carefully exercised responsible reasoning.

Human rights are certainly becoming increasingly important in international practice and are a very strong counterweight to any other international legal obligation.[95] Interpretative principles have been developed that aim to take

---

90 ILC Fragmentation Report, para. 474.

91 L. Brilmayer, 'The Structure of International Human Rights Agreements' (2007) 77 *British Yearbook of International Law* 163, 165.

92 Cf. K. Mechlem, 'Treaty Bodies and the Interpretation of Human Rights' (2009) 42 *Vanderbilt Journal of Transnational Law* 905, 912; B. Simma, 'Universality of International Law from the Perspective of a Practitioner' (2009) 20 *European Journal of International Law* 265, 277.

93 Cf. J. Klabbers, 'Reluctant Grundnormen: Articles 31(3)(c) and 42 of the Vienna Convention on the Law of the Treaties and the Fragmentation of International Law' in M. Craven *et al.*, *Time, History and International Law*, Nijhoff Publishers, Leiden 2007, p. 143.

94 ILC Fragmentation Report, para. 253.

95 J. Vidmar, 'Rethinking Jus Cogens after Germany v. Italy: Back to Article 53?' (2013) LX *Netherlands International Law Review* 1, 24.

account of the character of human rights treaties. These include terms such as 'autonomous concepts', 'living instrument' and 'practicality'.[96] These principles all derive from the consensus that interpretations that have no actual effect for human rights protection do not cohere with good faith interpretations of the wording and context of human rights treaties.[97]

As a multilateral treaty, the UNCAC has its legitimate and important objects and purposes, too, which should be adequately considered – not least due to the principle of good faith. The object and purposes of the UNCAC therefore likewise deserve to be considered within a process of striking a balance between its norms and human rights obligations. Based on a responsible case-by-case analysis, the principle of good faith and the object and purpose of the UNCAC and a given human rights obligation require preferably striking a balance that enables obligations from both regimes – the UNCAC's anti-corruption regime and the international human rights regime – to have appropriate effects as far as possible.

In this process, the character of human rights calls for a consideration that ensures their practical effect for the individual concerned.[98] This consideration certainly depends upon the circumstances and the particular human rights concerned in a given case.[99] In any case, nevertheless, the aspect of effectiveness regarding human rights treaties should be understood as shifting the burden of proof from the individual to the State in justifying the infringement of, or lack of measures for, protecting rights.[100]

In addition, the weight to be given to the rights and obligations should reflect the fact that some rules of international law are 'more important' than others.[101] These include: (1) recognised hierarchical relations that express a strong weight by the substance of the rules (*jus cogens*); (2) 'quasi-hierarchical relations' by virtue of a treaty provision (Article 103 UN Charter); or (3) rules specifying obligations owed to the international community as a whole (obligations *erga omnes*). The effects of these concepts have to be considered as important aspects in the process of balancing. Of practical relevance for the UNCAC will be the first and the last categories. A norm of the UNCAC could conflict with a human

---

96 See, for instance, the ECtHR in *Tyrer v. UK*, no. 5856/72, para. 31; *Chassagnou et al. v. France*, nos 25088/94 *et al.*, para. 100; *Selmouni v. France*, no. 25803/94, para. 101.

97 B. Çali, above n. 31, p. 538.

98 For instance, the ECtHR in *Airey v. Ireland*, no. 6289/73, para. 24; and *Chassagnou et al. v. France*, nos 25088/94 *et al.*, para. 100.

99 See, further, on specific approaches to interpret human rights treaties to the extent required by the interpretative task, J. Tobin, 'Seeking to Persuade: A Constructive Approach to Human Rights Treaty Interpretation' (2010) 23 *Harvard Human Rights Journal* 1.

100 B. Çali, above n. 31, p. 540.

101 Cf. Z. Galicki, 'Hierarchy in International Law within the Context of Its Fragmentation' in I. Buffard *et al.* (eds), *International Law between Universalism and Fragmentation*, Nijhoff Publishers, Leiden 2008, pp. 55 *et seq.*; ILC Fragmentation Report, para. 407.

rights obligation valid in an *erga omnes* way and with a human right of a *jus cogens* character. In this connection it has to be noted that a *jus cogens* norm necessarily has the procedural scope of an *erga omnes* norm. Not all *erga omnes* obligations, however, have a *jus cogens* character.[102] The concept of obligations *erga-omnes* is nevertheless aimed at the widest application of such obligations.[103] In addition, there is no question that a treaty must not be interpreted so as to produce effects that are in violation of norms of a *jus cogens* character.[104]

5.4.4. In Essence

In the event of conflict between the UNCAC and human rights obligations of an *erga omnes* character and/or *jus cogens* character, the UNCAC should, to the extent that is possible, be interpreted as being consistent with the latter. If this is not possible, the human rights obligation of an *erga omnes* character and/or *jus cogens* character prevails.[105] This scenario is, however, very unlikely; the language of the UNCAC offers enough flexibility to be adjusted to human rights obligations of such categories. In general, conflicts between the UNCAC and international human rights obligations should be resolved pursuant to the principle of systemic integration by striking a balance between the conflicting norms. This balance should enable both obligations – as far as possible – to have appropriate effects. The case of a narrow conflict – that is to say, a situation in which the UNCAC norm and the human rights obligation are irreconcilable – is unlikely. This finding is mainly based upon the discretionary and open-textured wording of the UNCAC's provisions, having an aspirational character that indicates that this treaty not merely allows for accordance with obligations on human rights protection including subsequent developments but even encourages it. Among all international anti-corruption frameworks the UNCAC is certainly the most far-reaching. The guidelines, previously identified, on how to deal with conflicting norms may therefore also be applicable to other anti-corruption regimes and/or other frameworks addressing transnational crime.

The question whether international anti-corruption frameworks and other frameworks against transnational crime prove successful is certainly not a purely legal question. It is predominantly dependent upon effective international cooperation between criminal law authorities and security agencies. This largely

---

102 See, further, on the distinction between norms valid in an *erga omnes* way and norms of a *jus cogens* character P. Picone, 'The Distinction between *Jus Cogens* and Obligations *Erga Omnes*' in E. Cannizzaro (ed.), *The Law of Treaties beyond the Vienna Convention*, Oxford University Press, Oxford 2011, pp. 411–24; ILC Fragmentation Report, para. 408.

103 Cf. Z. Galicki, above n. 101, pp. 55 *et seq.*

104 Separate opinion of Judge Simma in *Oil Platforms (Islamic Republic of Iran v. United States of America), ICJ Reports 2003*, p. 324 (para. 9); D. French, above n. 64, p. 285; see Art. 53 VCLT.

105 Cf. ILC Fragmentation Report, Conclusions, para. 42.

involves practical aspects such as liaising intensely and efficiently, considering that the different States involved may have different legal standards. Coping with these differences comes with negotiation and exchange. In balancing the conflicting norms, it is of essential relevance to consider that it is not about a technical triumph of one norm over another. Whenever a norm conflict with human rights in the field of criminal law arises, it is about striking a fair balance between the contradicting interests of public security, including the fight against impunity and rights of individuals. This balance should clearly reflect the special character of human rights[106] and fundamental legal principles such as proportionality and fairness, taking public confidence into account. In doing so, an inherent element of international treaty interpretation unfolds quite naturally: diplomacy that seeks the accommodation of differing interests.

106 See above section 3.2.

PART III

CONVERGENCES AND DIVERGENCES BETWEEN INTERNATIONAL HUMAN RIGHTS LAW AND INTERNATIONAL HUMANITARIAN LAW

'IT WAS THE BEST OF TIMES, IT WAS THE WORST OF TIMES': A TALE OF DETENTION IN TIME OF EMERGENCY

Federica FAVUZZA

*It was the best of times, it was the worst of times, it was the age of wisdom, it was the age of foolishness, it was the epoch of belief, it was the epoch of incredulity, it was the season of Light, it was the season of Darkness, it was the spring of hope, it was the winter of despair, we had everything before us, we had nothing before us, we were all going direct to Heaven, we were all going direct the other way.**

* C. Dickens, *A Tale of Two Cities*, 1859.

1. INTRODUCTION

Over these past few years, the human right to personal liberty has become one of the hottest topics in international law. Despite the relevance that it had already acquired in recent times, especially in the context of the war on terror,[1] the implications of public emergencies on this right have recently been addressed by international courts and human rights mechanisms.[2] While existing legal scholarship has dealt extensively with the complex issue of the interaction between human rights norms and those of other branches of international law, especially international humanitarian law (IHL), this chapter's aim is to assess the impact of public emergencies on the right to personal liberty from a victim's perspective.

To this end, the chapter will tell the story of a fictional character, Dr Alexandre Manette (clearly borrowed from Dickens' novel *A Tale of Two Cities*), who is suddenly deprived of his liberty by administrative authorities on security grounds,[3] being therefore subjected to what is generally defined as a 'security detention', i.e. a deprivation of personal liberty imposed on an individual 'not in contemplation of prosecution on a criminal charge'.[4] It will be a tale of two countries, as it will compare Dr Manette's situation in two alternative scenarios: while in the first scenario he will be detained by a State party only to the International Covenant on Civil and Political Rights (ICCPR),[5] in the second one he will be detained by a State party only to the European Convention on Human Rights (ECHR).[6] Sections 2 and 3 will assess Dr Manette's situation in these two alternative scenarios, assuming that he is being detained for security reasons outside the context of a public emergency. Section 4 will then analyse Dr Manette's security detention in time of emergency, distinguishing among three different cases: section 4.1 will deal with a situation of public emergency not

---

1 See, inter alia: S. Borelli, 'Casting Light on the Legal Black Hole: International Law and Detentions Abroad in the "War on Terror"' (2005) 87 *International Review of the Red Cross* 39.

2 See, inter alia: *Hassan v. UK* [GC], no. 29750/09, ECHR, 2014; UNCHR, 'General Comment 35 – Article 9 (Liberty and Security of Person)' (16 December 2014) UN Doc CCPR/C/GC/35; UNCHR, 'Report of the Working Group on Arbitrary Detention – United Nations Basic Principles and Guidelines on remedies and procedures on the right of anyone deprived of their liberty to bring proceedings before a court' (24 May 2015) UN Doc WGAD/CRP.1/2015.

3 Thus, the investigation will only deal with the case of deprivation of liberty for security reasons, leaving out the issue of detentions carried out in connection with criminal charges.

4 UNCHR, 'General Comment 35 – Article 9 (Liberty and Security of Person)' (16 December 2014) UN Doc CCPR/C/GC/35 [15].

5 International Covenant on Civil and Political Rights (adopted 16 December 1966, entered into force 23 March 1976) 999 UNTS 171 (ICCPR).

6 Convention for the Protection of Human Rights and Fundamental Freedoms (European Convention on Human Rights, as amended) (ECHR).

involving an armed conflict; section 4.2 will address the case of an international armed conflict (IAC); section 4.3 will examine the case of a non-international armed conflict (NIAC).[7] Through this two-fold comparison, this chapter will assess whether individuals administratively deprived of their liberty on security grounds in a situation of public emergency have a better chance of seeing their complaints succeed before the Human Rights Committee (HRC) or before the European Court of Human Rights (ECtHR).

The investigation will be limited to grounds for detention and procedural guarantees, neglecting the important (yet less controversial) issue of detention conditions. Moreover, for the sake of argument, this chapter will assume that the extraterritorial application of human rights treaty norms is universally accepted. Suffice it to say that, at least in the event of agents of a State exercising control and authority over an individual (as in the case of detention), extraterritorial jurisdiction is generally accepted by relevant treaty bodies.[8]

2. FIRST SCENARIO: DR ALEXANDRE MANETTE IS DETAINED BY A STATE PARTY TO THE ICCPR

In this first hypothetical scenario, Dr Manette is suddenly deprived of his liberty by the administrative authorities of a State party to the ICCPR (State A) outside the context of a public emergency. He is being held on security grounds and no criminal charge is pressed against him. Clearly, the question arises whether Dr Manette's deprivation of liberty under these circumstances would be considered as lawful or unlawful under the ICCPR.

In order to answer this question and determine whether the HRC would find that Dr Manette's right to personal liberty has been violated in the present case, this section will examine the right to liberty and security of person enshrined in Article 9 paragraph 1 ICCPR, which reads as follows:

> Everyone has the right to liberty and security of person. No one shall be subjected to arbitrary arrest or detention. No one shall be deprived of his liberty except on such grounds and in accordance with such procedure as are established by law.

As stressed by the HRC in its General Comment No 35, 'arrest within the meaning of Article 9 need not involve a formal arrest as defined under domestic law'.[9] Such provision is thus applicable to all deprivations of liberty, rather

---

7 This chapter will refer to only treaty law, leaving aside relevant customary international law.

8 See, inter alia: N. Lubell, 'Human Rights Obligations in Military Occupation' (2012) 94 *International Review of the Red Cross* 317.

9 UNCHR, 'General Comment 35 – Article 9 (Liberty and Security of Person)' (16 December 2014) UN Doc CCPR/C/GC/35 [13].

than being limited to those taking place in connection with criminal charges. Examples of deprivation of liberty may include, but are not limited to, police custody, imprisonment after conviction, house arrest, administrative detention and involuntary hospitalisation.[10]

In the ICCPR system, the right to liberty and security of person is far from absolute, as anyone could be deprived of his or her liberty. However, as with other rights and liberties enshrined in the Covenant, the right to personal liberty under Article 9 can only be made subject to those limitations that are necessary (as no alternative measures are available) and proportionate (as a balance is to be struck between the purpose of such limitation and the effective protection of human rights).[11] Moreover, Article 9 specifically requires that any deprivation of liberty be neither arbitrary nor unlawful.

As regards the notion of lawfulness, it is both substantive and procedural, as it refers to both the substantive grounds for a deprivation of liberty – which 'must be prescribed by law and … defined with sufficient precision to avoid overly broad or arbitrary interpretation or application'[12] – and the procedures to carry out such deprivation of liberty – which should also be provided by law. The term 'law' is to be interpreted in its strict sense as 'a parliamentary statute or an equivalent, unwritten norm of common law, accessible to all individuals subject to the relevant jurisdiction'.[13] Therefore, administrative provisions would not normally be sufficient for the purposes of Article 9 and any administrative act providing for a deprivation of liberty would be acceptable only if it took place in enforcement of a law clearly providing for such 'interference' and regulating the procedure to be followed.[14]

As for the notion of arbitrariness, it is undoubtedly difficult to define. In General Comment No 35, the HRC reiterates what it has already stressed in the renowned *Van Alphen* case,[15] underlining that the notion of arbitrariness 'is not to be equated with "against the law", but must be interpreted more broadly' as it should 'include elements of inappropriateness, injustice, lack of predictability and due process of law, as well as elements of reasonableness, necessity and proportionality'.[16]

---

10 Ibid., [4]–[5].

11 L. Pineschi, 'Il Patto delle Nazioni Unite sui diritti civili e politici' in L. Pineschi (ed.), *La tutela internazionale dei diritti umani: Norme, garanzie, prassi*, Giuffrè, Milano 2006, p. 83.

12 UNCHR, 'General Comment 35 – Article 9 (Liberty and Security of Person)' (16 December 2014) UN Doc CCPR/C/GC/35 [22].

13 M. Nowak, *UN Covenant on Civil and Political Rights: CCPR Commentary*, (Engel, Kehl 2005, p. 224.

14 Ibid.

15 UNCHR, 'H. van Alphen v The Netherlands' (15 August 1990) UN Doc CCPR/C/71/D/305/1988 [5.8].

16 Ibid.

Still, the ICCPR does not provide for any enumeration of permissible grounds for detention. It only 'expressly recognizes that individuals may be detained on criminal charges' (Article 9) and 'expressly prohibits' imprisonment on the ground of inability to fulfil a contractual obligation (Article 11).[17] In the HRC's view, any other regime involving a deprivation of liberty is admissible insofar as it is 'established by law', it does not 'amount to an evasion of the limits on the criminal justice system by providing the equivalent of criminal punishment without the applicable protections'[18] and it is 'accompanied by procedures that prevent arbitrary detention'.[19]

As a matter of fact, paragraphs 2 to 5 of Article 9 provide for specific safeguards for persons deprived of their liberty: the right to be informed, at the time of arrest, of the reasons for their arrest and to be promptly informed of any possible charges against them (paragraph 2); the right of those arrested or detained on criminal charges to be brought promptly before a judge or other officer authorised by law to exercise judicial power and be entitled to trial within a reasonable time or to release (paragraph 3); the right to *habeas corpus* proceedings (paragraph 4); and the right to compensation in the event of unlawful arrest or detention (paragraph 5). As clearly stated in General Comment No 35:

> Paragraphs 2 to 5 of article 9 set out specific safeguards for the protection of liberty and security of person. Some of the provisions of article 9 (part of paragraph 2 and the whole of paragraph 3) apply only in connection with criminal charges. But the rest, in particular the important guarantee laid down in paragraph 4, i.e. the right to review by a court of the legality of detention, applies to all persons deprived of liberty.[20]

Therefore, even deprivations of liberty not taking place in connection with criminal charges must be necessary and proportionate, as well as lawful and non-arbitrary, while also respecting the aforementioned set of procedural safeguards set out in paragraphs 2, 4 and 5 of Article 9.

Out of all these safeguards, the most important one for persons deprived of their liberty is definitely the right to *habeas corpus* under paragraph 4, which entitles anyone who is deprived of his or her liberty 'to take proceedings before a court, in order that that court may decide without delay on the lawfulness of his detention and order his release if the detention is not lawful'. This right 'applies to all detention by official action or pursuant to official authorization, including detention in connection with criminal proceedings, military detention, security

17 UNCHR, 'General Comment 35 – Article 9 (Liberty and Security of Person)' (16 December 2014) UN Doc CCPR/C/GC/35 [14].

18 Ibid.

19 Ibid.

20 Ibid., [4].

detention' and 'immigration detention', the only exception being that of prisoners 'serving the minimum duration of a prison sentence as decided by a court of law after a conviction'.[21]

It is important to highlight that the reviewing court 'must have the power to review the individual circumstances of detention and that to order release from unlawful detention'.[22] Such court 'should ordinarily be a court within the judiciary' or, exceptionally, a specialised tribunal, provided that it is established by law[23] and independent of the executive and legislative branches or, at least, capable of enjoying 'judicial independence in deciding legal matters in proceedings that are judicial in nature'.[24] Therefore, the notion of tribunal within the meaning of Article 9 is identical to that provided by Article 14 (on the right to a fair trial),[25] as any individual deprived of his or her liberty has a right to take *habeas corpus* proceedings before 'a competent, independent and impartial tribunal established by law'.[26] In particular, the requirement of independence entails that Judges or other members of a tribunal must not be 'subject to directives or in some other manner dependent on other State organs in the exercise of their office', whereas the notion of impartiality 'aims at the specific holding in a given case'.[27] As far as the judicial nature of proceedings is concerned, the HRC has often stressed the importance of the equality of arms[28] and cross-examination,[29] although such requirements are expressly mentioned only in Article 14. In addition, in order for the review to be effective, persons deprived of their liberty have a right 'not only to take proceedings, but also to receive a decision without delay'.[30] They should be afforded 'prompt and regular

---

21 Ibid., [40].

22 M. Nowak, above n. 13, p. 236. See also: UNCHR, 'General Comment 35 – Article 9 (Liberty and Security of Person)' (16 December 2014) UN Doc CCPR/C/GC/35 [41].

23 For the term 'law', see above on the notion of lawfulness.

24 UNCHR, 'General Comment 35 – Article 9 (Liberty and Security of Person)' (16 December 2014) UN Doc CCPR/C/GC/35 [45]. See also the *Vuolanne* case (UNCHR, 'Vuolanne v Finland' (2 May 1989) UN Doc Supp No 40 (A/44/40) at 311 [9.6]), in which the HRC did not 'accept the contention of the State party that the request for review before a superior military officer' was 'comparable to judicial scrutiny of an appeal and that the officials ordering detention' acted 'in a judicial or quasi-judicial manner', therefore concluding that 'the procedure followed in the case of Mr Vuolanne did not have a judicial character'.

25 M. Nowak, above n. 13, p. 235.

26 Ibid., p. 319.

27 Ibid., pp. 320–21.

28 See, inter alia: UNCHR, 'Concluding Observations on Tajikistan' (18 July 2005) UN Doc CCPR/CO/84/TJK [12–13].

29 See, inter alia: UNCHR, 'Concluding Observations on The United Kingdom' (30 July 2008) UN Doc CCPR/C/GBR/CO/6 [17].

30 UNCHR, 'General Comment 35 – Article 9 (Liberty and Security of Person)' (16 December 2014) UN Doc CCPR/C/GC/35 [47].

access to counsel'[31] and be informed, in a language they understand, of their right to *habeas corpus* under paragraph 4.[32]

Thus, should Dr Manette lodge a claim with the HRC, stating that his security detention by State A's authorities violated his right to personal liberty, his prospects of success would depend on whether his detention was carried out in a manner that ensured respect for all of his rights under Article 9 paragraphs 2 to 5 while, at the same time, being necessary and proportional, as well as lawful and non-arbitrary as prescribed by Article 9 paragraph 1. However, as already mentioned, the notion of arbitrariness under the ICCPR is not that easy to define.

In General Comment No 35, the HRC expressly mentions some 'egregious examples' of arbitrary detention, such as the holding of hostages, enforced disappearances, and arrest or detention as punishment for the legitimate exercise of the rights guaranteed by the Covenant or on discriminatory grounds.[33] As regards security detention – defined as a deprivation of personal liberty imposed on an individual 'not in contemplation of prosecution on a criminal charge'[34] – the HRC includes it among the types of detention that, in light of their very essence or their key features, may present 'severe risks of arbitrary deprivation of liberty'.[35]

In the HRC's opinion, security detention would not, *per se*, be arbitrary. As a matter of fact, 'under the most exceptional circumstances', the imposition of security detention could be justified as long as the State concerned could prove that the detained individual constituted 'a present, direct and imperative threat' that could not be addressed by alternative measures.[36] However, the HRC also notes that, in some instances, such detention could turn out to be arbitrary, especially when other effective measures addressing the threat, including the criminal justice system, are available.[37] In addition, it stresses that a regime

31 See, among others: ibid., [46]; UNCHR, '*Berry v Jamaica*' (26 April 1994) UN Doc CCPR/C/50/D/330/1988 [11.1]; UNCHR, 'Kelly v Jamaica' (8 April 1991) UN Doc CCPR/C/41/D/253/1987 [5.6]; UNCHR, 'Concluding Observations on Turkey' (13 November 2012) UN Doc CCPR/C/TUR/CO/1 [17]; UNCHR, 'Concluding Observations on The United Kingdom' (30 July 2008) UN Doc CCPR/C/GBR/CO/6 [16]; UNCHR, 'Concluding Observations on Israel' (21 August 2003) UN Doc CCPR/C/78/ISR [12]–[13]. See also: UNCHR, 'Basic Principles on the Role of Lawyers' (adopted by the Eighth United Nations Congress on the Prevention of Crime and the Treatment of Offenders, Havana, Cuba, 27 August to 7 September 1990) [7] <www.refworld.org/docid/3ddb9f034.html> accessed 02.02.2017.

32 UNCHR, 'General Comment 35 – Article 9 (Liberty and Security of Person)' (16 December 2014) UN Doc CCPR/C/GC/35 [46].

33 Ibid., [16].

34 Ibid., [15].

35 Ibid.

36 Ibid.

37 UNCHR, 'General Comment 35 – Article 9 (Liberty and Security of Person)' (16 December 2014) UN Doc CCPR/C/GC/35 [15].

of security detention could not last longer than absolutely necessary, that the overall length of any possible security detention must be limited, and that any detention must fully respect the guarantees set out by Article 9. In particular, the HRC underlines the importance of 'prompt and regular review by a court or other tribunal possessing the same attributes of independence and impartiality as the judiciary', as well as that of access to counsel and 'disclosure to the detainee of, at least, the essence of the evidence on which the decision is taken'.[38]

Taking all the above mentioned elements together, Dr Manette's security detention by State A's authorities would likely be considered as lawful under the ICCPR, despite the fact that it did not take place in contemplation of criminal prosecution, provided that: (a) he represented a 'present, direct and imperative threat';[39] (b) such a threat could not be addressed by alternative means, as no other effective measure 'addressing the threat, including the criminal justice system', was available;[40] (c) the overall length of his detention was limited; and (d) his detention fully respected the safeguards set out by Article 9, especially with regard to *habeas corpus* proceedings. Therefore, under these circumstances, it is unlikely that Dr Manette's complaint before the HRC would succeed.

3. SECOND SCENARIO: DR ALEXANDRE MANETTE IS DETAINED BY A STATE PARTY TO THE ECHR

In this second hypothetical scenario, Dr Manette is suddenly deprived of his liberty by the administrative authorities of a State party to the ECHR (State B) outside the context of a public emergency. Once again, he is being held on security grounds and no criminal charge is pressed against him. This section aims to determine whether Dr Manette's deprivation of liberty under these circumstances would be a violation of the ECHR, trying also to ascertain whether, once seized, the ECtHR would rule in favour of Dr Manette or in favour of State B.

Article 5 ECHR states that 'everyone has the right to liberty and security of person' but, at the same time, admits that, under certain circumstances, this right can be subject to limitations and an individual can be deprived of his or her liberty.[41] As with the ICCPR system, Article 5 paragraph 1 introduces a

38 Ibid.

39 Ibid., [15].

40 Ibid.

41 In general, any limitation on the rights enshrined in the ECHR must be necessary, proportionate and prescribed by law. See M. Pedrazzi, 'La Convenzione europea sui diritti umani e il suo sistema di controllo' in L. Pineschi, above n. 11, p. 286.

requirement of lawfulness, stating that any deprivation of liberty must take place 'in accordance with a procedure prescribed by law'. However, this provision differs from Article 9 ICCPR, as it does not mention the notion of arbitrariness. Still, the ECtHR has repeatedly held that, 'in a democratic society subscribing to the rule of law, no detention that is arbitrary can ever be regarded as "lawful"'.[42] In the ECtHR's opinion, the notion of arbitrariness within the meaning of Article 5 paragraph 1 'extends beyond lack of conformity with national law, so that a deprivation of liberty may be lawful in terms of domestic law but still arbitrary and thus contrary to the Convention'.[43]

The main difference between Article 5 ECHR and Article 9 ICCPR relates to the grounds for arrest and detention and lies in the fact that, while the latter only prohibits arbitrary deprivations of liberty without clarifying which types of deprivation of liberty are, in fact, prohibited, the former contains an exhaustive list of permissible grounds for arrest and detention. Outside the six hypotheses included in Article 5 paragraph 1(a) to (f), no deprivation of liberty could ever be lawful under the ECHR.

Out of these six cases, the one provided for under lit. (c) is certainly worth mentioning, in light of the preventive nature of one of the grounds envisaged. As a matter of fact, the provision refers to 'the lawful arrest or detention of a person effected for the purpose of bringing him before the competent legal authority on reasonable suspicion of having committed an offence or when it is reasonably considered necessary to prevent his committing an offence or fleeing after having done so'. Therefore, under lit. (c), an individual may be deprived of his or her liberty whenever there is reasonable suspicion that he or she might commit an offence in the future. However, the ECtHR has often stressed that a person may be detained within the meaning of this provision only in the context of criminal proceedings.[44] As a matter of fact, Article 5 paragraph 3 states that anyone arrested or detained in accordance with the provisions of paragraph 1(c) 'shall be brought promptly before a judge or other officer authorised by law to exercise judicial power and shall be entitled to trial within a reasonable time or to release pending trial'. Therefore, 'the said clause permits deprivation of liberty only when such deprivation is effected for the purpose of bringing the person arrested or detained before the competent judicial authority'.[45] The review 'must be automatic and cannot depend on the application of the detained person'.[46] It serves both the purpose of ensuring release of individuals held

[42] *Winterwerp v. Netherlands*, no. 6301/73, 1979, Series A no. 33 [39].
[43] *Saadi v. UK* [GC], no. 13229/03, ECHR, 2008-II 145 [68].
[44] *Ječius v. Lithuania*, no. 34578/97, ECHR, 2000-IX 235 [50].
[45] *Lawless v. Ireland (No. 3)*, no. 332/57, 1961 Series A no. 3 [14].
[46] *McKay v. UK* [GC], no. 543/03, ECHR 2006-X 325 [34].

on a mere suspicion whenever it ceases to be reasonable[47] and that of making sure that no one is indefinitely held in pre-trial detention. Thus, it is clear that, though contemplating some type of preventive detention, 'the list of grounds of permissible detention' in Article 5 paragraph 1 'does not include internment or preventive detention where there is no intention to bring criminal charges within a reasonable time'.[48]

Similarly to Article 9 ICCPR, Article 5 paragraphs 2 to 5 ECHR set out several important safeguards for persons deprived of their liberty on either one of the grounds provided for under paragraph 1. Paragraph 2 refers to the right of persons deprived of their liberty to be informed promptly, in a language they understand, of the reasons for their arrest and of any charge against them. Paragraph 5 prescribes that 'everyone who has been the victim of arrest or detention in contravention of the provisions of this Article shall have an enforceable right to compensation'. Paragraph 4 deals with the right to *habeas corpus* proceedings, stating that anyone who is deprived of his or her liberty by arrest or detention shall be entitled to take proceedings by which the lawfulness of such detention shall be decided speedily by a court and his or her release ordered if the detention is unlawful.

The right to *habeas corpus* proceedings under paragraph 4 is clearly one of the most important safeguards for persons deprived of their liberty, especially when – as in Dr Manette's case – such detention has been ordered by an administrative authority and no criminal charge has been pressed.[49] As the ECtHR has clearly put it, the 'court' referred to in Article 5 paragraph 4 'does not necessarily have to be a court of law of the classic kind integrated within the standard judicial machinery of the country'.[50] The term simply denotes bodies that exhibit 'common fundamental features', such as 'independence of the executive and of the parties to the case', as well as the guarantees of a judicial procedure.[51] Of course, these guarantees must be 'appropriate to the kind of deprivation of liberty in question' and their forms 'may vary from one domain to another'.[52] The ECtHR's case law has also made it clear that 'the body in question must not have merely

47 Cf. K. Reid, *A Practitioner's Guide to the European Convention on Human Rights*, Sweet & Maxwell, London 2004, p. 417.

48 *Al-Jedda v. UK* [GC], no. 27021/08, ECHR 2011-IV 305 [100].

49 The ECtHR noted that 'where the decision depriving a person of his liberty is taken by an administrative body', Art. 5 para. 4 ECHR clearly 'obliges the Contracting State to make available to the person detained a right of recourse to a court'. By contrast, where such decision 'is made by a court at the close of judicial proceedings, ... the supervision required by Article 5 para 4 is incorporated in the decision'. *De Wilde, Ooms and Versyp ('Vagrancy') v. Belgium*, nos 2832/66 *et al.*, 1971, Series A no, 12 [76].

50 *Weeks v. UK*, no. 9787/82, (1987) Series A no. 114 [61].

51 Ibid.

52 Ibid.

advisory functions but must have the competence to "decide" the "lawfulness" of the detention and to order release if the detention is unlawful'.[53] In addition, it has stressed that, 'in view of the dramatic impact of deprivation of liberty on the fundamental rights of the person concerned, proceedings conducted under Article 5 para 4 of the Convention should in principle also meet, to the largest extent possible under the circumstances of an on-going investigation, the basic requirements of a fair trial'.[54] Thus, 'the proceedings must be adversarial and must always ensure "equality of arms" between the parties such as the right to an adversarial procedure'.[55] In particular, the ECtHR has made it clear that the detained person must be granted legal representation and that 'equality of arms is not ensured if counsel is denied access to those documents in the investigation file which are essential in order effectively to challenge the lawfulness of his client's detention'.[56]

All the above mentioned elements considered, under Article 5(1)(c) ECHR, State B's authorities could indeed arrest and detain Dr Manette without pressing criminal charges, but only for a limited period of time and provided that there was a reasonable suspicion of his having committed an offence or being about to commit an offence. Except for this hypothesis, any deprivation of liberty of a preventive nature – such as security detentions – would likely be considered unlawful by the ECtHR. Indeed, in its case law on counterterrorism policies,[57] the ECtHR has consistently held that security detention would normally amount to a violation of the ECHR. As regards procedural safeguards, in the ECHR system, Dr Manette would have the right to be brought promptly before a Judge (or other officer authorised by law to exercise judicial power) 'for the purpose of examining the question of deprivation of liberty or for the purpose of deciding on the merits' of his case. Moreover, State B would need to make sure that Dr Manette, while detained awaiting charges to be pressed against him, enjoyed all of the safeguards enshrined in paragraphs 2 to 5 of Article 5, especially the right to challenge the lawfulness of his arrest and detention before a competent court, the right to legal representation, and the right of access to all information essential to assess the lawfulness of his detention.[58]

---

53 Ibid.

54 *Garcia Alva v. Germany*, no. 23541/94, ECHR 2001 [39].

55 Ibid.

56 Ibid.

57 See, inter alia: *Lawless v. Ireland (No 3)*, no. 332/57, 1961, Series A no. 3; *Brogan and Others v. UK*, nos 11209/84 and others, 1988, Series A no. 145-B; *Brannigan and McBride v. UK*, nos 14553/89 and others, 1993, Series A no. 258-B; *A and Others v. UK* [GC], no. 3455/05, ECHR 2009-II 137.

58 Cf, 'Guide on Article 5 – Right to Liberty and Security under the European Convention on Human Rights (Article 5)' (INTERIGHTS manual for lawyers, September 2007) 45–46 <www.interights.org/document/105/index.html> accessed 02.02.2017. See also: K. Reid, above n. 47, pp. 487–88.

4. SECURITY DETENTION IN TIME OF EMERGENCY

Recent events have dramatically shown how States' reaction to public emergencies can significantly impact human rights protection.[59] Although any State might, at any time, need or wish to detain certain individuals on security grounds without pressing any criminal charges, it is obviously more likely in time of national emergency. As mentioned, in order to determine how Dr Manette's situation would be affected by the existence of such an emergency and assess his potential complaint's prospects of success before the HRC and/or the ECtHR, this section will separately analyse the legal framework applicable in the case of any national emergency that threatens the life of the nation (case 1 at section 4.1), that of an IAC (case 2 at section 4.2), and that of a NIAC (case 3 at section 4.3).

4.1. CASE 1: ANY PUBLIC EMERGENCY THAT THREATENS THE LIFE OF THE NATION

Under both the ICCPR and the ECHR, States parties may take measures derogating from their obligations. Article 4 ICCPR allows for derogations 'in time of public emergency which threatens the life of the nation and the existence of which is officially proclaimed'. Under Article 15 ECHR, 'war or other public emergency threatening the life of the nation' may justify the adoption of derogating measures. Both articles prescribe that a State party is allowed to take only those derogating measures that are 'strictly required by the exigencies of the situation' and 'provided that such measures are not inconsistent with its other obligations under international law'. The ICCPR also requires that these measures 'do not involve discrimination solely on the ground of race, colour, sex, language, religion or social origin'. In addition, any State party to the ICCPR or the ECHR availing itself of the right to derogation must inform the other States parties of the measures taken and the reasons for them, as well as the date on which these measures cease to operate.

---

59 Both France and Turkey have recently declared a state of emergency. As regards France's declaration and renewal of the state of emergency, see: Decrees Nos 2015-1475, 2015-1476 and 2015-1478 of 29 February 2016 and Nos 2015-1493 and 2015-1494 of 18 November 2015 applying Act No. 55-385 of 3 April 1955 on the state of emergency, as modified by Act No. 2015-1501 of 20 November 2015, which extends the state of emergency for three months as of 26 November 2015. The state of emergency has subsequently been extended several times. For detailed information, see: <www.interieur.gouv.fr/fr/Actualites/L-actu-du-Ministere/Qu-est-ce-que-l-etat-d-urgence> accessed 02.02.2017. As regards Turkey's declaration of a state of emergency, see: Decision of the Council of Ministers No. 2016/9064 of 20 July 2016 (English translation available at <www.coe.int/it/web/conventions/search-on-treaties/-/conventions/treaty/005/declarations> accessed 02.02.2017).

Thus, the key feature of any derogating measures adopted under Articles 4 ICCPR and 15 ECHR is that the emergency justifying their adoption must be the type of emergency that could jeopardise the survival of the very nation. Clearly, in the event of such an emergency, the right to personal liberty is likely to be derogated from. As a matter of fact, while both Article 4 ICCPR and Article 15 ECHR include a list of rights that cannot be derogated from (such as the right to life under Articles 6 ICCPR and 2 ECHR), the right to liberty and security of person is not included in either list. Still, as regards the question whether it can be made subject to valid derogation, the HRC's approach considerably differs from the ECtHR's.

While the ECtHR has repeatedly recognised States parties' right to derogate from Article 5 under certain circumstances, the HRC has contended that 'there are limits on States parties' power to derogate' from Article 9.[60] In the HRC's opinion, 'there are some elements in Article 9 that … cannot be made subject to lawful derogation under Article 4'.[61] First, it refers to the prohibition of arbitrariness, as even the gravest public emergency threatening the life of the nation 'cannot justify a deprivation of liberty that is unreasonable or unnecessary under the circumstances';[62] indeed, the considerations invoked by a State in order to justify derogating measures 'are already factored into the arbitrariness standard itself',[63] so that the 'existence and nature' of such an emergency is 'relevant to a determination of whether a particular arrest or detention is arbitrary' to begin with.[64] Secondly, according to the HRC, 'the procedural guarantees protecting liberty of person may never be made subject to measures of derogation that would circumvent the protection of non-derogable rights'.[65] In order to protect these rights, the right to *habeas corpus* proceedings cannot be derogated from.[66]

In light of the above, in the ICCPR system, it is not entirely clear to what extent the existence of a national emergency would affect individuals' right to personal liberty. As already mentioned, even under normal circumstances,

---

60 UNCHR, 'General Comment 35 – Article 9 (Liberty and Security of Person)' (16 December 2014) UN Doc CCPR/C/GC/35 [65].

61 Ibid.

62 Ibid., [66]. Some experts have gone so far as to affirm that the prohibition of arbitrary deprivation of liberty 'constitutes a *jus cogens* norm'. See: UNCHR, 'Report of the Working Group on Arbitrary Detention' (24 December 2012) UN Doc A/HRC/22/44 [51].

63 UNCHR, 'Report of the Working Group on Arbitrary Detention' (24 December 2012) UN Doc A/HRC/22/44 [48].

64 UNCHR, 'General Comment 35 – Article 9 (Liberty and Security of Person)' (16 December 2014) UN Doc CCPR/C/GC/35 [66].

65 Ibid., [67].

66 Ibid. See also: UNCHR, 'Concluding Observations: Israel' (18 August 1998) UN Doc CCPR/C/79/Add.93. For a thorough examination of diverging opinions on such delicate and still (at least to some extent) controversial issue, see: 'Internment in Armed Conflict: Basic Rules and Challenges' (ICRC Opinion Paper, November 2014) 7 <www.icrc.org/en/download/file/1980/security-detention-position-paper-icrc-11-2014.pdf> accessed 02.02.2017.

Dr Manette's security detention by State A's authorities would be considered as lawful under the ICCPR – despite its administrative nature and the fact that it did not take place in contemplation of criminal prosecution – as long as: (a) Dr Manette represented a 'present, direct and imperative threat'; (b) such threat could not be addressed by alternative measures, as 'no other effective measures addressing the threat, including the criminal justice system', was available; (c) the overall length of his detention was limited; and (d) his detention fully respected the safeguards set out by Article 9, especially the right to *habeas corpus* proceedings. Considering that much leeway already seems to be given to States parties outside emergency situations and that no derogation leading to the arbitrariness of a deprivation of liberty or impairing the right to *habeas corpus* would be considered as lawful by the HRC,[67] one might wonder what is left to derogate from. In other words, given the significant tolerance towards security detention shown by the HRC, the impact of a national emergency on individuals' right to personal liberty is not clear.

In this respect, the ECHR system significantly differs from the ICCPR system. Under normal circumstances, the former appears to be far more stringent than the latter in respect of security detention. Indeed, as repeatedly stated in the ECtHR case law regarding States parties' counterterrorism policies,[68] security detention would normally amount to a violation of the ECHR, unless the State concerned adopted a lawful derogation under Article 15. Thus, in the ECHR system, the existence of a public emergency threatening the life of the nation would significantly affect Dr Manette's situation, as the adoption of a lawful derogation from Article 15 would make his security detention by State B's authorities lawful.[69] Nevertheless, as regards the nature and seriousness of such threat, the ECtHR has often stressed that States 'do not enjoy an unlimited power of appreciation' in deciding whether derogating measures – especially their special powers of arrest and detention – are strictly required by the exigencies of the situation, as 'the domestic margin of appreciation' must be 'accompanied by a European supervision'.[70] Therefore, the requirements of strict necessity and proportionality limit States parties' power to derogate from Article 5.

---

67 In particular, the HRC highlighted the importance of the judicial nature of the body entrusted with such proceedings and access to legal advice, as well as 'disclosure to the detainee of, at least, the essence of the evidence on which the decision is taken': UNCHR, 'General Comment 35 – Article 9 (Liberty and Security of Person)' (16 December 2014) UN Doc CCPR/C/GC/35 [15].

68 Text to n. 57.

69 In the case of *Brannigan and McBride v. UK*, nos 14553/89 and others, 1993, Series A no. 258-B [37]–[38]), the ECtHR noted that the Government itself had 'conceded that the requirement of promptness had not been respected' and that, 'in the absence of an enforceable right to compensation in respect of the breach of Article 5 para 3, Article 4 para 5 had not been complied with'. However, it also noted that 'the failure to observe these requirements of Article 5 had been met by their derogation of 23 December 1988 under Article 15'.

70 Ibid.

These conclusions are partially supported by relatively recent events in France.[71] Following the terrorist attacks of November 2015 in Paris, the French Government has declared a state of emergency[72] that, inter alia, entrusts the Minister of the Interior with the power to subject any individual to '*assignation à résidence*' to a place to be determined by the Minister when there are serious reasons to believe that he or she constitutes a threat to public order and safety. This may entail: the confinement to the said place for a timeframe to be determined by the Minister (up to 12 hours per day); the obligation periodically to report to the police or *gendarmerie*; the obligation to hand over one's passport and ID; the prohibition on entertaining relations with certain individuals; and the obligation to wear electronic surveillance equipment under certain circumstances.[73] The individuals concerned may apply to administrative courts ('*juge administratif*') to challenge any measure taken under the state of emergency law.[74] In less than a week from the declaration of the state of emergency, more than 160 individuals were subjected to '*assignation à résidence*' under this law.[75] The French authorities' prompt notification to the Secretary General of the Council of Europe of 'a number of state of emergency measures' that could 'involve a derogation from certain rights guaranteed' by the ECHR[76] can be considered as confirmation of the need for a derogation from the ECHR whenever, in a situation of public emergency, States parties subject individuals to deprivations of liberty not envisaged by Article 5.[77] Interestingly, however, despite the significant tolerance shown by the HRC towards security detention, the French authorities have also informed the Secretary General of the United Nations of the measures taken following the Paris attacks, insofar as they could involve a derogation from the obligations under the ICCPR, 'and particularly

---

71 In July 2016, after a failed coup attempt, Turkey also declared a state of emergency and informed the Secretary General of the Council of Europe that measures taken could involve derogation from the obligations under the ECHR. However, nothing was expressly said on possible deprivations of liberty on security grounds. For Turkey's notification, see: Declaration contained in a letter from the Permanent Representative of Turkey, dated 21 July 2016, registered at the Secretariat General on 21 July 2016 <www.coe.int/it/web/conventions/search-on-treaties/-/conventions/treaty/005/declarations> accessed 02.02.2017. An English translation of Turkey's Law No. 2935 on State of Emergency is available at <www.legislationline.org/documents/id/6974> accessed 02.02.2017.

72 Text to n. 59.

73 Article 6 of Act No. 55-385 of 3 April 1955 on the state of emergency.

74 Ibid., Art. 14-1.

75 See:<www.interieur.gouv.fr/Actualites/Communiques/Point-sur-les-operations-menees-depuis-l-entree-en-vigueur-de-l-etat-d-urgence> accessed 02.02.2017.

76 See: <www.coe.int/en/web/secretary-general/news/-/asset_publisher/EYlBJNjXtA5U/content/france-informs-secretary-general-of-article-15-derogation-of-the-european-convention-on-human-rights> accessed 02.02.2017.

77 Note, however, that the measure of '*assignation à résidence*' may be considered a restriction to an individual's freedom of movement rather than to his or her personal liberty. See: Conseil constitutionnel, Décision n° 2015-527 QPC du 22 décembre 2015 [5]–[6].

its Articles 9, 12 and 17'.[78] This probably confirms that at least some of the procedural safeguards provided by Article 9 could or should be made subject to lawful derogation in time of emergency.

4.2. CASE 2: INTERNATIONAL ARMED CONFLICT

Of all the public emergencies that might threaten the life of a nation, therefore justifying the adoption of derogating measures by States parties to the ICCPR and/or the ECHR, an IAC is certainly one that raises complex yet interesting questions for the purposes of this chapter. Indeed, in the event of this type of armed conflict, a set of specific IHL rules – providing for standards of protection of individuals generally different than those provided by human rights norms – becomes applicable.[79]

This section aims to ascertain whether and how the existence of an IAC affects Dr Manette's situation and his chances of seeing a violation of his right to personal liberty acknowledged by the HRC or the ECtHR. To this end, after briefly examining IHL rules relating to internment of enemy civilians,[80] a comparison will be drawn between such rules and the detention regimes envisaged by Articles 9 ICCPR and 5 ECHR, with a view to investigating the contentious issue of their interaction.

4.2.1. IHL Provisions on Administrative Detention

Article 27 of the fourth Geneva Convention (IVGC)[81] allows the parties to the conflict to 'take such measures of control and security in regard to protected persons as may be necessary as a result of the war'. One of the most severe measures that can be imposed on civilians is internment (or administrative detention).[82] Unlike pre-trial detention, internment is ordered by administrative

---

78 UN Secretary-General, C.N.703.2015.TREATIES-IV.4 (Depositary Notification) (23 November 2015) <treaties.un.org/doc/Publication/CN/2015/CN.703.2015-Eng.pdf> accessed 02.02.2017.

79 Clearly, applicable rules differ on the basis of the qualification of the conflict as an IAC or a NIAC.

80 The investigation will leave aside the issue of the deprivation of liberty of prisoners of war.

81 Geneva Convention relative to the protection of civilian persons in time of war (adopted 12 August 1949, entered into force 21 October 1950) 75 UNTS 973 (IV Geneva Convention).

82 Art. 41 para. 1 defines assigned residence and internment as the 'most severe' measures that 'the Power in whose hands protected persons may be' can take, provided that any other measure of control mentioned in the Convention is not deemed to be adequate. The difference between assigned residence and internment merely lies in their intensity: while the latter results in an individual being held with other internees in a place specially created by a belligerent, the former entails the mere displacement of an individual to an isolated area.

authorities and no criminal charge is pressed against the individual concerned.[83] As the Israeli Supreme Court Judge Zamir clearly put it, 'administrative detention deprives an individual of his liberty in the most severe fashion', as 'liberty is denied, not by the court, but rather by an administrative authority; not by a judicial proceeding, but rather by an administrative decision'.[84] Its key feature is that it is 'preventive, rather than punitive in nature',[85] as it can only be imposed on an individual for security reasons, whereas anyone suspected of having committed a crime shall be indicted and tried in the context of criminal proceedings.[86]

The IVGC contains several provisions regarding all protected persons, but also some specific provisions relating either to aliens in the territory of a party to the conflict (Part III, section II) or to civilians in occupied territories (Part III, section III).[87]

As regards aliens in the territory of a party to the conflict, Article 42 paragraph 1 states that the internment 'of protected persons may be ordered only if the security of the Detaining Power makes it absolutely necessary'.[88] The Convention does not give any indications as to what may constitute a sufficient threat to the security of a belligerent, so that such determination 'is left largely to the authorities of that State'.[89] Clearly, the State must have serious and legitimate

---

The choice between these two measures ultimately depends on the circumstances of each case and the seriousness of the threat posed by that individual. See, among others: J.S. Pictet, *Commentary to Geneva Convention IV Relative to the Protection of Civilian Persons in Time of War*, ICRC, Geneva 1958, p. 257; *Prosecutor v. Kordić & Čerkez* (Judgment) ICTY-95-14/2-T (26 February 2001) [283].

83 R. Kolb and S. Vité, *Le droit de l'occupation militaire: perspectives historiques et enjeux juridiques actuels*, Bruylant, Bruxelles 2009, pp. 368–69.

84 HCJ 2320/98 *El-Amla v. Commander of the IDF Forces in the West Bank* IsrSC 52(3) 246, as cited in HCJ 5591/02 *Yassin et al. v. Commander of the Kziot Military Camp – Kziot Detention Facility* [2002] IsrSC 57(1) 403 [7].

85 Y. Dinstein, *The International Law of Belligerent Occupation*, Cambridge University Press, Cambridge 2009, p. 173.

86 R. Kolb and S. Vité, above n. 83, p. 369. The distinction between internment and 'penal repression' is particularly important in order to avoid that the former is 'used as a substandard system of penal repression in the hands of the executive power, bypassing the one sanctioned by a country's legislature and courts'. Cf. J. Pejic, 'Procedural Principles and Safeguards for Internment/Administrative Detention in Armed Conflict and other Situations of Violence' (2005) 87 *International Review of the Red Cross* 375, 381. See also: HCJ 5784/03, 6024/03, 6025/03 *Salama et al. v. Israeli Defence Force (IDF) Commander in Judea and Samaria* [2003] IsrSC [6].

87 The first section of Part III contains provisions common to the territories of the parties to the conflict and to occupied territories.

88 The second paragraph of the same article deals with voluntary internment. For a detailed examination, see: J.S. Pictet, above n. 82.

89 *Prosecutor v. Delalić, Mucić, Delić and Landzo* (Judgment) ICTY-96-21-A (20 February 2001) [574].

reasons to believe 'that the person concerned, by his activities, knowledge or qualifications, represents a real threat to its present or future security'.[90]

Article 43 provides for important procedural safeguards for internees. First, 'any protected person who has been interned … shall be entitled to have such action reconsidered as soon as possible by an appropriate court or administrative board designated by the Detaining Power for that purpose'. This review does not take place automatically, but only after a request by the internee. In addition, in the event that the appeal is rejected and the internment maintained, the aforementioned 'court or administrative board shall periodically, and at least twice yearly, give consideration to his/her case, with a view to the favourable amendment of the initial decision, if circumstances permit'. Unlike the initial review, 'these periodical reconsiderations' are 'automatic once a protected person has made his first application to the responsible authority'.[91] The rationale behind this provision is that no protected person should be interned 'for a longer time than the security of the Detaining State demands'.[92] In fact, other provisions of the IVGC require that any internee be released once the reasons justifying his or her internment no longer exist.[93]

As regards civilians in occupied territories, under Article 78 paragraph 1, the Occupying Power may subject protected persons to internment only 'for imperative reasons of security'. Once again, the Convention does not define the notion of security. It is certainly possible to interpret this provision by analogy to Article 42, thus assuming that, also in occupied territories, a belligerent may subject civilians to internment whenever they pose a threat to its own security. However, Article 78 should also be interpreted in light of other relevant IHL provisions applicable in occupied territories, especially Article 43 of the Hague Regulations,[94] which states that the occupant 'shall take all the measures in his power to restore, and ensure, as far as possible, public order and safety'. Therefore, the phrase 'reasons of security' contained in Article 78 could be interpreted as referring to both the security of the Occupying Power and that of the civilian population.[95]

Article 78 paragraph 2 provides for procedural safeguards similar to those recognised by Article 43 in respect of aliens in the territory of a belligerent. Any decisions regarding internment 'shall be made according to a regular procedure', that shall 'be prescribed by the Occupying Power in accordance with' the

90 J.S. Pictet, above n. 82, p. 257.
91 Ibid., p. 259.
92 Ibid.
93 Art. 132.
94 Regulations concerning the Laws and Customs of War on Land annexed to the Convention (IV) respecting the Laws and Customs of War on Land (adopted 18 October 1907, entered into force 26 January 1910) (The Hague Regulations).
95 R. Kolb and S. Vité, above n. 83, p. 368.

Convention and 'include the right of appeal for the parties concerned'. Appeals shall 'be decided with the least possible delay'. Should the appeal be rejected, the internment decision 'shall be subject to periodical review, if possible every six months, by a competent body set up' by the Detaining Power. Though Article 78 does not mention any specific qualities of the 'competent body' entrusted with the appeals, one may interpret it by analogy to Article 43 and conclude that this body could be either a court or an administrative board.[96]

It is also worth mentioning that, under Article 75 paragraph 3 of the first Additional Protocol (API), 'any person arrested, detained or interned for actions related to the armed conflict shall be informed promptly, in a language he understands, of the reasons why these measures have been taken'. This person should 'be released with the minimum delay possible and in any event as soon as the circumstances justifying the arrest, detention or internment have ceased to exist'.

In light of the above, in the event of an IAC, IHL would allow Dr Manette's administrative detention on security grounds as either an alien in the territory of a belligerent or a civilian in an occupied territory. However, in both cases, IHL rules would provide for a set of procedural safeguards, such as the right to reconsideration or appeal and that to be informed of the reasons for internment.

4.2.2. A Comparison between IHL and IHRL Provisions as Regards Security Detention

The different detention regimes described so far all share the ultimate goal of protecting the individual from abuse. However, they do so in rather different ways and, as far as IHL is concerned, only to some extent. As a matter of fact, although both IHL and IHRL provide for important procedural safeguards, there are also significant differences.

The first fundamental difference – maybe the most dangerous one – concerns the grounds for a deprivation of liberty. IHL rules admit that individuals are deprived of their liberty for security reasons – i.e. the security of the Detaining Power or, in occupied territories, that of the civilian population – and as long as the circumstances justifying the deprivation of liberty exist. In contrast, under Article 5 ECHR, a State party would only be allowed to arrest and detain an individual without pressing criminal charges for a limited period of time and provided that there was a reasonable suspicion of his having committed an offence or being about to commit an offence. Clearly, in this respect, the ECHR system is much more stringent than IHL rules, as any deprivation of liberty not in contemplation of criminal prosecution – such as internment within the

96 Cf. J.S. Pictet, above n. 82, p. 367; R. Kolb and S. Vité, above n. 83, p. 383.

meaning of Articles 42, 43 and 78 IVGC – would be considered unlawful under the ECHR.[97]

The situation is not as clear when it comes to the ICCPR. Article 9 prohibits only unlawful and arbitrary detentions. Unlike Article 5 ECHR, it does not contain an exhaustive list of permissible grounds for a deprivation of liberty. Therefore, the question whether internment could be considered as lawful under the ICCPR is still controversial. As already mentioned, the HRC has recently stressed that – although security detention 'would normally amount to arbitrary detention as other effective measures addressing the threat, including the criminal justice system, would be available'[98] – the imposition of this type of detention could be justified 'under the most exceptional circumstances', provided that the State concerned could prove that the detained individual constituted 'a present, direct and imperative threat'.[99] However, some doubts remain as regards the nature of the threat. It is not clear which criteria the HRC is supposed to follow in order to determine whether, in each case, the threat posed by an individual is indeed 'present, direct and imperative': such terms are not mentioned in the ICCPR nor have they ever appeared in the HRC's Concluding Observations or Views on individual communications. Clearly, the lawfulness of internment under the ICCPR ultimately depends on the interpretation of this phrase.

Another major difference between IHL rules on internment and IHRL provisions on the right to personal liberty concerns procedural safeguards. True, IHL provides for a right to reconsideration or appeal. However, it does not mention the right to legal counsel for interned civilians and provides for only a limited right to access information on the reasons for internment. A duty of the Detaining Power to provide such information promptly is found in Article 75 paragraph 3 API[100] but, unlike the universally accepted Geneva Conventions, this Protocol is still awaiting ratification by several States. Moreover, State practice shows that one of the key features of internment is that it mostly relies on classified information that cannot be shared with the internee without compromising the security of the Detaining State.[101] This need for confidentiality inherent to internment clearly collides with the right to information enshrined in Articles 9 ICCPR and 5 ECHR.

---

97 See, inter alia: *Al-Jedda v. UK* [GC], no. 27021/08, ECHR, 2011-IV 305 [100]; *Hassan v. UK* [GC], no. 29750/09, ECHR, 16 September 2014 [97].

98 UNCHR, 'General Comment 35 – Article 9 (Liberty and Security of Person)' (16 December 2014) UN Doc CCPR/C/GC/35 [15].

99 Ibid.

100 Protocol Additional to the Geneva Conventions of 12 August 1949, and relating to the Protection of Victims of International Armed Conflicts (Protocol I) (adopted 8 June 1977, entered into force 7 December 1978) 1125 UNTS 3.

101 See, inter alia: HCJ 1139/04 *Abd el Rahman el Ahmar v. Commander of IDF Forces in the West Bank* [2004] IsrSC [4].

In addition, while both the HRC and the ECtHR have repeatedly stressed that the court entrusted with *habeas corpus* proceedings 'should ordinarily be a court within the judiciary'[102] or, exceptionally, a specialised tribunal that exhibits 'common fundamental features' – such as 'independence of the executive and of the parties to the case' – and the guarantees of a judicial procedure,[103] IHL expressly admits that the competent body dealing with the reconsideration or the appeal could also be an administrative board. Under IHL rules, there is no guarantee of independence from the authorities that took the internment decision in the first place, nor any assurances as regards the judicial nature of the proceedings, as these rules do not expressly provide for important safeguards such as the equality of arms and cross-examination.

It should also be recalled that, contrary to the IHL rules considered, both the ICCPR and the ECHR provide for an 'enforceable right to compensation' for any individual who has been the victim of unlawful arrest or detention.

In light of the above, it is reasonable to conclude that Dr Manette's situation would be significantly affected by the existence of an IAC because of the coexistence of two different legal regimes. As regards the right to personal liberty, the relationship between IHL and IHRL norms may be described as a potential conflict of norms.[104] Adopting a broad definition of conflict of norms as the situation in which a norm 'constitutes, has led to, or may lead to, a breach' of another norm,[105] the notion of potential conflict may be used to define the relationship between two norms that, when applied, lead 'to two opposite results'.[106] Indeed, while it is true that IHL is far less stringent than both the ICCPR and the ECHR as regards the protection of the rights of individuals deprived of their liberty, as any belligerent merely applying IHL provisions on internment would inevitably incur in a violation of both Article 9 ICCPR and Article 5 ECHR, it is still possible for a State party to either one of these human rights treaties to guarantee a wider protection of individual rights than that provided for under IHL by choosing to fully apply IHRL provisions even in the context of an IAC.

Therefore, should State A and State B decide to apply only IHL standards, Dr Manette's right to personal liberty would definitely be infringed. Dr Manette

102 UNCHR, 'General Comment 35 – Article 9 (Liberty and Security of Person)' (16 December 2014) UN Doc CCPR/C/GC/35 [45].

103 *Weeks v. UK*, no. 9787/82, 1987, Series A no. 114 [61].

104 Cf. M. Milanović, 'Norm Conflicts, International Humanitarian Law and Human Rights Law' in O. Ben-Naftali (ed.), *International Humanitarian Law and International Human Rights Law – Pas de Deux*, Oxford University Press, Oxford 2011, p. 116.

105 J. Pauwelyn, *Conflict of Norms in Public International Law: How WTO Law Relates to Other Rules of International Law*, Cambridge University Press, Cambridge 2003, pp. 176–77. See also: ibid., p. 101.

106 M. Milanović, above n. 104, p. 102.

would then have the right to lodge an individual complaint with the HRC or an application with the ECtHR. As regards the ICCPR, he could make a complaint regarding the alleged violation of the prohibition of arbitrary deprivation of liberty (Article 9 paragraph 1), as well as the right to information (paragraph 2), *habeas corpus* proceedings (paragraph 4), and compensation (paragraph 5). As regards the ECHR, he could make a complaint regarding a violation of Article 5 paragraph 1 in respect of the grounds for detention, as well as paragraphs 2 to 5 in relation to access to information, *habeas corpus* proceedings and the 'enforceable right to compensation'. The question is: what would the HRC and the ECtHR decide? The answer ultimately depends on how these judicial and quasi-judicial bodies tackle the problem of the conflict between IHL and IHRL norms.

4.2.3. Interaction between the Two Regimes: What Is and What Should Be

When it comes to the interaction between IHRL and IHL norms, the difference between conflict avoidance and conflict resolution should be recalled.[107] On the one hand, conflict avoidance 'interprets away any incompatibility'[108] by harmoniously interpreting two apparently conflicting norms, in line with Article 31 paragraph 3(c) of the Vienna Convention on the Law of Treaties (VCLT). This provision states that 'any relevant rules of international law applicable in the relations between the parties' shall be taken into account while interpreting a treaty. Nevertheless, conflict avoidance is possible only when the term to be interpreted is 'broad and ambiguous enough to allow for input by other rules' and the other rules say indeed something about what such a term means.[109] As a matter of fact, 'the input of other rules of international law in the interpretation of a treaty norm' must be 'limited to giving meaning to explicit treaty terms',[110] as 'other rules cannot add meaning' to a term 'that goes *beyond* or *against* the clear meaning' of such a term.[111]

On the other hand, conflict resolution 'requires one conflicting norm to prevail or have priority over the other'.[112] Possible methods of norm conflict resolution are explicit conflict clauses inserted in treaties, as well as recourse to the *lex posterior* or *lex specialis* principles. However, none of these methods is actually applicable in the relation between IHRL and IHL. First, the treaties concerned in the case at hand do not contain any conflict clauses. Secondly, at

[107] This difference was clearly explained in a seminal paper on the relationship between IHL and IHR: M. Milanović, above n. 104, p. 101.
[108] Ibid., p. 102.
[109] J. Pauwelyn, above n. 105, p. 245.
[110] Ibid., p. 262.
[111] Ibid., p. 245.
[112] M. Milanović, above n. 104, p. 102.

least in respect of the relation between IHL and IHRL norms,[113] neither the *lex specialis* principle nor the *lex posterior* principle is of any use. In particular, as regards the former, 'there is simply no evidence' that it is 'a rule of norm conflict resolution'.[114] It rather appears to be 'a method of norm conflict avoidance',[115] as a particular rule 'may give instructions on what a general rule requires in the case at hand'.[116] It has indeed been used as such by the International Court of Justice in the advisory opinion on nuclear weapons.[117]

Whenever conflict avoidance is not possible and, given the lack of any viable methods of norm conflict resolution, there is no way to establish the prevalence of one conflicting norm over the other, the conflict clearly turns out to be both 'unavoidable and unresolvable'.[118] In this event, the State concerned would have to decide which norm to apply and, should it choose to apply the less stringent one, it would incur in a violation of the other.

In the following subsections, these general considerations will be applied to the case of security detention in the context of an IAC, with a view to determine whether the conflict between IHL rules on internment and the right to personal liberty under Article 9 ICCPR (section 4.2.4) and Article 5 ECHR (section 4.2.5) can be either avoided or solved in any way.

4.2.4. The Conflict between Article 9 ICCPR and IHL Rules on Internment

The prohibition of arbitrary detention enshrined in Article 9 paragraph 1 could easily be interpreted as allowing States parties to intern individuals in conformity with IHL rules in the event of an IAC. In General Comment No 35, the HRC points out that 'Article 9 applies also in situations of armed conflict to which the rules of international humanitarian law are applicable' and highlights that, although such rules 'may be relevant for the purposes of the interpretation

---

113 Indeed, the International Law Commission's study group on the fragmentation of international law has included both IHRL and IHL in the category of 'self contained regimes' defined in a broad sense. See: ILC, 'Report of the Study Group of the International Law Commission (finalised by M. Koskenniemi) – Fragmentation of International Law: Difficulties Arising from the Diversification and Expansion of International Law' (13 April 2006) UN Doc A/CN.4/L.682 [123]–[185].

114 M. Milanović, above n. 104, p. 115. See also: N. Prud'homme, '*Lex Specialis*: Oversimplifying a More Complex and Multifaceted Relationship?' (2007) 40 *Israel Law Review* 380–81.

115 M. Milanović, above n. 104, p. 115.

116 ILC, 'Study on the Function and Scope of the *Lex Specialis* Rule and the Question of "Self Contained Regimes": Preliminary Report: Addendum (by M. Koskenniemi)' (4 May 2004) UN Doc. [A/CN.4/]ILC(LVI)/SG/FIL/CRD.1/Add.1 [2.1].

117 *Legality of the Threat or Use of Nuclear Weapons* (Advisory Opinion) 1996 <http://www.icj-cij.org/docket/index.php?p1=3&p2=4&k=e1&p3=4&case=95> accessed 02.02.2017 [25].

118 M. Milanović, above n. 104, p. 108.

of Article 9, both spheres of law are complementary, not mutually exclusive'.[119] Therefore, the HRC excludes that one sphere of law could prevail over the other, but admits that Article 9 could be interpreted in light of IHL rules. It then points out that security detention, 'when authorized and regulated by and complying with international humanitarian law', would 'in principle' not be arbitrary.[120] Hence, the potential conflict between this provision and IHL rules on internment could definitely be avoided by means of interpretation.

In contrast, when it comes to the alleged violation of the procedural safeguards enshrined in paragraphs 2 to 5, the conflict with IHL rules cannot be avoided, as the terms used in the ICCPR are neither broad nor ambiguous enough. Therefore, considering the unavailability of any method of norm conflict resolution in this context, State A would be confronted with the choice either to fully apply Article 9 paragraphs 2 to 5 ICCPR or to take derogating measures under Article 4. Nevertheless, should it choose the latter option, it would still have to take into account the HRC's stance in respect of the non-derogable nature of some elements of Article 9, especially paragraph 4 on the right to *habeas corpus* proceedings.

In light of the above, in its Views on Dr Manette's communication, the HRC would probably find that, as regards Dr Manette's internment in the context of an IAC, no violation of Article 9 paragraph 1 ICCPR had occurred, but – lacking any lawful derogations to the subsequent paragraphs and considering that no derogation to paragraph 4 is ever admissible – it could still find a violation of paragraphs 2 to 5.

4.2.5. The Conflict between Article 5 ECHR and IHL Rules on Internment

Given the exhaustive nature of the list of permissible grounds for detention included in Article 5 paragraph 1 ECHR, conflict avoidance by means of interpretation does not seem to be possible, since any interpretation of this provision as allowing internment would clearly be *contra legem*. Indeed, in the *Al-Jedda* case, the ECtHR highlighted that no deprivation of liberty would be compatible with Article 5 paragraph 1, unless it fell within one of the grounds provided for by (a) to (f) or was provided for by a lawful derogation under Article 15.[121] Clearly, the same is true as regards the procedural safeguards contained in paragraphs 2 to 5, as no conflict avoidance seems to be possible.

Therefore, considering the aforementioned unavailability of any method of norm conflict resolution applicable in the context of the interaction between IHRL and IHL norms, it seems reasonable to conclude that Dr Manette's

---

119 UNCHR, 'General Comment 35 – Article 9 (Liberty and Security of Person)' (16 December 2014) UN Doc CCPR/C/GC/35 [64].

120 Ibid.

121 *Al-Jedda v. UK* [GC], no. 27021/08, ECHR, 2011-IV 305 [99].

internment by State B's authorities would not be allowed under the ECHR, unless State B had previously adopted a valid derogation under Article 15.

Nevertheless, in the ECHR system, *what should be* and *what is* do not seem to correspond. In the *Hassan* case, the ECtHR openly dealt with the relationship between Article 5 and IHL rules on internment. As one would expect, the ECtHR noted that Mr Hassan's detention, though perfectly lawful under IHL, was not included in the list of admissible grounds for detention provided for by (a) to (f) and that the United Kingdom had not notified any derogations. However, relying on Article 31 paragraph 3 (b) VCLT on subsequent practice, the ECtHR held that, in the context of an IAC, State practice was not to derogate from their obligations under Article 5 in order to detain individuals on the basis of the IVGC, hence concluding that no derogation was needed. Then, relying on the abovementioned Article 31 paragraph 3 (c) VCLT on other relevant rules of international law, the ECtHR stated that

> By reason of the co-existence of the safeguards provided by international humanitarian law and by the Convention in time of armed conflict, the grounds of permitted deprivation of liberty set out in subparagraphs (a) to (f) of that provision should be accommodated, as far as possible, with the taking of prisoners of war and the detention of civilians who pose a risk to security under the Third and Fourth Geneva Conventions.[122]

Hence, the ECtHR unsurprisingly stated that 'even in situations of IAC, the safeguards under the Convention continue to apply'.[123] However, what is indeed surprising is that it also held that these safeguards were to be 'interpreted against the background of the provisions of international humanitarian law'.[124] In the ECtHR's opinion

> Internment in peacetime does not fall within the scheme of deprivation of liberty governed by Article 5 of the Convention without the exercise of the power of derogation under Article 15 .... It can only be in cases of IAC, where the taking of prisoners of war and the detention of civilians who pose a threat to security are accepted features of international humanitarian law, that Article 5 could be interpreted as permitting the exercise of such broad powers.[125]

Clearly, these findings are at the very least surprising. As brilliantly put in a partly dissenting opinion by Judge Robert R. Spano, the judgment in the *Hassan* case constituted 'an attempt to reconcile norms of international law that are irreconcilable', as the ECtHR's judgment did 'not conform with the text, object

122 *Hassan v. UK* [GC], no. 29750/09, ECHR, 16 September 2014 [104].
123 Ibid.
124 Ibid.
125 Ibid.

or purpose of Article 5 para 1 of the Convention', as this provision had been 'consistently interpreted' by the Court for decades, 'and the structural mechanism of derogation in times of war provided by Article 15'.[126]

Still, what the ECtHR decided in the *Hassan* case would probably be applied in Dr Manette's case as well. The ECtHR would most likely find that no violation of Article 5 occurred, provided that his detention complied 'with the rules of international humanitarian law and, most importantly', that it was 'in keeping with the fundamental purpose of Article 5 para 1, which is to protect the individual from arbitrariness'.[127] The same reasoning applies to the alleged violation of the subsequent paras of Article 5, as the ECtHR seems to believe that, 'in relation to detention taking place during an IAC, Article 5 paras 2 and 4 must also be interpreted in a manner which takes into account the context and the applicable rules of international humanitarian law'.[128]

4.3. CASE 3: NON-INTERNATIONAL ARMED CONFLICT

NIACs are generally defined as 'armed conflicts between governmental forces and insurgents or between armed groups'.[129] Compared to IACs, NIACs are much less regulated.[130] In respect of security detention, IHL applicable to this type of conflict only addresses the treatment of 'persons deprived of their liberty for reasons related to the armed conflict' and provides for judicial guarantees for those held on criminal charges (also related to the conflict). Although both Article 5 of Additional Protocol II (APII) – which specifically deals with persons whose liberty has been restricted – and Article 6 APII – regulating penal prosecution – make reference to internment, nothing is said on the grounds for internment or the procedure to be followed.[131] Hence, while not expressly prohibited, internment does not seem to find any legal basis in treaty law applicable to NIACs.[132] Neither does a legal basis for internment seem to be available under

---

126 *Hassan v. UK* [GC], no. 29750/09, ECHR, 16 September 2014 (partly Dissenting Opinion of Judge Spano, joined by Judges Nicolaou, Bianku and Kalaydjieva) [6].

127 *Hassan v. UK* [GC], no. 29750/09, ECHR, 16 September 2014 [105].

128 Ibid., [106].

129 R. Kolb, *Advanced Introduction to International Humanitarian Law*, Edward Elgar, Cheltenham 2014, p. 22.

130 For a thorough analysis of treaty law applicable to NIACs, see, inter alia: ibid.; Y. Dinstein, *Non-International Armed Conflicts in International Law*, Cambridge University Press, Cambridge 2014; L. Moir, *The Law of Internal Armed Conflict*, Cambridge University Press, Cambridge 2002.

131 Cf M. Sassòli, 'The Relationship between International Humanitarian and Human Rights Law where it Matters: Admissible Killings and Internment of Fighters in Non-international Armed Conflicts' (2008) 90 *International Review of the Red Cross* 599, 618.

132 Cf. L. Hill-Cawthorne, *Detention in Non-International Armed Conflict*, Oxford University Press, Oxford 2016, p. 69.

customary IHL, as neither practice nor *opinio juris* uncontentiously points to the existence of customary rule on this issue.[133]

This is precisely what UK courts have recently held in the *Serdar Mohammed* case.[134] The case originated from the detention of Serdar Mohammed (SM) on security grounds in 2010 by UK armed forces operating in Afghanistan under ISAF and raised the question as to whether the UK Government had any right in law to imprison people in Afghanistan. The Judge in the High Court case concluded, inter alia, that the UK had no legal basis under IHL for detaining SM. In the Judge's opinion, the argument advanced by the Government that relevant IHL rules (namely Common Article 3 to the Geneva Conventions and Article 5 APII) *implicitly* provided for a legal power to detain had to be rejected, as: (a) if these rules 'had indeed been intended to provide' such power 'they would have done so expressly'; (b) these provisions seem only to contemplate that during NIACs 'people will *in fact* be detained', but nothing in the language used suggests that they are 'intended to authorise or themselves confer legality on any such detentions'; (c) the notion that the provisions concerned are intended to provide a legal basis for detention is inconsistent with their aim, that is to guarantee certain minimum standards of treatment to all individuals irrespective of whether their detention is legally justified; (d) States subscribing to the treaties concerned 'would not have agreed to establish by treaty a power to detain' in NIACs as, considering that Common Article 3 and APII apply to 'each Party to the conflict' (including armed groups who are able to implement them), 'providing a power to detain would have meant authorizing detention by dissident and rebel groups'; and (e) given that neither Common Article 3 nor APII 'specifies who may be detained, on what grounds, in accordance with what procedures, or for how long', they could not 'possibly have been intended

133 For a detailed examination of this issue, see: ibid., p. 70. *Contra*, inter alia: R.E. Barnsby, 'Yes We Can: The Authority to Detain as Customary International Law' (2009) 202 *Military Law Review* 53.

134 *Serdar Mohammed v. Ministry of Defence* [2014] EWHC 1369 (QB); *Serdar Mohammed and Others v. Ministry of Defence* [2015] EWCA Civ 843; *Abd Ali Hameed Al-Waheed v. Ministry of Defence* and *Serdar Mohammed v. Ministry of Defence* [2017] UKSC 2. For interesting analyses of these judgments, see: M. Milanović, 'High Court Rules that the UK Lacks IHL Detention Authority in Afghanistan' (3 May 2014) <www.ejiltalk.org/high-court-rules-that-the-uk-lacks-ihl-detention-authority-in-afghanistan/> accessed 02.02.2017; L. Hill-Cawthorne and D. Akande, 'Does IHL Provide a Legal Basis for Detention in Non-International Armed Conflicts?' (7 May 2014) <www.ejiltalk.org/does-ihl-provide-a-legal-basis-for-detention-in-non-international-armed-conflicts/> accessed 02.02.2017; M. Milanović, 'Some Thoughts on the *Serdar Mohammed* Appeals Judgment' (10 August 2015) <www.ejiltalk.org/some-thoughts-on-the-serdar-mohammed-appeals-judgment/> accessed 02.02.2017; M. Milanović, 'A Trio of Blockbuster Judgments from the UK Supreme Court' (17 January 2017) <www.ejiltalk.org/a-trio-of-blockbuster-judgments-from-the-uk-supreme-court/> accessed 02.02.2017.

to provide a power to detain', 'nor they could reasonably be interpreted as doing so'.[135]

The absence of any legal basis in IHL does not mean that States cannot intern individuals on security grounds in NIACs, as internment is certainly not prohibited under applicable IHL rules. However, such lack of legal basis does mean that, given the lawfulness requirement of any deprivation of liberty under IHRL, any State wishing to intern individuals in the context of a NIAC will have to find the legal basis elsewhere, i.e. in domestic law[136] or in sources other than IHL.[137] Clearly, this lack of IHL norms applicable to internment in NIACs – except, as already mentioned, those relating to the treatment of detainees – has major consequences when it comes to security detention and the interaction between IHL and IHRL norms.

As regards the ICCPR system, the question whether a legal basis for security detention could be found in IHL is especially relevant, as Article 9 ICCPR only prohibits arbitrary deprivations of liberty and, as already mentioned, can be interpreted in light of other relevant rules of international law. In the context of an IAC this led to the conclusion that a security detention authorised by and complying with IHL would not be considered arbitrary within the meaning of Article 9 ICCPR.[138] By contrast, in the context of a NIAC, the absence of any relevant IHL rules to be used in order to interpret the non-arbitrariness requirement of Article 9 entails that only international human rights norms are applicable. The HRC seems to agree with this view as, in General Comment

---

135 *Serdar Mohammed v. Ministry of Defence* [2014] EWHC 1369 (QB) [242]–[246]. Note, however, that the UK Supreme Court later held, inter alia, that 'HM forces had legal power to detain SM in excess of 96 hours pursuant to UN Security Council Resolutions 1386 (2001), 1510 (2003) and 1890 (2009) in cases where this was necessary for imperative reasons of security'. See *Abd Ali Hameed Al-Waheed v. Ministry of Defence* and *Serdar Mohammed v. Ministry of Defence* [2017] UKSC 2 [111].

136 L. Hill-Cawthorne and D. Akande, above n. 132.

137 Cf. L. Hill-Cawthorne, above n. 132, p. 71. The author refers, in particular, to 'those situations where often no domestic law can be relied upon, such as certain extraterritorial non-international armed conflicts', and mentions the practice of some States relying on UN Security Council Resolutions and/or the right of self-defence under Art. 51 of the UN Charter. L. Hill-Cawthorne, above n. 132, p. 75. Indeed, this seems to be the conclusion reached by the UK Supreme Court in the abovementioned *Serdar Mohammed* case. See text to n. 136. However, the author also notes that, as regards UN Security Council Resolutions adopted under Chapter VII of the UN Charter and merely authorising States to 'take all necessary measures', they 'speak principally to legality under the *ius ad bellum*' and, therefore, 'it is questionable whether they could in principle provide a sufficient legal basis for specific actions such as internment'. Similarly, as regards the right of self-defence under Art. 51 of the UN Charter, the author points out that it 'speaks only to the inter-state relationship, acting as an exception to the prohibition on the use of force between states' and thus 'has no bearing … on the conduct of hostilities' and 'is certainly not sufficiently precise to constitute a legal basis to detain'. L. Hill-Cawthorne, above n. 132, p. 75.

138 See above at section 4.2.

No 35, it expressly differentiated a situation of IAC – in which 'substantive and procedural rules' of IHL 'remain applicable and limit the ability to derogate' – from any other situation, in which 'the requirements of strict necessity and proportionality constrain any derogating measures involving security detention, which must be limited in duration and accompanied by procedures to prevent arbitrary application'.[139] Therefore, in the context of a NIAC, the HRC would probably consider Dr Manette's security detention to be lawful under the ICCPR under the same conditions envisaged in time of peace. However, as NIACs undoubtedly qualify as public emergencies that threaten the life of the nation within the meaning of Article 4 ICCPR, States parties would have the power to derogate from, at least, some elements of Article 9 in NIACs just like in IACs. Indeed, in some instances of NIAC, such as the one taking place in Colombia in the 1990s,[140] States have done so, thus 'confirming their view that that provision would apply in full but for the derogation'.[141]

As regards the ECHR system, the question whether IHL rules provide for a legal basis for internment would not normally be relevant, as preventive detention not in contemplation of prosecution on criminal charges does not fall within any of the permissible grounds for detention exhaustively listed in Article 5 paragraph 1 ECHR. However, as already mentioned, the ECtHR has recently tried to 'accommodate' the grounds of permitted deprivation of liberty set out in (a) to (f) with the types of security detention authorised under IHL applicable to IACs. Clearly, the absence of any legal basis for internment in IHL applicable to NIACs entails that this 'accommodation' is not possible in respect of NIACs and that Article 5 must be fully applied.[142] This conclusion seems to be confirmed by the approach taken by the ECtHR in the *Al-Jedda* case relating to the internment of an individual in Iraq in October 2004 (in the context of a NIAC).

139 UNCHR, 'General Comment 35 – Article 9 (Liberty and Security of Person)' (16 December 2014) UN Doc CCPR/C/GC/35 [66].

140 On several occasions, Colombia informed the Secretary-General that it had adopted measures of derogation from Art. 9. On 21 June 1996, for instance, the Government wrote that 'by Decree No. 900 of 22 May 1996, measures were adopted to control the activities of criminal and terrorist organizations in special public-order zones' and that 'the provisions of the Pact which were derogated from are articles 9 (1) and 12'. See: <treaties.un.org/Pages/ViewDetails.aspx?src=TREATY&mtdsg_no=IV-4&chapter=4&clang=_en#EndDec> accessed 02.02.2017. For further State practice, see: L. Hill-Cawthorne, above n. 132, p. 164.

141 L. Hill-Cawthorne, above n. 132, p. 172.

142 See, however, the aforementioned UK Supreme Court judgment in the case of *Serdar Mohammed*, in which the majority held that Art. 5 para. 1 ECHR 'should be read so as to accommodate, as permissible grounds, detention pursuant to' the power to detain flowing from relevant UN Security Council Resolutions, while at the same time finding that 'the arrangements for SM's detention were not compatible with' Art. 5 para. 4 ECHR 'in that he did not have any effective means of challenging the lawfulness of his detention': *Abd Ali Hameed Al-Waheed v. Ministry of Defence* and *Serdar Mohammed v. Ministry of Defence* [2017] UKSC 2 [111].

In this case, the ECtHR held, inter alia, that no deprivation of liberty would be compatible with Article 5 paragraph 1 unless it fell within one of the grounds expressly envisaged by the said provision or unless it was provided for by a lawful derogation under Article 15.[143] Therefore, the ECtHR would probably consider Dr Manette's administrative detention on mere security grounds in the context of a NIAC as unlawful under the ECHR, unless the State concerned adopted lawful derogating measures under Article 15.

5. CONCLUDING REMARKS

In order to assess the impact of public emergencies on the right to personal liberty and ascertain whether an individual deprived of his liberty on security grounds would enjoy a wider protection in the ICCPR system or in the ECHR system, this chapter has told the story of a fictional character, Dr Alexandre Manette, who was deprived of his liberty by administrative authorities on security grounds, while no criminal charge was pressed against him. In light of the findings of the previous sections, it is possible to draw the following conclusions.

First, outside the context of a public emergency, Dr Manette's situation in State A, which is only party to the ICCPR, would considerably differ from his situation in State B, which is only party to the ECHR, at least insofar as grounds for detention are concerned.[144] In the former case, his security detention might be considered as lawful by the HRC, given that Article 9 ICCPR only sets a rather general prohibition of unlawfulness and arbitrariness. In this respect, the HRC practice leads to the conclusion that, notwithstanding the fact that Dr Manette's security detention by State A's authorities did not take place in contemplation of criminal prosecution, it would not be considered as arbitrary, provided that: (a) Dr Manette represented a 'present, direct and imperative threat';[145] (b) such threat could not be addressed by alternative means, as no other effective measure 'addressing the threat, including the criminal justice system', was available;[146] (c) the overall length of his detention was limited; (d) his detention fully respected the safeguards set out by Article 9, especially with respect to *habeas corpus* proceedings. In contrast, in the latter case, the ECtHR would undoubtedly consider Dr Manette's security detention as unlawful under the

143 *Al-Jedda v. UK* [GC], no. 27021/08, ECHR, 2011-IV 305 [99]. The ECtHR also excluded that, in the case at hand, UN Security Council Resolution 1546 disapplied the requirements of Art. 5: ibid., [102].

144 When it comes to procedural safeguards, the protection afforded under normal circumstances seems to be equivalent in the two systems considered.

145 UNCHR, 'General Comment 35 – Article 9 (Liberty and Security of Person)' (16 December 2014) UN Doc CCPR/C/GC/35 [15].

146 Ibid.

ECHR, as Article 5 ECHR only allows State B to detain an individual without pressing criminal charges for a limited period of time and provided that there is a reasonable suspicion of him having committed an offence or being about to commit an offence. While contemplating some type of preventive detention, the list of admissible grounds for detention in Article 5 does not include 'preventive detention where there is no intention to bring criminal charges within a reasonable time'.[147] Therefore, outside the context of a public emergency, Dr Manette would enjoy a wider protection of his right to personal liberty in a State party to the ECHR and would have a better chance of seeing his complaint succeed before the ECtHR.

Secondly, in the event of a public emergency that threatens the life of the nation, Dr Manette's right to personal liberty would undoubtedly enjoy a higher degree of protection in a State party to the ICCPR. As a matter of fact, although both the ECHR and the ICCPR allow States parties to derogate from the right to personal liberty, the HRC has repeatedly held that some elements of this right cannot be made subject to lawful derogation, especially the right to *habeas corpus* proceedings. Thus, Dr Manette would have better chances of seeing a violation of his right to personal liberty acknowledged, should he choose to submit a communication to the HRC.

Thirdly, in the event of a NIAC, even though IHL is clearly applicable, the lack of any specific rules on the grounds for internment or the procedure to be followed – hence the unavailability of any legal basis for internment under IHL – ends up making Dr Manette's situation in this case identical to his situation in the event of any other public emergency. Therefore, in light of the HRC's take on the non-derogable nature of some elements of the right to personal liberty enshrined in Article 9, a State party to the ICCPR would have to ensure a higher degree of protection of Dr Manette's right to personal liberty.

Fourthly, when it comes to an IAC, the difference between the ICCPR system and the ECHR system lies in the way the potential conflict between relevant IHRL norms on the right to personal liberty and IHL rules on internment is solved. In its Views on Dr Manette's communication, the HRC would probably find that no violation of Article 9 paragraph 1 ICCPR occurred, as the prohibition of arbitrariness enshrined in this provision can be interpreted as allowing States parties to intern individuals in conformity with IHL rules applicable to IACs. However, lacking any lawful derogations to the subsequent paras of Article 9 and considering that no derogation to paragraph 4 on *habeas corpus* proceedings is considered to be admissible, it would probably find a violation of the procedural safeguards set out by paragraphs 2 to 5. By contrast, the ECtHR would most likely find that no violation of any element of the right to personal liberty under

147 *Al-Jedda v. UK* [GC], no. 27021/08, ECHR, 2011-IV 305 [100].

Article 5 paragraphs 1 to 5 occurred, provided that Dr Manette's detention complied with IHL rules.[148] As a matter of fact, despite the exhaustive nature of the list of admissible grounds for detention provided by paragraph 1 of Article 5, the ECtHR has recently solved the conflict between this provision and IHL rules on internment by interpreting the said list 'against the background' of IHL provisions, therefore finding that, even in the absence of any derogating measures, a security detention taking place in the context of an IAC and fully complying with IHL rules would be lawful under the ECHR.[149] Therefore, considering the HRC's stand on the non-derogable nature of fundamental procedural safeguards, Dr Manette would probably enjoy a wider protection of his right to personal liberty in a State party to the ICCPR and he would have a much better chance of seeing his complaint succeed before the HRC.

In the final analysis, this chapter has shown that individuals detained on security grounds in time of emergency enjoy varying degrees of protection of their right to personal liberty, depending on whether the State holding them is a party to the ICCPR or the ECHR and whether they choose to lodge a complaint with the HRC or an application with the ECtHR. Most importantly (at least from a victim's perspective), this chapter has shown that the approach taken by different human rights mechanisms in respect of the interaction between different branches of international law, namely IHRL and IHL, significantly affects the degree of protection afforded to individuals' right to personal liberty in time of emergency and might end up impairing individuals' chances of seeing potential violations of their right acknowledged.

---

148 *Hassan v. UK* [GC], no. 29750/09, ECHR, 16 September 2014 [105].
149 Ibid.

THE EUROPEAN COURT OF HUMAN RIGHTS' APPROACH TO ARMED CONFLICT AND HUMANITARIAN LAW: IVORY TOWER OR PAS DE DEUX?

Cedric De Koker

1. INTRODUCTION

The European system of human rights protection came into being in 1950 with the adoption of the European Convention for the Protection of Human Rights and Fundamental Freedoms (ECHR) by the then newly formed Council of Europe.[1] The European Convention laid down a series of fundamental guarantees accorded to all individuals as protection against undue government interference and institutionalised human rights protection through the creation of the European Court of Human Rights (ECtHR). Interestingly, although the ECHR was adopted in the immediate aftermath of World War Two, the possibility of its provisions being applied to situations of armed conflict was not given serious thought during the drafting process and the ECHR was therefore principally conceived to apply in times of peace. In spite of this, the ECtHR has, in past decades, increasingly been called upon to apply its provisions in cases in

[1] Council of Europe, European Convention for the Protection of Human Rights and Fundamental Freedoms, 4 November 2015, European Treaty Series 5.

which the conduct of the military forces of one of the States parties in the course of armed conflicts was at the heart of the issue. Applications filed in the wake of and in relation to the Turkish occupation of Cyprus or the Kosovo, Chechnya and Iraqi conflicts are cases in point.

Considering this reality, two particular and overarching questions come to mind, each of which will be discussed in detail below. The first relates to the processes leading up to the increased engagement of the ECtHR with cases stemming out of armed conflict. As mentioned above, at the time of its inception, it was assumed that the Convention's scope of application would not extend to situations of armed conflict. These were to be governed by international humanitarian law (IHL), the body of law specifically designed to regulate the means and methods of warfare and to provide protection for persons who were not participating in the fighting. This has meant that, for the better part of its existence, the ECtHR did not need to consider cases relating to the conduct of hostilities. Looking at the number of applications that have been filed in the past two decades in relation to alleged violations committed by the armed forces of State parties in the course of military operations, one might wonder what has changed. As an understanding of the underlying processes is key to contextualising and comprehending the ECtHR's dealings with armed conflict-related cases, this chapter will examine, in section 2, which trends and evolutions have rendered the strict compartmentalisation between the *jus in pace* and the *jus in bello* untenable and have led to the introduction of armed conflict-related applications to the Strasbourg Court.

The second question concerns the way in which the ECtHR has approached such cases. The attitude of the Strasbourg Court towards cases concerning armed conflict will, in large part, determine the extent to which States will consider it an appropriate, legitimate and credible forum for discussing and settling issues relating to the conduct of hostilities. In this regard, it has been argued that an uninformed application of Convention rights to situations of armed conflict would burden States with obligations that, given the circumstances, are too onerous to comply with and that would severely restrict military bodies' freedom of manoeuvre, thereby undermining operational effectiveness.[2] To gauge the truth behind such statements, section 3 examines how the ECtHR

2 As Gioia has, for example, noted, 'even the most enthusiastic supporters of [international human rights law] sometimes agree that it would be unrealistic and, indeed, dangerous to assume that [international human rights law] is to be applied in exactly the same way irrespective of whether or not the interested state is involved in an armed conflict, e.g. by categorically forbidding killing in a combat situation or otherwise making compliance with the law and victory impossible to achieve at once': see A. Gioia, 'The Role of the European Court of Human Rights in Monitoring Compliance with Humanitarian Law in Armed Conflict' in O. Ben-Naftali (ed.), *International Humanitarian Law and International Human Rights Law – Pas de Deux*, Oxford University Press, Oxford 2011, p. 218.

went about applying the European Convention to the actions of the armed forces of State parties engaged in military operations. Have the Judges simply resorted to examining possible human rights questions as they would have done in other (peacetime) cases, and thus applied the norms and standards contained in the ECHR and its Protocols in a 'business as usual' type of way, even considering that the norms and standards are not necessarily particularly well suited to being applied in times of armed conflict? Or has the Strasbourg Court applied the Convention in a context-specific manner, displaying a degree of sensitivity to the need to take account of the special circumstances presented by emergency situations and making reasonable allowances for considerations of military necessity?

If the latter is the case, a particularly interesting issue is the extent to which the ECtHR has resorted to IHL when interpreting human rights norms. The competence of the Strasbourg Court is limited to the interpretation and application of the ECHR and its Protocols (see Article 32 ECHR) and there is no specific mandate to monitor norms other than the ones contained therein. As such, the Strasbourg Court has no direct competence 'to determine State responsibility for breaches of IHL, nor can it attribute individual criminal responsibility for war crimes or grave breaches of the Geneva Conventions'.[3] Yet, there are compelling reasons for the ECtHR to take account of IHL and not simply to dismiss this body of law outright: as the norms and standards of IHL were crafted precisely to regulate situations of armed conflict, they might inform the interpretation of the rights contained in the ECHR, which are mostly formulated in general terms and require further specification to be applied to a particular situation. Furthermore, referring to IHL while interpreting the Convention rights would have the added benefit of lending 'some unity and coherence to the otherwise fragmented standards governing armed conflicts' and ensuring that States are not faced with irreconcilable legal obligations under the two bodies of law.[4] In section 3, it will therefore also be determined whether the ECtHR has adopted an 'ivory tower' attitude, ignoring questions of IHL and showing tunnel vision with regard to human rights issues, or whether the Judges have performed an elegant 'pas de deux', providing a workable theory for the application of the ECHR in situations of armed conflict and the concurrent application of the Convention with IHL.

---

3 S. Hartridge, 'The European Court of Human Rights' Engagement with International Humanitarian Law' in D. Jinks, J. Nyamuya Maogoto and S. Solomon (eds), *Applying International Humanitarian Law in Judicial and Quasi-Judicial Bodies: International and Domestic Aspects*, TMC Asser Press, The Hague 2014, p. 259.

4 W. Abresch, 'A Human Rights Law of Internal Armed Conflict: The European Court of Human Rights in Chechnya' (2005) 16 *European Journal of International Law* 741, 759. In a similar sense, F.J. Hampson and N. Lubell, *Amicus Curiae Brief Submitted in the Case of Hassan v. United Kingdom* (2013), available at <https://www.essex.ac.uk/hrc/documents/practice/amicus-curae.pdf> (accessed 04.03.2018).

2. A CHANGING LEGAL LANDSCAPE: THE STRASBOURG COURT'S INCREASED ENGAGEMENT WITH CASES STEMMING FROM ARMED CONFLICT

In classic public international law, IHL and international human rights law (IHRL) (of which the ECHR forms part) were considered to be two distinct and mutually exclusive bodies of law, conceived for different situations and with different theoretical considerations in mind.[5] The origins of human rights law can be traced back to domestic constitutional law. In that it strived to ensure just treatment for individuals by the authorities through the imposition of 'a wide range of legal obligations on States affecting their relationship with the governed', human rights law intended to regulate an internal affair between a government and its citizens and became part of international law only after the adoption of the Universal Declaration of Human Rights (1948).[6] IHL – at the time commonly referred to as the law of armed conflict –, on the other hand, was part of international law from the outset because it represented an agreement between States on the rules of conduct during hostilities. Thus, whereas human rights law focused on a vertical, imbalanced relationship between State and individual, IHL regulated the interactions of more or less equal legal subjects and was initially concerned with safeguarding mutual interests (such as the fair treatment of each other's troops), rather than with the protection of the less powerful.

These different historical and doctrinal roots have traditionally been raised in support of a strict separation between the law of war (i.e. IHL) and the law of peace (i.e. human rights law) and, as Heintze has correctly noted, 'depending on the state of international relations, either the *corpus juris* of the law of peace or that of the law of war was applied'.[7] Given that these bodies of law had little in common at first and developed largely independently of each other, the

---

[5] For an account of the history of the relationship between, and the converging development of, international humanitarian law and human rights law, see N. Quénivet, 'The History of the Relationship Between International Humanitarian Law and Human Rights Law' in R. Arnold and N. Quénivet (eds), *International Humanitarian Law and Human Rights Law: Towards a New Merger in International Law*, Martinus Nijhoff Publishers, Leiden 2008, pp. 1–12.

[6] G. Verdirame, 'Human Rights in Wartime: A Framework for Analysis', (2008) 6 *European Human Rights Law Review* 689, 694.

[7] H.-J. Heintze, 'On the Relationship between Human Rights Law Protection and International Humanitarian Law' (2004) 86 *International Review of the Red Cross* 789, 789. The strict separation theory has its adherents even today, see, e.g., M.J. Dennis, 'Application of Human Rights Treaties Extraterritorially to Detention of Combatants and Security Internees: Fuzzy Thinking all Around?' (2006) 12 *ILSA Journal of International and Comparative Law* 459.

introduction of applications relating to armed conflict at the ECtHR was not self-evident. In essence, three developments, among other factors, have played a determinative role in eroding this strict separation and bringing about the current situation.

The first development relates to the perceived inadequacy of the traditional enforcement mechanisms of IHL to 'regularly, consistently and independently monitor situations of armed violence, compel parties to the conflict to end violations, and provide appropriate remedies to victims'.[8] Whether it is because those mechanisms are considered counterproductive and out of sync with the contemporary emphasis on humanitarianism (for example, belligerent reprisals) or because States simply do not resort to them (for example, the Protecting Powers system or the International Humanitarian Fact-Finding Commission), the means and methods that IHL has to offer to secure respect for the law are largely considered ineffective and have, until now, garnered little success.[9] Therefore, victims and their lawyers hoping to obtain individual damages or reparations have started couching their armed conflict-related claims in terms of ECHR rights, as the latter body of law 'benefits from an enforcement machinery that, for all its faults and limits, is still much better developed than what [IHL] offers'.[10]

The lack of effective monitoring mechanisms under IHL helps to clarify the introduction of conflict-related cases at the ECtHR. It does not explain, however, why (and at what moment) the Strasbourg Judges decided to break through the traditional separation between the *jus in bello* and the *jus in pace* and open themselves up to claims stemming from armed conflict. This evolution can be attributed to a second development, namely the recognition of the continued applicability of the ECHR in times of armed conflict. The main driver behind the acceptance of continued applicability was the idea of the universality of human rights protection, i.e. that all human beings are holders of human rights independent of what they do, where they come from or what environment they happen to live in. Taking this idea to its logical conclusion, awareness grew that victims of armed conflict could not be denied protection under IHRL in general or the ECHR in particular merely because they found themselves in close proximity to hostilities. It must be noted that this recognition was the result of a gradual process. The notion that human rights law was relevant and remained applicable during armed conflict only gained support over time, initially within the international community and academia and subsequently

[8] G. Oberleitner, *Human Rights in Armed Conflict: Law, Practice, Policy*, Cambridge University Press, Cambridge 2015, p. 318.

[9] Ibid.

[10] G. Verdirame, above n. 6, 691.

among Judges of international judicial and quasi-judicial bodies.[11] Specifically within the European realm, the tipping point came with the report of the European Commission of Human Rights – which, until 1998, served as a filtering mechanism for cases that had less chance of succeeding – in the case of *Cyprus v. Turkey.*[12] Here, the Commission held, in its admissibility decision, that the ECHR continued to apply during the occupation of northern Cyprus. At this point and as a result of the impressive body of case law of the ECtHR affirming the continuous relevance during armed conflict of the ECHR, its continued applicability can no longer be reasonably disputed.[13]

A third and final development ensured that the Judges could apply the ECHR across the board of armed conflicts, namely extraterritorial application. Traditionally, and for a long time, Article 1 ECHR – the jurisdiction clause of the Convention – was explained in a primarily territorial sense, meaning that a State Party could be held accountable only for violations committed on its own territory. While it was accepted that certain actions and omissions committed in a foreign State could establish jurisdiction and thus lead to extraterritorial application of the ECHR, these bases of jurisdiction were considered to be highly exceptional and required special justification in the particular circumstances of each case.[14] The conduct of a State's security forces in the territory was not considered as one of those bases, and States have firmly and continuously advocated against extending the scope of application of the ECHR to include military conduct abroad.[15] Seen from this perspective, the relevance of the ECHR in times of armed conflict was limited to the actions of the armed forces of a State Party during a non-international armed conflict (NIAC) or an international armed conflict (IAC) when the actual fighting took place within the confines of the national territory. Once the armed forces had crossed a border, whether in the context of an international military operation deployed to a faraway land under the auspices of an international organisation, as part of a coalition of the willing or at the request of other States involved in NIACs taking place on their territory, the Convention would lose its value.

11 C. Droege, 'Elective Affinities? Human Rights and Humanitarian Law' (2008) 90 *International Review of the Red Cross* 501, 503–07.

12 European Commission on Human Rights, *Cyprus v. Turkey*, Decision on the Admissibility of the Applications (26 May 1975), Appl. Nos 6780/74 and 6950/75.

13 As to a general overview of the important conflict-related cases at the ECtHR, see ECtHR, *Factsheet – Armed Conflicts*, June 2015, available at <http://www.echr.coe.int/Documents/FS_Armed_conflicts_ENG.pdf> (accessed 04.03.2018).

14 It has long been accepted that extraterritorial jurisdiction exists when acts of diplomatic and consular agents are involved or when it concerns the State's conduct on the high seas. Other existing grounds for extraterritorial jurisdiction under international law include: (1) the active personality principle: (2) the passive personality principle; (3) the protective principle; and (4) the universality principle. See C. Ryngaert, *Jurisdiction in International Law*, 2nd ed. Oxford University Press, Oxford, 2015, pp. 101–44.

15 G. Oberleitner, above n. 8, p. 145.

While this stance was very much in line with the original conception of human rights law – as mentioned above, that of a body of law imposing a wide range of legal obligations on States affecting their relationship with the governed –, it is no longer tenable. Inspired by the notion that it would be unconscionable to permit States to perpetrate violations of the ECHR on the territory of another State that it could not perpetrate on its own territory, the ECtHR has, over time, developed an extensive body of case law that recognises that the ECHR applies not only within the territory of its contracting parties but also, under certain circumstances, to the extraterritorial activities of these parties.[16] For present purposes, suffice it to say that there is a growing consensus towards accepting extraterritorial application where, as a consequence of military action, a State exercises effective control of an area situated outside its national territory or where persons are found to be under the aforementioned State's authority and control through its agents operating abroad.[17] In such cases, the ECtHR would be able to examine alleged violations committed by the armed forces of States during the active phase of hostilities, even when committed on the territory of another State.

3. HOW HAS THE STRASBOURG COURT DEALT WITH SITUATIONS OF ARMED CONFLICT?

Having examined what processes have led to the introduction and consideration at the ECtHR of cases relating to the conduct of armed forces in the course of military operations, the second and perhaps more important question is how the Strasbourg Court has dealt with those cases. The fact that claims relating to alleged violations of the Convention have been filed in Strasbourg raises issues of law and policy, after all. The main question relates to whether the ECtHR is considered an appropriate forum to decide on cases stemming from armed conflict and whether it can (and should) supersede the largely dysfunctional implementation mechanisms under IHL. This question, in turn, elicits a range of subsidiary issues. To what extent does the Strasbourg Court have the

16 The press unit of the Strasbourg Court has listed some of the main judgments relating to extraterritoriality in ECtHR, *Factsheet – Extra-territorial Jurisdiction of States Parties to the European Convention on Human Rights* (July 2015), available at <http://www.echr.coe.int/Documents/FS_Extra-territorial_jurisdiction_ENG.pdf> (accessed 04.03.2018).

17 For a starting point for research on the topic, see F. Coomans and M. Kamminga, *Extraterritorial Application of Human Rights Treaties*, Intersentia, Cambridge 2004; K. Da Costa, *The Extraterritorial Application of Selected Human Rights Treaties*, Martinus Nijhoff Publishers, Leiden 2012; M. Gondek, *The Reach of Human Rights in a Globalising World: Extraterritorial Application of Human Rights Treaties*, Intersentia, Cambridge 2009; and M. Milanović, *Extraterritorial Application of Human Rights Treaties: Law, Principles and Policy*, Oxford University Press, Oxford 2011.

organisational capacity and expertise to deal with the rapidly growing conflict-related caseload? To what extent do the judgments of the ECtHR interpret the legal obligations imposed on States in a 'realistic way', conveying clear and precise guidance on the conduct of hostilities that can be applied in battlefield operations? How effective is 'a rights-based approach [...] in bringing the needed protection to individuals during periods of armed conflict'?[18] In the end, one can only offer an informed opinion and thoroughly discuss these issues once a clear picture has emerged of the approach that the ECtHR has taken in this regard. This section aims to help clarify this picture and will therefore provide an overview of the main cases stemming from armed conflict, identify the legal questions with which the ECtHR has been confronted and attempt to discern any traceable position that the Strasbourg Court has taken in this regard.

It has already been stated that the engagement of the ECtHR with IHL will receive particular attention in this chapter, simply because it is impossible to evaluate the ECtHR's conflict-related jurisprudence without considering the role of IHL and its potential impact on the application of the ECHR. Before going into the detail of the specific cases, the ECtHR has considered it is therefore necessary, as a preliminary point, to determine whether and to what extent the Strasbourg Court can resort to the norms of IHL in its interpretative work. As mentioned above, the Convention limits the competence of the Strasbourg Court to the interpretation and application of its provisions and its Protocols (see Article 32 ECHR). There is no specific mandate to monitor and ensure compliance with norms of IHL. However, this should not necessarily be construed as a legal impediment to the Court's consideration of the latter body of law. In fact, several possible avenues have been identified in legal literature that would allow the ECtHR indirectly to take account of IHL.

A first such avenue exists when the norms of the ECHR themselves provide the hooks for examining other sources of international law. A *renvoi*, i.e. a referral to international legal norms outside the human rights framework, can be found in several provisions of the ECHR, and since 'the purpose of *renvois* in the ECHR is precisely to link the treaty to rules of other bodies of international law', these provisions invite the Judges to analyse and interpret those 'external' norms, which could very well be norms of IHL.[19] The *renvoi* most often cited to illustrate this point can be found in the derogation clause of the European Convention (Article 15 ECHR), which stipulates that '*in time of war or other public emergency* threatening the life of the nation any High Contracting Party may take measures derogating from its obligations under this Convention to

18 R. Provost, *International Human Rights Law and Humanitarian Law*, Cambridge University Press, Cambridge 2002, p. 349.

19 G. Pinzauti, 'The European Court of Human Rights' Incidental Application of International Criminal Law and Humanitarian Law' (2008) 6 *Journal of International Criminal Justice* 1043, 1046.

the extent strictly required by the exigencies of the situation, provided that such measures are not inconsistent with *its other obligations under international law*' (emphasis added). A second possible avenue is provided by the general rules on the interpretation of treaties, as embodied in the Vienna Convention on the Law of Treaties (VCLT). Here, Article 31, §3 (c) VCLT lays down the principle that, in interpreting treaty norms, account is to be taken of any other relevant rules of international law applicable in the relation between parties. Referring to this principle, the Strasbourg Court has posited, on multiple occasions, that the ECHR cannot be interpreted and applied in a vacuum and that its norms and standards should be interpreted, as far as possible, in harmony with other rules of international law, of which it forms part.[20] Again, this undoubtedly opens the door for consideration of IHL, as it would be hard to argue that when applying the ECHR to situations of armed conflict this body of law could not be considered as being one of 'other relevant rules of international law'.

In other words, the Strasbourg Court has ample opportunity to draw on the norms and standards of IHL when examining armed conflict-related cases. What approach has the Court taken, and why? Drawing upon an analysis of the ECtHR's conflict-related jurisprudence, this chapter will demonstrate that the approach taken by the Strasbourg Court differs depending on the type of conflict during which the alleged violations of the ECtHR have taken place, with the Court being increasingly willing to reach out to IHL in cases stemming from IACs, while displaying a marked reluctance to use IHL as an interpretative tool when applying the ECHR to NIACs.

4. INTERNATIONAL ARMED CONFLICTS AND SITUATIONS OF OCCUPATION

Over the years, and especially after the end of the Cold War and the dissolution of the USSR, members of the Council of Europe – the parent organisation of the ECHR – have fought in IACs against each other. For example, in 1974, Turkey invaded and occupied northern Cyprus; from 1991 until the signing of a ceasefire agreement in 1994, Armenia and Azerbaijan fought over the Nagorno-Karabak region; and when NATO launched its air campaign against Serb troops, it internationalised the internal conflict in the former Yugoslavia. More recently, one can point to the IACs between Russia and two other former Soviet States: Georgia and Ukraine. As the warring parties in all these conflicts had previously

---

20 See *Loizidou v. Turkey*, no. 15318/89, ECHR, 1996, para. 43; *Al-Adsani v. United Kingdom*, no. 35763/97, ECHR, 2001, para. 55; *Banković and Others v. Belgium and 16 Other Contracting States*, Decision on Admissibility, no. 52207/99, ECHR, 2001, para. 57.

entered into the ECHR – all new members of the Council of Europe are required to sign and ratify the ECHR as a prerequisite for their accession – and had thus agreed to respect and ensure respect for the obligations contained therein, the ECtHR was provided with the opportunity to pronounce on cases relating to the conduct of the State Parties' armed forces during these conflicts. Along the same lines, when States Parties to the ECHR have supplied troops to the international military operations deployed in past decades to IACs around the world (such as Iraq and Afghanistan), the Strasbourg Court could once again scrutinise compliance with the Convention, to the extent that these States exercised effective control over an area situated outside their national territories or were found to have exerted authority and control over persons through their agents operating abroad (cf. above).

Examining the case law produced by the ECtHR relating to these IACs, it is immediately apparent that the Judges have had to pronounce on a diverse set of topics, as allegations relating to, among others, extrajudicial killings, detention *incommunicado*, enforced disappearances, forcible displacement of the civilian population, the destruction of property, torture and other forms of inhuman and degrading treatment have been filed. In addressing these complaints, the Strasbourg Court has proceeded along established lines. When analysing the admissibility of the complaints, the judges have continuously affirmed the relevance of the ECHR during armed conflict, and have examined whether the conduct should be attributed to the respondent State or an international organisation in cases in which the former was involved in an international military operation. Then, after careful consideration of the concrete facts, the Judges have established on each occasion whether or not the events complained of fell within the (extraterritorial) jurisdiction of the respondent State, as required under Article 1 ECHR. If the case passed the admissibility stage, the Strasbourg Court would next set out the different complaints, summarise the arguments of both sides, and recall its established jurisprudence, referring to the principles that have been deduced from it to determine how these principles would translate in the context of an armed conflict. Over the years, the Judges have, on multiple occasions, found violations of different ECHR provisions, but most often of Articles 2 (right to life), 3 (prohibition of torture), 5 (right to liberty), 8 (right to respect for private and family life) and 13 (right to remedy) ECHR.

Key features of its jurisprudence have been: that the Strasbourg Court had to overcome difficulties with regard to fact finding (non-disclosure of domestic case files and hindrance on the part of the respondent States has been a real issue); that the ECtHR has been very critical of any 'negligence of [State Parties'] investigatory authorities in responding to wholly credible allegations' of violations of the ECHR; that the judges have placed great emphasis on operational planning and proportionality in attack; that they have 'evaluated tactics in light of the permitted aims of law enforcement in a democratic society'; and finally that, when finding a violation, the policy has been to accord monetary reparation as just satisfaction under Article 41 ECHR rather than non-pecuniary measures (which could, for example, include orders for fresh investigations, public apologies, requiring domestic laws or judgments to be changed, etc.).[21]

What role has IHL played in the consideration of these cases by the Strasbourg Court? If compared with the body of law relating to NIACs, the rules and standards dealing with IACs contain the most extensive regulation of the means and methods of warfare and the protection of those adversely affected by the conflict, and there is a significant substantive overlap with human rights law, with norms at times complementing and contradicting each other. As a result, the issues relating to the interplay and relationship between both bodies of law are in full effect here. Therefore, if the ECtHR were willing to take account of IHL and adopt an outward-looking perspective – which remains to be seen –, one might expect the Strasbourg Court to engage with this body of law and set out the main parameters of its approach in these cases. However, on examining the Strasbourg Court's early case law, it immediately becomes clear that the Judges were initially rather reluctant to resort to IHL when deciding cases, even where the relevant standards of the latter body of law could have been raised in support of the findings made on the basis of the ECHR. The lack of enthusiasm to engage with IHL became evident as early as 1976, when the now-defunct European Commission of Human Rights had to pronounce on the case of *Cyprus v. Turkey*.[22] In this inter-State dispute, Cyprus had alleged that in the course of the occupation of the northern part of its territory, Turkish armed forces were committing numerous breaches of the ECHR, including:

- indiscriminately killing civilians, in violation of Article 2 ECHR;
- subjecting persons of both sexes and all ages to torture, inhuman and degrading treatment and punishment, in violation of Article 3 ECHR;
- detaining hundreds of people in Cyprus and Turkey arbitrarily and with no lawful authority, in violation of Article 5 ECHR;
- subjecting the said persons to forced labour under conditions amounting to slavery or servitude, in violation of Article 4 ECHR;

21 These key features are not exclusive to the ECtHR's jurisprudence on international armed conflicts and situations of occupation, but equally apply to its case law relating to non-international armed conflict. See, among others, A. Gioia, above n. 2, pp. 218–45; G. Oberleitner, above n. 8, pp. 295–311; W. Abresch, above n. 4, 751–67; P. Leach, 'The Chechen Conflict: Analysing the Oversight of the European Court of Human Rights', (2008) 6 *European Human Rights Law Review* 732; K. Koroteev, 'Legal Remedies for Human Rights Violations in the Armed Conflict in Chechnya: The Approach of the European Court of Human Rights in Context' (2010) 1(2) *Journal of International Humanitarian Legal Studies* 275.

22 European Commission on Human Rights, *Cyprus v. Turkey*, Report (10 July 1976), Appl. Nos 6780/74 and 6950/75.

- interfering with the rights to private life and the free enjoyment of property as a result of the displacement of thousands of persons from their places of residence and refusal to allow them to return thereto, in violation of Article 8 ECHR *juncto* Article 1 of the First Protocol.[23]

Undoubtedly, since the facts under review took place during an occupation and both the Hague Convention of 1907 and the Fourth Geneva Convention (GCIV) extensively regulate such situations, these treaty norms could have informed the application of the ECHR. Article 49 GCIV, for example, contains a prohibition on individual or mass forcible transfers, unless the security of the population or imperative military reasons so demand (which was not the case in the circumstances under review) and, as such, could have been of assistance when the Strasbourg Court examined whether the displacement of thousands of persons conformed to Article 8 ECHR. Other provisions (such as Article 51 GCIV, with regard to forced labour, or Article 33 GCIV, which prohibits pillage) could have served a comparable purpose. Nevertheless, aside from a passing reference to the Third Geneva Convention's norms on prisoners of war when discussing the deprivation of liberty of military personnel, the Commission remained remarkably silent on the issue and refrained from explicitly invoking specific norms of IHL in its decision.[24]

The disinclination to deal with IHL persisted in subsequent cases decided by the ECtHR in relation to the occupation of northern Cyprus, such as *Loizidou v. Turkey*.[25] In this case, the claimant, a Cypriot national who owned several plots of land on the northern part of the island, was repeatedly refused entry to her property by Turkish armed forces following the invasion on 20 July 1974, and argued that the continued denial of access constituted a violation of the right to respect for her home (Article 8 ECHR) and a breach of the right of peaceful use of her property (Article 1 of Protocol No.1). Ultimately, the ECtHR (partly) sided with the applicant and decided that the continued denial of access indeed amounted to an unjustified interference with the peaceful

23 Ibid., paras 19–23.

24 The Commission noted that it 'has taken account of the fact that both Cyprus and Turkey are Parties to the (Third) Geneva Convention of 12 August 1949, relative to the treatment of prisoners-of-war, and that, in connection with the events in the summer of 1974, Turkey in particular assured the International Committee of the Red Cross (ICRC) of its intention to apply the Geneva Conventions and its willingness to grant all necessary facilities for humanitarian action': ibid., para. 313.

25 *Loizidou v. Turkey*, no. 15318/89, ECHR, 1996. Other relevant cases include: *Cyprus v. Turkey*, no. 25781/94, ECHR, 2001; *Demades v. Turkey*, no. 16219/90, ECHR, 2003; *Xenidis-Arestis v. Turkey*, no. 46347/99, ECHR, 2005; *Solomou and others v. Turkey*, no. 36832/97, ECHR, 2008; *Isaak v. Turkey*, no. 44587/98, ECHR, 2008; *Andreou v. Turkey*, no. 45653/99, ECHR, 2009; *Demopoulos and others v. Turkey*, Grand Chamber Admissibility Decision, nos 46113/99, 3843/02, 13751/02, 13466/03, 10200/04, 14163/04, 19993/04, 21819/04, ECHR 2010; *Cyprus v. Turkey*, Grand Chamber Judgment, no. 25781/94, ECHR, 2014.

enjoyment of her possessions, yet it did so without referring to IHL. While the Judges referred to the 'occupation of Cyprus' in their judgment, at no point did they examine whether the situation could actually be considered as such. This has been a deplorable constant in ECtHR case law with regard to Cyprus and other situations of occupation. Judges have refused to examine whether the situation could qualify as a belligerent occupation to which IHL applied. The majority view in legal literature, however, has been that the ECtHR's findings in *Loizidou*, and its decisions in comparable cases, could have been reinforced by having reference to the relevant norms of IHL.[26] The determination that a belligerent occupation under IHL existed could, for example, have assisted in establishing whether Turkey exercised effective control over northern Cyprus and thus whether it had the jurisdiction required under Article 1 ECHR for extraterritorial application of the Convention. Similarly, as already mentioned above, IHL treaty norms could have informed the application of the ECHR to the facts under review.

Along the same lines, when the Strasbourg Court got around to addressing cases concerning actual combat operations during IACs, as opposed to issues stemming from the existence of an occupation, issues of IHL were initially also not considered. The case most often cited in this regard is *Banković and Others v. Belgium and Others*, which concerned the NATO bombing of the Belgrade headquarters of 'Radio Television of Serbia' on 23 April 1999, as part of the Kosovo War. The applicants, four relatives of victims of the aerial attack, complained that the bombing had violated the right to life, the right to freedom of expression and the right to an effective legal remedy as laid down in Articles 2, 10 and 13 of the ECHR respectively. Importantly, the applicants had based part of their argumentation on IHL, thus once again providing the ECtHR with the opportunity to clarify the possible role of IHL in its decision-making processes and to address some of the complex and multifaceted questions that arise as a result of the simultaneous application of IHL and the ECHR.[27] However, as the case was declared inadmissible for falling outside the territorial scope of application of the Convention, the Judges did not have the opportunity to discuss these questions. It was simply no longer necessary to take the points of the application dealing with IHL into consideration.

Interestingly, inadmissibility also prevented the ECtHR from considering other cases relating to violation committed during IACs and where IHL was

---

26 See, e.g., A. Gioia, above n. 2, pp. 220–21; G. Oberleitner, above n. 8, p. 297; and H.-J. Heintze, above n. 7, 807–08. The dissenting opinion of Judge Pettiti in *Loizidou v. Turkey* is also noteworthy here, as he argued that the ECtHR should have explained the situation in northern Cyprus by clarifying the notions 'occupation' and 'annexation' and by examining the 'territorial application of the Geneva Conventions in Northern Cyprus'.

27 For a discussion of the application's reference to IHL, see H.-J. Heintze, 'The European Court of Human Rights and the Implementation of Human Rights Standards During Armed Conflicts' (2002) 45 *German Yearbook of International Law* 60, 69–70.

either invoked or could have proven informative in deciding upon the merits. In *Issa and others v. Turkey*, where an application was filed in relation to the killing and mutilation of shepherds living in Northern Iraq by Turkish soldiers during a military operation in the region, the Strasbourg Court dismissed the case, considering that it had not been established to the required standard of proof that the Turkish armed forces were involved in the series of events complained of, and thus that the victims came within Turkey's 'jurisdiction' for the purposes of Article 1 of the ECHR.[28] Similarly, when the ECtHR had to examine a couple of complaints stemming from the IAC in the former Yugoslavia and which dealt with the failure to remove undetonated cluster bombs (*Behrami v. France*) on the one hand and the treatment of individuals during detention (*Saramati v. France, Germany and Norway*) on the other, the Grand Chamber also struck out the application.[29] This time because the Judges believed that the conduct allegedly violating the ECHR had to be attributed to the United Nations and that, therefore, no jurisdictional link with the respondent States could be established. There is something to say about all these different judgments, and in particular the decisions in the latter two cases have been severely (and rightly) criticised for misinterpreting and misapplying the law.[30] According to Uriarte, the fact that the Judges have declared these cases inadmissible as easily as they did speaks 'volumes because it shows how eager the Court is to dismiss any application related to peacekeeping missions' deployed in IACs in order to avoid having to deal with IHL.[31]

Regardless of whether one agrees with this statement or not, what is certain is that, in previous years, and for a long time, the ECtHR chose not to take 'any traceable position on whether or not the Court can and should use international humanitarian law to interpret the Convention' even when it had the opportunity to do so.[32] The fact that the Strasbourg Court has glossed over issues of IHL in cases stemming from IACs or situations of occupation has been met with harsh criticism, in essence because the Judges neglected the will of States, embodied in the Geneva Conventions, to regulate armed conflict in a certain way, and supplanted it with their own views. More recently, however,

---

28 *Issa and others v. Turkey*, no. 31821/96, ECHR, 2004.

29 *Behrami and Behrami v. France* and *Saramati v. France, Germany and Norway*, Grand Chamber, Decision on Admissibility, nos 71412/01 and 78166/01, ECHR 2007.

30 See, e.g., M. Milanović and T. Papic, 'As Bad as It Gets: The European Court of Human Rights' Behrami and Saramati Decision and General International Law' (2009) 58 *International and Comparative Law Quarterly* 267.

31 J. Abrisketa Uriarte, 'The Problems the European Court of Human Rights Faces in Applying International Humanitarian Law' in P. Gibbons and H.-J. Heintze (eds), *The Humanitarian Challenge: 20 Years European Network on Humanitarian Action (NOHA)*, Springer International Publishing, 2015, p. 210.

32 G. Oberleitner, above n. 8, p. 309.

and perhaps in response to this criticism, the Strasbourg Court appears to have taken a different approach and the apparent unwillingness to engage with the norms of humanitarian law relating to these types of armed conflict seems to have been replaced by an increased open-mindedness towards the body of law. The first indication of this changed attitude came with the case of *Varnava and others v. Turkey*.[33] In yet another case originating in the Turkish occupation of Cyprus, the ECtHR had to pronounce on applications relating to nine people who had gone missing in northern Cyprus in the wake of the Turkish military operation of 1974. As the applicants were last seen in the custody of agents of the respondent State and subsequently disappeared in a context that could be considered life threatening, the case gave rise to issues relating to enforced disappearances – a prohibited practice under both the ECtHR and IHL. Ultimately, the Strasbourg Court found violations of the positive obligation to investigate these disappearances in light of Article 2 ECHR: the right not to be subjected to torture or cruel, inhuman or degrading treatment and the right not to be arbitrarily arrested or detained. Most importantly for present purposes, however, is that the ECtHR acknowledged that, in times of armed conflict, the European Convention 'must be interpreted in so far as possible in light of the general principles of international law, including the rules of international humanitarian law which play an indispensable and universally-accepted role in mitigating the savagery and inhumanity of armed conflict'.[34] Thus, for the very first time, and in contrast with its previous case law, the ECtHR referred to IHL and used it as an interpretative tool to inform the application in times of armed conflict of norms originally conceived to apply in situations of peace.

The *Varnava* case represented a turning point in the Strasbourg Court's approach to IHL and opened the door for increased engagement with the body of law in future cases. As a result, when the ECtHR was confronted with complaints relating to the conduct of British armed forces, acting as an occupying power in Iraq from 2003 onwards, the Judges displayed an increased awareness of the relevance of IHL and have started citing the norms of IHL in the 'applicable law' section of their judgments.[35] Admittedly, in several cases, the cited norms were not further discussed throughout the judgment, and thus did not did not have a significant impact on the ECtHR's deliberations. In other cases, the Strasbourg Court's approach to IHL attracted harsh criticism. The decision in the *Al-Jedda v. United Kingdom* case, for example, was said to constitute 'a potential and serious

---

33 *Varnava and others v. Turkey*, nos 16064/90, 16065/90, 16066/90, 16068/90, 16069/90, 16070/90, 16071/90, 16072/90 and 16073/90, ECHR 2009.

34 Ibid., para. 185.

35 See *Al Skeini and others v. United Kingdom*, Grand Chamber Judgment, no. 55721/07, ECHR 2011; *Al-Saadoon and Mufdhi v. United Kingdom*, no. 61498/08, ECHR, 2010; *Al Jedda v. United Kingdom*, Grand Chamber Judgment, no. 47708/08, ECHR, 2014.

revision of a legal regime agreed to by all States in the world and one generally considered to constitute the applicable *lex specialis* in IACs'.[36] Nevertheless, as Van den Herik and Duffy have correctly noted, these judgments are 'significant in at least acknowledging in principle the potential relevance of IHL to the interpretation of the Convention in conflict situations'.[37]

The current end point of the evolution is the case of *Hassan v. United Kingdom.*[38] Here, the Grand Chamber of the European Court of Human Rights reviewed the deprivation of liberty of a young male by British armed forces during the phase of active hostilities in Iraq. Central to the case was the fact that in detaining the person in question the UK had relied on IHL, and more specifically on the Third and Fourth Geneva Conventions, which provide a legal basis and the procedure to intern combatants and civilians posing a threat to security during armed conflict. Yet, as the list of grounds of permissible detention in Article 5 ECHR does not include internment or preventive detention where there is no intention to bring criminal charges within a reasonable time, the applicant had argued that absent any derogation under Article 15 ECHR, the United Kingdom had violated its international commitments under the Convention. As a result of the centrality of this norm conflict and thus of the interplay between the ECHR and IHL, the ECtHR had to clarify how the dual application of the two bodies plays out in a specific case. Ultimately, in an attempt to provide a workable model for the concurrent application of both bodies of law it chose to allow the more permissive regime of IHL to step in through a reading-down of Article 5 ECHR, thereby reconciling the two bodies of law. In doing so, the ECtHR took another step forward with the explicit engagement with IHL. In the words of the Strasbourg Court:

> By reason of the co-existence of the safeguards provided by international humanitarian law and by the Convention in time of armed conflict, the grounds of permitted deprivation of liberty set out in subparagraphs (a) to (f) of that provision should be accommodated, as far as possible, with the taking of prisoners of war and the detention of civilians who pose a risk to security under the Third and Fourth Geneva Conventions. The Court is mindful of the fact that internment in peacetime does not fall within the scheme of deprivation of liberty governed by Article 5 of the Convention without the exercise of the power of derogation under Article 15 (see paragraph 97 above). It can only be in cases of international armed conflict, where the taking of prisoners of war

36 J. Pejic, 'The European Court of Human Rights' Al-Jedda Judgment: the Oversight of International Humanitarian Law' (2011) 93 *International Review of the Red Cross* 837, 851.

37 See L. van den Herik and H. Duffy, 'Human Rights Bodies and International Humanitarian Law: Common but Differentiated Approaches', Grotius Centre Working Paper 2014/020-IHL, Universiteit Leiden, at <http://papers.ssrn.com/sol3/papers.cfm?abstract_id=2448146>, 20 (accessed 04.03.2018).

38 *Hassan v. United Kingdom*, Grand Chamber Judgment,no. 29750/09, ECHR, 2014.

> and the detention of civilians who pose a threat to security are accepted features of international humanitarian law, that Article 5 could be interpreted as permitting the exercise of such broad powers.[39]

Undoubtedly, the judgment does not resolve all questions relating to the relationship between IHL and the ECHR. Since the Judges expressly limited their findings to the right not to be arbitrarily deprived of liberty and IACs, the decision provides limited guidance on how to approach the issue in other cases and with regard to other articles. Future cases will need to bring additional clarity in this regard. Nonetheless, being the first judgment in which the interplay between IHL and the ECHR was thoroughly discussed, the decision might indicate a change in the position of the ECtHR, signal its willingness to engage in a more detailed manner with the ways in which IHL affects the application of the ECHR in conflict situations and set the tone for the future. As a result, and while it can hardly be said that the Strasbourg Court is performing an elegant 'pas de deux', providing a workable theory for the application of the ECHR in situations of armed conflict and the concurrent application of the Convention with IHL, there is, at least, noticeable progress as the Judges are becoming familiar with the issues involved. This stands in sharp contrast to the ECtHR's approach in cases relating to NIACs, to which the chapter will turn next.

5. NON-INTERNATIONAL ARMED CONFLICTS

Since the 1980s, several State Parties to the ECHR have been confronted with situations of internal instability, some of which have eventually deteriorated and led to intra-State violence, pitting a State's military and security forces against non-State armed groups. Although these clashes differed tremendously in terms of their duration and intensity, in certain cases the skirmishes have resulted in the use of combat weapons, artillery attacks and aerial bombardment. It should come as no surprise, therefore, that such armed confrontations have proven to be fertile ground for complaints to the ECtHR. The situation in Northern Ireland, for example, led to a series of communications relating to the measures that the United Kingdom had taken to halt the Irish Republican Army (IRA), a paramilitary organisation that committed terrorist attacks throughout Great Britain and that sought to liberate Northern Ireland from the United Kingdom's rule. Similarly, the skirmishes between the Turkish armed forces and the Kurdistan Workers' Party (PKK) in south-east Turkey, which were characterised by the violent oppression of Kurds by the Turkish authorities on the one hand and guerilla-style warfare by the PKK on the other, required the Strasbourg Court to

---

39 Ibid., para. 104.

examine the conduct of the Turkish authorities. Finally, the Russian response to the large-scale and high-intensity insurgency taking place in Chechnya similarly resulted in an impressive number of applications alleging misconduct on the part of Russian armed forces. Altogether, these cases provided the ECtHR with ample opportunity to examine how the rights contained in the ECHR translate and apply to situations of internal strife.

As was the case with regard to the complaints stemming from IACs and occupation, the applications relating to NIACs dealt with allegations of extrajudicial killings, detention *incommunicado*, enforced disappearances, forcible displacement of the civilian population, the destruction of property, torture and other forms of inhuman and degrading treatment. Interestingly, in examining these cases the ECtHR has proceeded in much the same way as it did when examining cases relating to IACs. The Judges have similarly stressed due diligence in operational planning, proportionality in attack and the necessity of providing effective remedies to victims of misconduct. Once again, they have accorded monetary rather than other forms of reparations. There is one important difference, however. Whereas the Strasbourg Court has gradually opened up to the prospect of considering IHL in relation to IACs, the Strasbourg Court has ignored IHL when examining complaints relating to the intra-State violence in Northern Ireland, south-east Turkey and Chechnya, and to this day continues to do so in more recent cases.

With regard to the allegations concerning the UK's actions in response to IRA attacks, the absence of any reference to the body of law could still be understood. As the IRA numbered only in the hundreds and the fighting was of a relatively low intensity and occurred only sporadically, it could reasonably be argued – as the UK Government did – that the events were nothing more than internal disturbances to which IHL did not apply because the threshold of Common Article 3 was not met. The same does not hold true, however, for the armed violence in south-east Turkey and Chechnya, which objectively constituted NIACs.[40] As a result, the norms of IHL relating to NIACs applied as a matter of law. Still, in deciding cases relating to south-east Turkey and Chechnya, the Strasbourg Court did not pay attention to the body of law, despite the applicants and intervening non-governmental organisations (NGOs) regularly raising arguments under IHL and thus inviting the ECtHR to do so. Instead, the Judges applied the principles they developed in their jurisprudence

---

40 Both conflicts satisfy the threshold criteria of Common Article 3 as the fighting was between a State and a non-State armed group and the non-State armed groups were organised and carried out protracted hostilities. It has been argued that the conflict in Chechnya could even fulfil the requirements for application of the Second Additional Protocol of 1977, because the insurgents were under responsible command and had sufficient control to carry out sustained and concerted military operations. For more on the qualifications of these conflicts, see, e.g., W. Abresch, above n. 4, 754–56.

on law enforcement operations to situations of conflict, thus creating a single regime of basic rules applicable to all situations ranging from riots and situations of violence falling just short of the armed conflict threshold, through relatively small-scale skirmishes in a low-intensity conflict, to cases of protracted and full-blown armed confrontations between State armies and/or non-State actors (for example, rebel groups).[41]

The Strasbourg Court still adheres to this approach and how this plays out in practice is especially visible in the context of the 'right to life' cases under Article 2 ECHR, where the judgment in *McCann and others v. United Kingdom* served as the model for the decisions in other cases.[42] This case related to the killing by British armed forces of three IRA members who intended to set off a car bomb in Gibraltar. Having received intelligence about the impending attack, the UK had begun to make preparations to thwart the assault and the operation to counter the danger posed by the IRA members was set up as one of law enforcement, meaning that the suspects were to be arrested using minimum force, that they were to be disarmed and that evidence was to be gathered for a court trial. Yet, when push came to shove, the British soldiers shot the terrorists, mistakenly assuming that they were about to detonate the bomb or otherwise open fire. Because subsequent investigations had revealed that there were no explosive devices in the vicinity and that the IRA members were not carrying weapons, their next of kin filed an application, alleging that the operation carried out by the United Kingdom was neither planned nor executed in accordance with the right to life, as laid down by Article 2 ECHR. In their defence, the British authorities rejected the applicants' claim and argued that the use of force was justified by Article 2, §2 (a) ECHR as it was 'no more than absolutely necessary in defence of the people of Gibraltar from unlawful violence'.[43] Ultimately, and although the ECtHR followed the United Kingdom's argument that the special forces honestly believed, in the light of the information that they had been given, that it was necessary to shoot the suspects in order to prevent them from detonating a bomb and causing serious loss of life, and that their actions did not, in themselves, give rise to a violation, the Judges nevertheless found that the UK had breached Article 2 ECHR. More precisely, the Judges found that there had been a lack of appropriate care in the control and organisation of the arrest operation in that the anti-terrorist operation was not planned and controlled

41 In the same sense, see L. Moir, 'The European Court of Human Rights and International Humanitarian Law' in R. Kolb and G. Gaggioli (eds), *Research Handbook on Human Rights and Humanitarian Law*, Edward Elgar Publishing, Cheltenham 2013, pp. 483–84; S. Hartridge, above n. 3, 273–78; J. Abrisketa Uriarte, above n. 31, p. 217; W. Abresch, above n. 4, 752–53.

42 *McCann and others v. United Kingdom*, Grand Chamber Judgment, no. 18984/91, ECHR, 1995.

43 Ibid., para. 143.

by the authorities so as to minimise, to the greatest extent possible, recourse to lethal force.[44]

From the *McCann* judgment the Strasbourg Court deduced several general principles guiding the use of force, namely that every operation had to be carefully planned and that, in any case, the resort to use of force was to be allowed only if it were '(a) absolutely necessary in the prevailing circumstances, (b) proportionate to the threat posed and to the legitimate aims set out in Article 2 (2) and (c) limited to circumstances where arrest or detention is either not possible, or else too dangerous'.[45] These benchmarks were then consistently applied in future 'right to life' cases, irrespective of whether the concrete facts giving rise to the complaints took place in the context of a law enforcement operation or during the conduct of hostilities. For example, in two of the leading cases stemming from the armed conflict in south-east Turkey, *Ergi v. Turkey* and *Güleç v. Turkey*, the Strasbourg Court extensively referred to the *McCann* rules in finding violations of Article 2 ECHR, even though both these cases lent themselves perfectly to the consideration of IHL.[46] The first case concerned an ambush operation staged by Turkish armed forces to catch a group of PKK members, during the course of which the State's armed forces had indiscriminately bombarded civilian houses, resulting in several civilian deaths, including that of the applicant. In the second case, the shooting of a young adolescent during a popular demonstration that had turned violent, with protesters throwing sticks and stones at security officers, was the central issue. In both cases the Judges had found that a violation of Article 2 had been committed, because in both instances the Turkish Government had failed to plan the operation with the requisite care for the civilian population and had applied force that was not strictly proportionate to the achievement of its proposed aims. In *Ergi*, the ECtHR had held that the Turkish forces had placed the villagers at considerable risk of being caught in the cross-fire between security forces and any PKK terrorists and that they had failed to choose the appropriate means and methods of a security operation mounted against an opposing group with a view to avoiding and, in any event, to minimising incidental loss of civilian life. In *Güleç* it was stated that although the use of force was justified – Article 2, §2 (c) ECHR allows the use of force to quell a riot –, the balance between the aim pursued and the means employed to achieve it was skewed because the Turkish armed personnel had used a very powerful weapon to disperse the demonstrators – an automatic rifle mounted on an armoured vehicle – because they apparently did not have truncheons, riot shields, water cannon, rubber bullets or tear gas. Importantly, in deciding the two cases the

44 Ibid., paras 194 and 202–14.

45 L. Moir, above n. 41, p. 483.

46 *Ergi v. Turkey*, no. 66/1997/850/1057, ECHR 1998; *Gülec v. Turkey*, no. 54/1997/838/1044, ECHR 1998.

ECtHR remained solely within the confines of the ECHR and did not make any explicit references to IHL, setting the baseline for other cases relating to the Turkish/PKK conflict.[47]

The Strasbourg Court did much the same thing with regard to the 'right of life' cases stemming from the Chechnya conflict. When, for example, an application was filed in *Isayeva, Yusupova and Bazayeva v. Russia* in relation to the attacks of Russian fighter planes, using air-to-ground missiles, on a convoy consisting of civilians and Red Cross personnel who believed they were passing through a humanitarian corridor, the ECtHR reiterated the core principle that any use of force must be no more than is 'absolutely necessary' for the achievement of one or more of the purposes set out in sub-paragraphs (a) to (c) of Article 2 ECHR and that the force used must be strictly proportionate to the achievement of these permitted aims.[48] Although the ECtHR considered the actions of the Russian forces against the Chechen rebels to be law enforcement operations, the Judges, strangely enough, accepted that the situation that existed in Chechnya at the relevant time called for exceptional measures on behalf of the State to suppress the illegal armed insurgency and that such measures could include the employment of military aviation equipped with heavy combat weapons.[49] Still, the Strasbourg Court found that a violation of Article 2 had occurred, stating that 'even assuming that the military were pursuing a legitimate aim in launching 12 S-24 non-guided air-to-ground missiles on 29 October 1999, the Court does not accept that the operation near the village of Shaami-Yurt was planned and executed with the requisite care for the lives of the civilian population'.[50] Likewise, in *Isayeva v. Russia*, in which the ECtHR had to pronounce on the use of free-falling high-explosive weapons by the Russian military in a densely populated area that was allegedly declared a safe zone and where a large group of Chechen fighters were believed to be present,[51] the Strasbourg Court found the use of lethal force in confronting the Chechen rebels justified and followed the Russian Government's argument that the use of force had been necessary 'to suppress the active resistance of the illegal armed groups, whose actions were a real threat to the life and health of the servicemen and civilians, as well as to the general interests of society and the State'.[52] As in the previous case, however, the ECtHR also found that the force applied was disproportionate

47 *Oğur v. Turkey*, no. 21594/93, ECHR, 1999; *Ahmet Özkan and others v. Turkey*, no. 21689/93, ECHR, 2004; ECtHR, *Mansuroğlu v. Turkey*, no. 43443/98, ECHR, 2008; *Benzer and others v. Turkey*, no. 23502/06, ECHR, 2015.

48 *Isayeva, Yusupova and Bazayeva v. Russia*, no. 57947/00, 57948/00 and 57949/00, ECHR, 2005.

49 Ibid., para. 178.

50 Ibid., para. 199.

51 *Isayeva v. Russia*, no. 57950/00, ECHR, 2005.

52 Ibid., para. 170.

to the aims pursued, deciding that 'using [heavy free-falling high-explosion aviation bombs with a damage radius exceeding 1,000 meters] in a populated area, outside wartime and without prior evacuation of the civilians is impossible to reconcile with the degree of caution expected from a law-enforcement body in a democratic society'.[53] As a result, the ECtHR concluded that 'the massive use of indiscriminate weapons stands in flagrant contrast with this aim and cannot be considered compatible with the standard of care prerequisite to an operation of this kind involving the use of lethal force by State agents'.[54] As was the case with south-east Turkey, references to IHL were entirely absent from the decisions in these two cases and the Strasbourg Court limited itself to finding a violation of Article 2 ECHR without considering the possible impact that IHL could have had on the application of the Convention. Again, and despite the fact that the applicants and intervening non-governmental organisations continued to frame their claims with reference to both the ECHR and IHL, this became the trademark of the judges' approach to 'right to life' issues in subsequent cases on Chechnya and other NIACs.[55]

Notwithstanding the lack of explicit references to IHL in the ECtHR's judgments, some commentators have argued that the Judges have nonetheless applied the body of law *sub silentio*. In this regard, they have pointed to the language used by the Court, which at times resembles very closely the vocabulary of IHL and which has been taken as 'evidence of the almost surreptitious application of humanitarian law rules and principles'.[56] These commentators are only partly correct. It is undeniable that the Strasbourg Court has, at times, expressed itself in terms that bear a striking resemblance to the formulation of certain norms of IHL. Compare, for example, the findings in *Ergi v. Turkey* and *Isayeva v. Russia* that a State's responsibility under Article 2 ECHR can be engaged where it fails to take all feasible precautions in the choice of means and methods of a security operation mounted against an opposing group with a view to avoiding and, in any event, to minimising incidental loss of civilian life with Article 57(2)(a)(ii) of Additional Protocol I, which regulates precaution in attack.[57] Undoubtedly, by using concepts such as 'legitimate targets', 'indiscriminate weapons' and

---

53 Ibid., para. 191.

54 Ibid., para. 191.

55 *Khashiyev and Akayeva v. Russia*, nos 57942/00 and 57945/00, ECHR, 2005; *Estamirov and others v. Russia*, no. 60272/00, ECHR, 2006; *Umayeva v. Russia*, no. 1200/03, ECHR, 2008; *Abdulkhanov and others v. Russia*, no. 22782/06, ECHR, 2013; *Esmukhambetov and others v. Russia*, no. 23445/03, ECHR, 2011.

56 L. Moir, above n. 41, p. 484.

57 Art. 57(2)(a)(ii) of Additional Protocol I reads as follows: 'Those who plan or decide upon an attack shall [...] take all feasible precautions in the choice of means and methods of attack with a view to avoiding, and in any event to minimizing, incidental loss of civilian life, injury to civilians and damage to civilian objects.'

'incidental loss of civilian life' the Judges have formulated their decisions in terms clearly reminiscent of IHL. Yet, concluding from the use of similar language that the ECtHR has implicitly applied the body of law would stretch the argument too far. The language used by the Strasbourg Court is not unique to IHL and, as Abresch has correctly noted, 'comparison between the ECtHR's holdings and the rules of humanitarian law reveals that if the ECtHR is attempting to apply humanitarian law, it is doing so in a highly imprecise manner'.[58] The conditions imposed by the Strasbourg Court go beyond what is required under IHL, where lethal force used against combatants (those not placed *hors de combat*) and civilians taking direct part in hostilities is considered lawful *per se* and the rule of proportionality is much looser (reducing casualties to a minimum versus avoiding excessive incidental damage). As a result, the Strasbourg Court has denounced the use of lethal force with referral to Article 2 ECHR and the *McCann* rules in cases where it would have been lawful under IHL.

One may wonder why the ECtHR has not resorted to IHL when confronted with cases stemming from NIACs, as it had gradually done in its IAC-related judgments. As the judges did not give their precise view on the possible impact of IHL on the application of the ECHR, it is hard to make definitive statements in this regard. Yet, with States often refusing to acknowledge that an armed conflict is occurring in their territory (and thus that IHL applies) or declining the opportunity offered by Article 15 ECHR to derogate from their human rights obligations in times of war or other public emergencies threatening the life of the nation, it has been speculated that the ECtHR took the easiest route and decided to settle the cases within the confines of the ECHR, thereby avoiding having to deal with politically sensitive and highly complex legal issues such as the threshold of application of IHL and the uncertainty surrounding the content of the norms and standards relating to NIACs.[59]

Whatever the case may be, the fact remains that, absent derogation, the ECtHR has applied the ECHR against a 'normal legal background' and did not have recourse to IHL, regardless of the views of the parties that have pressed the Strasbourg Court to do so. While some authors have heralded this approach because of its apparent 'potential to drive military reform and improvement at the institutional level' and because it may arguably 'prove to be both more protective of victims and more politically viable than [IHL]', the majority of commentators has been fairly critical, as is the present writer.[60] The European Court's silence on IHL has, for example, been criticised as 'disconnected from reality', as 'contributing to the fragmentation of international law', as 'making

58 W. Abresch, above n. 4, 746.
59 G. Oberleitner, above n. 8, p. 309.
60 Ibid., pp. 764 and 767.

compliance with the law and victory in battle impossible to achieve at once' and as being the embodiment of 'judicial imperialism' for singlehandedly substituting the applicable rules of IHL with those of IHRL.[61] Ultimately, the problem lies not so much with the concrete outcome of the decided cases. Aside from a couple of cases in which the Strasbourg Court found a violation for conduct that would have been lawful under IHL, the end result would have been the same in most cases, even if the ECtHR had taken account of IHL. Nor does the real issue lie with the application of the ECHR over IHL in times of armed conflict. There are multiple reasons imaginable that would justify coming to such a conclusion. It is, for example, a well-known fact that the norms of IHL with regard to NIACs are scarce in comparison with those relating to IACs and that they leave gaps in the protection offered to those adversely affected by the conflict. Here, the ECHR could fill the lacunae, providing more detailed rules and, indeed, often better protection. In addition, at times, the facts under review will resemble more closely the circumstances for which the ECHR was conceived (i.e. a law enforcement operation), rather than those of IHL (i.e. the conduct of hostilities). Once again, this might bring the ECtHR to conclude that the ECHR is better suited to apply. But as Hartridge has noted, 'such a conclusion should be reached through a transparent process of reasoning, which is conspicuously absent in the decided cases'.[62] By continuously '[constructing] the situation before it as a law enforcement operation regardless of the context and the views of the parties even when this means feigning a "normal legal background" in the midst of heaviest fighting', the Strasbourg Court has neglected to take account of the body of law where references to its norms could have proven informative or even necessary to apply the ECHR in a realistic way.[63] At no point did the ECtHR explain why it has done so, and therefore the ECtHR has arguably approached these conflict-related cases with an 'ivory tower' mindset.

6. CONCLUSION

Although initially contested, it is now an established fact that the ECHR continues to apply in times of armed conflict and under certain circumstances, even to the activities of military personnel on foreign soil. This has opened the ECtHR up to claims alleging rights-violating conduct on the part of the armed

---

61 See, e.g., F.J. Hampson and N. Lubell, above n. 4; R. Ekins, J. Morgan and T. Tugendhat, *Clearing the Fog of Law: Saving Our Armed Forces from Defeat by Judicial Diktat*, London, 2015, <http://www.policyexchange.org.uk/images/publications/clearing+20the%20fog%20of%20law.pdf> (accessed 04.03.2018), 11.

62 S. Hartridge, above n. 3, p. 274.

63 G. Oberleitner, above n. 8, p. 309.

forces of the State Parties and has required Judges to examine questions relating to how the ECHR translates into such settings, to what extent they can take account of IHL and how the ECHR relates to IHL. However, the Strasbourg Court's approach to these questions has – as Van den Herik and Duffy have noted and as has hopefully been substantiated throughout this chapter – been myopic, or at least opaque, with the ECtHR often having 'regard to the realities of armed conflict in interpreting and applying the Convention', without engaging 'in a detailed manner with the ways in which IHL may affect the ECHR in conflict situations'.[64] As argued above, for the better part of its existence, the ECtHR has neglected IHL and examined conflict-related cases as though they merited no different treatment than cases relating to violence during internal disturbances. This 'ivory tower' mindset still persists in cases relating to NIACs today, where the Judges apply a single regime of basic rules applicable to all situations ranging from riots and situations of violence falling just short of the armed conflict threshold, through relatively small-scale skirmishes in a low-intensity conflict, to cases of protracted and full-blown armed confrontations between State armies and/or non-State actors. This has resulted in decisions that 'are likely to be received by specialists in humanitarian law with some disquiet'.[65] In more recent IAC cases, on the other hand, the ECtHR has displayed an increased open-mindedness towards the body of law and has specifically examined how the norms of IHL interact with Article 2 ECHR. While, as mentioned, this hardly means that the Strasbourg Court is performing an elegant 'pas de deux', providing a workable theory for the application of the ECHR in situations of armed conflict and the concurrent application of the Convention with IHL, there is, at least, noticeable progress as the Judges are becoming familiar with the issues involved.

Now, what do these findings mean in practical terms? Without a doubt, the jurisprudence of the ECtHR has several concrete consequences for the stakeholders involved. Two final observations are in order in this regard. First, it stands to reason that for the victims of violent misconduct committed by the armed forces of a State party, the continued applicability of the ECHR in times of armed conflict and the supervision by the ECtHR has been a largely positive development as it has strengthened their legal position. It has provided them with an additional forum in which to file their grievances – one that has proven to be more effective in enforcing their rights than the traditional mechanisms of IHL, since the ECtHR has, on multiple occasions, held States accountable for their transgressions and has accorded (mainly pecuniary) remedies where appropriate. Moreover, it has resulted in broader protection for

---

64 L. van den Herik and H. Duffy, above n. 37, 21.

65 W. Abresch, above n. 4, 767.

those affected by armed conflict, especially in NIACs where rules of IHL are scarce and large gaps in regulation exist. For these reasons, victims of armed conflict will understandably continue to file cases claiming violations of human rights with the ECtHR. This brings us to our second consideration: both States and the Strasbourg Court will have to be prepared to deal with this new-found reality, which will require certain adjustments on their part. As has been argued elsewhere, States have, for example, tended to maintain their current litigation strategy, which consists of defending cases on the basis that the ECHR does not apply in the specific circumstances of the case (for example, because it is not covered by the established models of extraterritorial application) and arguing that IHL as *lex specialis* should take precedence.[66] Yet, this has proven to be counterproductive, as they have suffered one courtroom defeat after another, with Judges reaffirming the continued applicability of human rights law in times of armed conflict. If they do not want to be left at the mercy of the magistrates and take back control of the legal development in this area, they will have to proactively start engaging with the host of complex legal issues raised by the application of the ECHR during armed conflict and its relationship with IHL instead of trying to turn back the clock to the time of compartmentalising the *jus in bello* and the *jus in pace*. This will require States to reconsider their policies and enter into a constructive dialogue with the ECtHR, among other actors.

The Judges of the ECtHR, for their part, will have to be willing to listen to the lamentations of States and to take into account IHL and considerations of military necessity, otherwise risking a backlash against its jurisdiction and legitimacy. Additionally, it is recommendable that they proceed on a more principled basis. After all, although they have already come a long way, it remains difficult to draw specific and concrete conclusions from their rather ad hoc judgments, since the ECtHR generally decides only what it absolutely needs to on the facts of the case.[67] Although this is understandable from the perspective of the Strasbourg Court itself, the most important drawback is that it provides only limited guidance for the future. With the number of conflict-related applications to be adjudicated upon ever more increasing, however, the time is now for the Strasbourg Court to speak clear language and set out the contours of its approach. Only when the Judges have explicitly elaborated on the ECtHR's view on how the rights enclosed in the ECHR apply to situations of armed conflict and on how they see the interplay between the ECHR and norms of IHL play out in concrete cases will the ECtHR contribute to legal certainty and allow a proper discussion

---

66 C. De Koker and T. Ruys, 'Foregoing lex specialis? Alternative models for the concurrent application of international humanitarian and human rights law' (2016) 49 *Revue Belge de Droit International* 244.

67 M. Milanović, 'A Few Thoughts on *Hassan v United Kingdom*', *EJIL:Talk!* (2014), at <http://www.ejiltalk.org/a-few-thoughts-on-hassan-v-united-kingdom/> (accessed 04.03.2018).

on the issues of law and policy involved. This is more than necessary, because any haziness in this regard will persist in military manuals, standard operating procedures and rules of engagement – an undesirable result, indeed. After all, in the words of Corn, 'in an era of an already complex and often confused battle space, there can be little tolerance for adding complexity and confusion to the rules that war-fighters must apply in the execution of their missions'.[68]

[68] G. Corn, 'Mixing Apples and Hand Grenades: The Logical Limit of Applying Human Rights Norms to Armed Conflict' (2010) 1 *International Humanitarian Legal Studies 52*; 54.

PROHIBITIONS ON ARBITRARY DISPLACEMENT IN INTERNATIONAL HUMANITARIAN LAW AND HUMAN RIGHTS: A TIME AND A PLACE FOR EVERYTHING

Deborah CASALIN

1. INTRODUCTION

It is largely a settled matter that both international humanitarian law (IHL) and international human rights law (IHRL) have their place in armed conflict. However, there is no single formula governing their exact positioning in relation to each other. This is determined with reference to the specific subject matter, and a number of constellations have been developed to describe varying modes of interaction between IHL and IHRL rules. Some of these indicate greater convergence but, where a clear divergence appears, *lex specialis* remains an important mechanism to resolve this. Analyses of such interactions between specific, overlapping rules of IHL and IHRL have focused primarily on the use of force and detention.[1]

[1] E.g. ICRC, 'International humanitarian law and the challenges of contemporary armed conflicts: Report prepared for the 31st International Conference of the Red Cross and Red Crescent' (October 2011) Doc No 31IC/11/5.1.2, 15–22 <https://www.icrc.org/eng/assets/files/red-cross-crescent-movement/31st-international-conference/31-int-conference-ihl-challenges-report-11-5-1-2-en.pdf> (all websites accessed 25.02.2016); M. Sassòli and

This chapter aims to make a further contribution by examining the relationship between the IHL and IHRL rules prohibiting arbitrary displacement. Though the IHL/IHRL interaction in this subject area has not received extensive attention, a number of legal disparities can be observed that may have consequences in practice, most notably for the assessment of the legality of displacement events in the context of an armed conflict or occupation. In ambiguous situations, a clear analysis of the IHL/IHRL relationship may be key to delineating the difference between a justified measure and a potential war crime on the part of armed forces and their commanders. This will accordingly have implications for the response of actors such as Judges, third State agents, international bodies and aid organisations.

This chapter aims to provide a framework for such an analysis by outlining the normative content of these prohibitions and mapping their interaction in situations in which IHL applies (i.e. international armed conflict (IAC) – both in conduct of hostilities and under occupation – and non-international armed conflict (NIAC)). The above is conducted in light of general principles and models of IHL/IHRL interaction that have been set out previously by scholars.

It will be shown that in the situations examined (i.e. IAC, occupation, and NIAC), more specific IHL rules act as *lex specialis*. In the conduct of hostilities in IAC, this results in deviation from stricter IHRL norms, in recognition of the specificities of conflict (as is also the case with regard to the right to life in armed conflict). However, the cases of occupation and NIAC represent examples of a less commonly encountered paradigm, in which IHL as *lex specialis* provides more stringent protection for civilians.

The relevance of the careful resolution of such legal divergences in practice, particularly for third States' and international bodies' responses to displacement situations, will then be illustrated through the case of the planned mass displacement of Bedouin herder communities in the occupied Palestinian territory.

2. GENERAL PRINCIPLES OF INTERACTION BETWEEN IHL AND IHRL

While it is generally accepted that IHRL continues to apply in situations in which IHL comes into operation (i.e. IAC, including occupation, and NIAC),[2]

L.M. Olson, 'The Relationship between International Humanitarian and Human Rights Law Where it Matters: Admissible Killing and Internment of Fighters in Non-international Armed Conflicts' (2008) 90 *International Review of the Red Cross* 599, 610–27; C. Droege, 'Elective Affinities? Human Rights and Humanitarian Law' (2008) 90 *International Review of the Red Cross* 501, 535–39; D. Casalin, 'Taking Prisoners: Reviewing the International Humanitarian Law Grounds for Deprivation of Liberty by Armed Opposition Groups' (2011) 93 *International Review of the Red Cross* 743, 749–57.

2 On the scope of IHL in international armed conflict, see Geneva Conventions (I–IV) of 1949 (adopted 12 August 1949, entered into force 21 October 1950) 75 UNTS 31 common

the precise interplay between these bodies of law has been the subject of much debate and analysis.[3] Although IHL and IHRL share common aims of protecting human dignity,[4] they were originally designed to perform distinct functions,[5] with IHL traditionally serving the pragmatic objective of striking the balance between military exigencies and civilian protection.[6] The relationship that has developed between IHL and IHRL may affect this balance, and thus inevitably touches upon sensitivities relating to core interests of both States and individuals.

Though debate over balancing these interests will no doubt continue, general guidelines on the IHL/IHRL relationship have been established in three cases by the International Court of Justice (ICJ). In its *Nuclear Weapons* opinion, the ICJ first explicitly confirmed the concurrent application of IHL and IHRL, and found that IHL was to be considered the *lex specialis* in interpreting the human rights concept of 'arbitrary deprivation of life' in armed conflict, since the IHL norm was specifically designed to regulate the conduct of hostilities.[7] The ICJ confirmed this position in its *Wall* opinion, and further held that, in armed conflict, some matters may fall exclusively under the purview of IHL or IHRL, while others may concern both branches of law and require both IHL and IHRL to be taken into account. In the case at hand, concerning the law of occupation, the ICJ held that IHL would be considered *lex specialis*.[8] Thus, the ICJ clarified that the interaction

---

Art. 2(1); J.S. Pictet (ed.), *The Geneva Conventions of 12 August 1949: Commentary*, ICRC, Geneva 1958, p. 20; C. Greenwood, 'Scope of Application of International Humanitarian Law' in D. Fleck (ed.), *The Handbook of International Humanitarian Law*, 2nd ed., Oxford University Press, Oxford 2008, p. 46. On occupation, see Geneva Conventions (I–IV) of 1949 common, Art. 2(2); Hague Convention IV – Laws and Customs of War on Land (adopted 18 October 1907, entered into force 26 January 1910) 205 CTS 277 (Hague Convention IV), Art. 42; *Legal Consequences of the Construction of a Wall in the Occupied Palestinian Territory* (advisory opinion) [2004] ICJ Rep 136 (*Wall*) [95]. On non-international armed conflict, see Geneva Conventions (I–IV) of 1949 common Art. 3; J.S. Pictet, above, pp. 35–36; Protocol Additional to the Geneva Conventions of 12 August 1949 and Relating to the Protection of Victims of Non-International Armed Conflicts (adopted 8 June 1977, entered into force 7 December 1978) 1125 UNTS 609 (APII), Art. 1(1); C. Greenwood, above n. 2, pp. 54–55.

3 ICRC, above n. 1, 15. On overall State acceptance of IHRL's applicability in armed conflict, see I. Siatitsa and M. Titberidze, 'Human Rights in Armed Conflict from the Perspective of the Contemporary State Practice in the United Nations: Factual Answers to Certain Hypothetical Challenges' (Research Paper, Rule of Law in Armed Conflict Project 2011) 8–11 <http://www.geneva-academy.ch/RULAC/pdf/Human-Rights-Law-in-Armed-Conflict.pdf>.

4 As early as the adoption of the 1949 Geneva Conventions, the president of the diplomatic conference expressed that the '[t]he Universal Declaration of the Rights of Man and the Geneva Conventions are both derived from one and the same ideal' – 'Final Record of the Diplomatic Conference of Geneva of 1949' (Geneva, 21 April–12 August 1949) (Federal Political Department, Berne 1963), vol. II s. B 536.

5 C. Droege, above n. 1, 503–07; L. Doswald-Beck and S. Vité, 'International Humanitarian Law and Human Rights Law' (1993) *International Review of the Red Cross* 93, 95–105.

6 C. Greenwood, 'Historical Development and Legal Basis' in D. Fleck (ed.), above n. 2, p. 37.

7 *Legality of the Threat or Use of Nuclear Weapons* (advisory opinion) 1996 ICJ Rep 226 (*Nuclear Weapons*) [25].

8 *Wall*, above n. 2, [106].

between IHL and IHRL is not determined at a systemic level, but rather rule by rule, depending on the subject matter.[9] Later, in the *Armed Activities* case, the ICJ confirmed that both IHL and IHRL need to be taken into account in determining the responsibilities of an occupying power, and found that a number of IHL and IHRL treaties were all applicable 'as relevant'.[10] The ICJ did not elaborate further on the precise interaction of IHL and IHRL in this case, nor on the *lex specialis* issue. However, the right to life and the right to freedom from torture and ill treatment were the only IHRL provisions to which the ICJ's conclusions explicitly referred, while the rest of the acts under consideration (such as indiscriminate attacks and destruction of civilian objects) were covered by reference to IHL treaties.[11] This may implicitly indicate that the latter were primarily applied as *lex specialis*, with IHRL being used in a complementary manner to determine the (il)legality of conduct not covered specifically by the IHL treaties.

In light of the above, the relationship between IHL and IHRL is today generally understood as being mutually reinforcing, guided by the principles of complementarity and *lex specialis*.[12] In order to develop these principles further and provide more concrete guidance in specific cases, scholars have elaborated more detailed IHL/IHRL constellations. The most comprehensive typology, proposed by Sassòli, describes six categories of interactions:[13]

(1) IHL may be exclusively applicable to matters on which IHRL is silent (for example, use of the Red Cross/Red Crescent emblem).

---

9 Confirming that this shows IHRL is not overridden '*en bloc*', see H. Krieger, 'A Conflict of Norms: The Relationship between Humanitarian Law and Human Rights Law in the ICRC Customary Law Study' (2007) Berliner Online-Beiträge zum Völker- und Verfassungsrecht 2, 5 <www.jura.fu-berlin.de/fachbereich/einrichtungen/oeffentliches-recht/lehrende/kriegerh/berliner_online_beitraege/Nr3_Krieger/index.html>.

10 *Armed Activities on the Territory of the Congo (Democratic Republic of the Congo v. Uganda)* 2005 ICJ Rep 168 (*Armed Activities*) [216]–[218].

11 Ibid., [206]–[211], [219].

12 C. Droege, above n. 1, 520–24; United Nations (UN) Human Rights Committee (HRC), 'General Comment 31' in 'Note by the Secretariat, Compilation of General Comments and General Recommendations adopted by Human Rights Treaty Bodies' (27 May 2008) UN Doc HRI/GEN/1/Rev.9 (Vol. I) 243 [11]; Vienna Convention on the Law of Treaties (adopted 23 May 1969, entered into force 27 January 1980) 1155 UNTS 331 (VCLT), Art. 31(3)(c); C. Greenwood, above n. 2, p. 75. There has been critique regarding application of the *lex specialis* principle – e.g. G. Oberleitner, *Human Rights in Armed Conflict: Law, Practice, Policy*, Cambridge University Press, Cambridge 2015, pp. 84–104. However, while acknowledging this, the ICRC considers *lex specialis* indispensable in assessing the IHL/IHRL relationship: ICRC, above n. 1, 15.

13 M. Sassòli, 'Le droit international humanitaire, une lex specialis par rapport aux droits humains?' in A. Auer, A. Flückiger and M. Hottelier (eds), *Les droits de l'homme et la constitution, Etudes en l'honneur du Professeur Giorgio Malinverni*, Schulthess, Geneva 2007, pp. 375–95. The explanations of these categories below, as well as examples, are based on the same source unless otherwise stated. See also R. Kolb and S. Vité, *Le droit de l'occupation militaire: perspectives historiques et enjeux juridiques actuels* (Collection of the Geneva Academy of International Humanitarian Law and Human Rights, Bruylant, Brussels 2009, pp. 441–44.

(2) An IHL rule may prevail over an IHRL rule where there is an inconsistency regarding a particular subject matter, and it appears that the IHL rule is the *lex specialis*. For example, the basis for detention of prisoners of war in IAC (i.e. their status as enemy combatants) deviates from the default situation under IHRL, which generally requires detention to be based on an individual judicial decision. In order to determine the *lex specialis* in a given case, Sassòli and Olson refer to objective criteria of speciality and precision. Speciality entails that the *lex specialis* norm has a narrower or more precise scope, and applies more specifically to the facts at hand. Precision means that the norm addresses the issue explicitly, in more detail than the *lex generalis*, or with more focus on the specifics of the problem.[14] Where this objective test is not conclusive, a teleological approach in light of the systemic aims of IHL and IHRL may be followed to resolve the conflict.[15] According to Kolb and Vité, the IHRL norm is not discarded in such situations, but rather given an interpretation that is harmonised with IHL.[16]

(3) An IHL rule may clarify an IHRL rule in situations in which the former translates the latter into concrete rules of conduct (for example, detailed IHL rules on the treatment of prisoners of war provide a precise and practical guide to applying more general IHRL principles in this particular situation). In such cases, the IHL rule will already take the armed conflict context into account and incorporate any necessary limitations to the IHRL rule.

(4) An IHL rule may be clarified by or interpreted in light of IHRL (for example, in certain cases, extensive human rights jurisprudence may assist in interpreting concepts that also appear in IHL, such as 'inhumane treatment'). This configuration effectively leaves room for the possibility, raised by Droege, that IHL will not necessarily act as *lex specialis* in every situation arising in armed conflict: the more specific and clear rule that is most adapted to the situation should prevail.[17] Kolb and Vité suggest that this may occur where IHL lacks sufficient detail (for example, where IHL requires respect for particular standards but does not elaborate on their content).[18]

(5) A rule of IHL may be developed or updated in light of subsequent IHRL norms, where the IHL rule as originally conceived no longer conforms to more modern IHRL concepts (for example, the IHL obligation to repatriate prisoners of war at the end of hostilities has been tempered by the later IHRL non-refoulement principle).

---

14 M. Sassòli and L. Olson, above n. 1, 604.

15 Ibid., 605.

16 R. Kolb and S. Vité, above n. 13, p. 441.

17 C. Droege, above n. 1, 524.

18 R. Kolb and S. Vité, above n. 13, p. 442.

(6) IHRL may be exclusively applicable to issues that are not addressed in IHL (such as the rights to freedom of expression and association). Such IHRL norms may nevertheless be subject to derogations in light of the conflict situation.

Some authors further refer to a cumulative approach. According to Kolb and Vité, this entails simultaneously applying distinct elements from each body of law – retaining the most detailed aspects of each – to create a new rule by synthesis. In the event of differing content, the rules' common denominator would be applied.[19] Heintze emphasises that, in such an approach, the interpretation of rights and duties must refer to both IHRL and IHL, with the former 'providing a more exact formulation of State obligations; and the latter spelling out State duties with regard to particular issues.[20] Heintze nevertheless reaffirms the importance of *lex specialis* where the cumulative approach reveals conflicts between IHL and IHRL.[21]

3. INTERNATIONAL PROHIBITIONS ON ARBITRARY DISPLACEMENT

Affecting almost 60 million people worldwide, displacement is driven to a large extent by armed conflict.[22] Nevertheless, other human-driven causes that are not always linked to conflict, such as persecution, generalised violence and human rights violations (including forced evictions) are also prominent.[23] For the purposes of this chapter, 'arbitrary displacement' – defined as 'coerced population movement'[24] – will be used as a broad umbrella term. Specific legal

---

19 Ibid., p. 443.

20 H.-J. Heintze, 'On the Relationship between Human Rights Law Protection and International Humanitarian Law' (2004) 86 *International Review of the Red Cross* 789, 795.

21 Ibid., 794.

22 UNHCR, 'Global Trends: Forced Displacement in 2014', Geneva 2015, 2.

23 Ibid.; UN HABITAT and Office of the High Commissioner for Human Rights (OHCHR), 'Forced Evictions' (2014) Fact Sheet No 25/Rev.1, 1–2 <http://www.ohchr.org/Documents/Publications/FS25.Rev.1.pdf>.

24 This general definition is taken from M. Stavropoulou, 'The Right Not to Be Displaced' (1994) 9 *American University International Law Review* 687, 692, where it is asserted that 'a violation of the right not to be displaced manifests itself in the form of a coerced population movement'. This early analysis, which predates much of the treaty body jurisprudence and soft law cited below, examines displacement as a cross-cutting phenomenon in a wide range of contexts. Stavropoulou's definition is therefore an appropriate general point of departure from which more specific IHRL and IHL content can be approached. The qualifier 'arbitrary' is used in line with the Guiding Principles on Internal Displacement (UNCHR, 'Report of the Representative of the Secretary-General, Mr Francis M. Deng, submitted pursuant to Commission resolution 1997/39' (11 February 1998) UN Doc E/CN.4/1998/53/Add.2, Addendum) (GPID), in order to clarify that the displacement in question would not be justified on any grounds foreseen by international law.

terms describing particular forms of arbitrary displacement, such as 'forced eviction' and 'forcible transfer', will then be defined and used as appropriate in context.

Both IHL and IHRL contain rules that can be said to amount to general prohibitions on arbitrary displacement. This is reflected, inter alia, in the Guiding Principles on Internal Displacement and the Pinheiro Principles:[25] two sets of global standards, covering both conflict and non-conflict situations, which have been developed to reflect existing IHL and IHRL.[26] This section will outline the specific content of these prohibitions in IHL and IHRL respectively, and will reveal a divergence in the criteria set out by the two bodies of law to determine arbitrariness, particularly with regard to potential exceptions to the prohibitions (for example, evacuation versus public interest), and the necessary conditions for these (for example, necessity, proportionality, consultation, consent and provision of alternatives).

There follow a few notes on the scope of arbitrary displacement as addressed in this section: first, as the eventual destination of persons displaced in armed conflict generally has little bearing on the arbitrariness of the initial act of displacement, no distinction will be made between internal and external displacement unless explicitly indicated. Secondly, as the removal of non-nationals from a country[27] and the transfer of detained or interned persons[28] are largely subject to distinct provisions in international law, they will not be addressed here. Thirdly, this section covers only the rules determining the legality of the act of displacement, not those relating to protection and assistance of persons already displaced. Finally, as the aim is to determine the content of

---

25 GPID, above n. 24, s. III [6.1]; UNCHR (Sub-commission), 'Final report of the Special Rapporteur Paulo Sérgio Pinheiro: Principles on housing and property restitution for refugees and displaced persons' (28 June 2005) UN Doc E/CN.4/Sub.2/2005/17 (Pinheiro Principles), s. III [5.1].

26 GPID, above n. 24, [3]; Pinheiro Principles, above n. 25, introduction [4], s. I [1.2], s. VII [23.1]. On the broad international acceptance of the GPID, see M. Jacques, *Armed Conflict and Displacement: The Protection of Refugees and Displaced Persons under International Humanitarian Law*, Cambridge 2012, pp. 15–16. The Pinheiro Principles were adopted by the former UN Sub-Commission on the Promotion and Protection of Human Rights: see UNCHR (Sub-Commission) Res 21 (2005) E/CN.4/Sub.2/RES/2005/21, [5].

27 E.g. International Covenant on Civil and Political Rights (adopted 16 December 1966, entered into force 23 March 1976) 999 UNTS 171 (ICCPR), Art. 13; HRC, 'General Comment 15' in 'Note by the Secretariat', above n. 12, [9]–[10]; Geneva Convention (IV) relative to the Protection of Civilian Persons in Time of War (adopted 12 August 1949, entered into force 21 October 1950) 75 UNTS 287 (GC IV), arts 35–36; Convention Relating to the Status of Refugees (adopted 28 July 1951, entered into force 22 April 1954) 189 UNTS 137, art. 33. See also generally J.-M. Henckaerts, *Mass Expulsion in Modern International Law and Practice*, Kluwer Law International, The Hague 1995.

28 E.g. Geneva Convention (III) relative to the Treatment of Prisoners of War (adopted 12 August 1949, entered into force 21 October 1950) 75 UNTS 135 (GCIII), Art. 12; GCIV, Art. 45.

these rules in a generally applicable manner, global (as opposed to regional) instruments and jurisprudence will be emphasised.

3.1. NORMATIVE CONTENT IN IHRL

3.1.1. General Prohibition

In international human rights treaties, several provisions collectively can be said to constitute a general prohibition on arbitrary displacement. The existence of such a prohibition is clearly supported by treaty bodies' authoritative interpretation of these rights, as well as an explicit corresponding protective principle in global soft law standards.[29]

The International Covenant on Civil and Political Rights (ICCPR) guarantees the right of everyone lawfully present in a State to freedom of movement within the territory, which encompasses the freedom to choose their residence.[30] The Human Rights Committee has interpreted the latter as entailing 'protection against all forms of forced internal displacement'.[31] Further, according to the Pinheiro Principles, the freedom to choose one's residence also generally requires that 'no one shall be arbitrarily or unlawfully forced to leave a certain territory, area or region'.[32]

The scope of protection is not limited to internal displacement: the Human Rights Committee has interpreted the right of a person to enter her or his own country[33] as implying 'the right to remain in one's own country', as well as 'prohibition of enforced population transfers or mass expulsions to other countries'.[34] This is in line with the Universal Declaration of Human Rights' provision that '[n]o one shall be subjected to arbitrary ... exile',[35] which has been indicated as a customary prohibition with regard to nationals and permanent residents.[36]

The Human Rights Committee has additionally found that forced evictions and home demolitions, as well as duress and discrimination leading people to leave their residences, violate Article 17 ICCPR (right to freedom from arbitrary interference with the home).[37]

---

29 GPID, above n. 24, principle 6.1; Pinheiro Principles, above n. 25, s. III [5.1].

30 ICCPR, Art. 12(1).

31 HRC, 'General Comment 27' in 'Note by the Secretariat', above n. 12, 223, [7].

32 Pinheiro Principles, above n. 25, s. III [9.1].

33 ICCPR, Art. 12(4).

34 HRC, 'General Comment 27', above n. 31, [18].

35 Universal Declaration of Human Rights (adopted 10 December 1948 UNGA Res 217 A(III), Art. 9.

36 J.M. Henckaerts, above n. 27, pp. 78–79.

37 HRC, 'Concluding observations of the Human Rights Committee: Kenya' (29 April 2005) UN Doc CCPR/CO/83/KEN [22]; HRC, *Liliana Assenova Naidenova et al v. Bulgaria* (30 October 2012)

The International Covenant on Economic, Social and Cultural Rights (ICESCR) effectively prohibits arbitrary displacement by guaranteeing the right to adequate housing,[38] namely 'the right to live somewhere in security, peace and dignity'.[39] In interpreting this right, the Committee on Economic, Social and Cultural Rights (CESCR) has found that forced evictions, namely 'the permanent or temporary removal against their will of individuals, families and/or communities from the homes and/or land which they occupy, without the provision of, and access to, appropriate forms of legal or other protection',[40] are '*prima facie* incompatible' with ICESCR.[41] This general prohibition on forced eviction is a key expression of a State's duty to respect housing solutions that people have found for themselves.[42]

Flowing from States' duty to protect the right to adequate housing, positive obligations to prevent forced evictions have also been outlined, particularly by CESCR.[43] In particular, States must 'ensure that all persons have sufficient security of tenure to guarantee legal protection against forced eviction, harassment and other threats',[44] as well as ensuring the availability of domestic legal remedies.[45] States are further required to protect this right from interference by private actors – for example, by enacting and enforcing laws prohibiting them from conducting evictions without proper safeguards.[46]

3.1.2. Limitations

As shown above, the displacement of a person lawfully present in a country may be considered a *prima facie* direct violation of that person's right to choose their residence freely, their right to freedom from arbitrary interference with

UN Doc CCPR/C/106/D/2073/2011 [15]; HRC, *Dušan Vojnović v. Croatia* (28 April 2009) UN Doc CCPR/C/95/D/1510/2006 [8.7]. For the corresponding provision in other global instruments, see Convention on the Rights of the Child (adopted 20 November 1989, entered into force 20 September 1990) 1577 UNTS 3, Art. 16; Pinheiro Principles, above n. 25, s. III[6].

38 International Covenant on Economic, Social and Cultural Rights (adopted 16 December 1966, entered into force 1 March 1976) 993 UNTS 3 (ICESCR), Art. 11(1).

39 Committee on Economic, Social and Cultural Rights (CESCR) 'General Comment 4' in 'Note by the Secretariat', above n. 12, 11, [7].

40 CESCR, 'General Comment 7' in 'Note by the Secretariat', above n. 12, 38, [3].

41 CESCR, 'General Comment 4', above n. 39, [18].

42 A. Eide, 'Adequate Standard of Living' in D. Moeckli, S. Shah, S. Sivakumaran and D. Harris (eds), *International Human Rights Law*, 2nd ed., Oxford University Press, Oxford 2014, p. 204.

43 Ibid.

44 CESCR, 'General Comment 4', above n. 39, [8a].

45 Ibid., [17a].

46 HRC, 'General Comment 16' in 'Note by the Secretariat', above n. 12, 191, [1]; CESCR, 'General Comment 7', above n. 40, [8]–[9]; Pinheiro Principles, above n. 25, s. III, [5.4].

the home, and their right to adequate housing.[47] In order for such an act of displacement to be justified, and thus considered consistent with these rights, a number of conditions must be met.

In the ICCPR, the right to choose one's residence freely is subject to a set of explicit and specific limitations.[48] Further, the Human Rights Committee has clarified the conditions on restricting freedom from arbitrary or unlawful interference with the home.[49] The right to adequate housing is subject to ICESCR's general limitations clause (Article 4), and CESCR has found that forced evictions may be justified only in 'the most exceptional circumstances, and in accordance with the relevant principles of international law'.[50] CESCR has further developed a body of conditions to be met and safeguards that must be in place for an eviction to be considered consistent with ICESCR. Many have been incorporated into the Guiding Principles on Internal Displacement and other instruments relating to displacement in specific situations.[51] Taking the above into account, the limitation conditions on the IHRL prohibition on arbitrary displacement can be summarised as: lawfulness; necessity; proportionality; consultation, informed consent and participation; safeguards during relocation; and provision of alternatives and remedies.[52] These are briefly elucidated below.

3.1.2.1. Lawfulness

Any restriction on the abovementioned rights must have a basis in law.[53] In particular, an act of displacement must be based on a specific decision taken by

---

47 This does not exclude the possibility that a number of other rights may be violated, depending on the particular circumstances: see CESCR, 'General Comment 7', above n. 40. Indeed, forced evictions are considered to 'violate, directly and indirectly, the full spectrum of civil, cultural, economic, political and social rights enshrined in international instruments': UN HABITAT and OHCHR, above n. 23, 5–6.

48 ICCPR, Art. 12(3).

49 HRC, 'General Comment 16', above n. 46, [3]–[4]; Pinheiro Principles, above n. 25, s. III, [6.2] referring to a duty on States to ensure that 'everyone is provided with safeguards of due process' against such interference.

50 CESCR, 'General Comment 4', above n. 39, [18].

51 E.g. International Labour Organization Convention No. 169 concerning Indigenous and Tribal Peoples in Independent Countries (adopted 27 June 1989, entered into force 5 September 1991) (1989) 28 ILM 1382, art. 16; Basic Principles And Guidelines On Development-Based Evictions And Displacement, in Human Rights Council, 'Report of the Special Rapporteur on adequate housing as a component of the right to an adequate standard of living, Miloon Kothari' (5 February 2007) UN Doc A/HRC/4/18 (Annex 1).

52 For displacement to be consistent with IHRL, the limitation conditions applicable to all directly affected rights would need to be met. This cumulative approach to limitation conditions also appears in GPID, above n. 24, principles 7–9, and UN HABITAT and OHCHR, above n. 23, 26–34.

53 ICCPR, Art. 12(3); HRC, 'General Comment 16', above n. 46, [3]; CESCR, 'General Comment 7', above n. 40, [11].

an authority empowered to do so by law.[54] The decision (as well as the underlying law) must be consistent with other human rights,[55] particularly 'the fundamental principles of equality and non-discrimination',[56] and should be reasonable under the circumstances.[57]

3.1.2.2. Necessity

The restriction must be necessary to protect national security, public order, health or morals, or the rights and freedoms of others, including the general welfare.[58] This should be viewed in the context of a democratic society.[59]

3.1.2.3. Proportionality

The restriction should be proportionate to the legitimate interest to be protected, appropriate to achieve this protection, and the least intrusive means available.[60] Displacement should be carried out only as a last resort – i.e. where no feasible alternatives exist. In such cases, all measures must be taken to minimise the use of displacement, as well as its negative impact.[61]

3.1.2.4. Consultation, Informed Consent and Participation

Prior to displacement, there should be an opportunity for genuine consultation with affected persons.[62] This should first of all entail an exploration of all feasible alternatives, with a view to avoiding displacement altogether.[63]

Where alternatives to displacement do not exist, affected persons' free and informed consent must be sought.[64] Adequate steps must be taken to ensure that they are fully informed in reasonable time about the reasons for displacement and procedures to be followed.[65] In this regard, the existence of transparent policies and procedures is key.[66] Where relevant, affected persons should also be

---

54 GPID, above n. 24, principle 7.3.a.

55 ICCPR, Art. 12(3); HRC, 'General Comment 16', above n. 46, [3]; HRC, 'General Comment 31', above n. 12, [6]; CESCR, 'General Comment 7', above n. 40, [11].

56 HRC, 'General Comment 27', above n. 31, [18].

57 HRC, 'General Comment 16', above n. 46, [4].

58 ICCPR, Art. 12(3); ICESCR, Art. 4.

59 HRC, 'General Comment 27', above n. 31, [11]; ICESCR, Art. 4.

60 HRC, 'General Comment 27', above n. 31, [14]; HRC, 'General Comment 31', above n. 12, [6].

61 GPID, above n. 24, principle 7.1.

62 CESCR, 'General Comment 7', above n. 40, [16a]; HRC, 'Concluding observations: Kenya', above n. 39, [22].

63 CESCR, 'General Comment 7', above n. 40, [13]; GPID, above n. 24, principle 7.1.

64 GPID, above n. 24, principle 7.3.c.

65 GPID, above n. 24, principle 7.3.b.

66 HRC, 'Concluding observations: Kenya', above n. 39, [22].

informed about compensation, relocation, and the alternative use to which the vacated land or housing will be put.[67]

Finally, efforts must be made to involve affected persons (especially women) in planning and managing their relocation.[68] All affected persons must be given adequate and reasonable notice of the date of displacement, in order to give them the chance to participate in the process and defend their rights.[69]

3.1.2.5. Safeguards during Relocation

The process of relocation itself must also be carried out in strict compliance with IHRL.[70] Government officials should be present,[71] and enforcement measures should be carried out only by competent legal authorities,[72] with all persons involved being properly identified.[73] Relocation should not be carried out at night or in especially bad weather.[74] Affected persons should be properly accommodated in satisfactory conditions, and family members should not be separated.[75]

3.1.2.6. Provision of Alternatives and Remedies

Evictions should not be undertaken where affected persons will be made homeless or vulnerable to violations of other rights.[76] In such cases, appropriate resettlement plans should be in place.[77] Where affected persons are unable to provide for themselves, States must take all appropriate measures within their means to make alternative housing available.[78]

Affected persons must have access to legal recourses and remedies, including judicial review of the decision and adequate compensation for any affected property.[79] Where possible, legal aid must be provided so that affected persons can approach the courts.[80]

---

67 GPID, above n. 24, principle 7.3.b; CESCR, 'General Comment 7', above n. 40, [16c].
68 GPID, above n. 24, principle 7.3.d.
69 CESCR, *IDG v. Spain* (17 June 2015) UN Doc E/C.12/55/D/2/2014, [12.2].
70 CESCR, 'General Comment 7', above n. 40, [14]; GPID, above n. 24, principle 8.
71 CESCR, 'General Comment 7', above n 40, [15d].
72 GPID, Principle 7(3)(e).
73 CESCR, 'General Comment 7', above n. 40, [15e].
74 Ibid., [15f].
75 GPID, above n. 24, principle 7.2.
76 CESCR, 'General Comment 7', above n. 40, [16].
77 HRC, 'Concluding observations: Kenya', above n. 39, [22].
78 CESCR, 'General Comment 7', above n. 40, [16].
79 ICCPR art 2(3); CESCR, 'General Comment 7', above n. 40, [11], [13], [15g]; GPID, Principle 7(3)(f).
80 CESCR, 'General Comment 7', above n. 40, [15h].

3.2. NORMATIVE CONTENT IN IHL

3.2.1. International Armed Conflict – Conduct of Hostilities

3.2.1.1. Rules Flowing from Principle of Distinction

One of the main purposes of IHL is to place limits on armed conflict that spare non-participants from its effects as far as possible. Overall respect for IHL – in particular, the fundamental principle of distinction and the rules flowing from it[81] – should minimise the displacement of civilians. However, as noted by a former President of the International Committee of the Red Cross (ICRC): '[w]hen civilians flee a conflict zone, it is a good indication that the warring parties are indifferent to their rights under humanitarian law, or are deliberately ignoring their responsibilities'.[82]

Possibly owing to an assumption that the principle of distinction afforded sufficient protection, global IHL treaties do not clearly set out a stand-alone, general prohibition on causing displacement in international armed conflict (outside the context of occupation). This also does not appear in the body of customary IHL as determined by the ICRC. In the ICJ *Armed Activities* case, the conflict-related displacement of thousands of people was also not named as an IHL violation independently of the unlawful acts that contributed to it.[83] According to Jacques, the absence of such a prohibition constitutes a 'legal gap in the existing protection regime'.[84]

3.2.1.2. An Emerging Independent IHL Prohibition on Arbitrary Displacement?

In the face of this apparent lacuna (and despite such a rule not having been expressly included in the study itself), the commentary on the ICRC customary IHL study maintains that its extensive survey of state practice supports 'the duty of parties to a conflict to prevent displacement caused by their own acts, at least

81 J.-M. Henckaerts and L. Doswald-Beck, *Customary International Humanitarian Law: Volume I – Rules*, ICRC/Cambridge University Press, Geneva 2005, rr. 1, 7, 11, 14–24 <https://www.icrc.org/customary-ihl/eng/docs/v1>; Protocol Additional to the Geneva Conventions of 12 August 1949 and Relating to the Protection of Victims of International Armed Conflicts (adopted 8 June 1977, entered into force 7 December 1978) 1125 UNTS 3 (API), Arts 48–58.

82 J. Kellenberger, 'The ICRC's Response to Internal Displacement: Strengths, Challenges and Constraints' (2009) 91 *International Review of the Red Cross* 475, 478.

83 *Armed Activities*, above n. 10, [208]–[209], [211], [219]. Among the facts considered were two incidents of fighting which caused tens of thousands of people to flee, as well as land seizures in the context of an ethnic conflict. The ICJ did not find that these incidents of displacement as such constituted violations of IHL and IHRL.

84 M. Jacques, above n. 26, p. 22.

those acts which are prohibited in and of themselves'.[85] The Guiding Principles on Internal Displacement are further invoked in support – in particular, their exhortation to all authorities and international actors to respect and ensure respect for IHL 'so as to prevent and avoid conditions that might lead to displacement of persons'.[86]

The Pinheiro Principles, explicitly applicable to both conflict and non-conflict situations, further appear to substantiate this position. In general, they affirm a duty on States to 'take steps to ensure that no one is subjected to displacement by either state or non-state actors';[87] in a provision apparently directed at conflict situations, they outline a duty on states to prohibit forced eviction, home demolitions, destruction of agricultural land or land appropriation/confiscation 'as a punitive measure or as a means or method of war'.[88]

Finally, where expulsion or other coercive acts are employed to displace persons forcibly from an area where they are lawfully present, this will constitute a crime against humanity where it takes place as part of a widespread and systematic attack on a civilian population and without justification under international law.[89] Thus, in the context of such an attack, the act of displacement itself is deemed unlawful if not justified in terms of IHL (i.e. the applicable body of international law).

3.2.1.3. Limitations

The above texts, suggesting that a more general IHL prohibition on arbitrary displacement may be emerging, refer mainly to displacement as a result of practices that are already unlawful under IHL. Thus, it appears that such a prohibition would be limited to displacement caused by 'acts which are prohibited in and of themselves'.[90] The African Union's Kampala Convention goes further in this regard, as it includes 'generalized violence and violations of human rights' and 'harmful practices' as prohibited grounds for displacement in themselves (over and above IHL violations).[91] However, the fact that these

---

85 J.M. Henckaerts and L. Doswald-Beck, above n. 81, r. 129 (commentary).

86 GPID, above n. 24, principle 5.

87 Pinheiro Principles, above n. 25, s. III [5.4].

88 Ibid., s. III [5.3].

89 Rome Statute of the International Criminal Court (adopted 17 July 1998, entered into force 1 July 2002) 2187 UNTS 90 (Rome Statute), Arts 7(1)(d) and (2)(d); International Criminal Court (ICC), *Elements of Crimes*, ICC, The Hague 2011, p. 6.

90 J.M. Henckaerts and L. Doswald-Beck, above n. 81, r. 129 (commentary).

91 African Union Convention for the Protection and Assistance of Internally Displaced Persons in Africa (adopted 23 October 2009, entered into force 6 December 2012), Art. 4(d)–(e) <http://www.au.int/en/treaties/african-union-convention-protection-and-assistance-internally-displaced-persons-africa>.

provisions were considered innovative when adopted would indicate that they do not yet reflect universally applicable custom.[92]

3.2.2. *International Armed Conflict – Occupation*

3.2.2.1. Explicit Prohibition on Forcible Transfer/Deportation

While the law of IAC contains no explicit general prohibition on arbitrary displacement, such a rule is present in the sub-category of this law that applies under occupation. In such contexts, the Fourth 1949 Geneva Convention (GCIV) provides that individual and mass forcible transfers, as well as deportations of protected persons from occupied territory, are prohibited 'regardless of motive'.[93] 'Forcible transfer' has been defined broadly by the International Criminal Tribunal for the former Yugoslavia (ICTY) as the 'movement of individuals under duress from where they reside to a place that is not of their choosing'.[94] In this sense, the element of force has been construed to include the threat of force, coercion through 'fear of violence, duress, detention, psychological oppression or abuse of power', or taking advantage of a 'coercive environment'.[95] Ultimately, transfer is rendered unlawful by the 'lack of genuine choice', which is to be determined in light of the circumstances (such as the prevailing situation and atmosphere at the time that affected persons expressed their will).[96]

Unlawful transfers of protected persons constitute grave breaches of GCIV and the First Additional Protocol, as well as war crimes.[97] Grave breaches give rise to a duty on all States to search for suspects and either bring them before their courts or extradite them to a State that is willing to do so.[98] Given that grave breaches are among the most serious violations of IHL, their underlying prohibitions can be considered as basic rules of IHL that have the character of peremptory norms of international law.[99] Accordingly, third States are bound

---

92 See M. Asplet and M. Bradley, 'Strengthened Protection for Internally Displaced Persons in Africa: The Kampala Convention Comes Into Force' (2012) 16 (36) *American Society of International Law Insights* <www.asil.org/insights/volume/16/issue/36/strengthened-protection-internally-displaced-persons-africa-kampala>.

93 GCIV, Art. 49(1); for the corresponding customary IHL rule, see J.M. Henckaerts and L. Doswald-Beck, above n. 81, r. 129A. The category of 'protected persons' in this context would generally encompass civilians without the nationality of the occupying power: GCIV, Art. 4.

94 *Prosecutor v. Mladen Naletilić & Vinko Martinović* (Judgment), ICTY-98-34-T (31 March 2003) [519].

95 *Prosecutor v. Milomir Stakić* (Judgment), ICTY-97-24-A (22 March 2006) [281].

96 *Prosecutor v. Milorad Krnojelac* (Judgment) ICTY-97-25-A (17 September 2003) [229].

97 GCIV, Art. 147; API, Art. 85(4)(a); Rome Statute, Art. 8(2)(a)(vii).

98 GCIV, Art. 146.

99 See International Law Commission, 'Draft Articles on Responsibility of States for Internationally Wrongful Acts (with commentaries)' in 'Report of the International Law

not to recognise, aid or assist in maintaining the illegal situation created by a grave breach, and to cooperate in ending it.[100] Therefore, for example, a foreign State that provides an occupying power with logistical support to displace part of an occupied population, or that obstructs international efforts to prevent such an action, may also be in breach of its international obligations.

3.2.2.2. Exceptions

In the 1949 Geneva Conventions and customary IHL, the only exception foreseen to the prohibition on forcible transfer is evacuation, where this is required for the security of the civilians involved or on grounds of imperative military necessity.[101] This may occur to protect civilians from hostilities, or where they will impede operations. The evacuation must respond to an existing necessity: in the case of military reasons, the legitimacy of evacuation will cease when these are no longer imperative, such as where the danger posed by military operations has passed.[102] Article 49 of GCIV is deemed to create a presumption of the unlawfulness of transfer – accordingly, the burden of proof regarding the state of exception rests on the occupier.[103] An even heavier burden exists in cases of evacuation outside an occupied territory, as this is not permitted unless it is materially (i.e. physically) impossible to do otherwise.[104]

In all cases, evacuated persons must be transferred back to their homes 'as soon as hostilities in the area in question have ceased'.[105] During the evacuation, the occupying power is responsible for ensuring as far as possible that evacuees are provided with proper accommodation; that satisfactory safety, nutrition, health and hygiene standards are maintained; and that family members are not separated.[106]

3.2.3. *Normative Content in IHL of Non-International Armed Conflict*

3.2.3.1. Explicit Prohibitions on Displacement Related to the Conflict

The Second Additional Protocol to the 1949 Geneva Conventions (APII), applicable in non-international armed conflict, prohibits ordering the displacement of civilians within a territory (i.e. internally) for reasons connected

Commission on the work of its 53rd session' (23 April–1 June and 2 July–10 August 2001) UN Doc A/56/10 GAOR 56th Session, Supp 10, 113, [5].

100 Ibid., Arts 40–41.

101 GCIV, Art. 49(2); J.M. Henckaerts and L. Doswald-Beck, above n. 81, r. 129A.

102 J.S. Pictet, above n. 2, pp. 280, 282.

103 M. Jacques, above n. 26, p. 32.

104 GCIV, Art. 49(2); J.S. Pictet, above n. 2, p. 280.

105 GCIV, Art. 49(2); J.S. Pictet, above n. 2, p. 281.

106 GCIV, Art. 49(3); J.M. Henckaerts and L. Doswald-Beck, above n. 81, r. 131.

to the conflict.[107] This prohibition reflects customary IHL, and contravening it is a war crime.[108]

The ICC's *Elements of Crimes* asserts that the perpetrator of such displacement must give an explicit order, and be in a position to do so.[109] However, based on an analysis of subsequent treaty practice, Willms suggests that displacement through coercion may also violate this prohibition.[110] This is comparable to the ICTY's interpretation of GCIV Article 49.[111]

APII further provides that civilians may not be compelled to leave their territory (i.e. be displaced externally) for reasons connected to the conflict.[112] This applies to both individuals and groups, and does not require an explicit order. Although this provision was traditionally intended to refer to displacement of civilians across a border, the 1987 commentary to APII suggests that the phrase 'their own territory' is broad enough to prohibit non-State parties from displacing civilians outside territories under their control.[113]

3.2.3.2. Exceptions

As in situations of occupation, the only permissible exception in NIAC is where evacuation is required for the security of the civilians involved or imperative military reasons.[114] The former exception aims to prevent civilians from being exposed to serious danger, while the latter is to be used only in exceptional circumstances, which should be strictly scrutinised.[115] Evacuation does not justify displacement of civilians outside the territory of the state:[116] the prohibition on deportation in this context therefore appears absolute.

4. RELATIONSHIP BETWEEN THE IHL AND IHRL PROHIBITIONS ON ARBITRARY DISPLACEMENT

This section will examine the relationship between the IHL and IHRL prohibitions on arbitrary displacement outlined in section 3, in light of the general principles

107 APII, Art. 17(1).

108 J.M. Henckaerts and L. Doswald-Beck, above n. 81, r. 129B; Rome Statute, Art. 8(2)(e)(viii).

109 ICC, *Elements of Crimes*, above n. 89, p. 39.

110 J. Willms, 'Without Order, Anything Goes? The Prohibition on Forced Displacement in Non-International Armed Conflict' (2009) 91 *International Review of the Red Cross* 547, 551–59, 564–65.

111 Text to nn. 94–96.

112 Y. Sandoz, C. Swinarski and B. Zimmermann (eds), *Commentary on the Additional Protocols of 8 June 1977 to the Geneva Conventions of 12 August 1949*, ICRC/Martinus Nijhoff, Geneva 1987, p. 1472.

113 Ibid., p. 1474.

114 Ibid., p. 1472; J.M. Henckaerts and L. Doswald-Beck, above n. 81, r. 129 B.

115 Y. Sandoz, C. Swinarski and B. Zimmermann, above n. 112, pp. 1472–73.

116 APII, Art. 17(2); J.M. Henckaerts and L. Doswald-Beck, above n. 81, r. 129 (commentary).

of interaction set out in section 2. In particular, it will examine how the operation of the IHRL prohibition on arbitrary displacement is modified by the application of the respective IHL prohibitions in situations of IAC, occupation and NIAC. Given the divergence between the IHL and IHRL prohibitions on arbitrary displacement, it is determined that of the models of interaction outlined in section 2, the *lex specialis* model is the most applicable. Further insight is also provided into why other models, such as a cumulative approach, may not be workable. Sassòli and Olson's objective criteria of speciality and precision – and, where necessary, a teleological approach – are further applied to analyse why and how the *lex specialis* interaction model impacts the assessment of the legality of a displacement incident.

4.1. INTERACTION IN THE CONDUCT OF HOSTILITIES IN INTERNATIONAL ARMED CONFLICT

As discussed above, an independent prohibition on arbitrary displacement may be emerging in the context of international armed conflict (outside occupation), with the criterion of arbitrariness defined by the unlawfulness of the cause of displacement under IHL. One of the observations leading to this assertion is the development of soft law instruments based on existing IHL and IHRL, which apply both to conflict and non-conflict situations and make explicit a right to protection from arbitrary displacement. The emergence of such an IHL-based norm would in itself be an example of the development of IHL under the influence of IHRL, and thus of further convergence between the two branches of law.

This development would be consistent with the general IHL principle that all civilians must be respected,[117] which requires that parties avoid 'all acts that might unjustifiably cause harm to a civilian'.[118] The interests protected by this rule are not exhaustively listed in the 1949 Geneva Conventions,[119] so arbitrary displacement as such could be deemed to constitute such an act. This would be in line with the overall purposes of both IHL and IHRL, considering the grave impact of arbitrary displacement on a range of human rights, as well as the fact that mass displacement indicates an overall lack of respect for fundamental IHL principles.

Assuming the acceptance of such an IHL-based prohibition, its scope would be limited to displacement caused by acts that are already prohibited by IHL – a remit that is much narrower than that of the IHRL prohibition on arbitrary

117 GCIV, Art. 27.
118 H.-P. Gasser, 'Protection of the Civilian Population' in D. Fleck, above n. 2, p. 240.
119 Ibid.

displacement. It is submitted that applying the latter in a complementary or cumulative manner – with the effect of also prohibiting displacement in armed conflict which is not caused by acts that are unlawful under IHL – is not feasible for three reasons:

(1) It may amount to outlawing the collateral effects of lawful attacks, defeating IHL's purpose of balancing civilian protection with military necessity. This could result in erosion of respect for the principle of distinction, thus further endangering civilians.[120] Moreover, if a party conducting a lawful attack were expected to stop civilians from leaving the area, this might contradict that party's responsibility to avoid or minimise the loss of civilian life.[121]
(2) IHRL limitation conditions, such as those relating to consultation, informed consent and safeguards during relocation, are not designed for situations of active hostilities, and unlikely to be practicable in such situations. 'Forced evictions', in the context of which these conditions were developed, are often characterised by prior planning and announcement.[122] This is unlikely to be the case in conflict situations in which the population is not under the control of the party displacing them. Indeed, these conditions presume responsibilities that go beyond those of a party without territorial control.
(3) In principle, permissibility of an act under IHL (in this case, lawfulness of an attack) is a ground of justification for a *prima facie* violation of IHRL in conflict situations.[123] Therefore, the consequences of such an act (in this case, displacement) cannot be viewed as IHRL violations in and of themselves.

Owing to its more precise and context-specific scope, the IHL-based prohibition on arbitrary displacement would rather act as *lex specialis* in relation to the IHRL prohibition. Consequently, the definition of what is to be considered 'arbitrary' displacement would be determined with reference to the IHL rules on conduct of hostilities.[124] In particular, the detailed rules governing the permissibility of an attack in IHL[125] would provide a guide to determining the lawfulness of any resultant displacement. Indeed, these rules contain a number of comparable (although differently interpreted) concepts such as proportionality, necessity and precautionary procedures. They appear to strive for similar aims (namely those protecting people from unjustified harm), and would be capable of

120 C. Tomuschat, 'Human Rights and International Humanitarian Law' (2010) 21 *European Journal of International Law* 15, 21.
121 API, Art. 57(2)(a)(ii); J.M. Henckaerts and L. Doswald-Beck, above n. 81, r. 15.
122 UNCHR, 'Explanatory Notes on the Principles on Housing and Property Restitution for Refugees and Displaced Persons' (11 July 2005) UN Doc E/CN.4/Sub.2/2005/17/Add.1, 5, [16].
123 H. Krieger, above n. 9, 6.
124 This approach is analogous to that applied to the right to life in *Nuclear Weapons*, above n. 7.
125 API, Arts 48–57; J.M. Henckaerts and L. Doswald-Beck, above n. 81, rr. 1, 7, 11 and 14–23.

fulfilling a similar function. However, given the context, these IHL principles will inevitably be more permissive than the rules generally determining arbitrariness of displacement in IHRL (for example, 'necessity' will encompass only military needs rather than the general welfare of a democratic society, while the requisite precautions will only extend to procedures preceding military action, rather than any kind of consultation).

On this note, it should be recalled that the discussion above relates to application of the prohibition on arbitrary displacement by a party conducting an attack in an area that it does not control,[126] such as a party conducting aerial bombing. From the perspective of the party holding control over its own population (namely the 'defending' party), the IHRL prohibitions would remain applicable by default (although derogations may be made in light of the conflict situation). However, the express IHL obligation to evacuate civilians from the vicinity of military objectives[127] would necessarily constitute a legal justification for displacement by the defending party. This would appear, in turn, to be an example of an IHRL rule being clarified by IHL.

4.2. INTERACTION IN SITUATIONS OF OCCUPATION

Coerced movement of civilians within or out of occupied territory would *prima facie* violate the explicit IHL prohibition on forcible transfer in this context (in GCIV Article 49(1)), and the more general IHRL prohibition on arbitrary displacement.[128] However, the scope of these prohibitions differs in terms of the permissible exceptions foreseen, with IHL foreseeing only the more restrictive exception of evacuation. How, then, do these rules interact under occupation?

The ICJ unfortunately did not clarify this question in its *Wall* advisory opinion, which inter alia concerned the involuntary movement of the occupied population. It was held that measures altering the demographics of the occupied population – particularly those contributing to the departure of population from certain areas – were unlawful in terms of GCIV, and impeded the exercise of certain human rights.[129] However, the ICJ did not apply GCIV Article 49(1) (prohibition on forcible transfer or deportation) in this analysis. Instead, it relied on Article 49(6) (prohibition on transfer of the occupier's population into

---

126 See API, Art. 49.

127 API, Art. 58(a); J.M. Henckaerts and L. Doswald-Beck, above n. 81, r. 24. Specific limits on evacuation of children abroad are outlined in API, Art. 78.

128 See, e.g., CESCR, 'General Comment 7', n. 40, [12], stating that punitive forced evictions and house demolitions are inconsistent with ICESCR, and taking note of the prohibitions on displacement of civilian population and destruction of private property in GCIV and APII in a discussion on the concept of forced eviction.

129 *Wall*, n. 2, [122], [133]–[134].

the occupied territory),[130] as the departure of the occupied population in this case was accompanied by the organised introduction of the occupying power's citizens into the territory. Therefore, in terms of potential exceptions, the ICJ did not examine whether those under Article 49(2) (relating to evacuation) were applicable. Instead, it was held that the conditions of the specific limitations clause in ICCPR Article 12(3) had not been met, and that the violations of ICESCR rights were not justified under ICESCR's general limitations clause.[131]

Thus, while finding that displacement of the occupied population violated both IHL and IHRL, the ICJ did not clarify the relationship between the potential grounds of justification presented by these bodies of law. In order to assess this, it is necessary to turn to the general principles on interaction between IHL and IHRL norms.

4.2.1. *Cumulative Approach or Interpretation in Light of IHRL is Inconsistent with Law of Occupation*

Despite its overall position in the *Wall* opinion that IHL was the *lex specialis*,[132] the ICJ appears to have cumulatively applied IHL and IHRL provisions protecting against arbitrary displacement, save for GCIV Article 49(1). It is submitted, however, that a cumulative application of the exceptions foreseen by this article and by human rights provisions protecting against arbitrary displacement (or a reinterpretation of the IHL grounds in light of the IHRL grounds) would result in broadening the permissible grounds for displacement beyond those foreseen in IHL.[133] This would contradict the ordinary, restrictive meaning of GCIV Article 49(2),[134] which provides only one strictly circumscribed exception to the prohibition on forcible transfer in Article 49(1) (i.e. temporary evacuation). This may lead to the situation, warned of by Gross, in which convergence of IHL and IHRL 'could justify excessive violations of the rights of people living under occupation', as their rights could 'be limited both for "public interest" or the rights of others and for military necessity'.[135]

Such an approach may also import IHRL requirements that are not necessarily adapted to the situation of occupation, and of which fulfilment would in fact extend beyond the powers of the occupier laid out in IHL.[136] This would

130 Ibid., [134].

131 Ibid., [135]–[136].

132 Ibid., [26].

133 For further analysis on the use of IHRL to create further exceptions to IHL protections under occupation, see A. Gross, 'Human Proportions: Are Human Rights the Emperor's New Clothes of the International Law of Occupation?' (2007) 18 *European Journal of International Law* 1, 9.

134 See VCLT, Art. 31(1).

135 A. Gross, above n. 133, 9.

136 In this line, Krieger cautions that the highly contextualised, individualised method of applying IHRL limitation clauses may restrict their applicability in armed conflict, as

contradict the aims of the law of occupation, which are to maintain the legal and institutional status quo in occupied territory, as well as protect the population from the actions of a foreign power that has assumed control over them in the place of their own State of nationality.[137]

For example, an occupier generally would not be able to justify displacement of the population on the basis of law, as it is obliged to respect the laws in force in the occupied territory except where absolutely prevented.[138] Occupation is in principle a provisional situation;[139] an occupying power is therefore generally precluded from making long-term decisions entailing far-reaching structural change, and is accordingly restricted even in the implementation of socio-economic rights.[140] As GCIV Article 49 is considered to be closely linked to the objective of maintaining the legal and social order,[141] a claim that the occupier is absolutely required to change local laws to displace the population, even for purportedly developmental reasons, is unlikely to stand. Further, attempts to base displacement on local law would still be limited by the 'status quo' principle.

Endeavours by an occupying power to obtain consent from the population, as generally required by IHRL, would also be problematic. The Pictet commentary to GCIV Article 49 refers to the fact that 'voluntary transfers' are permitted by implication, as some transfers 'might up to a certain point have the consent of those being transferred'.[142] However, Pictet's example of a 'voluntary transfer' – i.e. members of minorities who might wish to leave because of discrimination – does not correspond to any modern human rights notion of informed consent, but rather to the ICTY's definition of forcible transfer caused by coercive acts or taking advantage of a coercive environment.[143] Indeed, referring to this paragraph in the commentary, the ICTY has held that 'it is impossible to infer genuine choice from the fact that consent was expressed, given that the circumstances may deprive the consent of any value'.[144] The ICTY has further held that, given the broad prohibition on coercion of protected persons, the existence of such a genuine choice would have to be determined in each individual case.[145]

---

this is a manifestation of the 'basic difference between human rights law limiting regular governmental activities vis-à-vis the individual and humanitarian law applicable to the extraordinary circumstance of war': H. Krieger, above n. 9, 19.

137 R. Kolb and S. Vité, above n. 13, p. 187.

138 Hague Convention IV, Art. 43.

139 H.P. Gasser, above n. 118, p. 273.

140 R. Kolb and S. Vité, above n. 13, p. 312; S. Vité, 'The Interrelation of the Law of Occupation and Economic, Social and Cultural Rights' (2008) 90 *International Review of the Red Cross* 629, 634–36.

141 H.P. Gasser, above n. 118, pp. 241, 277.

142 J.S. Pictet, above n. 2, p. 279.

143 Text to n. 95.

144 *Krnojelac*, above n. 96, [229].

145 *Prosecutor v. Mladen Naletilić and Vinko Martinović* (Judgment), ICTY-98-34-T (31 March 2003) [519].

In this regard, '[w]hether a person would have wished to leave the area, absent circumstances of discrimination or persecution, may also be considered as indicative of a person's will'.[146]

In light of the above, it would be difficult to conclude that a departure from occupied territory because of discrimination or persecution by the occupier is voluntary: permission to leave does not erase the coercive nature of the circumstances leading to departure. Where protected persons choose to leave because of discrimination or persecution by third parties (for example, elements within the occupied population itself), the occupier would typically not seek their consent to the departure (but rather *vice versa*). Even in cases of legitimate resettlement requests by a minority, Gasser cautions that these should be verified and confirmed by a neutral party.[147]

It is further submitted that purported consent by representatives of the population would be nullified by GCIV Article 47, which invalidates any such waiver of the population's protections under GCIV. This rule specifically addresses the context of occupation, as this subjection to external control leaves the population open to coercion, and the population's leadership may thus be vulnerable to being pressured into harmful decisions.[148]

4.2.2. *The IHL Prohibition on Forcible Transfer Acts as* Lex Specialis

Given the above issues with the cumulative approach, it is clear that there are divergences between the IHL prohibition on forcible transfer and the general IHRL prohibition on arbitrary displacement. That the former prevails over the latter as *lex specialis* is supported by the commentary to GCIV Article 49, which states that the prohibition on forcible transfers 'is absolute and allows of no exceptions, apart from those stipulated in paragraph 2' (namely temporary evacuation for the safety of the civilians themselves or based on imperative military necessity).[149] This interpretation does not appear to admit any possibility of additional IHRL grounds of justification being amalgamated to these. Indeed, Kolb and Vité consider that limitation provisions of human rights treaties cannot be interpreted in a manner that is inconsistent with GCIV Article 49.[150]

---

146 *Prosecutor v. Blagoje Simić, Miroslav Tadić and Simo Zarić* (Judgment) ICTY-95-9-T (17 October 2003) [126].

147 H.P. Gasser, above n. 118, p. 285.

148 See J.S. Pictet, above n. 2, pp. 273–75. Pictet refers to the 'particularly great danger of the Occupying Power forcing the Power whose territory is occupied to conclude agreements prejudicial to protected persons' (pp. 274–75).

149 Ibid., p. 279.

150 R. Kolb and S. Vité, above n. 13, pp. 441–42, referring in particular to ICCPR, Art. 12(3). Examining the interaction of norms from another angle, Kolb and Vité consider that the protection of Art. 49 is maintained by interpreting IHRL limitations clauses in a manner consistent with IHL.

Such a view would also be consistent with the criteria of speciality and precision proposed by Sassòli and Olson to determine the *lex specialis*.[151] The IHL prohibition meets the requirement of speciality in that it has a narrower and more precise scope than the IHRL prohibition. While the IHRL prohibition in principle protects all people lawfully present in a place, the IHL rule's material scope is limited to situations of occupation, and its personal scope covers only protected persons in the sense of GCIV Article 4 (in short, non-nationals of the occupying power). The IHL prohibition also meets the criterion of precision, as it addresses the issue of displacement by an occupying power explicitly, and is tailored to the particularities of the situation. The latter is evident in the fact that the IHL prohibition expressly takes into account the occupying power's military needs and the civilian population's protection needs.

Further, it is submitted that the more stringent protection provided by the IHL prohibition aligns more closely with the systemic aims of both the IHL of occupation and IHRL. Regarding the former, the central aim of preserving the status quo of the occupied territory is served by ruling out additional IHRL grounds of justification, as these presuppose the exercise of powers beyond an occupier's remit (such as the competence to make decisions about long-term structural changes, such as large-scale development projects requiring the removal of population). Regarding the latter, the aim of protecting individuals' rights from abuse of power is achieved through a more absolute prohibition, as a context where a population lives under the military control of a foreign State is not conducive to applying the limitation conditions foreseen by IHRL (such as genuine consultation and obtaining informed consent).

4.3. INTERACTION IN NON-INTERNATIONAL ARMED CONFLICT

Similarly to the prohibition under occupation, the IHL prohibition on arbitrary displacement in NIAC (APII Article 17 and its corresponding customary rule) has a narrower personal and material scope than the IHRL prohibition, as it only protects people holding the status of civilians under the circumstances of armed conflict within a State. It is also far more restrictive in terms of the exceptions that it foresees: evacuation is the only one in the case of internal displacement, while no exceptions at all are provided to the prohibition on displacement outside the territory of the State in question. Given the precise scope of this rule and its strict limits on exceptions, the amalgamation of extra IHRL-based grounds of justification to the exception of evacuation – as may occur when IHL and IHRL are applied cumulatively – would quite evidently conflict with the plain meaning of the IHL rule.

151 Text to n. 14.

It is submitted that, in this case, the IHL prohibition on arbitrary displacement also prevails over the IHRL rule as *lex specialis*, as this would be required to give effect to the stricter IHL protection. Such protection is more specifically designed for the context, since, by definition, at least one of the parties addressed by the rule will be a non-State armed group, which is unlikely to have the authority to implement measures to meet the IHRL limitation conditions. Towards State addressees, the stricter prohibition also counteracts the vulnerability of civilians who, although nationals of the State, may be viewed as associated with the adversary. This is more likely to be the case in NIACs, where the distinction between non-State armed group members and civilians is typically much less clear than that between civilians and State combatants in an international conflict. It further takes into account that, like occupation, a NIAC context is not necessarily conducive to the effectiveness of IHRL safeguards such as consultation and seeking of informed consent.

Where conflict-related internal displacement results from coercive acts rather than a direct order, it is submitted that if Willms' view on interpreting APII Article 17(1) and its corresponding customary rule is followed,[152] this could be viewed as a clarification or interpretation of the IHL rule in light of IHRL. This would be consistent with a State's more extensive IHRL responsibilities in its own territory, which cannot be reconciled with inducing or tolerating the displacement of civilians through coercion.

In the territory of a State in which a NIAC is taking place, IHRL will continue to apply by default to displacement unrelated to the conflict, since this is not addressed by IHL. However, in examining the legality of such displacement, it is suggested that the factual situation should be assessed for possible indirect coercion or discrimination related to the conflict (for example, assumptions that the affected population is associated with an armed group based on ethnicity, religion, etc.), as this is likely to indicate inconsistency with IHRL.[153]

5. FINDINGS REGARDING CONVERGENCES AND DIVERGENCES

While IHL and IHRL both contain norms amounting to prohibitions on arbitrary displacement, the above analysis demonstrates a number of divergences between them, mainly hinging on what actions can be considered to give rise to 'arbitrary' displacement (or rather, what steps must be taken to avoid this categorisation). This clearly reflects the contexts in which these norms have been developed. The IHRL prohibition has mainly developed in response to forced evictions in

[152] Text to n. 112.

[153] HRC, 'General Comment 27', above n. 31, [18]; *Vojnović*, above n. 37, [8.7].

non-conflict situations (for example, in the context of urban redevelopment), and offers protections that are typically within the power of a State *vis-à-vis* its own residents. On the other hand, the rules of IHL reflect its traditional function of balancing military necessity and civilian protection in times of conflict. It has been submitted that in both IAC (whether hostilities or occupation) and NIAC, the IHL norms prevail as *lex specialis* over the more general IHRL norms, given the former's specific adaptation to the context and greater precision. However, the impact of this differs in each of the abovementioned situations.

In hostilities in IAC, an independent prohibition on arbitrary displacement only appears to be in the process of emerging. This reflects the position of the principle of distinction as the main mechanism for protecting civilians in such situations, and IHL's tolerance of incidental effects of attacks that are lawful by its standards (that is to say that damage to civilians is not necessarily unlawful if it results from a proportionate and necessary attack on a military target). Therefore, it can be said that the IHL criteria for determining the arbitrariness of displacement in international hostilities leave more scope for lawful displacement than those for IHRL. This corresponds to the common dynamic of IHL acting as *lex specialis* to pare down IHRL requirements, given that full application of all IHRL criteria would be near impossible to respect in a conflict situation. The protection of civilians is then achieved through the IHL principles of distinction, necessity and proportionality, as well as specific precautions to be taken in attack.

Conversely, in the cases of occupation and non-international conflict, a less common paradigm is revealed in which IHL operates as *lex specialis* in order to provide a more stringent standard of protection from displacement. This reflects the respective contexts: in the first case, the population is in the power of a foreign military force against which it has little influence or recourse; in the second, the nexus between the displacement and an internal conflict is deemed to require a stricter standard of protection than under IHRL, in order to counteract civilian vulnerability caused by a lower level of distinction between civilians and fighters.

The analysis regarding occupation in particular demonstrates the need for a considered, case-by-case approach when applying IHRL rules in situations within the scope of IHL. Scholars of occupation law such as Roberts[154] and Gross have long advocated such caution, with Gross warning of contexts in which IHRL may provide 'more rather than less justifications for limiting rights'.[155] The case below provides a practical illustration of some of the pitfalls of applying the IHL and IHRL prohibitions on arbitrary displacement – in

154 A. Roberts, 'Transformative Military Occupation: Applying the Laws of War and Human Rights' (2006) 100 *American Journal of International Law*, 580, 599–600.

155 A. Gross, above n. 133, 9.

particular, the possibility of human rights justifications creating ambiguity around a population's position under IHL. With such ambiguity comes the risk of arbitrary displacement gaining a more acceptable face towards the outside world, which may have an impact on third-party assessments and thus place protection efforts on a weaker footing.

6. PLAN FOR MASS TRANSFER OF BEDOUINS IN AREA C OF THE WEST BANK, OCCUPIED PALESTINIAN TERRITORY: AN ILLUSTRATION

6.1. BACKGROUND

Area C is a zone comprising about 62 per cent of the West Bank in the occupied Palestinian territory (OPT). It is under the complete control of Israel, the occupying power, which has designated 70 per cent of the area for Israeli settlements or military zones, while heavily restricting Palestinian building in the remaining 30 per cent. Humanitarian agencies report that it is almost impossible for the Palestinian population of Area C to obtain building permits and connections to essential infrastructure. Shelters and other structures are therefore built without permission from the occupying power, which then demolishes them on the basis that they are illegal. Around 60 per cent of demolitions take place in areas allocated to Israeli settlements.[156] Between 2008 and 2015, over 6,000 Palestinians were displaced by such demolitions in Area C.[157] Further factors contributing to displacement of Palestinians in this area include movement restrictions, the use of military firing zones, evictions and settler violence.[158]

Bedouin herding communities are particularly vulnerable to these pressures.[159] Having been displaced to the West Bank from Israel in the late 1940s,

156 UN Office for the Co-ordination of Humanitarian Affairs (OCHA) occupied Palestinian territory (OPT), 'Area C Humanitarian Response Plan' (August 2010) 1–2; UN OCHA OPT, 'Demolitions and Forced Displacement in the Occupied West Bank' (January 2012). All UN OCHA OPT documents are available at <www.ochaopt.org>.

157 Over 4,000 Palestinians were reported to have been displaced by demolitions in Area C in 2008–12; the total for 2013–15 was over 2,000. See UN OCHA OPT, 'Communities in the Jerusalem Periphery at Risk of Forced Displacement' (June 2013); UN OCHA OPT, 'Humanitarian Bulletin Monthly Report – Annex: Monthly Indicator Tables' (January 2016) 3.

158 UN OCHA OPT, 'The Humanitarian Impact of Israeli-Declared Firing Zones in the West Bank' (August 2012) [6]; UN OCHA OPT, 'Israeli Settler Violence in the West Bank' (November 2011) [5]; UN OCHA OPT, 'Area C of The West Bank: Key Humanitarian Concerns' (August 2014).

159 See UN Development Programme, 'In Focus: Bedouins in the occupied Palestinian territory'(2013) 4–6; UN Relief and Works Agency for Palestine Refugees in the Near East

these communities chose to maintain their traditional pastoral way of life instead of moving to refugee camps. However, the Israeli occupation of the West Bank in 1967 placed their livelihoods under pressure, as settlements and military zones restricted their access to necessary resources. Therefore, Bedouin communities started to settle more permanently along their seasonal migration route outside Jerusalem. This area was viewed as highly strategic for Israeli settlement expansion, so as from the 1980s, occupation authorities began to inform the Bedouin that they would have to leave permanently.[160] In the late 1990s, 150 families were indeed transferred to a semi-urban site near the municipal garbage dump to make way for the expansion of an Israeli settlement.[161] This involuntary move had extremely negative social and economic consequences, particularly for women, as social structures broke down, livelihoods were strained, and personal security was reduced.[162]

6.2. THE JERUSALEM PERIPHERY RELOCATION PLAN

In 2011, Israeli occupation authorities indicated their intention to accelerate transfer of the remaining Bedouin from Area C through a mass relocation plan. This would involve the phased removal of Bedouin communities into designated locations. About 2,400 Bedouin living in the hills east of Jerusalem would be moved in the first phase, so that a contiguous belt of settlements could be completed.[163] The relocation plan was initially put on hold to assess environmental concerns over moving the Bedouin to an existing relocation site near a garbage dump.[164] However, demolitions and demolition threats continued, as did restriction of access to grazing land and Israeli authorities' inadequate response to settler violence.[165] In April 2014, Israeli authorities announced the preparation of three Bedouin relocation areas adjacent to

(UNRWA), UN Children's Fund & World Food Programme, 'Food Security and Nutrition Survey for Herding Communities in Area C' (2010) 10; UN OCHA OPT, 'Communities in the Jerusalem Periphery', above n. 157.

160 UNRWA and Bimkom, 'Al-Jabal: a study on the transfer of Bedouin Palestine Refugees' (2013) 10–11.

161 Ibid., 14–16.

162 Ibid., 38–42.

163 UN OCHA OPT, 'Communities in the Jerusalem Periphery', above n. 157; UN OCHA OPT, 'Bedouin Communities at Risk of Forcible Transfer' (September 2014); Amira Hass, 'Israel to Forcibly Evict Bedouins From West Bank' *Ha'aretz* (Tel Aviv, 24 September 2011) <http://www.haaretz.com/print-edition/news/israel-to-forcibly-evict-bedouins-from-west-bank-1.384290>.

164 A. Hass, 'Israel Freezes Plan to Move East Jerusalem Bedouin to Site Near Garbage Dump' *Ha'aretz* (Tel Aviv, 29 June 2012) <http://www.haaretz.com/israel-news/israel-freezes-plan-to-move-east-jerusalem-bedouin-to-site-near-garbage-dump.premium-1.444793>.

165 UN OCHA OPT 'Communities in the Jerusalem Periphery', above n. 157, [2].

towns controlled by the Palestinian Authority. It appeared from these plans that as many as 12,000 people could be displaced to these areas, with Bedouin communities in the Jerusalem periphery remaining a high priority. At the same time, demolitions, eviction orders, and destruction of humanitarian aid in the communities in question were stepped up.[166] Advancement of the relocation plan – in particular, preparation of the relocation sites – is continuing, alongside demolitions in the target communities.[167]

6.3. POSITIONS OF THE OCCUPYING POWER AND OF THE AFFECTED POPULATION

Israeli authorities have motivated the relocation plan as a 'legal and planning solution' for the Bedouin, which will alleviate the difficulties arising from their lack of permission to connect to basic services in their current locations.[168] The plan is also described as being 'for the benefit of the area's Bedouin population', as it would allow them to live in a place with suitable infrastructure.[169] Israeli courts have reportedly recommended that authorities enter into dialogue with Bedouin communities on the plans,[170] while officials have repeatedly claimed that communities have been consulted and that their needs have been taken into account.[171]

Assurances regarding alternative housing have also been prominent in Israeli official positions.[172] In a committee meeting of the Israeli Parliament in

166 UN OCHA OPT 'Humanitarian Bulletin: Monthly Report' (April 2014) 8–9.

167 UN OCHA OPT 'Humanitarian Bulletin: Monthly Report' (October 2015) 13–14; UN OCHA OPT 'Humanitarian Bulletin: Monthly Report' (January 2016) 3.

168 Position of Israel Civil Administration (as cited in A. Hass, 'Dovish Ex-general Appointed to Liaise With Bedouin in West Bank' *Ha'aretz* (Tel Aviv, 6 March 2015) <http://www.haaretz.com/israel-news/.premium-1.645567>).

169 Remarks by Yuval Turgeman (Director of Bedouin Affairs, Israel Civil Administration) (as cited in A. Hass, 'Israeli Government Plans to Forcibly Relocate 12,500 Bedouin' *Ha'aretz* (Tel Aviv 16 September 2014) <http://www.haaretz.com/israel-news/.premium-1.615986?date=1446807630813>); The Media Line, 'Jahalin Bedouins fear new Israeli transfer plan' *YNet News* (Jerusalem, 20 April 2013) <http://www.ynetnews.com/articles/0,7340,L-4369710,00.html>.

170 Remarks by Uzi Vogelman (Israeli High Court Justice) (as cited in A. Hass, 'Israeli Government Plans', above n. 169).

171 A. Hass, 'Israeli Government Plans', above n. 169; A. Hass, 'West Bank Bedouin Fighting Israel's Plan for Forcible Relocation', *Ha'aretz* (Tel Aviv, 3 December 2014) <http://www.haaretz.com/middle-east-news/.premium-1.629715>; Letter from Captain Yaniv Ya'ari (Israeli military legal advisor's office in the West Bank) to Advocate Shlomo Lecker (legal representative of the Jahalin Bedouin) (as cited in A. Hass, 'Goal of Bedouin Relocation: To Expel as Many Palestinians from Their Land as Possible', *Ha'aretz* (Tel Aviv, 8 December 2014) <http://www.haaretz.com/middle-east-news/.premium-1.630522>).

172 T. Lazaroff, 'Civil Administration confiscates 11 solar panels from West Bank Beduin village' *Jerusalem Post* (14 January 2015) <http://www.jpost.com/Israel-News/Civil-Administration-confiscates-11-solar-panels-from-West-Bank-Beduin-village-395890>; A. Hass, 'Israel Steps

April 2014, the head of the Civil Administration (Israeli authority in the occupied territory) explained that the Israeli High Court had warned against evicting the Bedouin, as they had no alternative accommodation. Therefore, he emphasised the importance of preparing relocation sites, as this would give 'moral and legal validation for performance of the enforcement'.[173]

The Bedouin communities, on the other hand, claim that they were not consulted and have consistently opposed the plan, including through legal action in Israeli courts.[174] In terms of solutions for their precarious situation, the Bedouin have expressed that pending their return to their ancestral lands in the Negev Desert in Israel, they wish to remain in their current locations and be permitted to develop their communities, connect to infrastructure and improve their living conditions.[175]

6.4. INTERNATIONAL POSITIONS

A great number of UN officials and bodies clearly called for a stop to the relocation plan, which they referred to as potentially giving rise to forcible transfer in violation of GCIV, as well as human rights violations.[176]

Up Pace of Bedouin Home Demolitions' *Ha'aretz* (Tel Aviv, 24 September 2014) <http://www.haaretz.com/israel-news/.premium-1.617537>; A. Hass, 'Controversial Resettlement Plan: It's Not Just Settlers Who Oppose Israel's Plan to Relocate Bedouin in West Bank' *Ha'aretz* (Tel Aviv 16 May 2013) <http://www.haaretz.com/israel-news/it-s-not-just-settlers-who-oppose-israel-s-plan-to-relocate-bedouin-in-west-bank.premium-1.524176>; R. Ahren, 'Amnesty: Bedouin relocation plan possibly a "war crime"' *Times of Israel* (Jerusalem 9 February 2012) <http://www.timesofisrael.com/amnesty-israels-bedouin-relocation-plan-possibly-a-war-crime>.

173 Nineteenth Knesset, 'Minutes of the meeting of the Judea and Samaria Region Subcommittee of the Foreign Affairs and Defense Committee' (unofficial English translation 27 April 2014) 15 <http://jahalin.org/wp-content/uploads/2012/01/2014.04.27-Minutes-Judea-and-Samaria-Region-Subcommittee-of-the-Foreign-Affairs-and-Defense-Committee.pdf>.

174 A. Hass, 'West Bank Bedouin Fighting Israel's Plan', above n. 171; A. Hass, 'West Bank Bedouin Leaders Reject Relocation Plan' *Ha'aretz* (Tel Aviv 17 September 2014) <http://www.haaretz.com/israel-news/.premium-1.616163>.

175 UN OCHA OPT, 'Bedouin Communities at Risk', above n. 163, [1]; A. Hass, 'Controversial Resettlement Plan', above n. 172.

176 UNGA 'Report of the Secretary-General: Israeli practices affecting the human rights of the Palestinian people in the Occupied Palestinian Territory, including East Jerusalem' (2012) UN Doc A/67/372, [37], [55]; UNRWA, 'UNRWA urges donor community to take firm stand against mass forcible transfer of Palestinian Bedouins' (Press Release 21 September 2014) <http://www.unrwa.org/newsroom/press-releases/unrwa-urges-donor-community-take-firm-stand-against-mass-forcible-transfer>; UNRWA 'UN officials urge Israel to halt plans to transfer Palestinian Bedouins, expand settlements' (Press Release 20 May 2015) <http://www.unrwa.org/newsroom/press-releases/un-officials-israel-must-halt-plans-transfer-palestinian-bedouins>; OHCHR, 'UN human rights expert urges Israel to abandon plans to transfer Bedouins in the occupied West Bank' (Press Release 5 June 2015) <http://www.ohchr.org/EN/NewsEvents/Pages/DisplayNews.aspx?NewsID=16045&LangID=E>.

The UN Secretary General further specifically referred to a number of practices which he considered were already creating a coercive environment for the communities subjected to the plan, such as demolitions, restriction of access to grazing land, and limitations on building permits.[177] Outside the UN system, the European Union (EU) Foreign Affairs Council repeatedly called for an end to the plan, which it placed in the context of the illegal settlement enterprise and characterised as 'forced transfer'.[178] In a démarche, the EU expressed that the plan might amount to a serious violation of GCIV.[179]

In some positions, however, there was an apparent amalgamation of the IHL and IHRL grounds of justification for displacement, which potentially could be read as broadening the scope of permissible justifications beyond what is foreseen by IHL.

For example, the Office of the High Commissioner for Human Rights expressed that the demolition and permanent displacement of one Bedouin community in the Jerusalem periphery potentially violated GCIV Article 49, as well as the IHRL prohibition on forced eviction. However, it was also emphasised that '[n]o alternative locations or housing options were offered'[180] – a criterion imported from IHRL, which would not be relevant in assessing the legality of the action under IHL.

In reporting on the relocation plan, the Special Rapporteur on Adequate Housing focused on the lack of community consultation or participation.[181] The report did not refer to applicable IHL provisions, but rather based its position on Israel's duty to 'respect, protect and fulfil the right to housing of Palestinians living under occupation'. The main recommendation in this regard was an immediate stop to all home demolitions and evictions in the West Bank and East Jerusalem. However, the occupying power was further called upon – in line with IHRL-based requirements – to explore all possible alternatives prior to

---

177 Report of the Secretary-General, 'Israeli settlements in the Occupied Palestinian Territory, including East Jerusalem, and the occupied Syrian Golan' (2014) UN Doc A/69/348, [16].

178 European Union (EU) Foreign Affairs Council (FAC), 'Council Conclusions on the Middle East Peace Process (MEPP)' (10 July 2015) [6] <http://www.consilium.europa.eu/en/press/press-releases/2015/07/20-fac-mepp-conclusions/>; EU FAC, 'Council Conclusions on the MEPP' (10 December 2012) [3] <http://eeas.europa.eu/delegations/israel/press_corner/all_news/news/2012/20121210_02_en.htm>; EU FAC, 'Council Conclusions on the MEPP' (14 May 2012) [5]–[6] <http://eu-un.europa.eu/articles/en/article_15300_en.htm>.

179 EU démarche (as cited in B. Ravid, 'EU seeks talks with Israel over "red lines" in West Bank' *Ha'aretz* (Tel Aviv, 22 October 2014) <http://www.haaretz.com/israel-news/1.622099>).

180 UN News, 'UN rights office voices concern over forced evictions of Palestinians in West Bank' *UN News* (27 August 2013) <http://www.un.org/apps/news/story.asp?NewsID=45707#.ViTHi37hCM8>.

181 UN Human Rights Council, 'Report of the Special Rapporteur on adequate housing as a component of the right to an adequate standard of living, and on the right to non-discrimination in this context, Raquel Rolnik: Mission to Israel and to the Occupied Palestinian Territory' (24 December 2012) UN Doc A/HRC/22/46/Add.1 (Annex) [71].

evictions, consult with affected persons, and provide effective remedies.[182] Such recommendations similarly appear to broaden the scope of permissible transfers beyond what is foreseen by GCIV Article 49.

Ambiguity can also be noted in the EU's démarche on this issue: while expressing concern about the potential for a serious violation of IHL, the EU urged Israel to put the relocation plan on hold and 'search for other solutions together with the concerned populations and the Palestinian Authority'.[183] This encouragement of a consensual solution appears to overlook the problems inherent in an occupying power seeking the occupied population's consent to transfer.[184] It also does not appear to take into account the legal inability of the Palestinian Authority to make any decisions on behalf of protected persons which would waive their protection from forcible transfer.[185]

6.5. ANALYSIS

This case illustrates the relevance and importance of a clear analysis of the relationship between IHL and IHRL rules prohibiting displacement. Absence of such clarity leaves room, on the one hand, for misuse of human rights discourse by involved parties; and, on the other, for dilution of stricter IHL prohibitions, even through good faith application of IHRL norms.

The positions of the occupying power illustrate the potential use of human rights discourse to serve purposes that are not for the benefit for the population, and even internationally unlawful (in this case, the plan to expand settlements). A notable element here is the mirroring of this discourse by some international bodies, as opposed to an assertion of the absolute nature of the IHL prohibition on forcible transfer. It is unclear whether this dynamic resulted from mandate restrictions, from a lack of clarity on the interaction of the relevant norms, from application of a cumulative approach, or simply from a desire to address the occupying power's arguments directly. Regardless, in this case, the ultimate position of most of these international bodies was not affected, as almost all characterised the plan as a potential forcible transfer contrary to IHL.

However, in other cases, the facts may be more ambiguous – for example, representatives of the population may be pressured to express consent, or there may not be such an evident link to the transfer of the occupier's population into the occupied territory. In such situations, a clear understanding of the interplay between IHL and IHRL may be more decisive, even if only in determining the reaction of third States and international bodies. If IHL is not sufficiently taken

182 Ibid., [101.c.i].
183 EU démarche (as cited in B. Ravid, above n. 179).
184 See text to nn. 142–147.
185 See GCIV, Art. 47; text to n. 148.

into account, this may impact on third States' discharge of their obligation to cooperate to bring forcible transfer to an end, as endeavours to uphold a clear protective rule may give way to debates on the modalities of decisions which an occupying power is not permitted to take in the first place.

7. CONCLUSION

While the analysis and case presented above illustrate the relevance of the IHL/IHRL relationship regarding the topic of arbitrary displacement, they also underline the more general importance of continuing to develop clear analysis of IHL/IHRL interactions in specific subject areas.

In the abstract, a cumulative approach to applying IHL and IHRL may *prima facie* appear to be in the best interests of civilians in armed conflict, as it would combine the protections available in both systems of law. However, this may have the opposite effect where it results in an 'accumulation of exceptions', in situations where IHRL grounds of justification are broader than those foreseen by IHL. The analysis of the relationship between IHL and IHRL prohibitions on arbitrary displacement – particularly in situations of occupation and NIAC – provides examples of such situations, and demonstrates that the application of IHL as *lex specialis* may indeed provide more stringent protection for civilians. This operation of IHL as *lex specialis* to curb an 'accumulation of exceptions' is not merely desirable from a civilian point of view. In the case of the prohibition on arbitrary displacement, it is consistent with the general principles of the relationship between IHL and IHRL, and in line with the aims of both bodies of law. In particular, it maintains the more unequivocal nature of IHL prohibitions, which find their natural place in providing clear-cut rules of conduct in times of armed conflict.

The case presented begins to illustrate some of the possible implications of the above analysis for users of international law in armed conflict situations involving displacement. In particular, it shows how ambiguity could potentially have a negative impact on the efforts of international bodies and third States to cooperate in bringing violations to an end. Although not addressed in the case above, it may also be noted that in situations of conflict-related displacement, the IHL/IHRL relationship also has implications for external aid actors, as they will need to take IHL into account in order to ensure that they do not do harm by indirectly lending assistance in unlawful actions (such as agreeing to help build a relocation site for forcibly transferred communities).

While the case focused on the implications for third parties, the interaction between the IHL and IHRL prohibitions on displacement evidently also has consequences for involved duty-bearers and rights-holders/protected persons. In the first group, military actors are more likely to be well versed in IHL through their training, and therefore understand the circumstances under which IHL permits displacement or not. They may therefore have a role to play in situations in which directives from civilian policy-makers, which may be presented in terms of human rights discourse, contradict IHL. As for affected rights-holders/protected persons, a clear awareness of their position under IHL will strengthen their efforts to advocate for themselves, particularly as it may help to avoid unnecessary and harmful concessions of their rights. This point also applies to the representatives of such communities and civil society actors advocating for their rights/protection. Finally, in ultimately adjudicating the claims of the respective parties, it is important that Judges are sensitised to the interplay between the IHL and IHRL prohibitions in armed conflict, and apply each in its rightful time and place. In this way, rules intended to protect homes from the excesses of spatial planning can be kept from inadvertently weakening those that protect homes from war.

INVESTIGATIONS IN ARMED CONFLICT: UNDERSTANDING THE INTERACTION BETWEEN INTERNATIONAL HUMANITARIAN LAW AND HUMAN RIGHTS LAW

Vito TODESCHINI

1. INTRODUCTION

The purpose of the present chapter is to examine the interaction between international humanitarian law (IHL) and human rights law (HRL) in relation to the duty to investigate in armed conflict. Scholars have extensively discussed many of the normative and practical implications arising from the interplay between these branches of international law.[1] However, too little attention has

[1] See, inter alia, R. PROVOST, *International Human Rights and Humanitarian Law*, Cambridge University Press, Cambridge 2002; R. ARNOLD and N. QUENIVET (eds), *International*

been paid to how this interaction impacts the obligation to investigate.[2] The analysis will look into how IHL and HRL respectively regulate this duty: it will be shown that whereas the latter prescribes in detail the standards an investigation must follow in order to be deemed effective, the former does not. Accordingly, the research question is whether and how HRL may complement IHL and fill what is here considered a gap in the law. To answer this question, the following three aspects will be examined.

The first concerns how human rights treaty bodies have applied the duty to investigate and the standards of effectiveness in armed conflict situations.[3] It will be illustrated that an interpretive trend is emerging, according to which a State is required to take 'all reasonable steps' or 'all feasible measures' to investigate as effectively as possible under any circumstances. What this study terms the 'all reasonable steps'/'all feasible measures' test will be pertinent to the application of the standards of effectiveness to war crimes investigations.

The second important aspect regards how HRL may complement IHL in relation to the standards of effectiveness and the right to an investigation. To explore this possibility, the study will examine the way in which IHL and HRL relate to each other at the macro level, namely as legal regimes, and at the micro level, when specific norms interact. It will employ a theoretical framework grounded on two elements: (1) a perspective of complementarity between IHL and HRL; and (2) the employment of the principle of systemic integration to connect their norms. This approach will enable to understand how norms from one body of law may be used to fill relevant gaps in the other.

The third aspect concerns the interplay of IHL and HRL norms regulating investigations. The analysis will specifically focus on two scenarios: concurrent applicability of the two legal frameworks, and exclusive applicability of IHL. Against this background, it will explore how HRL may complement IHL either as a matter of law or as a matter of interpretation, depending on the scenario at stake.

Section 2 will provide an overview of how IHL and HRL regulate the obligation to investigate, highlighting similarities and differences between the

---

Humanitarian Law and Human Rights Law, Brill/Nijhoff, Leiden 2008; R. Kolb and G. Gaggioli (eds), *Research Handbook on Human Rights and Humanitarian Law*, Edward Elgar, Cheltenham 2013; E. De Wet and J. Kleffner (eds), *Convergence and Conflicts of Human Rights and International Humanitarian Law in Military Operations*, Pretoria University Law Press, Pretoria 2014; G. Oberleitner, *Human Rights in Armed Conflict: Law, Practice, Policy*, Cambridge University Press, Cambridge 2015; D. Murray (ed), *Practitioners' Guide to Human Rights Law in Armed Conflict*, Oxford University Press, Oxford 2016.

2 The phrases 'obligation to investigate' and 'duty to investigate' will be used interchangeably.

3 The phrases 'treaty bodies' and 'monitoring bodies' will be employed interchangeably. The human rights bodies considered by the present analysis are the Human Rights Committee (HRCtee), the Committee against Torture (CteeAT), the European Court of Human Rights (ECtHR), the African Commission of Human and Peoples' Rights (AComHPR), and the Inter-American Commission (IAComHR) and Court (IACtHR) of Human Rights.

two frameworks. Section 3 will in turn clarify the theoretical framework here employed to understand the relationship between the two bodies of law; it will also discuss the (ir)relevance of the *lex specialis* principle in this context. Section 4 will then show how the IHL and HRL norms governing investigations in armed conflict interact within the two abovementioned scenarios, specifically looking at the way HRL may affect the conduct of war crimes investigations.[4]

2. THE OBLIGATION TO INVESTIGATE IN ARMED CONFLICT

2.1. INTERNATIONAL HUMANITARIAN LAW

Under IHL, the obligation to investigate is connected to the criminalisation of an act as a war crime.[5] States must investigate and, if the case demands, prosecute, alleged war crimes committed by their nationals, on their territory, or over which they have jurisdiction on the basis of domestic legislation. As far as treaty law is concerned, this obligation derives from the so-called 'grave breaches' regime set out in the Geneva Conventions (GCs) I–IV and Additional Protocol I (API),[6] which apply to international armed conflicts (IACs) only.[7]

---

4 The analysis will only deal with the obligation of a State to investigate acts committed by its armed forces and agents. Investigations into alleged human rights violations and war crimes committed by private parties or organised armed groups fall outside the scope of the present research.

5 Public Commission to Examine the Maritime Incident of 31 May 2010 (Turkel Commission), 'Second Report: Israel's Mechanisms for Examining and Investigating Complaints and Claims of Violations of the Laws of Armed Conflict according to International Law' (Government of Israel, February 2013) <http://www.turkel-committee.gov.il/files/newDoc3/The%20Turkel%20Report%20for%20website.pdf> accessed 19.02.2018, 75–77. As defined by the International Criminal Tribunal for the former Yugoslavia (ICTY), a war crime is a serious violation of a conventional or customary rule of IHL that gives rise to individual criminal responsibility; *Prosecutor v. Tadić* (Decision) ICTY-94-1 (2 October 1995) 94.

6 Convention for the Amelioration of the Condition of the Wounded and Sick in Armed Forces in the Field (adopted 12 August 1949) 75 UNTS 31 (GCI), Arts. 49–50; Convention for the Amelioration of the Condition of Wounded, Sick and Shipwrecked Members of Armed Forces at Sea (adopted 12 August 1949) 75 UNTS 85 (GCII), Arts. 50–51; Convention relative to the Treatment of Prisoners of War (adopted 12 August 1949) 75 UNTS 135 (GCIII), Arts. 129–30; Convention relative to the Protection of Civilian Persons in Time of War (adopted 12 August 1949) 75 UNTS 287 (GCIV), Arts. 146–47; Protocol Additional to the Geneva Conventions of 12 August 1949, and relating to the Protection of Victims of International Armed Conflicts (adopted 8 June 1977) 1125 UNTS 3 (API), Arts. 11, 85. Grave breaches are part of the broader category of war crimes; see API, Art. 85(5).

7 ICTY *Tadić*, above n. 5, 81. An IAC exists when there is 'a resort to armed force between States', whereas a NIAC takes place when there is 'protracted armed violence between governmental authorities and organized armed groups or between such groups': ibid., 70. Moreover, two specific requirements must be met for a situation to classify as a NIAC: hostilities have to

Common Article 3 GCs and Additional Protocol II (APII),[8] namely the treaty law applicable in non-international armed conflicts (NIACs), do not criminalise breaches of their provisions and therefore do not prescribe an obligation to investigate. At the same time, a number of treaties that cover both types of conflicts, such as several conventions regulating specific means and methods of warfare and the Rome Statute of the International Criminal Court (ICC),[9] impose this duty. Moreover, the jurisprudence of international criminal tribunals and courts has extensively developed the law of war crimes in relation to NIACs, including the obligation to investigate.[10] At present, it is acknowledged that the duty to investigate alleged war crimes has attained customary status under IHL and applies to both IACs and NIACs.[11]

It must be noted that not all allegations of war crimes trigger the duty to investigate. According to State practice,[12] a credible allegation or reasonable suspicion that a war crime has been committed must exist.[13] This mainly relates to the use of force in armed conflict. IHL indeed allows for the targeting of individuals on the basis of their status or activity, respectively as combatants or civilians taking direct part in the hostilities.[14] Additionally, it is not unlawful

---

reach a certain level of intensity and the armed group must be organised; *Prosecutor v. Tadić* (Judgment) ICTY-94-1 (7 May 1997) 562.

8 Protocol Additional to the Geneva Conventions of 12 August 1949 and relating to the Protection of Victims of Non-International Armed Conflicts (adopted 8 June 1977) 1125 UNTS 610 (APII).

9 Cf. Convention for the Protection of Cultural Property in the Event of Armed Conflict (14 May 1954) 249 UNTS 240, Art. 28; Convention on the Prohibition of the Development, Production, Stockpiling and Use of Chemical Weapons and on Their Destruction (adopted 3 September 1992) 1974 UNTS 45, Art. VII(1); Protocol on Prohibitions or Restrictions on the Use of Mines, Booby-Traps and Other Devices, as amended on 3 May 1996, annexed to the Convention on Certain Conventional Weapons (adopted 3 May 1996) 2048 UNTS 93, Art. 14; Convention on the Prohibition of the Use, Stockpiling, Production and Transfer of Anti-Personnel Mines and on their Destruction (adopted 18 September 1997) 2056 UNTS 211, Art. 9; Second Protocol to the Hague Convention of 1954 for the Protection of Cultural Property in the Event of Armed Conflict (adopted 26 March 1999) 2253 UNTS 212, Arts. 15–17; Rome Statute of the International Criminal Court (adopted 17 July 1998) 2187 UNTS 3, Arts. 1, 17, 53. States may also criminalise any breaches of IHL at domestic level; see United States Department of Defence, *Law of War Manual*, June 2015, pp. 1073–74.

10 For an account in this respect, see S. Darcy, *Judges, Law and War: The Judicial Development of International Humanitarian Law*, Cambridge University Press, Cambridge 2014, pp. 279 ff.

11 J.-M. Henckaerts and L. Doswald-Beck (eds), *Customary International Humanitarian Law*, vol. 1, Cambridge University Press, Cambridge 2005, p. 607; M.N. Schmitt, 'Investigating Violations of International Law in Armed Conflict' (2011) 2 *Harvard National Security Journal* 31, 38–39, 47–48; Turkel Commission, above n. 5, 82.

12 Ibid., 256. The Commission studied the legislation and practice of the US, Canada, Australia, the UK, Germany and the Netherlands: ibid., Annex C, *The Comparative Survey*.

13 Ibid., 100, 110–11; M.N. Schmitt, above n. 11, 39, 83; A. Cohen and Y. Shany, 'Beyond the Grave Breaches Regime: The Duty to Investigate Alleged Violations of International Law Governing Armed Conflicts' (2011) 14 *Yearbook of International Humanitarian Law* 37, 51.

14 API, Arts. 43(2), 48, 51(3); APII, Art. 13(3).

under this framework to cause incidental civilian casualties as long as the principle of proportionality is respected.[15] It follows that not all allegations of death and injuries of civilians or destruction of civilian objects need to be investigated: only a credible allegation or reasonable suspicion in that regard triggers the duty to investigate. When attacks result in civilian casualties, the specific circumstances will determine the necessity to open an investigation.[16] At the same time, those acts that are prohibited under any circumstances, such as torture or rape, always require the initiation of an investigation.[17]

Effectiveness defines the content of the obligation to investigate. This concept expresses the capacity of investigators carefully to assess the factual circumstances surrounding an incident, verify the allegations, identify those allegedly responsible, and gather the evidence for possible prosecution.[18] It is worth noting that IHL does not specifically regulate the standards of effectiveness, namely the requirements that an investigation must meet in order to be considered effective.[19] Limited guidance may be found in Articles 121 GCIII and 131 GCIV: these provisions prescribe that any suspected death of prisoners of war or interned civilians must be immediately investigated, witnesses must be questioned, and those responsible prosecuted.[20]

The overarching requirement of effectiveness under IHL has been further elaborated upon by the ICTY case law. In general, a commander bears the duty to examine, investigate or report any allegations concerning breaches of IHL.[21] He or she is required to take all necessary and reasonable measures to that end. What is necessary and reasonable in a given situation will depend on the concrete circumstances: the actual material ability of a commander to investigate, report or punish a violation will shape his or her obligation.[22] The ICTY maintained that, in order to assess whether the minimum standard for the fulfilment of such a duty has been met, one has to examine 'what steps were taken to secure an adequate investigation capable of leading to the criminal prosecution of the perpetrators'.[23] The requirement that an investigation must be 'effective' or 'adequate' has consistently been affirmed in international case law.[24] Yet, no

15 API, Art. 51(5)(b).
16 Turkel Commission, above n. 5, 102.
17 Ibid., 100–01.
18 *Prosecutor v. Boškoski and Tarčulovski* (Judgement) ICTY-04-82-T (10 July 2008) 418.
19 The generally recognised standards of effectiveness are promptness, thoroughness, independence, impartiality, transparency, and victims' involvement. Such standards have been developed within HRL. See below section 2.2.
20 GCIII, Art. 121; GCIV, Art. 131.
21 API, Art. 87.
22 G. Mettreaux, *The Law of Command Responsibility*, Oxford University Press, Oxford 2009, p. 235, and case law cited therein.
23 *Prosecutor v. Popović et al* (Judgment) ICTY-05-88-A (30 January 2015) 1932.
24 *Prosecutor v. Strugar* (Judgment) ICTY-01-42-T (31 January 2005) 376, 378; *Boškoski*, above n. 18, 418; *Popović*, above n. 23, 1932; *Prosecutor v. Jean-Pierre Bemba Gombo* (Decision)

indication in respect of more specific standards of effectiveness has been offered. Although such case law relates to the individual responsibility of commanders, it is sensible to consider effectiveness as a more general standard that attaches to a State's obligation to investigate alleged war crimes.

To recap, under IHL States have an obligation to conduct an effective or adequate investigation when a credible allegation or reasonable suspicion that a war crime has been committed exists. One question is how to assess whether or not an investigation satisfies the general requirement of effectiveness. In the absence of precise guidance within IHL, it is useful to pay attention to HRL.[25] Broad consensus among commentators exists on the fact that war crimes investigations should in principle adhere, as far as the circumstances of armed conflict permit, to the standards of effectiveness provided for by HRL.[26] It will be argued below that this is a matter of legal obligation, due to either the parallel applicability of IHL and HRL or the very interpretation of the duty to investigate under IHL.[27]

Finally, it must be recalled that under IHL neither are States obliged to involve victims or their next of kin in the investigation proceedings, nor can the latter claim to have a right to an investigation. As will be illustrated shortly, this is another crucial difference in comparison with HRL.

2.2. HUMAN RIGHTS LAW

Most human rights treaties do not include a provision regulating the obligation to investigate. The Convention against Torture (CAT) and the International Convention for the Protection of All Persons from Enforced Disappearance (ICED) constitute an exception in this respect: they envisage the duty to investigate both as an individual right and as a State obligation.[28] As far as other

ICC-01/05-01/08 (15 June 2009) 439–43; *Prosecutor v. Jean-Pierre Bemba Gombo* (Judgment) ICC-01/05-01/08 (21 March 2016) 205–09.

25 Turkel Commission, above n. 5, 114.

26 Ibid., 115; M.N. Schmitt, above n. 11, 55–56; A. Cohen and Y. Shany, n. 13, 59; United Nations Human Rights Council, 'Report of the United Nations Fact-Finding Mission on the Gaza Conflict' UN Doc A/HRC/12/48 (25 September 2009) 1808, 1814. It is worth mentioning that as a matter of domestic law, policy or practice, some States already apply the HRL standards of effectiveness when carrying out war crimes investigations; Turkel Commission, above n. 5, 261–64.

27 See below section 4.

28 Convention against Torture and Other Cruel, Inhuman or Degrading Treatment or Punishment (adopted 10 December 1984) 1465 UNTS 85 (CAT), Arts. 12–13; International Convention for the Protection of All Persons from Enforced Disappearance (adopted 20 December 2006) 2716 UNTS 3 (ICED), Arts. 3, 10, 12. Various soft law instruments are also concerned with investigations: inter alia, Principles on the Effective Prevention and Investigation of Extra-Legal, Arbitrary and Summary Executions, UN Doc E/1989/89 Annex (January 1991), Principles 9–17; Principles on the Effective Investigation and Documentation of Torture and Other Cruel, Inhuman or Degrading Treatment or Punishment, UN Doc A/RES/55/89 Annex (4 December 2000).

human rights treaties are concerned, the matter has mainly been developed by the respective monitoring bodies, which similarly conceived of investigations both as a right and a procedural duty attached to a substantive obligation. It is important to highlight that the obligation to investigate generally arises in connection with arbitrary or unlawful killings, acts of torture and ill-treatment, or enforced disappearance.[29]

Human rights treaty bodies have developed the right to an investigation as a dimension of the right to a remedy. The European Court of Human Rights (ECtHR) stated that the former is an implied element of the latter,[30] enshrined in Article 13 of the European Convention on Human Rights (ECHR).[31] Similarly, the Human Rights Committee (HRCtee) affirmed that the obligation to investigate arises from a conjunctive reading between the right to an effective remedy, spelled out in Article 2(3) of the International Covenant on Civil and Political Rights (ICCPR),[32] and relevant substantive provisions of the Covenant, such as Article 6 on the right to life.[33] The Inter-American Court of Human Rights (IACtHR), in turn, linked the right to an investigation to the rights to a fair trial and to an effective remedy,[34] respectively enshrined in Articles 8 and 25 of the American Convention on Human Rights (ACHR).[35] More narrowly, the African Commission of Human and Peoples' Rights (AComHPR) affirmed the existence of a right to an investigation in relation to acts of torture and ill-treatment suffered in custody and to violence against women.[36] As mentioned, the CAT expressly provides that: 'any individual [...] has the right to complain to, and to have his case promptly and impartially examined by, its competent authorities'.[37] The consequence of envisaging a right to an investigation is that a

29 *Aksoy v. Turkey*, no. 21987/93, ECHR, 1996, 98; *Kurt v. Turkey*, no. 15/1997/799/1002, ECHR, 1998, 139–40; *Kaya v. Turkey*, no. 158/1996/777/978, ECHR, 1998, 106–07.

30 *Aksoy*, above n. 29, 98: 'the notion of an "effective remedy" entails, in addition to the payment of compensation where appropriate, a thorough and effective investigation capable of leading to the identification and punishment of those responsible and including effective access for the complainant to the investigatory procedure'.

31 Convention for the Protection of Human Rights and Fundamental Freedoms (adopted 4 November 1950) 213 UNTS 222 (ECHR).

32 International Covenant on Civil and Political Rights (adopted 16 December 1966) 999 UNTS 171 (ICCPR).

33 *Draft General Comment no 36: Article 6 (Right to Life)* HRCtee Doc CCPR/C/GC/R.36/Rev.2 (2 September 2015) 29.

34 *Blake v. Guatemala (Merits)* IACtHR Series C no. 36 (24 January 1998) 97; *Blake v. Guatemala (Reparations and Costs)* IACtHR Series C no. 48 (22 January 1999) 62–63; *Villagrán Morales et al. v. Guatemala (Merits)* IACtHR Series C no. 63 (19 November 1999) 225.

35 American Convention on Human Rights (Pact of San José) (adopted 22 November 1969) 1144 UNTS 144 (ACHR).

36 *Principles and Guidelines on the Right to a Fair Trial and Legal Assistance in Africa* AComHPR OS(XXX)247 (2003) Principle M(7)(h), Principle P(e).

37 CAT, Art. 13. See also ICED, Art. 12(1).

failure to investigate alleged human rights violations amounts to an autonomous breach of the treaty provision(s) to which it is connected,[38] chiefly the right to a remedy.

The obligation to investigate is also construed as a procedural duty attached to a State's general obligation to respect and ensure human rights. In the IACtHR's jurisprudence, a failure to investigate or ineffective investigations give rise to autonomous breaches of Articles 25 (right to judicial protection), 8 (right to a fair trial), 1(1) (obligation to respect rights), and the general obligation to counter impunity.[39] The ECtHR in turn inferred the obligation to investigate from a conjunctive reading between specific substantive provisions, for example Article 2 ECHR (right to life), and the general obligation to respect and ensure rights under Article 1.[40] An analogous interpretation has been adopted by the HRCtee.[41] With specific regard to the right to life, the AComHPR held that States bear a duty to conduct effective official investigations when individuals have allegedly been killed by State agents.[42] In its view, a failure to carry out investigations amounts to a violation of the provision protecting the right to life,[43] namely Article 4 of the African Charter on Human and Peoples' Rights (ACHPR).[44] Again, differently to the other treaties, the CAT includes a specific provision that requires States to investigate alleged acts of torture.[45]

Treaty bodies have paid special attention to investigations into alleged human rights violations perpetrated by State agents,[46] whose accountability requires that their action be independently and publicly scrutinised.[47]Accordingly, the mere knowledge by authorities that an unlawful act has occurred gives rise to the obligation to investigate, without the need for private parties to lodge a formal

38 *Armani Da Silva v. United Kingdom*, no. 5878/08, ECHR, 2016, 231.

39 *Valle Jaramillo et al v. Colombia (Reparations and Costs)* IACtHR Series C no. 192 (27 November 2008) 98; *Blake (Reparations)*, above n. 34, 63–64.

40 *McCann and others v. United Kingdom*, no. 18984/91, ECHR, 1995, 161; *Assenov and others v. Bulgaria*, no. 90/1997/874/1086, ECHR, 1998, 102; *Kurt*, above n. 29, 124.

41 *General Comment no 31: Nature of the General Legal Obligation on States Parties to the Covenant* HRCtee Doc CCPR/C/21/Rev.1/Add.13 (26 May 2004) 15; *Draft General Comment no 36*, above n. 33, 29.

42 *Sudan Human Rights and Centre on Human Rights and Evictions v. Sudan* Communications 279/03 and 296/05 AComHPR 28th Activity Report (May 2009) 147.

43 Ibid., 153; *General Comment no 3: The Right to Life (Article 4)* AComHPR 57th Ordinary Session (4–18 November 2015) 15.

44 African Charter on Human and Peoples' Rights (adopted 27 June 1981) 1582 UNTS 217 (ACHPR).

45 CAT, Art. 12: 'Each State Party shall ensure that its competent authorities proceed to a prompt and impartial investigation, wherever there is reasonable ground to believe that an act of torture has been committed in any territory under its jurisdiction'. See also ICED, Arts. 3, 10, 12.

46 *McCann*, above n. 40, 161; *Assenov*, above n. 40, 102; *Kurt*, above n. 29, 124.

47 *Kaya*, above n. 29, 87.

complaint.[48] This means that the threshold for opening an investigation under HRL is considerably lower than under IHL. It is also worth specifying that the duty to investigate is an obligation of means and not of result: investigators must take all required steps to ascertain the truth of the facts, but they are not supposed to achieve necessarily a positive outcome.[49]

Effectiveness constitutes an overarching requirement of investigations under HRL as well.[50] Monitoring bodies have elaborated in detail upon the standards that define effectiveness. These are promptness,[51] thoroughness,[52] independence,[53] impartiality,[54] transparency[55] and the involvement of victims or their next of kin in the proceedings.[56] A general understanding exists among treaty bodies that these are the standards that define an effective investigation.[57] Although the differences in the texts of the treaties and variants in the interpretation of the standards should not be overlooked, substantial interpretive convergence among treaty bodies may be observed. In light of this, it is possible to contend that HRL provides for general standards of effectiveness, which give content to the obligation to investigate under this framework.[58] As noted, this marks a significant difference with IHL.

---

48 IACtHR, *Valle Jaramillo*, above n. 39, 101; *Ergi v. Turkey*, no 66/1997/850/1057, ECHR, 1998, 82.

49 *Velásquez Rodríguez v. Honduras (Merits)* IACtHR Series C no. 4 (29 July 1988) 177; *Al-Skeini and others v. United Kingdom*, no. 55721/07, ECHR, 2011, 166.

50 *Cangöz and others v. Turkey*, no. 7469/06, ECHR, 2016, 114.

51 IACtHR, *Valle Jaramillo*, above n. 39, 101; *Encarnación Blanco Abad v. Spain* Communication no. 59/1996 CteeAT Doc CAT/C/20/D/59/1996 (19 June 1998) 8.2–8.5.

52 IACtHR, *Blake (Merits)*, above n. 34, 97; *Villafañe Chaparro et al v. Colombia* Communication no. 612/1995 HRCtee Doc CCPR/C/60/D/612/1995 (19 August 1997) 8.8; ECtHR *Al-Skeini*, above n. 49, 166.

53 IACtHR, *Velásquez Rodríguez*, above n. 49, 180; *Al-Skeini*, above n. 49, 167; *Amnesty International et al v. Sudan* Communications 48/90, 50/91, 52/91, 89/93 AComHPR 13th Annual Activity Report (November 1999) 51.

54 IACtHR, *Valle Jaramillo*, above n. 39, 101; *General Comment no 3: Implementation of Article 14 by States parties* CteeAT Doc CAT/C/GC/3 (13 December 2012) 23.

55 *Juan Humberto Sánchez v. Honduras (Preliminary Objection, Merits, Reparations and Costs)* IACtHR Series C no. 99 (7 June 2003) 186; *Al-Skeini*, above n. 49, 167; AComHPR, *Amnesty International*, above n. 53, 51.

56 The victims or their next of kin must have the possibility to participate in the investigatory proceedings, be heard by the competent bodies, and challenge the decision not to prosecute those allegedly responsible; *Kaya*, above n. 29, 107; IACtHR, *Villagrán*, above n. 34, 227.

57 HRCtee, *General Comment no 31*, above n. 41, 15; CteeAT, *General Comment no 3*, above n. 54, 23; IACtHR, *Velásquez Rodríguez*, above n. 49, 176–80; *Al-Skeini*, above n. 49, 165–67; AComHPR, *General Comment no 3*, above n. 43, 7, 15.

58 AComHPR, *Sudan Human Rights*, above n. 42, 150: 'In present communication, the state claims to have investigated the alleged abuses, put in place mechanisms to prevent further abuses and to provide remedies to victims. The question is – were all these initiatives done *in accordance with international standards*? Did they meet the *test of effective official investigations under international human rights law*?' (emphasis added). See also UN Human Rights Council, above n. 26, 1814.

2.3. APPLYING THE STANDARDS OF EFFECTIVENESS IN ARMED CONFLICT

The widespread violence and insecurity characterising armed conflict situations may prevent a State from complying entirely with the high standards applicable to normal police investigations. A full investigation may simply be impracticable due to factual circumstances:[59] security conditions may impede to carry out the basics of an investigation such as accessing the field, gathering evidence, and questioning testimonies.[60] As some commentators pointed out, during armed conflict there is 'the need to engage in constant balancing between the duty to investigate and battlefield conditions'.[61] This notwithstanding, a tenet of HRL is that States cannot simply abstain from fulfilling their obligation to investigate in an effective manner.[62]

Whereas the IACtHR seems to hold States to the abovementioned standards of effectiveness at all times,[63] the ECtHR and the AComHPR have considered the possible obstacles to investigations that armed conflicts may pose, as well as the corresponding need to evaluate effectiveness accordingly.[64] At the same time, they also held that investigations into alleged human rights violations must be carried out even in difficult security circumstances, including armed conflicts. In this sense, the ECtHR and the AComHPR respectively affirmed that a State must take 'all reasonable steps' or 'all feasible measures' to conduct an investigation as effectively as possible.[65] It is interesting to note that, with reference to emergency situations, the HRCtee stated that derogations from certain treaty provisions cannot diminish the 'duty to take *all feasible measures* to investigate, prosecute, punish and remedy violations of the right to life'.[66]

---

59 A. Cohen and Y. Shany, above n. 13, 50.

60 M.N. Schmitt, above n. 11, 54–55.

61 A. Cohen and Y. Shany, above n. 13, 50.

62 UN Special Rapporteur on Extrajudicial, Summary or Arbitrary Executions, 'Report of the Special Rapporteur, Philip Alston' UN Doc E/CN.4/2006/53 (8 March 2006) 36.

63 *Massacres of El Mozote and Nearby Places v. El Salvador (Merits, Reparations and Costs)* IACtHR Series C no. 252 (25 October 2012) 242–49; *Santo Domingo Massacre v. Colombia (Preliminary Objections, Merits and Reparations)* IACtHR Series C no. 259 (30 November 2012) 155–58.

64 *Isayeva v. Russia*, no. 57950/00, ECHR, 2005, 180; AComHPR, *General Comment no 3*, above n. 43, 20.

65 *Al-Skeini*, above n. 49, 164; *Jaloud v. The Netherlands*, no. 47708/08, ECHR, 2014, 186; AComHPR, *General Comment no 3*, above n. 43, 17, 20.

66 HRCtee, *Draft General Comment no 36*, above n. 33, 64 (emphasis added). Notably, the last draft prepared by the HRCtee Rapporteur provides that: '[States Parties must] investigate allegations of violations of article 6 in situations of armed conflict in accordance with the relevant in ternational standards'; *General Comment no 36 on article 6 of the International Covenant on Civil and Political Rights, on the Right to Life*, Revised Draft Prepared by the Rapporteur (August 2017) 67 <http://www.ohchr.org/Documents/HRBodies/CCPR/GCArticle6/GCArticle6_EN.pdf> accessed 19.02. 2018. See also OHCHR, *The Minnesota Protocol on the Investigation of Potentially Unlawful Death (2016)*, New York/Geneva 2017, 20–21.

The 'all reasonable steps'/'all feasible measures' test, as it will be referred to by the present analysis, bears the advantage of allowing a realistic application of the abovementioned standards while safeguarding the overarching requirement of effectiveness. Since its precise content is context dependent, the test also appears to be flexible enough to accommodate the needs of investigators when acting in armed conflict, especially extraterritorially.

The 'all reasonable steps' test is consolidated within the ECtHR's jurisprudence.[67] As far as the other monitoring bodies are concerned, the scarcity of case law does not yet allow the same conclusion to be reached. Whereas it cannot be concluded that the 'all reasonable steps'/'all feasible measures' test is as established within HRL as the general standards of effectiveness are, what can be affirmed is that an interpretive trend among treaty bodies is emerging. The similar wording they employed signals convergence of interpretations in this respect. Considering that this test enables the striking of a balance between the practical hindrances that a State may face when investigating in such contexts and the need to ensure that alleged human rights violations be effectively investigated, it is foreseeable that treaty bodies will confirm it in future pronouncements. For present purposes, the 'all reasonable steps'/'all feasible measures' test proves particularly useful when applying the standards of effectiveness to war crimes investigations.[68] Before exploring this point, the analysis will describe the methodological approach employed by the present study to understand the interaction between IHL and HRL.

3. INTERACTION BETWEEN IHL AND HRL: A THEORETICAL FRAMEWORK

3.1. COMPLEMENTARITY

IHL and human rights treaties present several cross-references. The APs contain provisions recalling States' obligations deriving from HRL,[69] while human rights treaties include provisions regulating their application in situations of armed conflict, especially in connection with derogations.[70] Moreover, the acknowledgement by international bodies that HRL continues to apply in

---

67 *Al-Skeini*, above n. 49, 164; *Jaloud*, above n. 65, 186. See also *Kaya*, above n. 29, 91; *Ergi*, above n. 48, 85; *Isayeva*, above n. 64, 181, 215–24.

68 See below section 4.

69 API, Art. 72; APII, Preambular para. 2.

70 ICCPR, Art. 4; ECHR, Art. 15; ACHR, Art. 27; CAT, Art. 2(2); ICED, Art. 1(2); Convention on the Rights of the Child (adopted 20 December 1989) 1577 UNTS 3, Art. 38; Optional Protocol to the Convention on the Rights of the Child on the Involvement of Children in Armed Conflict (adopted 25 May 2000) 2173 UNTS 222.

situations of armed conflict expands the possibility that rules pertaining to the two different regimes apply to the same case.[71]

IHL and HRL rules interact because the two frameworks partly regulate the same matter – action of States affecting individuals – and to a certain extent share the common aim of protecting human beings.[72] Interaction principally occurs in two ways. On the one hand, IHL and HRL rules may compete, namely point to different directions and possibly lead to a norm conflict.[73] In that case, the interpreter needs to decide which norm to apply and which not. On the other hand, if one regime presents a lacuna, rules from the other may be used as gap-fillers.

These two dimensions of the relationship between IHL and HRL have given rise to opposite perspectives: mutual exclusiveness and merger. In the present writer's opinion, neither catches the essence of the interplay between the two. The former position, advocated for mostly in the past,[74] has definitely been set aside by the jurisprudence of international bodies and domestic courts.[75] The perspective of merger,[76] in turn, bears the risk of overlooking the structural differences and rationales characterising IHL and HRL. It is submitted here that complementarity is the correct approach in this context, for it is capable to comprehend both convergence and divergence between the two frameworks.[77] This perspective is firmly grounded in the pronouncements of international bodies such the International Court of Justice (ICJ), human rights treaty bodies, and the ICTY.[78] The present analysis will endeavour to explore its normative significance and practical implications.

When considering the interplay between IHL and HRL, it is important to distinguish between the macro and micro levels.[79] The macro level refers to the relationship between the two as legal regimes; the micro level relates to the

---

71 *Legal Consequences of the Construction of a Wall in the Occupied Palestinian Territory* (Advisory Opinion) ICJ Rep 179 [2004] 106.

72 F. Hampson and I. Salama, 'Working Paper on the Relationship between Human Rights Law and International Humanitarian Law' UN Doc E/CN.4/Sub.2/2005/14 (21 June 2005) 3.

73 This is due to some fundamental divergences between the two bodies of law. As some commentators noted: 'Whilst both regimes seek to avoid unnecessary deaths, injuries and destruction, the starting point of [...] IHL is the soldier's right to kill. The starting point of HRL is the prohibition of arbitrary killing and the obligation to protect the right to life'; ibid., 45.

74 G. Draper, 'Humanitarian Law and Human Rights' (1979) *Acta Juridica* 193, 199, 205.

75 H.-J. Heintze, 'Theories on the Relationship between International Humanitarian Law and Human Rights Law' in R. Kolb and G. Gaggioli, above n. 1, pp. 55–56.

76 For an account of this perspective, see ibid., pp. 61–62.

77 Literally, the term conveys 'a relationship or situation in which two or more different things improve or emphasize each other's qualities; see *Oxford Dictionary Online* <http://www.oxforddictionaries.com/> accessed 19.02.2018.

78 See nn. 89–90.

79 R. Cryer, 'The Interplay of Human Rights and Humanitarian Law: The Approach of the ICTY' (2009) 14 *Journal of Conflict and Security Law* 1, 4.

interaction between their norms. At the macro level, complementarity means that the two frameworks partially converge when it comes to the protection of individuals from State action.[80] The outcome of this perspective is that IHL and HRL may be seen as mutually reinforcing, not exclusive,[81] and that each body may fill the other's gaps. However, when talking about complementarity and possible convergence, the differences between the two must be kept in mind: the object of IHL is the action of States during hostilities, whereas the object of HRL is the authority of States over persons and territory under their jurisdiction. The distinction as to the objects in turn leads to the different aims that each framework pursues in regulating State action.[82] Considering complementarity without paying sufficient attention to the structural differences between the two bodies of law might lead to overlooking possible instances of norm competition, which would render this approach methodologically useless when applied to concrete cases.

All this is mirrored by the interaction between IHL and HRL that occurs at the micro level, namely between specific norms. As mentioned, it may happen that rules pertaining to the two different regimes are both applicable and in competition, meaning that they regulate the same situation but point at different outcomes. It may also be that the same act is prohibited by both regimes – for example, torture – yet only one of them provides for detailed regulation. At this level, complementarity acquires different connotations depending on the situation at hand. When norms are in competition, for example in relation to the use of force or detention,[83] and the interpreter needs to make a choice about which rule to apply, complementarity has a narrower significance. It will mean that, when HRL is construed in light of IHL,[84] the former will still inform the interpretation of the latter.[85] On the other hand, when one regime presents some gaps – for example, in relation to the standards defining an effective investigation – complementarity means that the rules of the other regime may be used as gap-fillers.[86] In either case, the interpreter needs to be careful in transposing concepts, rules and principles from one regime to the other. He or she must always keep in mind the structural differences between IHL and HRL concerning their

[80] L. Doswald-Beck, *Human Right in Times of Conflict and Terrorism*, Oxford University Press, Oxford 2011, p. 122.

[81] HRCtee, *General Comment no 31*, above n. 41, 11.

[82] This is exemplified by how the two frameworks differently protect life and personal liberty; see nn. 132–40 and accompanying text.

[83] See nn. 132–40 and accompanying text.

[84] AComHPR, *General Comment no 3*, above n. 43, 33: 'In armed conflict, what constitutes an "arbitrary" deprivation of life during the conduct of hostilities is to be determined by reference to international humanitarian law'.

[85] For instance, the AComHPR affirmed that the protection of the right to life in armed conflict is better pursued by capturing an individual, rather than killing him or her, if military necessity allows; ibid., 34.

[86] Turkel Commission, above n. 5, 146.

objects, purposes, terminology, legal techniques, and operational principles.[87] The possible lack of expertise by the interpreter in either field is a further factor to be aware of.[88]

The ICJ, human rights treaty bodies and the ICTY have either expressly affirmed that IHL and HRL are complementary bodies of law;[89] or they underlined the common protective purpose the two legal frameworks share, implicitly assuming the same perspective.[90] While complementarity is the first leg of the theoretical approach here employed, the second is constituted by the principle of systemic integration. This interpretive tool indeed serves the purpose of connecting international rules pertaining to different legal regimes, and it is relevant both to work out instances of norm competition and to perform the gap-filling role between the regimes.

3.2. THE PRINCIPLE OF SYSTEMIC INTEGRATION

Systemic integration is one of the principles of interpretation codified in Article 31 of the Vienna Convention on the Law of Treaties (VCLT).[91] It is embodied in Article 31(3)(c), which provides that in the interpretation of a treaty '[t]here shall be taken into account, together with the context: [...] any relevant rules of international law applicable in the relations between the parties'.[92]

Article 31(3)(c) VCLT is a mandatory element of the interpretive process,[93] and it demands that the interpreter construe a norm in light of international law

87 Ibid., 470–71; H. Krieger, 'A Conflict of Norms: The Relationship between Humanitarian Law and Human Rights Law in the ICRC Customary Law Study' (2006) 11 *Journal of Conflict & Security Law* 265, 278–81.

88 F. Hampson, 'The Relationship between International Humanitarian Law and International Human Rights Law' in S. Sheeran and N. Rodley (eds), *Routledge Handbook of International Human Rights Law*, Routledge, Abingdon 2013, p. 192.

89 HRCtee, *General Comment no 31*, above n. 41, 11; IACtHR, *Massacres of El Mozote*, above n. 63, 141; *Prosecutor v. Kunarac et al.* (Judgment) ICTY-96-23-T and ICTY-96-23/1-T (22 February 2001) 467.

90 *Juan Carlos Abella v. Argentina (La Tablada case)* IAComHR Report no. 55/97 (18 November 1997) 158, 160; *Varnava and others v. Turkey*, nos 16064–66/90 and 16068–73/90, ECHR, 2009, 185; *Hassan v. United Kingdom*, no. 29750/09, ECHR, 2014, 102.

91 Vienna Convention on the Law of Treaties (adopted 23 May 1969) 1155 UNTS 331 (VCLT). The analysis will refer interchangeably to the principle of systemic integration and to Art. 31(3)(c) VCLT.

92 Art. 31 VCLT formally applies to the interpretation of treaties only. Yet, having attained customary status in its entirety, it may be employed to construe customary norms as well; see *Certain Questions of Mutual Assistance in Criminal Matters (Djibouti v. France)* (Merits) ICJ Rep 177 [2008] 112; P. Merkouris, *Article 31(3)(c) VCLT and the Principle of Systemic Integration*, Brill/Nijhoff, Leiden 2015, pp. 263–69, 298–300.

93 C. McLachlan, 'The Principle of Systemic Integration and Article 31(3)(c) of the Vienna Convention' (2005) 54 *International and Comparative Law Quarterly* 279, 290.

as a legal system.[94] As the ICJ affirmed, '[...] an international instrument has to be interpreted and applied within the framework of the entire legal system prevailing at the time of the interpretation'.[95] Accordingly, international rules must be interpreted in light of their normative environment,[96] which comprises all rules that are relevant at the time of interpretation.[97] Conceptually, the principle of systemic integration is based on the premise that international law is a unified legal system.[98] This perspective points towards the need for a systematic interpretation that considers norms originating from different legal regimes as 'a single set of compatible obligations'.[99] With regard to situations of armed conflict, IHL and HRL constitute each other's normative environment.

Under Article 31(3)(c) VCLT, an interpreter may take into account rules deriving from any of the sources of international law: treaties, custom, and general principles of law.[100] The reference to 'rules' requires to consider only norms that are part of the *lex lata*.[101] The term 'applicable', in turn, is construed in a similar fashion as excluding the possibility to consider non-binding rules.[102] The interpreter should therefore take into account only established norms of international law.[103] Further, the term 'parties' is understood as referring to the parties to whom the interpreted rule will apply.[104] Article 31(3)(c) also provides

---

94 M.E. Villiger, *Commentary on the 1969 Vienna Convention on the Law of Treaties*, Brill/Nijhoff, Leiden 2009, p. 432.

95 *Legal Consequences for States of the Continued Presence of South Africa in Namibia (South West Africa) notwithstanding Security Council Resolution 276 (1970)* (Advisory Opinion) ICJ Rep 16 [1971] 53. See also *The Right to Information on Consular Assistance in the Framework of the Guarantees of the Due Process of Law* Advisory Opinion OC-16/99 IACtHR Series A no. 16 (1 October 1999) 113.

96 International Law Commission (ILC), 'Fragmentation of International Law: Difficulties Arising from the Diversification and Expansion of International Law' UN Doc A/CN.4/L.682 (13 April 2006) 413.

97 Ibid., 475–78; C. McLachlan, above n. 93, 316–18.

98 J. d'Aspremont and E. Tranchez, 'The Quest for a Non-conflictual Coexistence of International Human Rights Law and Humanitarian Law: Which Role for the *Lex Specialis* Principle?' in R. Kolb and G. Gaggioli, above n. 1, pp. 235–36.

99 Ibid., p. 236.

100 C. McLachlan, above n. 93, 290.

101 Ibid.

102 M.E. Villiger, above n. 94, p. 433.

103 However, the ECtHR has explicitly referred to non-binding and emerging norms: *Demir and Baykara v. Turkey*, no. 34503/97, ECHR, 2008, 78 ff.

104 ILC, above n. 96, 472. For a different interpretation, U. Linderfalk, 'Who are "The Parties"? Article 31, paragraph 3(c) of the 1969 Vienna Convention and the "Principle of Systemic Integration" Revisited' (2008) 55 *Netherlands International Law Review* 343. It is worth highlighting that the ICJ, human rights monitoring bodies, and the ICTY, have employed the principle of systemic integration either in advisory opinions, general comments, or concluding observations to State reports, i.e. when no dispute was at stake; or in relation to individual complaints, in which disputes arise between an individual and a State. In terms of the VCLT, the 'parties' involved therein are the one or more respondent States only, since individuals do not have the legal capacity to become parties to it.

that the other rules to be taken into account must be 'relevant'. In this respect, the risk exists of an arbitrary choice of the relevant rules, which may eventually result in a change of the law applicable to a specific case.[105] The general tendency is primarily to consider rules that concern the same subject matter.[106]

Article 31(3)(c) VCLT has been employed by numerous international bodies, inter alia the ICJ,[107] the ECtHR,[108] the ICC,[109] the Court of Justice of the European Union[110] and the World Trade Organization dispute settlement bodies,[111] as well as by domestic courts.[112] In relation to the interaction between IHL and HRL, the ICJ, human rights treaty bodies and the ICTY have resorted to the principle of systemic integration implicitly,[113] or explicitly,[114] or on the basis of specific treaty provisions that have the same effect as Article 31(3)(c), such as Articles 29(b) ACHR and 60–61 ACHPR.[115] For present purposes, what the Inter-American Commission of Human Rights (IAComHR) affirmed in the *Molina* case is of special interest:

> Due to their similarity and the fact that both norms are based on the same principles and values, international human rights law and IHL may influence and reinforce each

---

105 *Oil Platforms (Islamic Republic of Iran v. United States of America)* (Merits) ICJ Rep 161 [2003] [Judge Buergenthal] 22–32; [Judge Higgins] 40–54; ICC *Bemba (Judgment)*, above n. 24, 79.

106 M.E. Villiger, above n. 94, p. 433; *European Communities and Certain Member States – Measures Affecting Trade in Large Civil Aircraft* (Appellate Report) WT/DS316/AB/R (18 May 2011) 846. One commentator suggested evaluating the relevance of a rule on the basis of its proximity with the interpreted norm. Such proximity should in turn be considered from a number of perspectives: terminological/linguistic; subject-matter; temporal; and shared parties/actor. See P. Merkouris, above n. 92, pp. 83–95.

107 ICJ, *Oil Platforms*, above n. 105, 41–42; *Djibouti v. France*, above n. 92, 112–14.

108 Inter alia: *Golder v. United Kingdom*, no. 4451/70, ECHR, 1975, 35–36; *Al-Adsani v. United Kingdom*, no. 35763/97, ECHR, 2001, 55–56; *Demir*, above n. 103, 74–86.

109 ICC, *Bemba (Judgment)*, above n. 24, 78–79; *Prosecutor v. Germain Katanga* (Judgment) ICC-01/04-01/07 (7 March 2014) 47.

110 *Council v. Polisario* Case C-104/16 P (21 December 2016) 86.

111 *United States – Import Prohibition of certain Shrimp and Shrimp Products* (Appellate Report) WT/DS58/AB/R (12 October 1998) 158; *European Communities – Measures Affecting the Approval and Marketing of Biotech Products* (Panel Report) WT/DS291/R, WT/DS292/R, WT/DS293/R (29 September 2006) 7.65 ff; *Large Civil Aircraft*, above n. 106, 845.

112 J. d'Aspremont, 'The Systemic Integration of International Law by Domestic Courts: Domestic Judges as Architects of the Consistency of the International Legal Order' in A. Nollkaemper and O.K. Fauchald (eds), *Unity or Fragmentation of International Law: The Role of International and National Tribunals*, Oxford University Press, Oxford 2011, pp. 154–56, and case law cited therein.

113 *Legality of the Threat or Use of Nuclear Weapons* (Advisory Opinion) ICJ Rep 226 [1996] 25; *General Comment no 35: Article 9 (Liberty and security of person)* HRCtee Doc CCPR/C/GC/35 (16 December 2014) 64; ICTY *Kunarac*, above n. 89, 470–88.

114 *Hassan*, above n. 90, 102.

115 *Avilan v. Colombia* IAComHR Report no. 26/97 (13 April 1998) 132; *Mapiripán Massacre v. Colombia (Merits, Reparations, and Costs)* IACtHR Series C no. 134 (15 September 2005) 115; *Democratic Republic of Congo (DRC) v. Burundi, Rwanda and Uganda* Communication 227/1999 AComHPR 33rd Ordinary Session (May 2003) 70, 78.

> other, following as a [*sic*] interpretative method that enshrined in Article 31(3)(c) of the Vienna Convention on the Law of Treaties, which establishes that in interpreting a norm 'any relevant rules of international law applicable in the relations between the parties' may be considered. The foregoing shows that international human rights law may be interpreted in the light of IHL and the latter may be interpreted in the light of international human rights law, as required.[116]

In this passage, the IAComHR not only expressly invoked systemic integration but also connected it to the complementary character of the two bodies of law. This shows that the principle of systemic integration is especially germane to the interplay between IHL and HRL at the micro level. Article 31(3)(c) not only allows but also requires, when the case demands it, to consider relevant rules of one of these legal frameworks to interpret those belonging to the other. As it enables putting in communication distinct legal regimes, the principle of systemic integration is crucial to addressing both norm competition and possible gaps in the law. Whereas the first aspect will be dealt with in the next sections, the latter will be examined in section 4 of this contribution.

3.3. THE (IR)RELEVANCE OF *LEX SPECIALIS*

Before considering the interaction of IHL and HRL rules with regard to investigations, it is necessary briefly to discuss *lex specialis*.[117] Its employment by the ICJ in the *Nuclear Weapons* and *Wall* advisory opinions has framed the subsequent debate among scholars.[118] In basic terms, *lex specialis* 'suggests that if a matter is being regulated by a general standard as well as a more specific rule, then the latter should take precedence over the former'.[119] The purpose of this section is to show that systemic integration, not *lex specialis*, is the principle that is apt to understand the interaction between these two bodies of law.

First, *lex specialis* may be a norm conflict-solving technique.[120] A norm conflict is a situation in which two applicable rules regulate the same subject

---

116 *Franklin Guillermo Aisalla Molina (Ecuador-Colombia) (Admissibility)* IAComHR Report no. 112/10 (21 October 2010) 121 (footnote omitted).

117 The whole maxim reads *'lex specialis derogat legi generali'*, which means that special law derogates from general law.

118 ICJ *Nuclear Weapons*, above n. 113, 25; *Wall*, above n. 71, 106; N. Prud'homme, '*Lex Specialis*: Oversimplifying a More Complex and Multifaceted Relationship?' (2007) 40 *Israel Law Review* 356. It is worth noting that, in its last case dealing with the interplay between IHL and HRL, the ICJ did not refer to *lex specialis*; *Armed Activities on the Territory of the Congo (Democratic Republic of the Congo v. Uganda)* (Merits) ICJ Rep 168 [2005] 216. Among the human rights treaty bodies, only the IAComHR has referred to it; see *Coard et al. v. United States (Merits)* IAComHR Report no. 109/99 (29 September 1999) 42; *Gregoria Herminia et al v. El Salvador (Admissibility)* IAComHR Report no. 11/05 (23 February 2005) 120.

119 ILC, above n. 96, 56.

120 Ibid., 57, 88.

matter and give rise to incompatible results.[121] Having chosen which norm to apply, the interpreter will then need to resort to tools of conflict solution such as *lex specialis*.[122] However, a norm conflict arises only after interpretation has failed to avoid it.[123] Possible conflicts may indeed be addressed at the interpretation stage, when norms are in competition yet not necessarily in conflict. The concept of norm competition indeed relies on a broad understanding of norm conflict, one that is capable to capture not only actual but also potential incompatibility between legal rules.[124] The consequence of considering competition between IHL and HRL norms, rather than conflict, is that *lex specialis* as a conflict-solving tool loses its relevance.

Secondly, *lex specialis* may be a principle of interpretation. Even under this perspective, however, such a principle is not useful to understand the interplay between IHL and HRL.[125] Some commentators have rightly pointed out that when the ICJ invoked *lex specialis*, it actually employed the principle of systemic integration.[126] In *Nuclear Weapons*, the ICJ affirmed that during armed conflict the right to life continues to be protected under Article 6 ICCPR. It subsequently stated that: 'The test of what is an arbitrary deprivation of life, however, then falls to be determined by the applicable *lex specialis*, namely [IHL].'[127] The ICJ took IHL into account in order to interpret the ICCPR: although invoking *lex specialis*, it in fact resorted to the principle of systemic integration.[128] A similar interpretive operation has been conducted by the IAComHR when it referred to *lex specialis*

121 This corresponds to a narrow understanding of norm conflict; see G. Marceau, 'Conflicts of Norms and Conflicts of Jurisdictions. The Relationship between the WTO Agreement and MEAs and other Treaties' (2001) 35 *Journal of World Trade* 6, 1081, 1084.

122 Other principles are '*lex superior derogat legi inferiori*' and '*lex posterior derogat legi priori*'.

123 J. d'Aspremont and E. Tranchez, above n. 98, p. 225.

124 Ibid., pp. 232–33.

125 Scholars have extensively discussed the unsuitability of *lex specialis* to describe the interplay between IHL and HRL. One major issue is that this principle is generally designed for vertical relationship between norms, where a defined normative hierarchy exists. The relationship between IHL and HRL is instead horizontal: it involves collisions between legal regimes where no hierarchical connection exist. See F. Hampson, above n. 88, p. 188; N. Prud'homme, above n. 118, 379–80. Moreover, whereas the *lex specialis* principle dictates that the special rule should prevail over the general, it does not in itself indicate how to distinguish between the special and the general rule. Since it tends to be vague and interpretable in different if not opposite ways, some commentators suggested to stop employing this principle to read the interplay between IHL and HRL. See ibid., 378–86; M. Milanović, *Extraterritorial Application of Human Rights Treaties: Law, Principles, and Policy*, Oxford University Press, Oxford 2011, pp. 250–52, 260; G. Oberleitner, above n. 1, pp. 95 ff.

126 J. d'Aspremont and E. Tranchez, above n. 98, pp. 234–35, 238–41. See also V. Gowlland-Debbas, 'The Relevance of Paragraph 25 of the ICJ's Advisory Opinion on Nuclear Weapons' (2004) 98 *American Society of International Law Proceedings* 358, 361, who advances a similar argument.

127 ICJ *Nuclear Weapons*, above n. 113, 25.

128 J. Pauwelyn, *Conflict of Norms in Public International Law: How WTO Law Relates to other Rules of International Law*, Cambridge University Press, Cambridge 2003, p. 410, who makes an analogous point without referring to systemic integration.

in order to read the relationship between IHL and HRL.[129] The employment of systemic integration under the guise of *lex specialis* shows that it is the former, not the latter, that matters in order to understand the interplay between the two legal frameworks.[130] Given the foregoing, the present writer does not consider *lex specialis* as relevant to understanding the relationship between IHL and HRL.

3.4. NORM COMPETITION BETWEEN IHL AND HRL

Competition between IHL and HRL rules is likely to arise in connection with use of force and detention. The protection of the individual in these areas is indeed differently regulated by the two frameworks. In this respect, one can observe divergence between permissive IHL rules and restrictive HRL rules.[131] IHL allows for the use of lethal force against combatants and civilians taking direct part in the hostilities.[132] HRL, on the other hand, imposes a general prohibition on arbitrary deprivation of life, which is a corollary of the protection of the right to life.[133] Force can be used by law enforcement agents under strict conditions: it must be necessary, proportionate and in pursuance of a legitimate aim, which most often will regard the protection of a person's life.[134] If one juxtaposes IHL and HRL rules in this area, it is apparent that in principle the targeting of individuals based on status or activity under the former would amount to an arbitrary deprivation of life under the latter.

A similar conclusion may be drawn with regard to detention of individuals in IACs.[135] GCIV allows for the detention of civilians – 'protected persons'[136] in terms of the Convention – who pose a threat to the security of the enemy belligerent party

129 IAComHR *Coard*, above n. 118, 42. See also *Serdar Mohammed v. Ministry of Defence* [2014] EWHC 1369 (QB) 288.

130 As shown above, the IAComHR expressly affirmed this point: *Molina*, above n. 116, 121.

131 The present analysis employs the terms 'permissive' and 'restrictive' in order to contrast the IHL (permissive) rules on targeting and detention with the HRL prohibitions (restrictive rules) of arbitrary deprivation of life and liberty.

132 API, Arts. 43(2); 48; 51(3); APII, Art. 13(3).

133 ICCPR, Art. 6; ACHR, Art. 4; ECHR, Art. 2; ACHPR, Art. 4.

134 N. Rodley, 'Integrity of the Person' in D. Moeckli, S. Shah and S. Sivakumaran (eds), *International Human Rights Law*, Oxford University Press, Oxford 2014, p. 186; *Guerrero v. Colombia* Communication no R.11/45 HRCtee Doc CCPR/C/15/D/45/1979 (31 March 1982) 13.1–13.3; *Zambrano Velez v. Ecuador (Merits, Reparations and Costs)* IACtHR Series C no. 166 (4 July 2007) 108; *McCann*, above n. 40, 193; AComHPR, *General Comment no 3*, above n. 43, 27. The legitimate aims are exemplified in Art. 2 ECHR, which provides that force can be used '(a) in defence of any person from unlawful violence; (b) in order to effect a lawful arrest or to prevent the escape of a person lawfully detained; (c) in action lawfully taken for the purpose of quelling a riot or insurrection'.

135 No provision in Common Article 3 GCs or APII regulates the grounds for detention and procedural safeguards in NIACs. The debate whether IHL provides for an implicit authorization to detain individuals on security grounds is still open; cf., in general, ICRC, *'Internment in Armed Conflict: Basic Rules and Challenges'* Opinion Paper (November 2014).

136 GCIV, Art. 4.

or the occupying power.[137] The decision to intern must be initially assessed by a competent judicial or administrative body, and reviewed at least every six months.[138] A person must be released as soon as the reasons of security that justified his or her internment cease to exist, and in any case at the end of the hostilities or as soon as possible thereafter.[139] In turn, HRL generally protects the right to personal liberty and security, and correspondingly prohibits unlawful and/or arbitrary deprivation of liberty; permitted detention typically forms part of criminal proceedings.[140] The prohibition of arbitrary deprivation of liberty entails that administrative detention on purely security grounds is absolutely forbidden.[141] It may be allowed only if derogations from relevant treaty provisions are in place.[142] As with norms regulating the use of force, it may be observed that IHL and HRL point to divergent directions in relation to the protection of individual liberty.

Norm competition between IHL and HRL arises because the prohibitions of arbitrary deprivation of life and liberty continue to apply in armed conflict.[143] Relevant international jurisprudence shows that this situation is addressed at the interpretation stage through the principle of systemic integration. The ICJ and human rights treaty bodies have taken IHL rules on targeting and detention into account to interpret the HRL prohibitions of arbitrary deprivation of life and liberty in armed conflict,[144] eventually avoiding norm conflict. The interpretive outcome is the following: acts that in peacetime amount to arbitrary deprivation of life or liberty, in armed conflict do not. This precludes a violation of the relevant HRL norms.[145] The corollary of this interpretive choice, on the other hand, is that a violation of the prevailing IHL norm *a fortiori* entails a violation of the background HRL norm.[146]

To recap, the present writer understands the relationship between IHL and HRL through a theoretical framework based on two components: a perspective of

---

137 GCIV, Arts. 42(1), 78(1).

138 GCIV, Arts. 43(1), 78(2).

139 GCIV, Arts. 46(1), 132(1), 133(1).

140 ICCPR, Art. 9; ACHR, Art. 7; ECHR, Art. 5; ACHPR, Art. 6.

141 *Hassan*, above n. 90, 97.

142 Whereas the right to life is non-derogable, the right to personal liberty may be derogated from; e.g. ICCPR, Art. 4. However, as clarified by the HRCtee, measures adopted under a derogation regime must 'not exceed those strictly required by the exigencies of the actual situation. […] [T]he requirements of strict necessity and proportionality constrain any derogating measures involving security detention', HRCtee, *General Comment no 35*, above n. 113, 65–66.

143 ICJ *Nuclear Weapons*, above n. 113, 25; *Hassan*, above n. 90, 104–06; AComHPR, *General Comment no 3*, above n. 43, 32; HRCtee, *Draft General Comment no 36*, above n. 33, 63; IACtHR, *Santo Domingo Massacre*, above n. 63, 211–37.

144 Ibid., 211; *Hassan*, above n. 90, 104–06.

145 HRCtee, *Draft General Comment no 36*, above n. 33, 63; *Hassan*, above n. 90, 104–06.

146 The normative consequences relevant to the obligation to investigate will be analysed in section 4.1.

complementarity that acknowledges both convergence and divergence between the two bodies of law as well as highlights their mutual gap-filling role; and the principle of systemic integration, which emerges as the principal interpretive tool instead of *lex specialis*, and operationalises complementarity at the micro level.

The next section will look at the interplay between IHL and HRL in relation to the duty to investigate. In particular, it will explore how HRL may complement IHL with regard to the standards of effectiveness and the right to an investigation, both when they apply concurrently and when IHL only is applicable.

4. THE IMPACT OF HRL ON WAR CRIMES INVESTIGATIONS

4.1. CONCURRENT APPLICABILITY OF IHL AND HRL

This scenario is based on the assumption that both bodies of law are applicable to an incident. For IHL to apply, an armed conflict must exist;[147] furthermore, this framework governs only acts that have a nexus with the conflict.[148] In turn, the basic condition for the application of HRL is that a State exercises jurisdiction, which in extraterritorial contexts means that it must have effective control over a territory or individuals.[149]

As discussed, IHL and HRL regulate use of force and detention in different ways. When these frameworks apply concurrently, relevant rules may be in competition. In that case, human rights treaty bodies tend to address this issue by interpreting HRL norms in light of relevant IHL norms, to the effect that what in peacetime would be an infringement of HRL, in armed conflict might not. The other side of the coin is that a violation of the IHL rule entails a violation of the corresponding HRL rule. As illustrated shortly, this clearly emerges from the pronouncements of human rights monitoring bodies.

In relation to the right to life, the AComHPR stated that:

> In armed conflict, what constitutes an 'arbitrary' deprivation of life during the conduct of hostilities is to be determined by reference to international humanitarian law.

147 See n. 7.

148 *Prosecutor v. Kunarac et al.* (Judgment) ICTY-96-23 and ICTY-96-23/1 (12 June 2002) 57–59.

149 M. Milanović, above n. 125, pp. 7–8. The extraterritorial applicability of human rights treaties is a wide and complicated topic, which will be dealt with below only in its essential features. For an extensive analysis, cf., in general, ibid.; F. Coomans and M.T. Kamminga (eds), *Extraterritorial Application of Human Rights Treaties*, Intersentia, Cambridge 2004; M. Gondek, *The Reach of Human Rights in a Globalising World: Extraterritorial Application of Human Rights Treaties*, Intersentia, Cambridge 2009. Section 4.2 will consider the scenario in which HRL does not apply for lack of jurisdiction.

> [...] Any violation of international humanitarian law resulting in death, including war crimes, will be an arbitrary deprivation of life.[150]

This is a logical conclusion: if an IHL rule is to be given prevalence over an HRL rule under certain circumstances, only a lawful application of the former can preclude a violation of the latter. It is relevant noting that the AComHPR is the first treaty body that makes this point explicitly. The HRCtee took the same view in its draft General Comment 36,[151] which to date has not yet been adopted. Previously, the IACtHR and the ECtHR reached a similar conclusion but did not convey it in express terms.[152]

In the present writer's opinion, this constitutes a more general principle concerning the relationship between IHL and HRL. In instances of norm competition in which a permissive IHL norm prevails over a restrictive HRL norm, the consequence of a violation of the former is a violation of the latter.[153] The outcome is that the HRL norm re-emerges, bringing along all normative consequences ensuing from a breach thereof. With regard to the obligation to investigate, two consequences are particularly relevant.

First, the HRL standards of effectiveness become *de jure* applicable to war crimes investigations, and in this regard the 'all reasonable steps'/'all feasible measures' test stands as especially pertinent. As discussed, this test demands that an investigation be carried out effectively; at the same time, it allows for some degree of flexibility by taking into account the special circumstances characterising armed conflicts, including the obstacles these situations may pose to investigators. It is submitted that this test stands as practically useful in two respects: on the one hand, it provides guidance to investigators as to the standards of conduct they are expected to follow; on the other hand, it sets a yardstick for domestic and international courts and bodies tasked with scrutinising whether an investigation has been conducted effectively.

Two further considerations should be made. Since the HRL norm re-emerges only when the IHL norm is breached, the opening of an investigation will be dependent upon the higher IHL threshold, namely the existence of a credible allegation or reasonable suspicion that a war crime has been committed. Yet, HRL will require that an investigation be opened as promptly as circumstances permit. Additionally, IHL allows for war crimes investigations to be carried out

---

150 AComHPR, *General Comment no 3*, above n. 43, 32.

151 HRCtee, *Draft General Comment no 36*, above n. 33, 63.

152 IACtHR, *Santo Domingo Massacre*, above n. 63, 230, 237; *Hassan*, above n. 90, 105.

153 The present writer expressed the same view elsewhere. See V. Todeschini, 'The Relationship between International Humanitarian Law and Human Rights Law in the African Commission's General Comment on the Right to Life' 2016 *EJIL Talk!* <http://www.ejiltalk.org/the-relationship-between-international-humanitarian-law-and-human-rights-law-in-the-african-commissions-general-comment-on-the-right-to-life/> accessed 19.02.2018.

by military personnel.[154] Although most treaty bodies criticise investigations carried out by the military into the conduct of the armed forces,[155] States may avail themselves of this option. Yet, HRL will definitely play a role in defining whether independence and impartiality are complied with.[156]

A second consequence of the re-emergence of HRL regards the right to an investigation, which, as mentioned, is not granted by any IHL provision. In that regard denying victims and their next of kin the possibility of being involved in the investigatory proceedings into alleged war crimes, including any preclusion to challenge the closure of an investigation or the decision not to prosecute those allegedly responsible, may give rise to an autonomous breach of the relevant HRL norm(s) granting the right to an investigation.[157] This arguably opens up new perspectives for victims of war crimes to seek redress and justice.

In sum, when IHL and HRL apply concurrently and an act allegedly violates relevant norms of both frameworks, the standards of effectiveness will apply to war crimes investigations as a matter of law.

4.2. EXCLUSIVE APPLICABILITY OF IHL

In armed conflict, an act may violate IHL without infringing HRL. First, HRL does not prohibit certain acts, such as the use of expanding bullets and riot-control agents:[158] their employment for law enforcement purposes is not unlawful as long as it complies with the HRL rules governing the use of force. Under IHL, in contrast, the use of expanding bullets and riot-control agents is absolutely forbidden for it amounts to a breach of the prohibition of unnecessary suffering – a fundamental principle governing both international armed conflicts (IACs) and non-international armed conflicts (NIACs).[159]

Secondly, an act may in principle violate both IHL and HRL norms; yet, HRL may not be applicable for lack of extraterritorial jurisdiction. Under the examined human rights treaties, jurisdiction constitutes a threshold criterion that triggers a State's obligations and responsibility.[160] Whereas jurisdiction is presumed on a State's territory, in extraterritorial contexts it becomes dependent on the factual exercise of effective control over a territory or individual(s).[161]

154 M.N. Schmitt, above n. 11, 80, 83.

155 IACtHR, *Velásquez Rodríguez*, above n. 49, 180; International Commission of Jurists, *The Right to a Remedy and Reparation for Gross Human Rights Violations: A Practitioner's Guide*, International Commission of Jurists, Geneva 2006, pp. 67–68, and case law cited therein.

156 *Al-Skeini*, above n. 49, 171–74.

157 See nn. 30–38 and accompanying text.

158 Such bullets expand on impact and produce injuries of great severity.

159 API, Art. 35(2); J.M. Henckaerts and L. Doswald-Beck, above n. 11, rr. 70, 75, 77.

160 ICCPR, Art. 2(1); CAT, Art. 2(1); ACHR, Art. 1(1); ECHR, Art. 1; AComHPR, *General Comment no 3*, above n. 43, 14; *Al-Skeini*, above n. 49, 130.

161 M. Milanović, above n. 125, pp. 7–8.

In the absence of jurisdiction, a human rights treaty does not apply to a certain situation or act. Issues in this respect mainly arise with reference to the ECtHR, which tends to deny that use of force by distance, such as shooting or bombing, brings an individual within a State's jurisdiction.[162] Only when a State exercises some degree of control over a territory does the ECtHR acknowledge that use of force by distance establishes a jurisdictional link between a State and an individual.[163] When HRL is not applicable, a State is not *de jure* bound by its norms. However, it is submitted that this framework can still inform the application of IHL, although in different terms than in the previous scenario.

As already discussed, general consensus exists on the fact that investigations into alleged war crimes should in principle adhere to the standards of effectiveness.[164] In the present writer's opinion, it is possible to maintain that this is a legal obligation of States, which derives from a combined reading of the obligation to investigate under IHL and the principle of systemic integration. To better explain this point, it is possible to break the reasoning into the following steps. First: IHL prescribes that investigations into alleged war crimes be effective, yet it does not prescribe specific standards of effectiveness. Secondly: the need to define effectiveness for the purposes of war crimes investigations leads the interpreter to look into the relevant standards developed within HRL. Thirdly: this interpretive operation is not only allowed, but also demanded by Article 31(3)(c), which is one of the mandatory principles of interpretation.[165] Fourthly: the standards of effectiveness may be adapted to the circumstances characterising armed conflict by employing the 'all reasonable steps'/'all feasible measures' test.

By reconnecting all these elements, it may be seen that States are bound by two norms: the IHL obligation prescribing that investigations must be effective, and Article 31(3)(c) requiring them to construe such international rule in light of its normative environment – in the present case, the HRL standards of

---

162 *Banković and others v. Belgium and other 16 Contracting States*, no. 52207/99, ECHR, 2001, 75. However, some cases depart from this interpretation: *Pad and others v. Turkey*, no. 60167/00, ECHR, 2007, 54–55; *Solomou and others v. Turkey*, no. 36832/97, ECHR, 2008, 51.

163 *Al-Skeini*, above n. 49, 149–50.

164 See n. 26.

165 The possibility of considering rules that are not *de jure* applicable to a given case owes to the fact that such principle belongs to the interpretation of the law, a stage that necessarily precedes its application. The term 'applicable', as found in Art. 31(3)(c) VCLT, means that the other international rules taken into account must be part of the *lex lata*, hence binding; not that they must be applicable to the case at hand; see M.E. Villiger, above n. 94, p. 433. This is demonstrated by the fact that monitoring bodies, when dealing with armed conflict situations, have taken into account IHL rules regardless of their applicability to the case at hand.

effectiveness. In this writer's opinion, the combined effect of these norms is that, even when only IHL applies, a State is under an obligation to conduct war crimes investigations following the standards of effectiveness, duly contextualised in light of the 'all reasonable steps'/'all feasible measures' test. Although such standards would become applicable not as a matter of law but as a matter of interpretation, it is submitted that this normative result is part of the *lex lata* concerning the obligation to investigate in armed conflict.

What stays out of the picture is the right to an investigation. Under IHL, there is no procedural remedy for individuals to the effect that they cannot assert a right to an investigation *vis-à-vis* States when HRL is not applicable. Whereas in relation to the standards of effectiveness the lacuna in IHL pertains to the content of effectiveness, with regard to the right to an investigation it concerns the existence of the norm. In this sense, the principle of systemic integration cannot be used to create a new rule.

Yet, such principle may constitute the basis for a proposal *de lege ferenda*, according to which States may grant victims or their next of kin such a right. Systemic integration indeed offers the possibility to take the right to an investigation into account in the context of war crimes investigations. This would allow victims to exercise this right even when HRL is not applicable, and to claim its autonomous violation. The proposal is based on a victim-oriented perspective of international law – one that places emphasis on the rights of victims in armed conflict.[166] This approach finds support in the UN Principles on Remedy and Reparation – a soft law instrument whose purpose is to identify 'mechanisms, modalities, procedures and methods for the implementation of existing legal obligations under [HRL and IHL]'.[167] These Principles affirm that victims should be granted substantial and procedural remedies against IHL and HRL violations, including '[e]qual and effective access to justice; [a]dequate, effective and prompt reparation for harm suffered; [a]ccess to relevant information concerning violations and reparation mechanisms'.[168]

Although victims cannot yet rely on an autonomous right to an investigation when HRL does not apply, it should be recalled that the involvement of victims is one of the standards of effectiveness, as such binding on States.

---

166 M.C. Bassiouni, 'International Recognition of Victims' Rights' (2006) 6 *Human Rights Law Review* 203, 204–06, 255.

167 UN Commission on Human Rights, 'Basic Principles and Guidelines on the Right to a Remedy and Reparation for Victims of Gross Violations of International Human Rights Law and Serious Violations of International Humanitarian Law, Commission on Human Rights' UN Doc E/CN.4/RES/2005/35 (19 April 2005), Preamble.

168 Ibid., 11(a).

5. CONCLUSION

The present chapter aimed at an understanding of the relationship between IHL and HRL. More specifically, it intended to explore how the interaction between the two bodies of law shapes a State's obligation to investigate in armed conflict.

The analysis observed that IHL prescribes for States a duty to investigate alleged war crimes. Whereas this framework also demands that an investigation be carried out effectively, it falls short of indicating the relevant standards of effectiveness. It was then proposed to look into HRL, within which human rights treaty bodies have elaborated in detail upon the standards that an investigation must follow in order to be deemed effective.

Some of the treaty bodies have considered the application of such standards to investigations carried out in the context of an armed conflict. They developed what has here been termed the 'all reasonable steps'/'all feasible measures' test. This test allows for a flexible application of the standards of effectiveness that takes into account the concrete obstacles State authorities may face while investigating in armed conflict. The question this chapter raised was whether such standards, and especially the 'all reasonable steps'/'all feasible measures' test, may be applied to war crimes investigations in order to fill the corresponding gap in IHL.

In order to determine how HRL may complement IHL, the study looked at how the two bodies of law interact both as legal regimes and at the level of specific norms. It accordingly delineated a theoretical framework based on a perspective of complementarity between the two, operationalised at the micro level through the principle of systemic integration. The appropriateness of this approach to understand the interaction between IHL and HRL is corroborated by relevant pronouncements of the ICJ, human rights treaty bodies, and the ICTY.

With specific regard to the obligation to investigate in armed conflict, the analysis considered two scenarios: concurrent applicability of IHL and HRL and exclusive applicability of IHL. It was shown that the standards of effectiveness, duly contextualised by means of the 'all reasonable steps'/'all feasible measures' test, may be applied to war crimes investigations in both scenarios. More precisely, whereas in the first scenario they apply as a matter of law, in the second they do so as a matter of interpretation through the principle of systemic integration.

This normative result also has practical consequences. First, States should know that, even when IHL only applies to a situation or incident, investigations into alleged war crimes must follow the standards of effectiveness; better said, a State is required to take 'all reasonable steps' or 'all feasible measures' to investigate as effectively as possible. In the present writer's view, this is a matter of legal obligation. Secondly, the 'all reasonable steps'/'all feasible measures' test provides guidance to competent State authorities as to how investigations in armed conflict must be conducted. It is thus relevant to practitioners in the field, who should know what standards of conduct they are required to follow. Thirdly, the test stands as a normative yardstick against which domestic or international bodies, entrusted with the task of scrutinising the conduct of an investigation, should evaluate whether or not the overarching requirement of effectiveness has been complied with. Such an evaluation is context dependent and can be made on a case-by-case basis only.

Overall, clarifying what the impact is of HRL on war crimes investigations serves the purpose of shedding light on how States are expected to fulfil their relevant legal obligations. This is important at the normative level, for it brings more clarity within international law. At the practical level, it may be of assistance to those who carry out investigations into armed conflict as well as to those who scrutinise the conduct of investigators.

CONCLUSION

Paul De Hert, Stefaan Smis and Mathias Holvoet

1. INTRODUCTION

This chapter offers some general conclusions that can be drawn from how the different authors in their respective chapters have analysed the ways in which international human rights law (IHRL), international criminal law (ICL) *stricto sensu*, transnational criminal law (TCL) and international humanitarian law (IHL) converge and diverge. We first identify the possible ways in which IHRL, ICL *stricto sensu*, TCL and IHL (can) converge (see below section 2). IHRL, ICL *stricto sensu* and *lato sensu*, TCL and IHL interact and overlap, but diverge at the same time. We therefore also look at the frictions, collisions and impairments that arise because of this. In this regard, we list the means proposed by some of the authors in this book to remedy conflicts born out of the interaction of IHRL, ICL *stricto sensu* and *lato sensu*, TCL and IHL (see below section 3).

2. POSSIBLE CONVERGENCES BETWEEN IHRL, ICL *STRICTO SENSU*, TCL AND IHL

2.1. ICL AND TCL's GAP-FILLING EFFECT THROUGH ENFORCING IHRL

As pointed out by Patrícia Pinto Soares and Gerhard Kreutzer, Damien Scalia and Valentina Milano, the fact that ICL *stricto sensu* and TCL serve as an enforcement vehicle for IHRL is one of the most straightforward ways in which ICL *stricto sensu*, TCL, and IHRL can converge. In the same vein, Milano contends that the strongest gap-filling effect of TCL on IHRL is to give 'teeth to the anti-trafficking response in terms of providing effective tools to combat and prosecute crime on the ground, where human rights law lacks these teeth and has been referred to as a "precious but blunted sword"'.

Pinto Soares and Kreutzer do not limit the enforcement potential of ICL *stricto sensu* for IHRL to enforcement through the criminal justice system. They contend that ICL can empower and work as the louder voice of IHRL, as discourse of ICL involves a strong emotional message condemning the gravity of the conduct under its scope.

2.2. IHRL AS A GAP-FILLER OF ICL *STRICTO SENSU*, TCL AND IHL

Throughout the chapters, various ways in which IHRL can serve as a gap-filler for ICL *stricto sensu*, TCL and IHRL have been identified.

Pinto Soares and Kreutzer point out, in their chapter entitled 'Catalytic, Gap-Filling or Retardant Effects of ICL on HRL: *Quid Juris*', that the convergence between ICL *stricto sensu* and IHRL is most straightforward in the context of due process guarantees. They hold that in this area 'the fundamentals of ICL and HRL are most similar; therefore, it is in this realm that a more direct application and influence of one branch on the other may legitimately take place'. However, both authors stress that there is no full convergence between ICL and IHRL in this area. This is highlighted by the fact that the ICC's judicial practice has adopted a 'holier than the Pope' mentality by granting the participants in international criminal trials fair trial rights that surpass the standards laid down by the European Court of Human Rights (ECtHR).

In his chapter, 'Use of Human Rights in International Criminal Law: Influence or Appearances of Legitimacy?', Scalia points out and illustrates that, when done judiciously, IHRL may be relied upon as a gap-filler to interpret substantive ICL, such as the individual acts of crimes against humanity.

In her contribution, 'Strengthening Action to End Forced Labour: The ILO Forced Labour Protocol and States' Positive Human Rights Obligations',

Amy Weatherburn asserts how IHRL can serve as a gap-filler to operationalise the 2014 ILO Protocol and Recommendation on Forced Labour (Supplementary Measures), as it will be facilitated by the enforcement of and adherence to States' positive human rights obligations. As an example, Weatherburn explains how human rights law jurisprudence came to accept that States have a duty to protect against non-State human rights abuses, such as forced labour, within their territory and/or jurisdiction.

In her chapter, 'The International Law of Human Trafficking: At the Forefront of the Convergence between Transnational Criminal Law and International Human Rights Law? Valentina Milano explains how IHRL has had a predominant gap-filling role towards TCL, and the law of human trafficking in particular. She specifies the following areas in which IHRL has addressed the loopholes of TCL: IHRL fills a significant gap in terms of victims' protection; IHRL calls for a much stronger response in terms of prevention; IHRL promotes State accountability; and, lastly, IHRL promotes civil society participation at national and international levels.

In his chapter, 'Investigations in Armed Conflict: Understanding the Interaction between International Humanitarian Law and Human Rights Law', Vito Todeschini determines how IHRL may serve as a gap-filler when States aim to fulfil their duty under IHL to investigate alleged war crimes. Because IHL fails short of indicating the relevant standard of effectiveness, Todeschini proposes looking into IHRL. He specifies how the 'all reasonable steps'/'all feasible measures' test developed by human rights treaty bodies may be applied to war crimes investigations in two scenarios. First, when there is concurrent applicability of IHRL and IHL, the 'all reasonable steps'/'all feasible measures' test applies as a matter of law. Secondly, when IHL applies exclusively, the 'all reasonable steps'/'all feasible measures' test can be invoked as a matter of interpretation through the principle of systemic integration.

3. FRICTIONS, COLLISIONS AND IMPAIRMENTS ARISING OUT OF THE INTERACTIONS BETWEEN IHRL, ICL *STRICTO SENSU*, TCL AND IHL

3.1. AN OVEREMPHASIS ON CRIMINAL LAW AND THE RISKS IT BEARS FOR ESTABLISHED HUMAN RIGHTS

Pinto Soares and Kreutzer posit that the seriousness of crimes under international law, the risk that they pose to the international community, and the eagerness and pressure to identify perpetrators speedily and hold them responsible has led to unwarranted derogations from certain fundamental rights. As the authors illustrate in their chapter, the fight against terrorism, in particular, has often been accompanied by serious derogations from fundamental rights, and especially violations of the prohibition of torture and inhuman and degrading treatment, as enshrined, for example, under Article 3 of the European Convention on Human Rights (ECHR).

In the same vein, Milano acknowledges that an expanded role of TCL may come at the expense of human rights law basic guarantees, in terms of, for example, fair trial, presumption of innocence or arbitrary detention.

3.2. POSSIBLE NORM CONFLICTS BETWEEN IHRL AND TCL/IHL AND THE VARIOUS MEANS TO RESOLVE THEM

As Mirja Ciesiolka illustrates in her chapter, 'International Security and Financial Stability: Resolving Norm Conflicts between Anti-Corruption and Individual Rights', various provisions of the United Nations Convention against Corruption (UNCAC) have the potential to come into a norm conflict with various established human rights under IHRL, such as the right to privacy and the right to a fair trial. Ciesiolka proposes resolving these norm conflicts through the operationalisation of the systemic integration principle, as enshrined under Article 31(3)(c) of the Vienna Convention on the Law of Treaties (VCLT). In general, applying the principle of systemic integration entails striking a balance between conflicting norms on a case-by-case basis, allowing both obligations under the UNCAC and obligations under IHRL to have appropriate effects. Because of the fact that UNCAC's provisions are worded in a discretionary and open-textured way and have an aspirational character, Ciesiolka is of the opinion that it not only allows for obligations on human rights protection but even encourages it.

Federica Favuzza's chapter, '"It was the Best of Times, It was the Worst of Times": A Tale of Detention in Time of Emergency', enquires into the potential conflict between IHRL norms on the right to personal liberty and IHL rules on internment in international armed conflict. She demonstrates how the approach taken by either the ECtHR or the Human Rights Committee (HRC), in respect of solving this potential conflict significantly affects the degree of protection afforded to individuals' right to personal liberty. More specifically, given its stance on the non-derogable nature of some of elements of the right to personal liberty, Favuzza argues that the HRC would find the IHL rules on internment to be in violation of some of the procedural safeguards under Article 9 of the International Covenant on Civil and Political Rights (ICCPR). By contrast, the ECtHR has solved the potential conflict between IHRL and IHL by interpreting Article 5 of the ECHR 'against the background' of IHL provisions. This would entail that a security detention taking place in the context of an IAC and fully complying with IHL rules would be lawful under the ECHR. Consequently, a State party to the ICCPR would have to ensure a higher degree of protection of an individual's right to personal liberty.

In her contribution entitled 'Prohibitions on Arbitrary Displacement in International Humanitarian Law and Human Rights: A Time and a Place for Everything', Deborah Casalin explains how IHL and IHRL norms on arbitrary displacement contain divergences, especially when it comes to which displacements can be categorised as 'arbitrary'. Casalin proposes resolving a possible norm conflict between IHL and IHRL rules on arbitrary displacement in both international armed conflict and non-international armed conflict by giving the IHL prevalence as *lex specialis* over the more general IHRL norms. As further explained by Casalin, the impact of the prevalence of IHL depends on the specific situation. In situations of international armed conflict, the IHL criteria for determining the arbitrariness of displacement give more leeway for lawful displacement than IHRL. Conversely, in cases of non-international conflict and occupation, IHL operates as *lex specialis* in order to provide a more stringent standard of protection.

3.3. MISUSES AND MISAPPLICATIONS OF IHRL AND IHL IN THE JURISPRUDENCE OF SUPRANATIONAL COURTS

In his chapter, Scalia highlights several instances of misuses and misapplications of IHRL by international criminal courts. First, he gives the example of the *nulla poena sine lege* principle, as enshrined in, inter alia, the ECHR and the ICCPR. Scalia specifies how both the Statutes and Rules of Procedure and Evidence of the International Criminal Court (ICC), International Criminal Tribunal for the former Yugoslavia (ICTY), and the International Criminal Tribunal for Rwanda (ICTR) fail to comply with the requisites of the *nulla poena* principle as identified in the ECtHR jurisprudence. Further, he gives the example of the *Galić* decision of the Mechanism for the International Criminal Tribunal (MICT) as an instance in which an international criminal court cherry-picked certain jurisprudence from the ECtHR to legitimise the refusal of early release of the accused, while ignoring other consistent authorities on the matter. Scalia's findings should relativise Pinto Soares and Kreutzer's chapter, as discussed above, as it demonstrates that certain well-established human rights principles and practices have been disregarded within ICL.

In his chapter, 'The European Court of Human Rights' Approach to Armed Conflict and Humanitarian Law: Ivory Tower or Pas de Deux?', Cedric De Koker first emphasises how the ECtHR has often failed to engage with IHL in cases involving armed conflict situations, thereby displaying an 'ivory tower' mindset. Nonetheless, in cases involving international armed conflict, the author discerns the increasing open-mindedness of the ECtHR towards IHL, and more specifically how norms of IHL interact with Article 2 of the ECHR.

Still, he recommends that the Strasbourg Judges provide a principled basis for the application of the ECHR in situations of armed conflict and the concurrent application of the Convention with IHL. In De Koker's view, only when the Judges have explicitly elaborated on the ECtHR's view on how the rights enclosed in the ECHR apply to situations of armed conflict and on how they see the interplay between the ECHR and norms of IHL play out in concrete cases will the ECtHR contribute to legal certainty and allow a proper discussion of the issues of law and policy involved.

3.4. THE IMPORTANCE OF JUDICIAL DISCRETION TO MITIGATE COLLISIONS BETWEEN DIVERGING BODIES OF LAW

By focusing on the *Al Senussi* decision, Marina Aksenova explores, in her chapter 'The Future of the International Criminal Court: A Non-Human Rights Body?', how IHRL and ICL *stricto sensu* interact with specific reference to the principle of complementarity. The *Al Senussi* decision is exemplary of the collisions that can arise between human rights concerns and considerations implicit in the framework and mandate of international criminal courts such as the ICC. In deciding whether to declare the case of *Al Senussi* admissible before the ICC, judges had to weigh due process guarantees against several other factors such as the importance of vesting trust into the local judiciary by upholding the principle of complementarity and the possible difficulties of apprehending the suspect. For Aksenova, the *Al Senussi* case highlights the power vested in international judges by virtue of their ability to exercise discretion and, more specifically, to mitigate the collisions that can arise because of conflicting considerations of IHRL and ICL. Aksenova's chapter is also supported by Favuzza's findings, as discussed above under section 3.2.

4. GENERAL CONCLUDING OBSERVATIONS

By covering a wide array of topics, the chapters in this volume give a deeper insight into the multiple ways in which the neighbouring fields of IHRL, IHL and ICL (both ICL *stricto sensu* and TCL) can interact, by identifying both convergences and divergences. The various contributions obviously provide only snapshots of the state of the law on a particular issue. The interactions between IHRL, IHL and ICL will most likely further increase and expand. In this regard, the possible convergences identified in the different chapters, – as well as the means proposed for remedying conflicts that arise out of the diverging nature of the three bodies of law, – could serve as meaningful guidelines.

INDEX

ABOUT THE EDITORS

Paul De Hert is a full-time professor at the Vrije Universiteit Brussel (VUB) and is an associated professor at Tilburg University. His research focuses on international fundamental rights (both in legal practice and more fundamental reflections about law); EU justice and home affairs; human rights in criminal law, health and the elderly; constitutionalism in an historical perspective; technology and data protection law; international, European and EU criminal law; national (Belgian) criminal law; legal theory and philosophy; and transnational police cooperation.

He currently holds 11 active memberships of editorial boards of scientific periodicals/editors and is also on the editorial boards of several national and international scientific journals such as the *Inter-American and European Human Rights Journal*, *Criminal Law & Philosophy*, *The Computer Law & Security Review* and the *International Journal on Advances in Security*. He is Co-Editor in Chief of the *Supranational Criminal Law Series* and of the *New Journal of European Criminal Law*.

Stefaan Smis is a professor of international and human rights law at the Faculty of Law and Criminology at Vrije Universiteit Brussel (VUB) and Reader in International Law at the School of Law of the University of Westminster. His research focuses on international law, international protection of human rights, settlement of international disputes, states in transition, the prosecution of grave violations of human rights, and international law from an African perspective.

He is Editor-in-Chief of the international peer reviewed journal *Human Rights & International Legal Discourse* and is a member of the editorial board of the *Revue de droit africain*. He is also a member of the Law&Dev (law and development) Inter-University Network and of Recherches et documentation Juridiques Africaines Asbl.

Mathias Holvoet holds a PhD in International Criminal Law from the Faculty of Law and Criminology of the Vrije Universiteit Brussel (VUB), where he is affiliated with the Fundamental Rights and Constitutionalism (FRC) Research Group and the Institute for European Studies (IES).

From April 2017 until September 2017, Mathias was a visiting professional within the Trial Division of the Chambers of the International Criminal Court. He has also been a visiting researcher at the Whitney R. Harris World Law Institute, Washington University in St. Louis, United States of America; Humboldt University, Berlin, where he was also *Lehrstuhl* of Professor Dr. Gerhard Werle;

and at the Institute for International Peace and Security Law, University of Cologne.

His work has been published in leading journals in the field of International Criminal Law such as the *Journal of International Criminal Justice*, *International Criminal Law Review* and *Criminal Law Forum*.

www.ingramcontent.com/pod-product-compliance
Ingram Content Group UK Ltd.
Pitfield, Milton Keynes, MK11 3LW, UK
UKHW051926100926
8556IPUK00022B/1393

9 781780 686400